# LARGE
## Numbers

# Recipes for LARGE Numbers

## Stephen Ashley
## Sean Anderson

with a special section
on Healthy Diet
by Sue Ross

**HOSPITALITY PRESS**
MELBOURNE

Hospitality Press Pty Ltd
38 Riddell Parade
P.O. Box 426
Elsternwick Victoria 3185 Australia
Telephone (03) 9528 5021  Fax (03) 9528 2645

*Recipes for Large Numbers*

First  published 1996. Reprinted 1999

National Library of Australia
Cataloguing-in-publication data:

Ashley, Stephen
      Recipes for large numbers

      Includes index.
      ISBN 1  86250  461 X


      1. Quantity cookery, 2. Health. 3. Nutrition. 4. Diet.
      I. Anderson, Sean. II. Ross, Sue, 1964-, III. Title.

641.57

Designed by John van Loon
Edited by Nicholas Scott and Frances Wade (Wade's Distractions)
Typeset by Eclipse, St Kilda, Vic.
Produced in Malaysia by SRM Production Services Sdn.Bhd., Petaling Jaya
Published by Hospitality Press Pty Ltd (ACN 006 473 454)

For Theresa and Christine

# PREFACE

*Recipes for Large Numbers* has been written for all those involved in providing catering to large numbers of people on a regular basis. Unfortunately, for far too long this section of the catering industry has been virtually ignored by the food media and has had little written to help it develop and achieve the recognition it deserves.

This large sector of the catering industry serves hundreds of thousands of meals every day, 365 days of the year, and employs thousands of professional caterers who strive to deliver good quality, innovative and nutritious food within often restrictive budgets. Large-scale catering is provided in such diverse settings as office complexes, factories, defence bases, health care facilities, factories, universities, colleges, schools, and function and conference centres.

This book is a companion to *Catering for Large Numbers* (Butterworth-Heinemann, 1993) and will aid experienced caterers, students and those new to the industry alike with recipes written for numbers of 25, 50 and 100. It also aims to support the authors' belief that producing food for large numbers of people is a unique style of cookery that requires great skill and dedication and therefore deserves recognition and support.

Stephen Ashley
Sean Anderson
April 1996

# TABLE OF CONTENTS

# ACKNOWLEDGEMENTS

The authors wish to thank:

- Theresa Hurst, Stephen's fiancée, and Christine Anderson, Sean's wife, for the many understanding hours while this book was being written
- Sue Ross, one of Sydney's leading dieticians, for her help and expert nutritional and specialised dietary advice
- our good friend Simon Hawkswell, who is a great chef, for his help with the cake and biscuit recipes
- the staff of Hospitality Press for making publication possible.

Stephen Ashley would also like to express thanks to Sydney staffing agents Blache Lepers, and especially all the staff at Allseasons, for allowing him the flexibility necessary to complete this book.

# STOCKS AND SAUCES

# STOCKS AND SAUCES

The sauces in this chapter are basic. They can be used in their own right or adapted to more complex sauces depending on your requirements. More complex sauce recipes are to be found throughout the book accompanying relevant dishes.

## STOCKS

The following stock recipes will yield approximately 8 L; this allows for evaporation during the cooking process. The loss will vary depending on the time the stock is allowed to simmer.

♥ **Health tip**    Traditional stock is generally more tasty and less salty than powdered stock. For people on a low salt diet, these recipes are suitable. Be careful with the amount of salt you add.

# Brown beef stock

**Ingredients**

| | |
|---|---|
| beef bones, raw | 6 kg |
| water | 12 L |
| onions, washed, roughly chopped | 500 g |
| carrots, washed, roughly chopped | 500 g |
| celery, washed, roughly chopped | 500 g |
| leeks, washed, roughly chopped | 500 g |
| thyme | 15 g |
| parsley, stalks | 25 g |
| peppercorns | 5 g |
| oil | as required |

**Method**
1 Roughly chop the bones and vegetables and brown either by:
  a Placing into a roasting tray and browning in a moderate oven (150–180°C);
  or
  b Browning carefully in a sauté pan over a moderate heat with a small amount of oil.
2 Place bones and vegetables into a stock pot.
3 Add the water and bring to the boil.
4 Skim off any impurities that may rise to the surface.
5 Add herbs and peppercorns. Simmer gently for approx. 4–6 hours.
6 Skim the surface of any impurities and strain stock.
7 Use immediately or cool to 4°C in four hours or less and refrigerate until needed.

To produce a white beef stock do not brown the bones or vegetables.

After stock has been refrigerated the fat that rises to the surface and sets can be used as the cooking medium when roasting potatoes, as it imparts an excellent flavour.

# Veal stock

**Ingredients**

| | |
|---|---|
| **raw veal**, bones | 6 kg |
| **water** | 12 L |
| **onions**, washed, roughly chopped | 500 g |
| **carrots**, washed, roughly chopped | 500 g |
| **celery**, washed, roughly chopped | 500 g |
| **leeks**, washed, roughly chopped | 500 g |
| **thyme** | 15 g |
| **parsley** | 25 g |
| **peppercorns** | 5 g |

**Method**

1 Remove any excess fat from the bones.
2 Place into a stock pot.
3 Cover with the water and bring to the boil.
4 Skim off any impurities that may rise to the surface.
5 Add the vegetables, herbs and peppercorns.
6 Simmer gently for approx. 4–6 hours.
7 Skim the surface of any impurities and strain.
8 Use immediately or cool to 4°C in four hours or less and refrigerate until needed.

If a lot of scum rises to the surface strain and wash bones, cover with another 12 L of water and bring to the boil.

After stock has been refrigerated the fat that rises to the surface and sets can be used as the cooking medium when roasting potatoes, as it imparts an excellent flavour.

# Chicken stock

**Ingredients**

| | |
|---|---|
| **chicken**, carcasses | 6 kg |
| **water** | 12 L |
| **onions**, washed, roughly chopped | 500 g |
| **carrots**, washed, roughly chopped | 500 g |
| **celery**, washed, roughly chopped | 500 g |
| **leeks**, washed, roughly chopped | 500 g |
| **thyme** | 15 g |
| **parsley**, stalks | 25 g |
| **peppercorns** | 5 g |

**Method**

1 Roughly chop carcasses.
2 Place into a stock pot.
3 Cover with water and bring to the boil.
4 Skim off any impurities that may rise to the surface.
5 Add the vegetables, herbs and peppercorns.
6 Simmer gently for approx. 4–6 hours.
7 Skim the surface of any impurities and strain.
8 Use immediately or cool to 4°C in four hours or less and refrigerate until needed.

 **Notes**

If a lot of scum rises to the surface strain and wash carcasses, cover with another 12 L of water and bring to the boil.

After stock has been refrigerated the fat that rises to the surface and sets can be used as the cooking medium when roasting potatoes, as it imparts an excellent flavour.

# Fish stock

**Ingredients**

| | |
|---|---|
| **butter** | 150 g |
| **onions**, sliced thinly | 700 g |
| **white fish bones**, washed | 6 kg |
| **bay-leaves** | 5 |
| **lemons**, juice | 4 |
| **parsley**, stalks | 25 g |
| **peppercorns** | 10 g |
| **water** | 12 L |

**Method**

1 Place a stockpot over a moderate heat. Melt butter, add onions and cook without colour until tender.
2 Add all other ingredients, except water. Cover with a lid and cook gently for approx. 5 minutes.
3 Add the water and bring to the boil.
4 Skim the surface of any scum and simmer gently for 20 minutes.
5 Strain and use immediately or cool to 4°C in four hours or less and refrigerate until needed.

If fish stock is simmered for more than twenty minutes the flavour will become bitter and impaired.

# Vegetable stock

**T**here is no set method or set group of ingredients that make up a vegetable stock. A good guide to a vegetable stock is as follows and can be varied as required.

Ingredients

| | |
|---|---|
| butter/olive oil/vegetable oil | 150 g/as required |
| onions, washed, roughly chopped | 1 kg |
| carrots, washed, roughly chopped | 1 kg |
| celery, washed, roughly chopped | 1 kg |
| leeks, washed, roughly chopped | 1 kg |
| tomatoes, washed, roughly chopped | 1 kg |
| parsnips, washed, roughly chopped | 1 kg |
| water | 12 L |
| parsley, stalks | 40 g |
| thyme | 15 g |
| peppercorns | 5 g |
| salt | to taste |

Method

1 Heat butter/oil over a moderate heat in a stock pot.
2 Add vegetables and mix well.
3 Cover with a lid and cook gently for 5–10 minutes.
4 Add water and other ingredients.
5 Bring to the boil and skim surface of any impurities.
6 Simmer gently for approx. 2–3 hours.
7 This stock can then either be strained ready for use or the strained vegetables can then be liquidised, strained and returned to the stock ready for use. Use immediately or cool to 4°C in four hours or less and refrigerate until needed.

 If the vegetables are liquidised, then consideration should be given when preparing a dish to the fact that puréed vegetables are a natural thickening agent.

# Powdered stock mixes

**T**here are alternatives on the market to making fresh stocks. These can either be in liquid form or more commonly in powdered form. These are now an accepted part of many kitchen stores and are invaluable when time or staff limitations have to be considered. Each brand of powdered stock base will have different strengths, so no accurate guide can be given; the proportions are usually in the region of 25–30 grams of powdered stock base to each litre of water. It is advised that powdered stocks should be whisked in small amounts to boiling water until the required strength is achieved.

**Notes**   Powdered stocks are also a good method of boosting the flavour of a home-made stock.

Powdered stock bases are usually salty so it may not be necessary to add salt, even though it may be required by the recipe.

# ROUX

**A** roux is a combination of flour and fat which is cooked together to form a thickening agent for liquids.
The quantities given in the mixes below will yield enough roux to thicken approx. 2/4/8 L of liquid to the consistency that will coat the back of a spoon.

♥ **Health tip**   Use polyunsaturated or monounsaturated margarine instead of butter, to make more suitable for cholesterol-lowering diets.

# White roux

**Ingredients**

| For a sauce yield of: | 2 L | 4 L | 8 L |
|---|---|---|---|
| butter | 150 g | 300 g | 600 g |
| flour, plain | 150 g | 300 g | 600 g |

**Method**

1 Melt the butter in a saucepan over a moderate heat.
2 Add the flour and mix well with butter using a wooden spoon.
3 Reduce heat and cook gently for approx. 2–3 minutes without colouring.
4 Remove from the heat and use as required.

# Blonde roux

**Ingredients**

| For a sauce yield of: | 2 L | 4 L | 8 L |
|---|---|---|---|
| butter | 150 g | 300 g | 600 g |
| flour, plain | 150 g | 300 g | 600 g |

**Method**

1 Melt the butter in a saucepan over a moderate heat.
2 Add the flour and mix well with butter using a wooden spoon.
3 Reduce heat and cook until a sandy texture is achieved. This will require a slightly longer cooking time than when making a white roux.
4 Remove from the heat and use as required.

# Brown roux

**Ingredients**

| For a sauce yield of: | 2 L | 4 L | 8 L |
|---|---|---|---|
| butter | 150 g | 300 g | 600 g |
| flour, plain | 150 g | 300 g | 600 g |

**Method**

1 Melt the butter in a saucepan over a moderate heat.
2 Add the flour and mix well with butter using a wooden spoon.
3 Reduce heat and cook until roux turns brown in colour. This will require a slightly longer cooking time than when making a blonde roux.
4 Remove from the heat and use as required.

# SAUCES, WHITE

**♥ Health tip**

Use low fat or reduced fat milk instead of full cream milk to make these suitable for low fat diets.

# White sauce (béchamel)

**Ingredients**

| | 25 | 50 | 100 |
|---|---|---|---|
| butter | 150 g | 300 g | 600 g |
| flour, plain | 150 g | 300 g | 600 g |
| milk | 2 L | 4 L | 8 L |
| salt and white pepper | to taste | | |

**Method**

1 Melt the butter in a saucepan over a moderate heat.
2 Add the flour and mix well with butter using a wooden spoon.
3 Reduce heat and cook gently for approx. 2–3 minutes without colouring.

continued

4 Gently warm the milk in a separate saucepan.
5 Slowly incorporate the milk in small amounts making sure each
   addition has mixed with the roux smoothly.
6 Reduce heat and cook out gently for approx. 10 minutes
   stirring regularly.
7 Remove from heat, strain and use as required.

 **Note** When making a white sauce/béchamel it is always advisable when possible to use butter over margarine as it will give a slightly richer flavour. Nonetheless margarine will give a good finished product. If a white sauce is being prepared for a vegan dish, margarine (with a vegetable oil base) must be used in place of butter and soya milk in place of milk.

 ♥ **Health tip** Use lite milk, not regular milk, for a low fat diet.

# Cheese sauce

| Ingredients | | 25 | 50 | 100 |
|---|---|---|---|---|
| butter | | 150 g | 300 g | 600 g |
| flour, plain | | 150 g | 300 g | 600 g |
| milk | | 2 L | 4 L | 8 L |
| cheese, Cheddar, grated | | 200 g | 400 g | 800 g |
| parsley, finely chopped | | 10 g | 20 g | 40 g |
| salt and white pepper | | to taste | | |

**Method**
1 Melt the butter in a saucepan over a moderate heat.
2 Add the flour and mix well with butter using a wooden spoon.
3 Reduce heat and cook gently for approximately 2–3 minutes
   without colouring.
4 Gently warm the milk in a separate saucepan.
5 Slowly incorporate the milk in small amounts making sure each
   addition has mixed with the roux smoothly.
6 Reduce heat and cook out gently for approx. 10 minutes
   stirring regularly.
7 Add grated cheese, chopped parsley and season to taste. Mix well.
8 Remove from heat and use as required.

 **Note** Other cheeses can be added with the Cheddar cheese in moderation. A good accompanying cheese to Cheddar cheese within this sauce is a little grated Parmesan. If strong cheeses are to be used such as blue cheese, add the crumbled cheese to the sauce a little at a time tasting regularly until the required flavour is achieved. To make a richer cheese sauce substitute 200 mL of the milk for 200 mL of cream for the last 2 minutes of cooking time making sure the sauce does not boil.

 ♥ **Health tip** Low fat cheese can be substituted for regular cheese to lower the fat content.

# Cream sauce

**Ingredients**

|  | 25 | 50 | 100 |
|---|---|---|---|
| butter | 150 g | 300 g | 600 g |
| flour, plain | 150 g | 300 g | 600 g |
| milk | 1 L | 2 L | 4 L |
| cream, single | 1 L | 2 L | 4 L |
| salt and white pepper | to taste | | |

**Method**

1 Melt the butter in a saucepan over a moderate heat.
2 Add the flour and mix well with butter using a wooden spoon.
3 Reduce heat and cook gently for approx. 2–3 minutes without colouring.
4 Gently warm the milk in a separate saucepan.
5 Slowly incorporate the milk in small amounts making sure each addition has mixed with the roux smoothly.
6 Reduce heat and cook out gently for approx. 5 minutes stirring regularly.
7 Gently warm the cream in a separate saucepan.
8 Add cream, season to taste and mix well.
9 Gently heat the sauce through without boiling.
10 Remove from heat and use as required.

**Health tip** Cream sauce is not suitable for a low fat diet.

# Mustard sauce

**Ingredients**

|  | 25 | 50 | 100 |
|---|---|---|---|
| butter | 150 g | 300 g | 600 g |
| flour, plain | 150 g | 300 g | 600 g |
| milk | 2 L | 4 L | 8 L |
| If a hot mustard is used such as | | | |
| **English mustard**, use approx. | 100 g | 200 g | 400 g |
| If a mild mustard is used such as | | | |
| **grain mustard**, use approx. | 150 g | 300 g | 600 g |

**Method**

1 Melt the butter in a saucepan over a moderate heat.
2 Add the flour and mix well with butter using a wooden spoon.
3 Reduce heat and cook gently for approx. 2–3 minutes without colouring.
4 Gently warm the milk in a separate saucepan.
5 Slowly incorporate the milk in small amounts making sure each addition has mixed with the roux smoothly.
6 Reduce heat and cook out gently for approx. 10 minutes stirring regularly.

continued

7 Thoroughly whisk mustard into sauce in small amounts and
  cook for a further 1–2 minutes.
8 Remove from heat and serve.

It is advisable with this sauce that the mustard be added in small amounts and tasted
frequently so as to save waste and the time of preparing a new sauce if too much
mustard is added by accident.

# VELOUTÉS

These are sauces prepared using a blonde roux which is used
with white stock such as veal, chicken and fish as opposed to
milk in white sauce/béchamel thickened with a white roux.
This is the only difference and preparation is basically the
same as for the white sauce recipes except for the amount of
time the roux (butter and flour mixture) is allowed to cook
out prior to the addition of any liquid. Veloutés served with
fish, chicken or veal dishes usually have a little cream
added just prior to service. If this is the case with the sauce
you choose, use only 1.8 L/3.6 L/7.2 L of stock and whisk in
200 mL/400 mL/800 mL of cream to the sauce just prior
to service.

After cream has been added to a sauce it must not be allowed to boil.

 **Health tip**   Velouté is low in fat; Diane, pepper and mushroom sauces are higher in fat content.

## Chicken/veal/fish velouté

| Ingredients | | 25 | 50 | 100 |
| --- | --- | --- | --- | --- |
| butter | | 150 g | 300 g | 600 g |
| flour, plain | | 150 g | 300 g | 600 g |
| stock, chicken or veal | | 2 L | 4 L | 8 L |
| salt and white pepper | | to taste | | |

**Method**

1 Melt the butter in a saucepan over a moderate heat.
2 Add the flour and mix well with butter using a wooden spoon.
3 Reduce heat and cook gently for approx. 3–4 minutes or until flour
  turns to a sandy texture.
4 Gently warm the stock in a separate suitably sized saucepan.

5 Slowly incorporate the stock in small amounts making sure each addition has mixed with the roux smoothly.

6 Reduce heat and cook gently for approx. 10 minutes stirring regularly. Season to taste.

7 Remove from heat and use as required.

**Note** This is the basic velouté recipe and all velouté based sauces are derivatives of this basic recipe, using other ingredients and flavourings as required to suit the relevant dish.

# Diane sauce

Ingredients

| | 25 | 50 | 100 |
|---|---|---|---|
| butter | 150 g | 300 g | 600 g |
| onions, finely diced | 250 g | 500 g | 1 kg |
| garlic, cloves, peeled, finely chopped | 3 | 5 | 7 |
| flour, plain | 150 g | 300 g | 600 g |
| stock, veal/chicken | 1.7 L | 3.4 L | 6.8 L |
| Worcestershire sauce | 50 mL | 100 mL | 200 mL |
| mustard, French | 150 g | 300 g | 600 g |
| tomato paste | 200 g | 400 g | 800 g |
| cream, single | 250 mL | 500 mL | 1 L |
| **salt and freshly milled black pepper** | to taste | | |

Method

1 Melt the butter in a saucepan over a moderate heat.

2 Add onions and garlic and cook without colour until onions are tender.

3 Add the flour and mix well with butter using a wooden spoon.

4 Reduce heat and cook gently for approx. 3–4 minutes or until flour turns to a sandy texture.

5 Gently warm the stock in a separate suitably sized saucepan.

6 Slowly incorporate the stock in small amounts making sure each addition has mixed with the roux smoothly.

7 Whisk in Worcestershire sauce, mustard and tomato paste.

8 Reduce heat and cook out gently for approx. 10 minutes stirring regularly.

9 Whisk in cream and season to taste.

10 Heat sauce through, do not allow to boil, remove from heat and use as required.

**Note** The strength of the Diane sauce can be adjusted by varying the quantity of the Worcestershire sauce and the mustard as required.

# Pepper sauce

Ingredients

| | 25 | 50 | 100 |
|---|---|---|---|
| butter | 150 g | 300 g | 600 g |
| onions, finely diced | 250 g | 500 g | 1 kg |
| flour, plain | 150 g | 300 g | 600 g |
| stock, chicken or veal | 1.75 L | 3.5 L | 7 L |
| peppercorns, green, approx. | 15–25 g | 30–50 g | 60–100 g |
| cream, single | 250 mL | 500 mL | 1 L |
| salt and freshly milled black pepper | to taste | | |

Method
1 Melt the butter in a saucepan over a moderate heat.
2 Add onions and cook without colour until onions are tender.
3 Add the flour and mix well with butter using a wooden spoon.
4 Reduce heat and cook gently for approx. 3–4 minutes or until flour turns to a sandy texture.
5 Gently warm the stock in a separate saucepan.
6 Slowly incorporate the stock in small amounts making sure each addition has mixed with the roux smoothly.
7 Whisk in peppercorns.
8 Reduce heat and cook out gently for approximately 10 minutes stirring regularly.
9 Whisk in cream and season to taste.
10 Heat sauce through; do not allow to boil.
11 Remove from heat and use as required.

**Note** If a dark pepper sauce is required whisk in small amounts of parisienne essence at stage 9 until the required colour is achieved.

# Mushroom sauce

Ingredients

| | 25 | 50 | 100 |
|---|---|---|---|
| butter | 150 g | 300 g | 600 g |
| onions, finely diced | 200 g | 400 g | 800 g |
| flour, plain | 150 g | 300 g | 600 g |
| stock, chicken | 1.8 L | 3.6 L | 7.2 L |
| mushrooms, button, finely sliced | 250 g | 500 g | 1 kg |
| cream, single | 200 mL | 400 mL | 800 mL |
| salt and freshly milled black pepper | to taste | | |

Method
1 Melt the butter in a saucepan over a moderate heat.
2 Add onions and mushrooms and cook without colour until onions are tender.
3 Add the flour and mix well with butter using a wooden spoon.

4 Reduce heat and cook for approx. 3–4 minutes or until flour turns to a sandy texture.
5 Gently warm the stock in a separate saucepan.
6 Slowly incorporate the stock in small amounts making sure each addition has mixed with the roux smoothly.
7 Reduce heat and cook out gently for approx. 10 minutes stirring regularly.
8 Whisk in cream and season to taste.
9 Heat sauce through; do not allow to boil.
10 Remove from heat and use as required.

# BROWN SAUCES

 **Health tip**   These are all quite low in fat.

## Basic gravy

| Ingredients | | 25 | 50 | 100 |
|---|---|---|---|---|
| **butter** | | 150 g | 300 g | 600 g |
| **onions**, finely diced | | 250 g | 500 g | 1 kg |
| **flour**, plain | | 150 g | 300 g | 600 g |
| **stock**, beef, veal, chicken or vegetable | | 2 L | 4 L | 8 L |
| **parisienne essence** | | to colour as required | | |
| **salt and freshly milled black pepper** | | to taste | | |

**Method**

1 Melt the butter in a saucepan over a moderate heat.
2 Add onions and cook without colour until onions are tender.
3 Add the flour and mix with butter using a wooden spoon.
4 Reduce heat and cook gently until roux turns brown in colour.
5 Gently warm the stock in a separate saucepan.
6 Slowly incorporate the stock in small amounts making sure each addition has mixed with the roux smoothly.
7 Whisk in parisienne essence until the required colour is achieved.
8 Reduce heat and cook out gently for approx. 10 minutes stirring regularly. Season to taste.
9 Remove from heat, strain, and use as required.

# Mustard flavoured gravy

| Ingredients | | 25 | 50 | 100 |
|---|---|---|---|---|
| **butter** | | 150 g | 300 g | 600 g |
| **onions**, finely diced | | 250 g | 500 g | 1 kg |
| **flour**, plain | | 150 g | 300 g | 600 g |
| **stock**, beef, veal, chicken or vegetable | | 2 L | 4 L | 8L |
| **mustard**, English | | 150 g | 300 g. | 600 g |
| **parisienne essence** | | to colour as required | | |
| **salt and freshly milled black pepper** | | to taste | | |

Method

1 Melt the butter in a saucepan over a moderate heat.
2 Add onions and cook without colour until onions are tender.
3 Add the flour and mix well with butter using a wooden spoon.
4 Reduce heat and cook gently until roux turns brown in colour.
5 Warm the stock in a separate saucepan.
6 Slowly incorporate the stock in small amounts making sure each addition has mixed with the roux smoothly.
7 Add mustard and mix well.
8 Whisk in parisienne essence until the required colour is achieved.
9 Reduce heat and cook out gently for approx. 10 minutes stirring regularly. Season to taste.
10 Remove from heat and use as required.

# Onion gravy

| Ingredients | | 25 | 50 | 100 |
|---|---|---|---|---|
| **butter** | | 150 g | 300 g | 600 g |
| **onions**, finely sliced | | 250 g | 500 g | 1 kg |
| **flour**, plain | | 150 g | 300 g | 600 g |
| **stock**, beef, veal, chicken or vegetable | | 2 L | 4 L | 8 L |
| **parisienne essence** | | to colour as required | | |
| **salt and freshly milled black pepper** | | to taste | | |

Method

1 Melt the butter in a saucepan over a moderate heat.
2 Add onions and cook without colour until onions are tender.
3 Add the flour and mix well with butter using a wooden spoon.
4 Reduce heat and cook gently until roux turns brown in colour.
5 Warm the stock in a separate saucepan.
6 Slowly incorporate the stock in small amounts making sure each addition has mixed with the roux smoothly.
7 Whisk in parisienne essence until the required colour is achieved.
8 Reduce heat and cook out gently for approx. 10 minutes stirring regularly. Season to taste.
9 Remove from heat and use as required.

# GENERAL BASIC SAUCES

**Health tip**    These are all low fat sauces.

## Basic tomato sauce

| | 25 | 50 | 100 |
|---|---|---|---|
| tomatoes, crushed, A10 tin | 2 | 4 | 8 |
| garlic, cloves, peeled, finely chopped | 3 | 6 | 12 |
| onions, finely chopped | 1 kg | 2 kg | 4 kg |
| basil, finely chopped | 15 g | 30 g | 60 g |
| sugar, white | 100 g | 200 g | 400 g |
| salt and freshly milled black pepper | to taste | | |

**Ingredients**

**Method**

1 Place all ingredients into a saucepan and bring to the boil.
2 Reduce heat and simmer gently.
3 Cover with a tight fitting lid and cook very gently for approx.
45 minutes–1 hour stirring regularly.
4 Season to taste.
5 Remove from heat and use as required.

## Quick tomato sauce

| | 25 | 50 | 100 |
|---|---|---|---|
| olive oil/vegetable oil | as required | | |
| garlic, cloves, peeled, finely chopped | 3 | 6 | 12 |
| onions, finely sliced | 750 g | 1.5 kg | 3 kg |
| tomatoes, crushed, A10 tin | 1.5 | 3 | 6 |
| basil, fresh, finely chopped | 40 g | 80 g | 160 g |
| vinegar, balsamic | to taste | | |
| salt and freshly milled black pepper | to taste | | |

**Ingredients**

**Method**

1 Heat a little oil in a pan over a moderate heat.
2 Add garlic and onions and cook until onions are tender without colour.
3 Add tomatoes, basil and balsamic vinegar and mix well.
4 Simmer gently for approx. 10–15 minutes over a low heat stirring regularly.
5 Season to taste and use as required.

# Basic curry sauce

Ingredients

|  | 25 | 50 | 100 |
|---|---|---|---|
| butter | 150 g | 300 g | 600 g |
| onions, finely sliced | 500 g | 1 kg | 2 kg |
| garlic, cloves, peeled, finely chopped | 4 | 6 | 10 |
| tomato paste | 100 g | 200 g | 400 g |
| curry powder, mild, approx. | 75 g | 150 g | 300 g |
| sugar, soft brown | 50 g | 100 g | 200 g |
| flour, plain | 150 g | 300 g | 600 g |
| stock, chicken | 2 L | 4 L | 8 L |
| salt and freshly milled black pepper | to taste | | |

Method

1 In a pan over a moderate heat, melt butter and gently fry onions and garlic until onions are tender.
2 Add tomato paste, curry powder and sugar and mix well with a wooden spoon.
3 Add the flour and mix well with butter using a wooden spoon.
4 Reduce heat and cook out gently for approximately 2–3 minutes.
5 Gently warm the stock in a separate saucepan.
6 Slowly incorporate the stock in small amounts making sure each addition has mixed with the roux smoothly.
7 Reduce heat and cook out gently for approx. 10 minutes stirring regularly.
8 Season to taste.
9 Remove from heat and use as required.

# Sweet and sour sauce

Ingredients

|  | 25 | 50 | 100 |
|---|---|---|---|
| olive oil/vegetable oil | as required | | |
| onions, finely chopped | 400 g | 1 kg | 2 kg |
| garlic, cloves, finely chopped | 5 | 9 | 12 |
| ginger, fresh, peeled, minced | 10 g | 20 g | 40 g |
| vinegar, white | 250 mL | 500 mL | 1 L |
| soya sauce | 100 mL | 200 mL | 400 mL |
| pineapples, rings, A10 tin | 1 | 2 | 4 |
| tomato purée | 200 g | 400 g | 800 g |
| sugar | to taste | | |
| cornflour | as required | | |
| water | as required | | |
| salt and freshly milled black pepper | to taste | | |

**Method**

1 In a saucepan over a moderate heat, gently fry onions, garlic and ginger until onions are tender.
2 Add vinegar, soya sauce, pineapple rings that have been finely minced and the pineapple juice, tomato purée and sugar. Whisk well.
3 Simmer gently for approx. 20 minutes.
4 Mix small amounts of cornflour with small amounts of water to a smooth paste. Whisk into sauce until the required consistency is reached, repeating process if required.
5 Season to taste.
6 Remove from heat and use as required.

# **S**OUPS

**♥ Health tips**

Soups can be made with light cream instead of regular cream for a low fat diet.

Skimmed or evaporated milk instead of cream is ideal.

**Note**

Soup recipes can be adapted to a vegetarian or vegan diet by substituting vegetable stock or water for meat stock, and a vegetable-based oil for butter. Where milk is specified, substitute soya milk.

\* Suitable for a vegetarian diet
† Suitable for a vegan diet

# Creamed pumpkin, coriander and sweet potato soup

Garnish: sprigs of coriander and a dash of sour cream.

Ingredients

| | 25 | 50 | 100 |
|---|---|---|---|
| **pumpkin**, peeled, seeded, rough dice | 2 kg | 4 kg | 8 kg |
| **sweet potatoes**, peeled, rough dice | 2 kg | 4 kg | 8 kg |
| **onions**, peeled, roughly chopped | 500 g | 1 kg | 2 kg |
| **stock**, chicken | 8 L | 16 L | 32 L |
| **coriander**, fresh, finely chopped | 20 g | 40 g | 80 g |
| **cream**, single | 300 mL | 600 mL | 1.2 L |
| **salt and freshly milled black pepper** | to taste | | |

Method

1 Put pumpkin, sweet potato and onion into a saucepan and cover with the chicken stock. Bring to a gentle simmer covered with a tight fitting lid. Cook until all ingredients are tender, approx. 45 minutes–1 hour.
2 Add all other ingredients and season to taste. Purée and serve.

 **Note**

After soup has been puréed it can be reduced over a low heat if a thicker consistency is required; it can be thinned down if necessary with small amounts of stock.

♥ **Health tip**

To reduce the fat content, omit the cream. Stir in plain yoghurt just prior to serving. Do not cook yoghurt, as it will curdle.

# Puréed pumpkin and parsnip soup

Garnish: a light sprinkling of paprika.

Ingredients

| | 25 | 50 | 100 |
|---|---|---|---|
| **pumpkin**, peeled, seeded, rough dice | 2 kg | 4 kg | 8 kg |
| **parsnips**, topped and tailed, peeled, rough dice | 2 kg | 4 kg | 8 kg |
| **onions**, peeled, roughly chopped | 500 g | 1 kg | 2 kg |
| **stock**, chicken | 8 L | 16 L | 32 L |
| **cream**, single | 300 mL | 600 mL | 1.2 L |
| **salt and freshly milled black pepper** | to taste | | |

Method

1 Put pumpkin, parsnip and onion into a saucepan and cover with the chicken stock. Bring to a gentle simmer covered with a tight fitting lid. Cook until all ingredients are tender, approx. 45 minutes–1 hour.
2 Add cream and season to taste. Purée and serve.

 **Note**

After soup has been puréed it can be reduced over a low heat if a thicker consistency is required; it can be thinned down if necessary with small amounts of stock.

♥ **Health tip**

To reduce the fat content, omit the cream. Stir in plain yoghurt just prior to serving. Do not cook yoghurt, as it will curdle.

# Cream of leek, bacon and potato soup

**G**arnish: finely chopped fresh parsley.

**Ingredients**

| | 25 | 50 | 100 |
|---|---|---|---|
| **potatoes**, peeled, rough dice | 3 kg | 6 kg | 12 kg |
| **bacon**, rind removed, finely diced | 300 g | 600 g | 1.2 kg |
| **leeks**, topped and tailed, outer leaves removed, finely sliced, washed | 2 kg | 4 kg | 8 kg |
| **onions**, peeled, roughly chopped | 500 g | 1 kg | 2 kg |
| **stock**, chicken | 8 L | 16 L | 32 L |
| **cream**, single | 500 mL | 1 L | 2 L |
| **salt and freshly milled black pepper** | to taste | | |

**Method**

1 Put potatoes, bacon, leeks and onions into a saucepan. Cover with chicken stock and bring to a gentle simmer covered with a tight fitting lid. Cook until all ingredients are tender, approx. 45 minutes–1 hour.

2 Add cream and season to taste. Purée and serve.

**Note**  After soup has been puréed it can be reduced over a low heat if a thicker consistency is required; it can be thinned down if necessary with the addition of small amounts of stock.

**Health tip**  To reduce the fat content, omit the cream. Stir in plain yoghurt just prior to serving. Do not cook yoghurt, as it will curdle.

# Cream of cauliflower soup

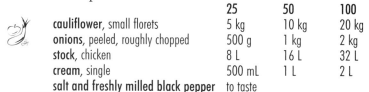

**G**arnish: crisp focaccia croûtons.

**Ingredients**

| | 25 | 50 | 100 |
|---|---|---|---|
| **cauliflower**, small florets | 5 kg | 10 kg | 20 kg |
| **onions**, peeled, roughly chopped | 500 g | 1 kg | 2 kg |
| **stock**, chicken | 8 L | 16 L | 32 L |
| **cream**, single | 500 mL | 1 L | 2 L |
| **salt and freshly milled black pepper** | to taste | | |

**Method**

1 Put cauliflower and onions into a saucepan. Cover with the chicken stock and bring to a gentle simmer covered with a tight fitting lid. Cook for approximately 45 minutes–1 hour.

2 Add cream and season to taste, purée and serve.

**Note**  After soup has been puréed it can be reduced over a low heat if a thicker consistency is required; it can be thinned down if necessary with the addition of small amounts of stock.

**Health tip**  To reduce the fat content, omit the cream. Stir in plain yoghurt just prior to serving. Do not cook yoghurt, as it will curdle. Alternatively, substitute buttermilk for cream.

# Potato, watercress and spinach soup

Garnish: finely chopped fresh parsley.

Ingredients

|  | | 25 | 50 | 100 |
|---|---|---|---|---|
| potatoes, peeled, rough dice | | 3 kg | 6 kg | 12 kg |
| watercress, sprigs | | 100 g | 200 g | 400 g |
| onions, peeled, roughly chopped | | 500 g | 1 kg | 2 kg |
| spinach, stalks removed, washed, roughly chopped | | 1 kg | 2 kg | 4 kg |
| stock, chicken | | 8 L | 16 L | 32 L |
| cream, single | | 500 mL | 1 L | 2 L |
| salt and freshly milled black pepper | | to taste | | |

Method

1 Put potato, watercress, onion and spinach into a saucepan and cover with the chicken stock. Bring to a gentle simmer, covered with a tight fitting lid. Cook until all ingredients are tender, approx. 45 minutes– 1 hour.

2 Add cream and season to taste. Purée and serve.

 Note

After soup has been puréed it can be reduced over a low heat if a thicker consistency is required; it can be thinned down if necessary with the addition of small amounts of stock.

Health tip

To reduce the fat content, omit the cream. Stir in plain yoghurt just prior to serving. Do not cook yoghurt, as it will curdle. Alternatively, substitute buttermilk for cream.

# Chicken, sweet corn and potato soup

Garnish: finely sliced chives.

Ingredients

|  | | 25 | 50 | 100 |
|---|---|---|---|---|
| potatoes, peeled, rough dice | | 2 kg | 4 kg | 8 kg |
| sweet corn niblets | | 2 kg | 4 kg | 8 kg |
| onions, peeled, roughly chopped | | 500 g | 1 kg | 2 kg |
| stock, chicken | | 8 L | 16 L | 32 L |
| cream, single | | 500 mL | 1 L | 2 L |
| parsley, fresh, finely chopped | | 15 g | 30 g | 60 g |
| salt and freshly milled black pepper | | to taste | | |

Method

1 Put potato, sweet corn and onion into a saucepan and cover with the chicken stock. Bring to a gentle simmer covered with a tight fitting lid. Cook until all ingredients are tender, approx. 45 minutes–1 hour.

2 Add cream and parsley. Season to taste. Purée and serve.

 Note

After soup has been puréed it can be reduced over a low heat if a thicker consistency is required; it can be thinned down if necessary with the addition of small amounts of stock.

**Health tip**    To reduce the fat content, omit the cream. Stir in plain yoghurt just prior to serving. Do not cook yoghurt, as it will curdle. Alternatively, substitute buttermilk for cream.

# Mushroom, bacon and parsley soup

Garnish: julienne of red capsicum.

| Ingredients | | 25 | 50 | 100 |
|---|---|---|---|---|
| | butter | 250 g | 500 g | 1 kg |
| | **onions**, finely sliced | 1 kg | 2 kg | 4 kg |
| | **garlic**, cloves, finely chopped | 3 | 5 | 9 |
| | **bacon**, rind removed, finely sliced | 250 g | 500 g | 1 kg |
| | **mushrooms**, finely sliced | 1.5 kg | 3 kg | 6 kg |
| | **flour**, plain | 250 g | 500 g | 1 kg |
| | **stock**, chicken, warmed | 8 L | 16 L | 32 L |
| | **salt and freshly milled black pepper** | to taste | | |
| | **parsley**, fresh, finely chopped | 25 g | 50 g | 100 g |

**Method**
1 Melt butter in a saucepan over a moderate heat. Add onions, garlic, bacon and mushrooms and cook until onions are soft.
2 Reduce heat and thoroughly incorporate flour. Gradually add warmed stock until all has been incorporated and simmer gently for approx. 45 minutes.
3 Season to taste, mix in parsley and serve.

**Health tip**    To make more suitable for cholesterol-lowering diets, use margarine instead of butter. Remove fat from bacon prior to cooking.

# Puréed garden vegetable soup

Garnish: finely chopped fresh parsley.

| Ingredients | | 25 | 50 | 100 |
|---|---|---|---|---|
| | **vegetables**, any combination, prepared, roughly chopped | 4 kg | 8 kg | 16 kg |
| | **onions**, peeled, roughly chopped | 500 g | 1 kg | 2 kg |
| | **stock**, chicken | 8 L | 16 L | 32 L |
| | **cream**, single | 500 mL | 1 L | 2 L |
| | **salt and freshly milled black pepper** | to taste | | |

**Method**
1 Put vegetables and onions into a saucepan; cover with the chicken stock and bring to a gentle simmer covered with a tight fitting lid. Cook until all ingredients are tender, approx. 45 minutes–1 hour.
2 Add cream and season to taste. Purée and serve.

continued

Note

After soup has been puréed it can be reduced over a low heat if a thicker consistency is required; it can be thinned down if necessary with the addition of small amounts of stock.

 **Health tip** To reduce the fat content, omit the cream. Stir in plain yoghurt just prior to serving. Do not cook yoghurt, as it will curdle. Alternatively, substitute buttermilk for cream.

# Asian-style egg noodle and chicken soup

**G**arnish: sprigs of fresh coriander.

**Ingredients**

| | 25 | 50 | 100 |
|---|---|---|---|
| **stock**, chicken | 8 L | 16 L | 32 L |
| **ginger**, fresh, peeled, grated | 25 g | 50 g | 100 g |
| **soya sauce** | 125 mL | 250 mL | 500 mL |
| **chillies**, fresh, topped and tailed, seeded, finely chopped | 2 | 4 | 8 |
| **bok choy**, trimmed, leaves roughly chopped | 2 kg | 4 kg | 8 kg |
| **spring onions**, topped and tailed, finely sliced | 250 g | 500 g | 1 kg |
| **mushrooms**, oyster, halved lengthways | 100 g | 200 g | 400 g |
| **chicken meat**, cooked, finely sliced | 1 kg | 2 kg | 4 kg |
| **egg noodles** | 1 kg | 2 kg | 4 kg |
| **beansprouts** | 200 g | 400 g | 800 g |
| **coriander**, fresh, roughly chopped | 15 g | 30 g | 60 g |
| **salt and freshly milled black pepper** | to taste | | |

**Method**

1 Put chicken stock, ginger, soya sauce, chillies, bok choy and spring onions in a saucepan over a moderate heat. Allow to come to the boil and simmer approx. 10 minutes.

2 Add oyster mushrooms, chicken meat and egg noodles and simmer gently until egg noodles are tender (approx. 10 minutes).

3 Add beansprouts and coriander. Cook for a further 2–3 minutes, season and serve, making sure to evenly distribute the hard ingredients.

 **Health tip** A meal in itself — very nutritious and low in fat.

# Chicken and tofu laksa

|  | 25 | 50 | 100 |
|---|---|---|---|
| **Ingredients**  **SOUP:** | | | |
| **oil**, sesame | as required | | |
| **onions**, white, finely chopped | 600 g | 1.2 kg | 2.4 kg |
| **garlic**, cloves, peeled, finely chopped | 4 | 8 | 16 |
| **chillies**, fresh, topped and tailed, seeded, finely chopped | 4 | 8 | 16 |
| **cumin**, ground | 10 g | 20 g | 40 g |
| **coriander**, ground | 10 g | 20 g | 40 g |
| **red Thai curry paste** | 50 g | 100 g | 200 g |
| **coconut milk** | 3 L | 6 L | 12 L |
| **soya sauce** | 50 mL | 100 mL | 200 mL |
| **stock**, chicken | 5 L | 10 L | 20 L |
| **salt and freshly milled black pepper** | to taste | | |
| **HARD INGREDIENTS:** | | | |
| **rice noodles**, cooked, refreshed, drained | 1.5 kg | 3 kg | 6 kg |
| **spring onions**, finely sliced | 200 g | 400 g | 800 g |
| **coriander**, fresh, roughly chopped | 100 g | 200 g | 400 g |
| **beansprouts** | 700 g | 1.4 kg | 2.8 kg |
| **tofu**, cut into 2 cm squares | 1.5 kg | 3 kg | 6 kg |
| **chicken meat**, cooked, finely sliced | 1 kg | 2 kg | 4 kg |

**Method**

1 Heat a little sesame oil in a saucepan over a moderate heat, add onions, garlic and chillies and cook until onions are tender.
2 Mix in cumin, coriander and Thai curry paste. Cook out for 1 minute mixing constantly.
3 Mix in coconut milk, soya sauce, chicken stock and bring to a simmer. Season to taste and simmer gently for approx. 4–5 minutes.
4 In a mixing bowl combine all hard ingredients and set aside for service.
5 To serve laksa, place equal amounts of the hard ingredients into soup bowls and just cover with the simmering soup. Serve immediately with a spoon and chopsticks.

**Health tip**  Coconut milk is high in saturated fat. Laksa is unsuitable for cholesterol-lowering and low fat diets.

# French onion soup

Garnish: crunchy croûtons.

| Ingredients | | | 25 | 50 | 100 |
|---|---|---|---|---|---|
| | | butter | 200 g | 400 g | 800 g |
| | | garlic, cloves, finely chopped | 3 | 5 | 9 |
| | | onions, white, finely sliced | 3 kg | 6 kg | 12 kg |
| | | stock, beef | 8 L | 16 L | 32 L |
| | | salt and freshly milled pepper | to taste | | |

Method

1 Melt butter in a saucepan over a moderate heat. Add garlic and onions and cook gently until onions are tender.
2 Add beef stock and simmer gently for approx. 45 minutes–1 hour; skim any scum or fat that may rise to the surface during the cooking process.
3 Remove from heat, season to taste and serve.

♥ Health tip  To make more suitable for cholesterol-lowering diets, use margarine instead of butter.


# Gazpacho soup

A chilled soup.
Garnish: finely chopped fresh basil.

| Ingredients | | | 25 | 50 | 100 |
|---|---|---|---|---|---|
| |  | tomatoes, crushed, A10 tin | 3 | 6 | 12 |
| | | cucumbers, peeled, seeded, finely diced | 500 g | 1 kg | 2 kg |
| | | onions, Spanish, roughly chopped | 500 g | 1 kg | 2 kg |
| | | capsicums, red, seeded, roughly chopped | 250 g | 500 g | 1 kg |
| | | capsicums, green, seeded, roughly chopped | 250 g | 500 g | 1 kg |
| | | garlic, cloves, finely chopped | 3 | 5 | 9 |
| | | lemon, juice and zest | 1 | 2 | 4 |
| | | vinegar, white | 50 mL | 100 mL | 200 mL |
| | | sugar | 50 g | 100 g | 200 g |
| | | salt and freshly milled black pepper | to taste | | |

Method

1 Combine all ingredients and purée.
2 Season to taste and refrigerate for at least four hours before serving.

♥ Health tip  Suitable for low fat diets.

# Our minestrone soup

Garnish: freshly grated Parmesan cheese.

| Ingredients | | 25 | 50 | 100 |
|---|---|---|---|---|
| butter | | 500 g | 1 kg | 2 kg |
| onions, Spanish, finely diced | | 500 g | 1 kg | 2 kg |
| garlic, cloves, finely chopped | | 3 | 5 | 9 |
| carrots, topped and tailed, peeled, finely diced | | 500 g | 1 kg | 2 kg |
| celery, finely diced | | 500 g | 1 kg | 2 kg |
| capsicums, red, seeded, finely diced | | 250 g | 500 g | 1 kg |
| capsicums, green, seeded, finely diced | | 250 g | 500 g | 1 kg |
| flour, plain | | 500 g | 1 kg | 2 kg |
| tomato purée | | 200 g | 400 g | 800 g |
| stock, chicken, warmed | | 8 L | 16 L | 32 L |
| spaghetti, broken into 2 cm pieces | | 200 g | 400 g | 800 g |
| salt and freshly milled black pepper | | to taste | | |
| basil, fresh, finely chopped | | 10 g | 20 g | 40 g |
| parsley, fresh, finely chopped | | 10 g | 20 g | 40 g |

## Method

1 Melt butter in a saucepan over a moderate heat. Add all vegetable ingredients mixing thoroughly. Cover pan with a tight fitting lid and cook gently until all vegetables are soft, stirring occasionally.
2 Reduce heat. Incorporate flour and mix in tomato purée well.
3 Add warmed stock slowly, incorporating thoroughly. Add spaghetti, season to taste and simmer gently for 45 minutes–1 hour.
4 Just prior to service, mix in basil and parsley and check seasoning.

 **Health tip** To make more suitable for cholesterol-lowering diets, use margarine instead of butter. Also, this soup is high in fibre. Serve with wholemeal bread to increase fibre content.

# Scotch broth

Garnish: a sprig of continental parsley.

| Ingredients | | 25 | 50 | 100 |
|---|---|---|---|---|
| stock, beef | | 9 L | 18 L | 36 L |
| barley | | 300 g | 600 g | 1.2 kg |
| onions, Spanish, finely diced | | 500 g | 1 kg | 2 kg |
| garlic, cloves, finely chopped | | 3 | 5 | 9 |
| carrots, topped and tailed, peeled, finely diced | | 300 g | 600 g | 1.2 kg |

continued

| | 300 g | 600 g | 1.2 kg |
| --- | --- | --- | --- |
| **celery**, finely diced | 300 g | 600 g | 1.2 kg |
| **parsnips**, peeled, topped and tailed, finely diced | 300 g | 600 g | 1.2 kg |
| **leeks**, topped and tailed, outer leaves removed, finely sliced, washed | 300 g | 600 g | 1.2 kg |
| **turnips**, peeled, finely diced | 300 g | 600 g | 1.2 kg |
| **salt and freshly milled black pepper** | to taste | | |

**Method**

1 Place beef stock in a saucepan over a moderate heat and add barley. Cover with a tightly fitting lid and simmer for approx. one hour.
2 Add vegetables to beef stock and bring back to the boil. Skim any scum from the surface once the stock has boiled. Reduce heat to a gentle simmer and cook for approx. 45 minutes–1 hour or until all ingredients are tender.
3 Season to taste and serve.

**♥ Health tip**

Barley is a good source of soluble fibre. Soluble fibre can help to lower cholesterol levels. Therefore this recipe is particularly recommended for people on a cholesterol-lowering diet.

# Tomato and roasted red capsicum soup flavoured with fresh basil

**G**arnish: freshly shaved parmesan cheese.

**Ingredients**

| | 25 | 50 | 100 |
| --- | --- | --- | --- |
| **olive oil/vegetable oil** | as required | | |
| **onions**, Spanish, finely chopped | 1 kg | 2 kg | 4 kg |
| **garlic**, cloves, finely chopped | 3 | 5 | 9 |
| **tomatoes**, crushed, A10 tin | 3 | 6 | 12 |
| **red capsicums**, roasted, finely chopped | 500 g | 1 kg | 2 kg |
| **basil**, fresh, roughly chopped | 20 g | 40 g | 80 g |
| **salt and freshly milled black pepper** | to taste | | |

**Method**

1 Put a little oil in a saucepan over a moderate heat. Add onions and garlic and cook until onions are tender.
2 Add tomato, red capsicum and basil. Bring to the boil and simmer gently for approx. 30 minutes or until required consistency is achieved.
3 Season to taste and serve.

**Note** Roast capsicum by removing stalk and seeds, quartering and roughly chopping. Place capsicum into a deep sided roasting tray tossed with a little olive oil and place into a pre-heated moderate oven (150–180°C) and roast, turning regularly, for approx. 30–45 minutes or until the flesh is soft, and the skin is easily removed.

# Cream of tomato soup

Garnish: finely chopped chives and a little sour cream.

Ingredients

| | 25 | 50 | 100 |
|---|---|---|---|
| olive oil/vegetable oil | as required | | |
| onions, white, finely chopped | 1 kg | 2 kg | 4 kg |
| garlic, cloves, finely chopped | 3 | 5 | 9 |
| tomatoes, crushed, A10 tin | 1 | 2 | 4 |
| tomato paste | 2 kg | 4 kg | 8 kg |
| water | 3.5 L | 7 L | 14 L |
| basil, fresh, roughly chopped | 20 g | 40 g | 80 g |
| sugar | 100 g | 200 g | 400 g |
| cream, single | 500 mL | 1 L | 2 L |
| salt and freshly milled black pepper | to taste | | |

Method

1 Heat a little oil in a saucepan over a moderate heat. Add onions and garlic and cook until onions are tender.
2 Add crushed tomatoes and paste, water, basil and sugar, whisk thoroughly. Bring to the boil and simmer gently for approx. 45 minutes or until required consistency is achieved.
3 Season to taste. Whisk in cream, re-heat, do not boil, and serve.

❤ Health tip  To reduce fat content, use low fat sour cream in place of regular cream.

# Hearty split yellow pea and ham soup

Garnish: croûtons.

Ingredients

| | 25 | 50 | 100 |
|---|---|---|---|
| stock, chicken | 4.5 L | 9 L | 18 L |
| water | 4.5 L | 9 L | 18 L |
| ham, hocks | 1 | 2 | 4 |
| split peas, yellow, pre-soaked | 1.5 kg | 3 kg | 6 kg |
| carrots, topped and tailed, peeled, finely chopped | 300 g | 600 g | 1.2 kg |
| celery, finely chopped | 300 g | 600 g | 1.2 kg |
| onions, white, finely chopped | 1 kg | 2 kg | 4 kg |
| salt and freshly milled black pepper | to taste | | |

Method

1 Place hocks into a saucepan and add chicken stock and water. Bring to the boil covered with a tight fitting lid. Simmer gently for one hour.
2 Remove ham hocks and cool. Remove all flesh and cut into 1 cm dice, skim any scum that has risen to the surface of the stock.
3 Add all ingredients, including meat, to stock and simmer gently for approx. 45 minutes–1 hour.
4 Correct seasoning and serve.

❤ Health tip  This soup is high in fibre.

# Mild curried lentil soup

Garnish: a sprig of fresh coriander.

| Ingredients | | 25 | 50 | 100 |
|---|---|---|---|---|
| olive oil/vegetable oil | | as required | | |
| onions, white, roughly chopped | | 1 kg | 2 kg | 4 kg |
| garlic, cloves, finely chopped | | 3 | 5 | 9 |
| lentils, pre-soaked | | 1.5 kg | 3 kg | 6 kg |
| curry powder, mild | | 100 g | 200 g | 400 g |
| stock, chicken, warmed | | 8 L | 16 L | 32 L |
| coconut cream | | 500 mL | 1 L | 2 L |
| salt and freshly milled black pepper | | to taste | | |

**Method**

1 Heat a little oil in a saucepan over a moderate heat. Add onions and garlic and cook until onions are soft.
2 Reduce heat, add lentils and curry powder and mix well.
3 Gradually mix in warmed stock until it is all incorporated and bring to the boil covered with a tight fitting lid. Reduce heat to a gentle simmer and cook for approx. 1 hour or until lentils are cooked.
4 Whisk in coconut cream, re-heat and season to taste and serve.

**Health tips**

This soup is high in fibre.

To make more suitable for low fat diets, use plain yoghurt instead of coconut cream.

# CHAPTER 3

# ENTRÉES

## Cold entrées

| | |
|---|---|
| **Caesar salad** with Caesar salad dressing | 32 |
| **Fresh asparagus spears** with cracked pepper, Parmesan cheese and an English mustard vinaigrette* | 33 |
| **Mixed melon and prosciutto salad** | 34 |
| **Individual antipasto plate** with herbed vinaigrette | 34 |
| **Rare roasted marinated beef and fresh mango salad** with a Thai-style dressing | 35 |
| **Rock oysters** served with a tomato and balsamic vinegar salsa | 36 |
| **Provençale-style mussels in the half shell** | 37 |

## Hot entrées

| | |
|---|---|
| **Crispy breaded mushroom caps** stuffed with pâté served with aïoli | 38 |
| **Warm tart of wild mushrooms, goat's cheese and roasted red capsicum** | 40 |
| **Japanese-style scallops** with a mirin and spring onion sauce served on a bed of soba noodles | 41 |
| **Warm asparagus** served with a lemon hollandaise sauce | 42 |
| **Tempura prawns** served with a Thai-style dipping sauce | 43 |
| **Italian-style risotto** flavoured with garlic, leeks, sun-dried tomatoes and Kalamata olives | 44 |
| **Italian-style slow baked eggplant** with ricotta cheese* | 45 |

* Suitable for a vegetarian diet

# COLD ENTRÉES

## Caesar salad with Caesar salad dressing

| Ingredients | | | 25 | 50 | 100 |
|---|---|---|---|---|---|
|  | **bread**, crusts removed | | 500 g | 1 kg | 2 kg |
| | **butter** | | 100 g | 200 g | 400 g |
| | **cos lettuce**, remove outer leaves and any leaves that are bruised or damaged and slice into strips approx. 3 cm wide, wash and place to one side to drain | | 5 | 10 | 20 |
| | **dressing** | | see following recipe | | |
| | **anchovy fillets**, roughly chopped, optional | | 25 | 50 | 100 |
| | **bacon**, rind removed, finely diced, cooked until crisp | | 500 g | 1 kg | 2 kg |
| | **Parmesan**, fresh, shaved | | 125 g | 250 g | 500 g |
| | **black pepper**, freshly milled | | to taste | | |

**Method**

1 Prepare croûtons by cutting bread into 1 cm dice.
2 Melt the butter in a sauté/frying pan over a moderate heat. Cook croûtons till crisp, remove and place on kitchen paper to drain excess oil.
3 Place leaves into a mixing bowl and pour over enough dressing to lightly coat the lettuce. Add anchovies, bacon, half of the Parmesan cheese and half the croûtons and mix well.
4 Immediately place even amounts of Caesar salad into required size serving bowls/plates. Evenly sprinkle over remaining Parmesan cheese and croûtons.
5 Season with freshly milled black pepper and serve immediately.

**Health tip**  Unsuitable for a low fat diet.

## Caesar salad dressing

Yields approx. 1 L.

| Ingredients | | |
|---|---|---|
|  | **garlic**, cloves, finely chopped | 4 |
| | **anchovy fillets**, finely chopped | 6 |
| | **mustard**, Dijon | 120 g |
| | **egg**, yolks | 4 |
| | **lemon**, juice | 120 mL |
| | **lemon**, zest | 1 |
| | **Worcestershire sauce** | 120 mL |
| | **extra virgin olive oil** | 600 mL |
| | **vinegar**, red wine | 120 mL |
| | **egg**, boiled for exactly 1 minute, peeled | 3 |
| | **salt** | to taste |

1 Put all ingredients except salt into a blender and blend until smooth.
2 Season to taste and serve.

# Fresh asparagus spears with cracked pepper, Parmesan cheese and an English mustard vinaigrette

Garnish: a sprig of fresh basil.

Ingredients

| | 25 | 50 | 100 |
|---|---|---|---|
| asparagus, spears, trimmed | 5 kg | 10 kg | 20 kg |
| English mustard vinaigrette | see following recipe | | |
| freshly milled black pepper | to taste | | |
| Parmesan cheese, fresh, shaved | 125 g | 250 g | 500 g |

Method   1 Plunge asparagus spears into boiling water and cook for one minute. Remove and refresh under cold running water and drain well.
2 Divide asparagus evenly and place onto the centre of plates in a random criss-cross fashion.
3 Just prior to serving, drizzle with a little English mustard vinaigrette.
4 Sprinkle asparagus with freshly milled black pepper and Parmesan cheese and serve.

## English mustard vinaigrette

Yields approx. 1 L.

Ingredients

| | |
|---|---|
| olive oil | 700 mL |
| mustard, English | 50 g |
| vinegar | 300 mL |
| sugar, castor | 200 g |
| salt and freshly milled black pepper | to taste |

Method   Combine all ingredients, whisk thoroughly and serve.

# Mixed melon and prosciutto salad

Garnish: half a lime.

Ingredients

| | 25 | 50 | 100 |
|---|---|---|---|
| melon, assorted, peeled, seeded, cut into 4 cm x 2 cm x 1 cm | 3.75 kg | 7.5 kg | 15 kg |
| prosciutto, very finely sliced | 75 slices | 150 slices | 300 slices |
| parsley, fresh, finely chopped | 20 g | 40 g | 80 g |
| paprika | as required | | |

Method

1 Divide melon evenly between plates, placing on the centre of the plate in a pyramid fashion.
2 Carefully drape melon with 3 slices of prosciutto to expose some of the colour of the melon.
3 Sprinkle the melon and prosciutto with a little of the chopped parsley and dust around the melon with a little paprika.
4 Serve with half a lime on the side of each plate.


# Individual antipasto plate with herbed vinaigrette

Garnish: finely chopped basil.

Ingredients

| | 25 | 50 | 100 |
|---|---|---|---|
| eggplant, topped and tailed, halved lengthways, sliced across the width, 1 cm thick | 2.5 kg | 5 kg | 10 kg |
| zucchini, topped and tailed, finely sliced lengthways | 2.5 kg | 5 kg | 10 kg |
| mushrooms, washed, quartered | 1.25 kg | 2.5 kg | 5 kg |
| olives, Kalamata | 75 | 150 | 300 |
| sun-dried tomatoes | 50 pieces | 100 pieces | 200 pieces |
| prosciutto ham, very finely sliced | 50 slices | 100 slices | 200 slices |
| red capsicum, roasted (see note) | 1.25 kg | 2.5 kg | 5 kg |
| herbed vinaigrette | see following recipe | | |

Method

1 On a lightly oiled pre-heated grill plate, cook eggplant and zucchini until lightly browned and tender, turning regularly.
2 Place cooked eggplant and zucchini into separate mixing bowls. Add a generous amount of herbed vinaigrette to each bowl and mix gently.
3 Place mushrooms into a mixing bowl. Add a generous amount of herbed vinaigrette and mix.

4 Evenly divide all ingredients and place creatively onto the plates making sure to drain any excess oil from ingredients. Garnish and serve.

**Note** Roast capsicum by removing stalk and seeds, quartering and roughly chopping. Place capsicum into a deep sided roasting tray tossed with a little olive oil and place into a pre-heated moderate oven (150–180°C) and roast, turning regularly, for approx. 30–45 minutes or until the flesh is soft, and the skin is easily removed.

## Herbed vinaigrette

**Y**ields approx. 1 L.

Ingredients

| | |
|---|---|
| olive oil | 700 mL |
| mustard, French | 50 g |
| vinegar | 150 mL |
| lemon, juice | 150 mL |
| chives, finely sliced | 10 g |
| parsley, finely chopped | 10 g |
| basil, finely chopped | 10 g |
| salt and freshly milled black pepper | to taste |

Method Combine all ingredients, whisk well and serve.

# Rare roasted marinated beef and fresh mango salad with a Thai-style dressing

**G**arnish: crispy julienne of leek and finely sliced roasted red capsicum.

Ingredients

| | 25 | 50 | 100 |
|---|---|---|---|
| beef, fillet, trimmed | 2.5 kg | 5 kg | 10 kg |
| Thai-style marinade/dressing | see following recipe | | |
| mango, skinned, cut into small strips | 6 | 12 | 24 |
| coral lettuce, leaves, washed, cut into 2 cm strips | 4 | 8 | 16 |
| cos lettuce, leaves, washed, cut into 2 cm strips | 4 | 8 | 16 |
| watercress, sprigs, picked, washed | 125 g | 250 g | 500 g |
| coriander, leaves, picked, washed | 125 g | 250 g | 500 g |
| basil, purple, leaves, picked, washed | 50 g | 100 g | 200 g |

continued

| Method | |
|---|---|
| | 1 Pre-heat oven to moderate (150–180°C). |
| | 2 Trim beef fillet/s of any excess fat and sinew. Sear on all sides over a high heat on a grill plate or in a pan with a little oil. |
| | 3 Place into oven and roast for 10–15 minutes. |
| | 4 Cool and refrigerate. |
| | 5 Finely slice fillet/s across the grain. |
| | 6 Place beef slices and mango into a mixing bowl. Add a little of the marinade and mix together gently. |
| | 7 Mix lettuce leaves and herbs together in a mixing bowl and place an even amount onto the centre of each plate. Place a small amount of the marinated beef and mango in the centre of the lettuce. |
| | 8 Gently drizzle a little of the remaining marinade/dressing over the meat and garnish. |
| | 9 Serve immediately. |

## Marinade/dressing

Yields approx. 1 L.

Ingredients

| Ingredient | Amount |
|---|---|
| soya sauce | 500 mL |
| vinegar, white | 400 mL |
| lemon, juice | 100 mL |
| sugar, castor | to taste |
| ginger, fresh, peeled, finely grated | 10 g |
| garlic, cloves, finely chopped | 2 |
| chillies, red, small, topped and tailed, seeded, finely chopped | 2 |
| coriander, leaves, finely chopped | 10 g |

**Method**  Mix all ingredients and refrigerate for approx. 2 hours.

# Rock oysters served with a tomato and balsamic vinegar salsa

Garnish: wedges of fresh lemon and lime.

| Ingredients | | 25 | 50 | 100 |
|---|---|---|---|---|
| oysters, rock, half shell | | 150 | 300 | 600 |

### TOMATO AND BALSAMIC VINEGAR SALSA:

| | | | |
|---|---|---|---|
| tomatoes | 13 | 25 | 50 |
| chillies, red, small | 4 | 8 | 16 |
| onions, Spanish, finely diced | 3 | 6 | 12 |
| garlic, cloves, peeled, finely chopped | 4 | 7 | 10 |
| olive oil | 50 mL | 100 mL | 200 mL |
| lemons/limes, juice and zest | 2 | 4 | 8 |
| vinegar, balsamic | to taste | | |
| salt and freshly milled black pepper | to taste | | |

**Method**

1 Score bottom of tomatoes and place into a pan of boiling water for approx. 20 seconds or until skin separates from tomato.
2 Refresh tomatoes immediately under cold running water and remove skin. Drain.
3 Quarter tomatoes, remove seeds and core. Finely dice the flesh.
4 Top and tail chillies, remove seeds and finely dice the flesh and mix with tomatoes in a bowl.
5 Add Spanish onion and garlic to tomatoes and combine.
6 Add olive oil, lemon/lime juice and zest, balsamic vinegar, salt and pepper. Combine.
7 Cover with cling wrap and refrigerate for at least 2–3 hours before serving.
8 Place a small amount of the salsa on top of each oyster and serve allowing six oysters per portion.

**Note**  **Salsa** is the Mexican word for sauce; it can be applied to cooked or uncooked mixtures. Salsa is classically made up of tomatoes, chillies and onions and can be used as an accompaniment to a wide variety of dishes.

# Provençale-style mussels in the half shell

Garnish: wedges of fresh lemon and a sprig of continental parsley.

**Ingredients**

| | 25 | 50 | 100 |
|---|---|---|---|
| olive oil/vegetable oil | as required | | |
| onions, Spanish, finely chopped | 500 g | 1 kg | 2 kg |
| garlic, cloves, finely chopped | 3 | 5 | 9 |
| tomatoes, crushed, A10 tin | 1/2 | 1 | 2 |
| vinegar, balsamic | 100 mL | 200 mL | 400 mL |
| basil, fresh, finely chopped | 20 g | 40 g | 80 g |
| parsley, fresh, finely chopped | 25 g | 50 g | 100 g |
| salt and freshly milled black pepper | to taste | | |
| mussels, small, black | 14 kg | 28 kg | 56 kg |

continued

**Method**

1 Put a little oil in a saucepan over a moderate heat. Cook onions and garlic until onions are soft.
2 Add crushed tomato, balsamic vinegar, basil and one-third of the parsley. Reduce heat, simmer and reduce until sauce thickens. Season to taste and remove from heat. Cool completely.
3 Wash mussels thoroughly under cold running water and remove the beard. Place mussels into a steamer and cook for approx. 2–4 minutes or until shells have opened and mussels are just cooked.
4 Remove mussels from steamer and cool. Break away the top half of the shell and discard.
5 Mix remaining parsley through tomato sauce and fill each mussel with a little of the provençale sauce and place neatly onto plates allowing approx. 8–12 mussels per portion.

**Note**

Any mussels purchased uncooked with their shells open, or any that fail to open after the cooking process, should be discarded.

# HOT ENTRÉES

## Crispy breaded mushroom caps stuffed with pâté served with aïoli

Garnish: finely chopped fresh parsley.

**Ingredients**

| | 25 | 50 | 100 |
|---|---|---|---|
| **mushrooms**, button, medium sized, washed and drained, stalks removed | 125 | 250 | 500 |
| **pâté** of your choice | 2.5 kg | 5 kg | 10 kg |
| **flour**, plain | as required | | |
| **eggs** | 10 | 20 | 40 |
| **milk** | 200 mL | 600 mL | 1.2 L |
| **breadcrumbs** | as required | | |
| **salt and freshly milled black pepper** | to taste | | |

**Method**

1 Pre-heat deep fryer to 170°C.
2 Take button mushrooms and using a teaspoon fill mushroom caps and smooth over so mushroom caps are filled just to the brim.
3 Place flour into a stainless steel bowl and the eggs, which have been beaten together with the milk, into a second bowl. Place the breadcrumbs into a third bowl.
4 Dredge mushroom caps through flour, egg mixture and breadcrumbs; gently shake off any excess breadcrumbs.
5 Gently place mushrooms into deep fryer in small batches and cook to a light golden brown. Remove from oil and drain any excess fat.
6 Serve onto warmed plates, allowing 5 per portion built into a pyramid shape on a bed of aïoli.

**Note** Extra pâté may be required, depending on the size of the mushroom caps.

# Aïoli

| Ingredients | | | 25 | 50 | 100 |
|---|---|---|---|---|---|
|  | **mayonnaise**, see following recipe | | 1 L | 2 L | 4 L |
| | **garlic**, cloves, peeled and minced | | 6 | 12 | 24 |
| | **salt and freshly milled black pepper** | | to taste | | |

**Method**
1 Combine mayonnaise and minced garlic. Season to taste.
2 Refrigerate until required, allowing one full dessertspoon per portion.

**Note** When refrigerating aïoli keep covered so that the garlic aroma does not interfere with other foods.

 **Health tip** Unsuitable for a low fat diet.

# Mayonnaise

**Y**ields 1 L.

| Ingredients | | |
|---|---|---|
|  | **egg**, yolks | 8 |
| | **mustard**, English | 25 g |
| | **vinegar**, white | 50 mL |
| | **salt and freshly milled black pepper** | to taste |
| | **olive oil**, room temperature | 1 L |

**Method**
1 Place egg yolks, mustard, vinegar, salt and pepper into a bowl and whisk well.
2 Slowly add oil, whisking continuously until all oil has been incorporated.
3 Correct seasoning and use as required.

**Notes** If mixture curdles add one egg yolk and a dash of vinegar to a clean mixing bowl. Whisking continuously, slowly add curdled mixture.

# Warm tart of wild mushrooms, goat's cheese and roasted red capsicum

Garnish: serve on a bed of mixed leaves tossed in a little vinaigrette dressing.

**Ingredients**

| | 25 | 50 | 100 |
|---|---|---|---|
| oil | as required | | |
| pastry, puff | as required | | |
| butter | 100 g | 200 g | 400 g |
| onions, white, finely chopped | 250 g | 500 g | 1 kg |
| garlic, cloves, finely chopped | 3 | 5 | 9 |
| mushrooms, Swiss brown, finely sliced | 250 g | 500 g | 1 kg |
| feta cheese | 200 g | 400 g | 800 g |
| red capsicum, roasted, cut into thin strips | 200 g  see following note | 400 g | 800 g |
| milk | 1 L | 2 L | 4 L |
| eggs | 6 | 12 | 24 |
| salt and freshly milled black pepper | to taste | | |

**Method**

1 Pre-heat oven to moderate (150–180°C).
2 Lightly grease individual tart moulds approx. 10 cm diameter x 2 cm deep. On a lightly floured surface, roll out puff pastry to a thickness of approx. 3 mm and line with tart moulds ensuring pastry is pressed firmly into mould.
3 Place 10 cm squares of greaseproof paper onto each mould and pour rice onto paper so all moulds are filled.
4 Place moulds into pre-heated moderate oven (150–180°C) and bake blind for approx. 5 minutes.
   Remove from oven and cool, retaining rice for further use.
5 Melt butter in a saucepan over moderate heat. Add onions and garlic and cook until onions are tender. Add mushrooms and cook until mushrooms are tender.
6 Remove from heat and drain in a colander.
7 Place mushroom mixture into a mixing bowl and crumble feta cheese into mixture. Mix together.
8 Beat eggs and milk together thoroughly. Season to taste.
9 Place mixture evenly into required amount of tart cases and carefully fill with egg and milk mixture.
10 Carefully place two strips of capsicum in a cross pattern on top of tart. Return tarts to low oven and cook for approx. 10–15 minutes or until tart has set.
11 Remove from oven and cool for approx. 2 minutes. Carefully remove from tart moulds.
12 Serve on warmed plates allowing one tart per portion.

**Note** Roast capsicum by removing stalk and seeds, quartering and roughly chopping. Place capsicum into a deep sided roasting tray tossed with a little olive oil and place into a pre-heated moderate oven (150–180°C) and roast, turning regularly, for approx. 30–45 minutes or until the flesh is soft, and the skin is easily removed.

❤ **Health tip** Unsuitable for a low fat diet.

# Japanese-style scallops with a mirin and spring onion sauce served on a bed of soba noodles

Garnish: a sprig of fresh mint.

| Ingredients | | 25 | 50 | 100 |
|---|---|---|---|---|
| soba noodles | | 2 kg | 4 kg | 8 kg |
| butter | | 200 g | 400 g | 800 g |
| garlic, cloves, finely chopped | | 6 | 10 | 15 |
| ginger, peeled, grated | | 50 g | 100 g | 200 g |
| spring onions, trimmed, finely sliced | | 250 g | 500 g | 1 kg |
| mirin, Japanese rice wine | | 1 L | 2 L | 4 L |
| scallops, cleaned | | 125 | 250 | 500 |

**Method**

1 Plunge soba noodles into lightly salted boiling water and cook until tender but firm. Remove from water and refresh under cold running water and drain thoroughly. Keep water simmering to re-heat soba noodles.

2 Melt butter in a sauté pan over a moderate heat. Add garlic, ginger and spring onions. Reduce heat and cook slowly without colour for approx. 4–5 minutes stirring occasionally.

3 Add mirin and simmer until sauce has reduced by one-quarter.

4 Place soba noodles back into boiling water for approx. 30 seconds–1 minute or until heated thoroughly. Remove and drain well.

5 While sauce is reducing, melt a little butter in a sauté pan/flat grill plate over a high heat. Once butter is hot, add scallops and sauté for approx. 1–3 minutes, agitating pan constantly until scallops are just cooked through.

6 Immediately place scallops in the reduced mirin sauce and mix well. Remove from heat.

7 Evenly divide soba noodles between warmed plates, placing them in the centre of the plates, and place 5 scallops on top of noodles. Spoon over a little of the sauce and serve immediately.

**Note** When preparing large amounts of scallops, cooking in batches is advisable.

# Warm asparagus served with a lemon hollandaise sauce

Garnish: a light sprinkle of paprika.

| Ingredients | | | 25 | 50 | 100 |
|---|---|---|---|---|---|
|  | **asparagus**, spears, trimmed | | 6 kg | 12 kg | 24 kg |
| | **LEMON HOLLANDAISE SAUCE:** | | | | |
| | **vinegar**, white | | 50 mL | 100 mL | 200 mL |
| | **lemon**, juice | | 50 mL | 100 mL | 200 mL |
| | **zest**, lemon | | 1/2 | 1 | 2 |
| | **freshly milled black pepper** | | to taste | | |
| | **egg**, yolks | | 4 | 8 | 16 |
| | **butter** | | 1 kg | 2 kg | 4 kg |
| | **salt and freshly milled black pepper** | | to taste | | |

**Method**

1  Place vinegar, lemon juice and zest and a little freshly milled black pepper into a saucepan over a moderate heat (150–180°C). Reduce by two-thirds and remove from heat.

2  Place butter into a pan and melt over a low heat. Remove from heat.

3  Place egg yolks into a stainless steel mixing bowl. Add cooled vinegar and lemon mixture and whisk well.

4  While whisking gradually incorporate melted butter until combined.

5  Check seasoning and stand to one side in a warm spot.

6  Plunge asparagus spears into boiling water and cook for one minute. Remove from water and drain well.

7  Place a little of the warm hollandaise sauce into the centre of the warm plates. Allowing 3–4 pieces of asparagus per serve, arrange in a random criss-cross fashion and serve immediately.

**Notes**

If a food processor is available, add egg yolks and the vinegar and lemon juice reduction and blend for a few seconds. While blender is running continuously, add the warm melted butter in a slow drizzle until all is incorporated.

Hollandaise sauce should **not** be re-heated as this will curdle the sauce. If the sauce does curdle add a tablespoon of boiling water and re-whisk. If this fails to reconstitute the sauce, repeat process with one egg yolk, whisking continually in a clean mixing bowl, gradually adding the curdled sauce.

# Tempura prawns served with a Thai-style dipping sauce

Garnish: roughly chopped fresh coriander.

Ingredients

| | 25 | 50 | 100 |
|---|---|---|---|
| cornflour | 1 kg | 2 kg | 4 kg |
| rice flour | 1 kg | 2 kg | 4 kg |
| vinegar, white | 20 mL | 40 mL | 80 mL |
| water, iced | as required | | |
| salt | to taste | | |
| flour, plain | 1 kg | 2 kg | 4 kg |
| prawns, green, shelled, tail on, de-veined, butterflied | 100 | 200 | 400 |
| Thai-style dipping sauce, chilled | see following recipe | | |

Method

1  Pre-heat deep fryer to 170°C.
2  In a mixing bowl combine cornflour, rice flour and vinegar. Slowly incorporate iced water until a consistency is reached that will thickly coat the back of a spoon. Season to taste.
3  Ensuring prawns are dry, lightly coat with flour and dip into batter mix making sure all the prawns are coated in the batter. Drain any excess mixture and carefully place into hot oil.
4  Cook prawns until they float to the surface and are golden brown.
5  Carefully remove prawns from oil and drain all excess fat.
6  Immediately place a little of the sauce on the centre of the warmed plates, arrange 4 prawns in a pyramid, and serve immediately.

# Thai-style dipping sauce

Yields: 1 L.

Ingredients

| | |
|---|---|
| soya sauce | 500 mL |
| vinegar, white | 400 mL |
| lemon, juice | 100 mL |
| sugar, castor | to taste |
| ginger, fresh, peeled, finely chopped | 10 g |
| garlic, cloves, finely chopped | 2 |
| chillies, red, small, topped and tailed, seeded, finely chopped | 2 |
| coriander, leaves, finely chopped | 10 g |

Method  Mix all ingredients and refrigerate for approx. 2 hours.

# Italian-style risotto flavoured with garlic, leeks, sun-dried tomatoes and Kalamata olives

Garnish: finely diced tomato concassé mixed with freshly chopped parsley.

**Ingredients**

| | 25 | 50 | 100 |
|---|---|---|---|
| olive oil/vegetable oil | as required | | |
| garlic, cloves, finely chopped | 4 | 6 | 8 |
| onions, white, finely chopped | 750 g | 1.5 kg | 3 kg |
| leeks, trimmed, washed, finely sliced | 1.5 kg | 3 kg | 6 kg |
| butter | 175 g | 350 g | 700 g |
| rice, Arborio or long grained | 1.2 kg | 2.4 kg | 4.8 kg |
| stock, chicken, warmed | 3 L | 6 L | 12 L |
| parsley, fresh, finely chopped | 30 g | 60 g | 120 g |
| olives, Kalamata, stoned, roughly chopped | 100 g | 200 g | 400 g |
| sun-dried tomatoes, finely shredded | 50 g | 100 g | 200 g |
| Parmesan cheese, shaved | 50 g | 100 g | 200 g |
| salt and freshly milled black pepper | to taste | | |

**Method**

1 Heat a little oil in a saucepan over a moderate heat. Add garlic and onion and cook until onion is soft.

2 Add leeks and cook for a further two minutes.

3 Reduce heat and add butter. When butter has melted, add rice and stir continually ensuring all rice is completely coated with butter.

4 Slowly add warmed stock until all has been incorporated stirring continuously.

5 Place a tight fitting lid over saucepan. Cook slowly, stirring regularly until all stock has been absorbed and the rice is tender.

6 Thoroughly mix in parsley, olives, sun-dried tomatoes and shaved Parmesan and cook for a further five minutes (stir regularly to ensure rice does not stick and burn to the bottom of the pan).

7 Season to taste, remove from heat and serve.

**Note**

**Risotto** is a classic Italian dish, usually made with Arborio rice. It is cooked slowly to allow the rice to absorb the many flavours and ingredients that can be used. Arborio rice, with its white core, stays firm while the rest of the grain leaks starch into the liquid, producing a velvety sauce. However, long grained rice can be substituted.

# Italian-style slow baked eggplant with ricotta cheese

Garnish: sprigs of fresh basil.

**Ingredients**

| | 25 | 50 | 100 |
|---|---|---|---|
| olive oil/vegetable oil | as required | | |
| onions, Spanish, finely chopped | 500 g | 1 kg | 2 kg |
| garlic, cloves, finely chopped | 3 | 5 | 9 |
| tomatoes, crushed, A10 tin | 1/2 | 1 | 2 |
| vinegar, balsamic | 100 mL | 200 mL | 400 mL |
| basil, fresh, finely chopped | 20 g | 40 g | 80 g |
| parsley, fresh, finely chopped | 25 g | 50 g | 100 g |
| salt and freshly milled black pepper | to taste | | |
| eggplant, topped and tailed, sliced lengthways 1 1/2 cm thick | 4.5 kg | 9 kg | 18 kg |
| tomatoes, Roma, cored, finely sliced lengthways | 2 kg | 4 kg | 8 kg |
| cheese, ricotta | 1.25 kg | 2.5 kg | 5 kg |
| mozzarella cheese, sliced | 500 g | 1 kg | 2 kg |

**Method**

1 Pre-heat oven to moderate (150–180°C).
2 Put a little oil in a saucepan over a moderate heat. Cook onions and garlic until onions are soft.
3 Add crushed tomatoes, balsamic vinegar, basil and one-third of the parsley. Reduce heat and simmer. Reduce until sauce thickens, season to taste and remove from heat. Cool completely.
4 Lightly brush a grill plate or sauté pan with a little oil over a moderate heat and lightly cook eggplant on both sides until lightly browned.
5 Onto lightly oiled baking tray/s, place one layer of eggplant slices keeping a small space between each one.
6 Place a layer of sliced tomato onto each piece of eggplant and top with a little of the prepared tomato sauce.
7 Spread a little of the ricotta cheese evenly over the tomato sauce. Sprinkle a little sliced mozzarella cheese over the ricotta cheese. Finally top with a slice of eggplant and press down gently.
8 Place tray/s into oven and cook for approx. 20–30 minutes.
9 Remove from oven and serve immediately on warmed plate. Allow one eggplant bake per portion.

**P**ASTA

\* Suitable for a vegetarian diet
† Suitable for a vegan diet

# A GUIDE TO SOME OF THE MOST COMMON PASTAS

Most pasta can be obtained either plain or flavoured/coloured with various ingredients such as herbs, spinach, tomatoes or numerous other puréed vegetables. Pasta can also be made using wholemeal flours.

| Name | Description |
| --- | --- |
| Agnolotti | Stuffed semi-circular pasta resembling ravioli. |
| Anelini | Small pasta rings, approx. 4–6 mm in diameter; excellent with sauces and in minestrone. |
| Bavette | Long, flat, thin strands. |
| Bucatini | Long, slim, hollow pasta tubes. |
| Cannelloni | Large hollow tubes, usually stuffed e.g. with spinach and ricotta cheese, covered with a sauce and baked. |
| Capellini | Long, thin strips of pasta, usually coiled to resemble a nest. |
| Diamantini | Very small diamond shapes for use in soups; will act as a thickening agent. |
| Eliche | Short, spiral shaped pasta. |
| Farfalle | Bow tie shaped pasta approx. 2–3 cm long. |
| Farfallini | Small bow tie shaped pasta with serrated edges; can act as a thickening agent when used in soups. |
| Fettuccine | Long, flat pasta approx. 1 cm in width. |
| Fusilli bucati | Hollow pasta that has been twisted. |
| Gnocchi | Pasta dough made into dumplings. |
| Lasagne | Sheets of flat pasta. |
| Linguine | Long, thin strips of pasta cut square. |
| Macaroni | Hollow, thick pasta approx. 3–4 cm in length. |
| Pappardelle | Long, flat, ribbon-like pasta. |
| Penne | Thick, hollow tubes with ends cut at 45 degrees. |
| Pipe rigate | Ridged, hollow, snail-like pasta. |
| Ravioli | Square, stuffed pasta. |
| Rigatoni | Long tubes of pasta with large ridges. |
| Rissoni | Small, rice-shaped pasta. |
| Spaghetti | Long, thin, round pasta; thickness may vary. |
| Tagliatelle | Long, flat, ribbon-like pasta. |
| Tortellini | Crescent-shaped, stuffed pasta. |

# PASTA RECIPES

## How to cook pasta

**A**llow approx. 80 g of dry pasta per person.
Always cook pasta in plenty of lightly salted boiling water to allow for its absorption by the pasta.

**Ingredients**

| | 25 | 50 | 100 |
|---|---|---|---|
| water | 7.5 L | 15 L | 30 L |
| olive oil/vegetable oil | 50 mL | 100 mL | 200 mL |
| salt, approx. | 20 g | 40 g | 80 g |
| pasta, dry | 2 kg | 4 kg | 8 kg |

**Method**

1 Fill a saucepan with water and bring to the boil.
2 Add oil and salt to water.
3 Plunge pasta into water and stir thoroughly making sure all pasta is separated.
4 Simmer until pasta is firm but tender — 'al dente'.
5 If not used immediately, drain pasta and refresh under cold running water.
6 To re-heat pasta, plunge it into a saucepan of boiling water until pasta is heated through, stirring constantly.
7 Strain and serve.

**Note**

Cooking times will vary depending on the amount and variety of pasta being cooked; careful monitoring is required.

**Health tip**

To make pasta dishes lower in fat:
• reduce cheese quantity
• use a low fat cheese
• use only a little oil when softening onions
• use reduced fat milk
• substitute cream with skim evaporated milk

# Farfalle pasta with our ratatouille

Garnish: fresh sprigs of basil.

## Farfalle pasta

Allow approx. 80 g of dry pasta per person.
Always cook pasta in plenty of lightly salted boiling water to allow for its absorption by the pasta.

| Ingredients | | | 25 | 50 | 100 |
|---|---|---|---|---|---|
| |  | water | 7.5 L | 15 L | 30 L |
| | | olive oil/vegetable oil | 50 mL | 100 mL | 200 mL |
| | | salt | 20 g | 40 g | 80 g |
| | | farfalle pasta, dry | 2 kg | 4 kg | 8 kg |

Method
1 Fill a saucepan with water and bring to the boil.
2 Add oil and salt to water.
3 Plunge pasta into water and stir thoroughly making sure all pasta is separated.
4 Simmer until pasta is firm but tender — 'al dente'.
5 If not used immediately, drain pasta and refresh under cold running water.
6 To re-heat pasta, plunge it into the boiling water until pasta is heated through, stirring constantly.
7 Strain and serve.

**Note** Cooking times will vary depending on the amount and variety of pasta being cooked; careful monitoring is required.

## Ratatouille

| Ingredients | | | 25 | 50 | 100 |
|---|---|---|---|---|---|
| |  | olive oil/vegetable oil | as required | | |
| | | onions, Spanish, large dice | 1 kg | 2 kg | 4 kg |
| | | garlic, cloves, peeled, finely chopped | 4 | 8 | 16 |
| | | basil, leaves, fresh, finely chopped | 25 g | 50 g | 100 g |
| | | marjoram, dried | 15 g | 30 g | 60 g |
| | | bay-leaves, dried | 2 | 4 | 8 |
| | | zucchini, top and tail, cut into 2 cm dice | 2 kg | 4 kg | 8 kg |
| | | eggplant, top and tail, cut into 2 cm dice | 1 kg | 2 kg | 4 kg |
| | | tomatoes, remove core, cut into 2 cm dice | 1 kg | 2 kg | 4 kg |
| | | tomatoes, crushed, A10 tin | 1 | 2 | 4 |
| | | sugar, white | to taste | | |
| | | salt and freshly milled black pepper | to taste | | |

| Method | 1 Heat oil in a saucepan over a moderate heat. |
|---|---|
| | 2 Add onions and garlic. Cook without colour until tender. |
| | 3 Add basil, marjoram, bay-leaves and mix well. |
| | 4 Add zucchini, eggplant, tomato and mix well. |
| | 5 Allow vegetables to sweat until softened, stirring occasionally. |
| | 6 Add crushed tomatoes and mix well. |
| | 7 Place a tight fitting lid onto pan and simmer gently for approx. 30–40 minutes, stirring occasionally. |
| | 8 Add sugar, salt and freshly milled pepper to taste. |
| | 9 Remove from heat. Serve ratatouille on a little of the farfalle pasta. |

**Health tip**   Good for vegetarian diets and all other diets.

# Beef lasagne al forno

Garnish: melted grated cheese.

## White sauce (béchamel)

| Ingredients | | | 25 | 50 | 100 |
|---|---|---|---|---|---|
| |  | butter | 150 g | 300 g | 600 g |
| | | flour, plain | 150 g | 300 g | 600 g |
| | | milk | 2 L | 4 L | 8 L |
| | | salt and white pepper | to taste | | |

| Method | 1 Melt the butter in a saucepan over a moderate heat. |
|---|---|
| | 2 Add the flour and thoroughly incorporate butter using a wooden spoon. |
| | 3 Reduce heat and cook gently for approx. 2–3 minutes without colouring. |
| | 4 Gently warm the milk in a separate saucepan. |
| | 5 Slowly incorporate the milk in small amounts, making sure each addition has mixed with the roux smoothly. |
| | 6 Reduce heat and cook out gently for approx. 10 minutes, stirring regularly. |
| | 7 Remove from heat, strain and use as required. |

**Note**   When making a white sauce/béchamel it is always advisable, when possible, to use butter over margarine as it will give a slightly richer flavour. Nonetheless margarine will give a good finished product.

continued

# Meat sauce

| Ingredients | | 25 | 50 | 100 |
|---|---|---|---|---|
| olive oil/vegetable oil | | as required | | |
| garlic, cloves, peeled, finely chopped | | 5 | 8 | 11 |
| onions, white, finely sliced | | 400 g | 800 g | 1.6 kg |
| beef, minced | | 5 kg | 10 kg | 20 kg |
| flour, plain | | 150 g | 300 g | 600 g |
| tomato paste | | 300 g | 600 g | 1.2 kg |
| tomatoes, crushed, A10 tin | | 1/2 | 1 | 2 |
| stock, beef | | 2 L | 4 L | 8 L |
| basil, finely chopped | | 25 g | 50 g | 100 g |
| oregano, finely chopped | | 25 g | 50 g | 100 g |
| Parmesan cheese, grated | | 150 g | 300 g | 600 g |
| salt and freshly milled black pepper | | to taste | | |
| lasagne sheets, cooked, approx. | | 1 kg | 2 kg | 4 kg |
| mozzarella cheese, grated | | 250 g | 500 g | 1 kg |
| Cheddar cheese, grated | | 250 g | 500 g | 1 kg |
| parsley, roughly chopped | | 20 g | 40 g | 80 g |

**Method**

1 Pre-heat oven to moderate (150–180°C).
2 Heat a little oil in a saucepan over a moderate heat.
3 Add garlic and onions and cook without colour until tender.
4 Add beef and mix thoroughly with garlic and onions. Cook, stirring occasionally until meat is lightly browned.
5 Add flour and mix well.
6 Add tomato paste, crushed tomato, beef stock and herbs. Mix well. Simmer gently and reduce until thickened to the required consistency.
7 Mix through Parmesan. Season to taste.
8 Remove from heat and cool slightly.
9 Using deep sided baking/serving tray/s, ladle a layer of mixture onto the bottom, then place one layer of lasagne sheets over the top to cover all of the meat sauce.
10 Repeat process until 2 cm from top of baking/serving tray/s.
11 Place one more layer of lasagne sheets over mixture, and then top evenly with white sauce.
12 Sprinkle top liberally with grated cheeses and parsley. Place into oven for approx. 30–40 minutes or until lasagne has cooked through.
13 Pre-portion and serve.

**Note**
**Al forno** is an Italian term for 'baked'. 'Al forno' can be used on a menu to signify any Italian dish that has been baked, e.g. macaroni cheese can become macaroni cheese al forno.

**Health tip**
To reduce fat content, use low fat milk in béchamel sauce, omit cheese from meat sauce and use low fat cheese sparingly on top of the lasagne.

# Spaghetti bolognese

**G**arnish: freshly grated Parmesan cheese.

## Spaghetti

**A**llow approx. 80 g of dry pasta per person.
Always cook pasta in plenty of lightly salted boiling water to
allow for its absorption by the pasta.

Ingredients

| | 25 | 50 | 100 |
|---|---|---|---|
| water | 7.5 L | 15 L | 30 L |
| olive oil/vegetable oil | 50 mL | 100 mL | 200 mL |
| salt | 20 g | 40 g | 80 g |
| spaghetti, dry | 2 kg | 4 kg | 8 kg |

Method

1 Fill a saucepan with water and bring to the boil.
2 Add oil and salt to water.
3 Plunge pasta into water and stir thoroughly making sure all pasta
  is separated.
4 Simmer until pasta is firm but tender — 'al dente'.
5 If not used immediately, drain pasta and refresh under cold running
  water.
6 To re-heat pasta, plunge it into the boiling water until pasta is heated
  through, stirring constantly.
7 Strain and serve.

**Note**

Cooking times will vary depending on the amount and variety of pasta being cooked;
careful monitoring is required.

## Bolognese sauce

Ingredients

| | 25 | 50 | 100 |
|---|---|---|---|
| olive oil/vegetable oil | as required | | |
| onions, white, finely sliced | 1 kg | 2 kg | 4 kg |
| garlic, cloves, crushed | 5 | 7 | 10 |
| beef, minced | 6 kg | 12 kg | 24 kg |
| flour, plain | 150 g | 300 g | 600 g |
| tomato paste | 250 g | 500 g | 1 kg |
| tomatoes, crushed, A10 tin | 1 | 2 | 4 |
| stock, chicken | 2 L | 4 L | 8 L |
| basil, finely chopped | 20 g | 40 g | 80 g |
| oregano, finely chopped | 20 g | 40 g | 80 g |
| salt and freshly milled black pepper | to taste | | |
| Parmesan cheese, grated | 300 g | 600 g | 1.2 kg |

continued

Method

1 Place a little oil in a saucepan over a moderate heat.
2 Add onion and garlic. Cook without colour until tender.
3 Add mince and mix well until meat is sealed and browned.
4 Add flour and tomato paste. Mix well.
5 Add crushed tomato, stock and herbs. Season to taste, and mix well.
6 Simmer gently and reduce until thickened to the required consistency.
7 Remove from heat. Serve on a bed of hot spaghetti and sprinkle lightly with a little grated Parmesan cheese.

# Macaroni in a three cheese sauce

Garnish: $^{1}/_{2}$ cm slices of chives.

## Macaroni

Allow approx. 80 g of dry pasta per person.
Always cook pasta in plenty of lightly salted boiling water to allow for its absorption by the pasta.

Ingredients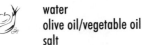

| | 25 | 50 | 100 |
|---|---|---|---|
| water | 7.5 L | 15 L | 30 L |
| olive oil/vegetable oil | 50 mL | 100 mL | 200 mL |
| salt | 20 g | 40 g | 80 g |
| macaroni, dry | 2 kg | 4 kg | 8 kg |

Method

1 Fill a saucepan with water and bring to the boil.
2 Add oil and salt to water.
3 Plunge pasta into water and stir thoroughly making sure all pasta is separated.
4 Simmer until pasta is firm but tender — 'al dente'.
5 If not used immediately, drain pasta and refresh under cold running water.
6 To re-heat pasta, plunge it into the boiling water until pasta is heated through, stirring constantly.
7 Strain and serve.

Note

Cooking times will vary depending on the amount and variety of pasta being cooked; careful monitoring is required.

# Three cheese sauce

| Ingredients | | 25 | 50 | 100 |
|---|---|---|---|---|
| butter | | 250 g | 500 g | 1 kg |
| flour, plain | | 250 g | 500 g | 1 kg |
| milk | | 3 L | 6 L | 12 L |
| mustard, English | | 200 g | 400 g | 800 g |
| Cheddar cheese, grated | | 250 g | 500 g | 1 kg |
| mozzarella, grated | | 250 g | 500 g | 1 kg |
| Parmesan, grated | | to taste | | |
| parsley, finely chopped | | 15 g | 30 g | 60 g |
| cream, single | | 1 L | 2 L | 4 L |
| salt and white pepper | | to taste | | |
| Cheddar cheese, grated | | 1 kg | 2 kg | 4 kg |

Method

1 Pre-heat oven to moderate (150–180°C).
2 Melt the butter in a saucepan over a moderate heat.
3 Add the flour and mix well with butter using a wooden spoon.
4 Reduce heat and cook gently for approx. 2–3 minutes without colouring.
5 Gently warm the milk in a separate saucepan.
6 Slowly incorporate the milk in small amounts, making sure each addition has mixed with the roux smoothly.
7 Reduce heat. Cook out gently for approx. 10 minutes, stirring regularly.
8 Add mustard, cheeses, chopped parsley and mix well.
9 Gently warm the cream in a separate saucepan.
10 Add cream, season to taste and mix well.
11 Gently heat the sauce through without boiling.

## Then

1 Combine sauce with the cooked and refreshed macaroni in a container.
2 Place mixture into baking/serving tray/s. Sprinkle evenly with grated Cheddar cheese.
3 Place tray/s into oven. Cook until pasta and sauce are heated through and cheese has melted.
4 Remove from oven, garnish and serve.

Health tip
Suitable for a soft diet. Unsuitable for low fat diets.

# Penne pasta tossed in a tomato sauce (Napoli)

**G**arnish: roughly chopped continental parsley.

## Penne pasta

**A**llow approx. 80 g of dry pasta per person.
Always cook pasta in plenty of lightly salted boiling water to allow for its absorption by the pasta.

Ingredients

| | 25 | 50 | 100 |
|---|---|---|---|
| water | 7.5 L | 15 L | 30 L |
| olive oil/vegetable oil | 50 mL | 100 mL | 200 mL |
| salt | 20 g | 40 g | 80 g |
| penne pasta, dry | 2 kg | 4 kg | 8 kg |

**Method**

1 Fill a saucepan with water and bring to the boil.
2 Add oil and salt to water.
3 Plunge pasta into water and stir thoroughly making sure all pasta is separated.
4 Simmer until pasta is firm but tender — 'al dente'.
5 If not used immediately, drain pasta and refresh under cold running water.
6 To re-heat pasta, plunge it into the boiling water until pasta is heated through, stirring constantly.
7 Strain and serve.

 **Note**  Cooking times will vary depending on the amount and variety of pasta being cooked; careful monitoring is required.

## Tomato sauce

Ingredients

| | 25 | 50 | 100 |
|---|---|---|---|
| olive oil/vegetable oil | as required | | |
| onions, white, finely sliced | 500 g | 1 kg | 2 kg |
| garlic, cloves, finely chopped | 4 | 7 | 10 |
| olives, black, stoned, roughly chopped | 300 g | 600 g | 1.2 kg |
| basil, fresh, finely chopped | 35 g | 70 g | 140 g |
| sugar, white | 100 g | 200 g | 400 g |
| tomatoes, crushed, A10 tin | 1½ | 3 | 6 |
| Parmesan cheese, grated | 200 g | 400 g | 800 g |
| salt and freshly milled black pepper | to lightly season | | |
| vinegar, balsamic | to taste | | |
| Cheddar cheese, grated | 1 kg | 2 kg | 4 kg |

**Method**
1 Pre-heat oven to moderate (150–180°C).
2 Place a little oil in a saucepan over a moderate heat. Add onions and garlic. Cook without colour until tender.
3 Reduce heat. Add all other ingredients. Season to taste. Add balsamic vinegar to taste and simmer gently until thickened to the required consistency, stirring regularly.

## Then

1 Combine sauce with the cooked and refreshed penne pasta in a container.
2 Place mixture into baking/serving tray/s. Sprinkle evenly with grated Cheddar cheese.
3 Place tray/s into oven. Cook until pasta and sauce are heated through and the cheese has melted.
4 Remove from oven. Garnish and serve.

 **Health tip**  To reduce fat content, omit the Cheddar cheese altogether.

# Pasta shells tossed in a creamy pesto and sun-dried tomato sauce

Garnish: fresh chives, finely sliced.

## Pasta shells

Allow approx. 80 g of dry pasta per person.
Always cook pasta in plenty of lightly salted boiling water to allow for its absorption by the pasta.

**Ingredients**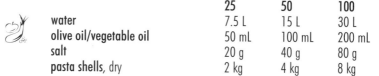

|  | 25 | 50 | 100 |
|---|---|---|---|
| water | 7.5 L | 15 L | 30 L |
| olive oil/vegetable oil | 50 mL | 100 mL | 200 mL |
| salt | 20 g | 40 g | 80 g |
| pasta shells, dry | 2 kg | 4 kg | 8 kg |

**Method**
1 Fill a saucepan with water and bring to the boil.
2 Add oil and salt to water.
3 Plunge pasta into water and stir thoroughly making sure all pasta is separated.
4 Simmer until pasta is firm but tender — 'al dente'.
5 If not used immediately, drain pasta and refresh under cold running water.
6 To re-heat pasta, plunge it into a saucepan of boiling water until pasta is heated through, stirring constantly.
7 Strain and serve.

continued

# Creamy pesto and sun-dried tomato sauce

Ingredients

| | 25 | 50 | 100 |
|---|---|---|---|
| butter | 250 g | 500 g | 1 kg |
| flour, plain | 250 g | 500 g | 1 kg |
| milk | 3 L | 6 L | 12 L |
| cream, single | 1 L | 2 L | 4 L |
| pesto, approx., see following recipe | 300 g | 600 g | 1.2 kg |
| sun-dried tomatoes, finely sliced | 200 g | 400 g | 800 g |
| salt and white pepper | to taste | | |

**TO FINISH DISH:**

| | | | |
|---|---|---|---|
| Cheddar cheese, grated | 500 g | 1 kg | 2 kg |
| chives, finely sliced | 50 g | 100 g | 200 g |
| Parmesan cheese, grated | 100 g | 200 g | 400 g |

Method

1 Melt the butter in a saucepan over a moderate heat.
2 Add the flour and mix well with butter using a wooden spoon.
3 Reduce heat. Cook gently for approx. 2–3 minutes without colouring.
4 Gently warm the milk in a separate saucepan.
5 Slowly incorporate the milk in small amounts, making sure each addition has mixed with the roux smoothly.
6 Reduce heat. Cook out gently for approx. 5 minutes, stirring regularly.
7 Gently warm the cream in a separate saucepan.
8 Add cream, pesto and sun-dried tomatoes. Season to taste and mix well.
9 Gently heat the sauce through without boiling.
10 Remove from heat and use as required.
11 Pre-heat oven to moderate (150–180°C).

# Then

1 Combine sauces in a container with the cooked and refreshed pasta shells, chives and half the grated Cheddar and Parmesan cheeses.
2 Place mixture into baking/serving tray/s. Sprinkle evenly with the remaining Cheddar and Parmesan cheeses.
3 Place tray/s into oven. Cook until pasta and sauce are heated through and the cheese has melted.
4 Remove from oven and serve.

## Pesto sauce

|  | | 25 | 50 | 100 |
|---|---|---|---|---|
| Ingredients 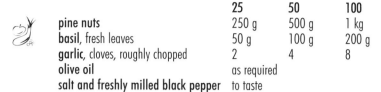 | pine nuts | 250 g | 500 g | 1 kg |
| | basil, fresh leaves | 50 g | 100 g | 200 g |
| | garlic, cloves, roughly chopped | 2 | 4 | 8 |
| | olive oil | as required | | |
| | salt and freshly milled black pepper | to taste | | |

**Method**

1 Roast pine nuts until a light golden brown. Place into a blender with basil and garlic, a little olive oil and blend.
2 Slowly add a little more olive oil whilst blending until firm but smooth. Season to taste.
3 Use pesto as required.

**Health tip**  This is a high protein meal, suitable for vegetarians and people on a soft diet. Unsuitable for a low fat diet. Use skim evaporated milk instead of cream.

# Tagliatelle tossed in a cream, mushroom, white wine and basil sauce

**G**arnish: finely chopped black olives.

## Tagliatelle

**A**llow approx. 80 g of dry pasta per person.
Always cook pasta in plenty of lightly salted boiling water to allow for its absorption by the pasta.

|  | | 25 | 50 | 100 |
|---|---|---|---|---|
| Ingredients | water | 7.5 L | 15 L | 30 L |
| | olive oil/vegetable oil | 50 mL | 100 mL | 200 mL |
| | salt | 20 g | 40 g | 80 g |
| | tagliatelle pasta, dry | 2 kg | 4 kg | 8 kg |

**Method**

1 Fill a saucepan with water and bring to the boil.
2 Add oil and salt to water.
3 Plunge pasta into water and stir thoroughly making sure all pasta is separated.
4 Simmer until pasta is firm but tender — 'al dente'.
5 If not used immediately, drain pasta and refresh under cold running water.
6 To re-heat pasta, plunge it into a saucepan of boiling water until pasta is heated through, stirring constantly.
7 Strain and serve.
8 Pre-heat oven to moderate (150–180°C).

continued

**Note** Cooking times will vary depending on the amount and variety of pasta being cooked; careful monitoring is required.

## Cream, mushroom, white wine and basil sauce

Ingredients

| | 25 | 50 | 100 |
|---|---|---|---|
| butter | 250 g | 500 g | 1 kg |
| onions, white, finely chopped | 250 g | 500 g | 1 kg |
| garlic, cloves, finely chopped | 4 | 7 | 10 |
| mushrooms, button, finely sliced | 500 g | 1 kg | 2 kg |
| flour, plain | 250 g | 500 g | 1 kg |
| milk | 3 L | 6 L | 12 L |
| cream, single | 750 mL | 1.5 L | 3 L |
| wine, white | 250 mL | 500 mL | 1 L |
| basil, fresh, finely chopped | 30 g | 60 g | 120 g |
| **salt and white pepper** | to taste | | |
| **Parmesan cheese**, grated | 400 g | 800 g | 1.6 kg |

Method

1 Melt the butter in a saucepan over a moderate heat.
2 Add onions and garlic, and cook until tender.
3 Add mushrooms and cook until softened.
4 Add the flour and thoroughly incorporate with butter and vegetables using a wooden spoon.
5 Reduce heat. Cook gently for approx. 2–3 minutes without colouring.
6 Gently warm the milk in a separate saucepan.
7 Slowly incorporate the milk in small amounts, making sure each addition has mixed with the roux smoothly.
8 Reduce heat. Cook out gently for approx. 5 minutes stirring regularly.
9 Gently warm the cream in a separate saucepan.
10 Add cream, white wine and basil. Season to taste and mix well.
11 Gently heat the sauce through without boiling.
12 Remove from heat.

## Then

1 Combine sauce in a container with the cooked and refreshed tagliatelle.
2 Place mixture into baking/serving tray/s. Sprinkle evenly with grated Parmesan cheese.
3 Place tray/s into oven. Cook until pasta and sauce are heated through and the Parmesan cheese is golden.
4 Remove from oven, garnish and serve.

 Health tip You could reduce the fat in this dish by using low fat milk, using evaporated milk instead of cream, and omitting the cheese.

# Cannelloni baked with a cheese sauce

Garnish: finely diced tomato and finely chopped parsley.

## Cannelloni

Recommended portion size is 2–4 pieces of cooked cannelloni per person.

### Cannelloni filling

| Ingredients | | | 25 | 50 | 100 |
|---|---|---|---|---|---|
|  | olive oil/vegetable oil | | as required | | |
| | onions, white, finely sliced | | 1 kg | 2 kg | 4 kg |
| | garlic, cloves, crushed | | 5 | 7 | 10 |
| | beef, minced | | 6 kg | 12 kg | 24 kg |
| | flour, plain | | 150 g | 300 g | 600 g |
| | tomato paste | | 250 g | 500 g | 1 kg |
| | tomatoes, crushed, A10 tin | | 1 | 2 | 4 |
| | stock, chicken | | 2 L | 4 L | 8 L |
| | basil, finely chopped | | 20 g | 40 g | 80 g |
| | oregano, finely chopped | | 20 g | 40 g | 80 g |
| | salt and freshly milled black pepper | | to taste | | |
| | Cheddar cheese, grated | | 500 g | 1 kg | 2 kg |

Method

1 Add a little oil in a saucepan over a moderate heat.
2 Add onion and garlic and cook until tender.
3 Add mince and mix well until meat has been sealed and browned.
4 Add flour and mix well.
5 Add tomato paste and mix well.
6 Add crushed tomato, stock and herbs. Season to taste. Mix well.
7 Simmer gently and reduce until thickened to the required consistency.
8 Remove from heat. Cool.

## Cheese sauce

| Ingredients | | 25 | 50 | 100 |
|---|---|---|---|---|
|  | butter | 200 g | 400 g | 800 g |
| | flour, plain | 200 g | 400 g | 800 g |
| | milk | 3 L | 6 L | 12 L |
| | Cheddar cheese, grated | 200 g | 400 g | 800 g |
| | parsley, finely chopped | 10 g | 20 g | 40 g |
| | salt and white pepper | to taste | | |

continued

Method
1 Melt the butter in a saucepan over a moderate heat.
2 Add the flour and mix well with butter using a wooden spoon.
3 Reduce heat and cook gently for approx. 2–3 minutes without colouring.
4 Gently warm the milk in a separate saucepan.
5 Slowly incorporate the milk in small amounts making sure each addition has mixed with the roux smoothly.
6 Reduce heat and cook out gently for approx. 10 minutes stirring regularly.
7 Add grated cheese, chopped parsley and season to taste. Mix well.
8 Remove from heat and use as required.

## Then

1 Pre-heat oven to moderate (150–180°C).
2 Using a piping bag fitted with a plain wide nozzle, half fill with cooled cannelloni filling.
3 Fill each cannelloni with filling.
4 As each cannelloni tube is filled, place in rows one layer deep into baking/serving tray/s.
5 Coat cannelloni with cheese sauce.
6 Lightly sprinkle with grated Cheddar cheese.
7 Place tray/s into oven. Cook until pasta and sauce are heated through and cheese has melted.
8 Remove from oven, garnish and serve.

 Health tip    You can reduce the fat content by using low fat milk and low fat cheese for the sauce. Use low fat cheese on top of the dish too.

# Eliche pasta in a rich sauce of tomato, Kalamata olives, Spanish onion and roasted red capsicum

Garnish: roughly chopped continental parsley.

## Eliche pasta

Allow approx. 80 g of dry pasta per person.
Always cook pasta in plenty of lightly salted boiling water to allow for its absorption by the pasta.

| Ingredients | | | 25 | 50 | 100 |
|---|---|---|---|---|---|
|  | | water | 7.5 L | 15 L | 30 L |
| | | olive oil | 50 mL | 100 mL | 200 mL |
| | | salt | 20 g | 40 g | 80 g |
| | | eliche pasta, dry | 2 kg | 4 kg | 8 kg |

Method

1 Fill a saucepan with water and bring to the boil.
2 Add oil and salt to water.
3 Plunge pasta into water and stir thoroughly making sure all pasta is separated.
4 Simmer until pasta is firm but tender — 'al dente'.
5 If not used immediately, drain pasta and refresh under cold running water.
6 To re-heat pasta, plunge it into a saucepan of boiling water until pasta is heated through, stirring constantly.
7 Strain and serve.

**Note** Cooking times will vary depending on the amount and variety of pasta being cooked; careful monitoring is required.

## Sauce

| Ingredients | | | 25 | 50 | 100 |
|---|---|---|---|---|---|
|  | | olive oil/vegetable oil | as required | | |
| | | garlic, cloves, finely chopped | 4 | 7 | 10 |
| | | onions, Spanish, finely sliced | 500 g | 1 kg | 2 kg |
| | | basil, fresh, finely chopped | 35 g | 70 g | 140 g |
| | | tomatoes, crushed, A10 tin | 1½ | 3 | 6 |
| | | red capsicums, roasted, finely chopped | 250 g | 500 g | 1 kg |
| | | olives, Kalamata, stoned, roughly chopped | 200 g | 400 g | 800 g |
| | | Parmesan cheese, grated | 200 g | 400 g | 800 g |
| | | salt and freshly milled black pepper | to taste | | |
| | | balsamic vinegar | to taste | | |

Method

1 Pre-heat oven to moderate (150–180°C).
2 In a saucepan over a moderate heat add a little olive oil and then the garlic and onions. Cook without colour until tender.
3 Reduce heat and add all other ingredients, using only half the Parmesan cheese. Season to taste. Add a little balsamic vinegar to taste and gently simmer until thickened to the required consistency, stirring regularly.

## Then

1 Combine sauce in a container with the cooked and refreshed eliche pasta.
2 Place mixture into baking/serving tray/s and sprinkle evenly with remaining Parmesan cheese.

continued

3 Place tray/s into oven. Cook until pasta and sauce are heated through and the Parmesan cheese is golden.
4 Remove from oven, garnish and serve.

**Notes**

Roast capsicum by removing stalk and seeds, quartering and roughly chopping. Place capsicum into a deep sided roasting tray tossed with a little olive oil and place into a pre-heated moderate oven (150–180°C) and roast, turning regularly, for approx. 30–45 minutes or until the flesh is soft, and the skin is easily removed.

**Balsamic vinegar** is a dark vinegar produced in Modena, Italy. It is made from the white Trebbiano grape that develops its flavour, colour and sweetness through ageing in barrels of different woods such as oak, chestnut, mulberry, juniper and cherrywood, each imparting its own flavour. The vinegar is aged for at least twenty years before it is bottled for sale.

# Rigatoni tossed in a walnut pesto with char-grilled shredded chicken

Garnish: finely sliced julienne of roasted red capsicum.

## Rigatoni

Allow approx. 80 g of dry pasta per person.
Always cook pasta in plenty of lightly salted boiling water to allow for its absorption by the pasta.

**Ingredients**

|  | 25 | 50 | 100 |
|---|---|---|---|
| water | 7.5 L | 15 L | 30 L |
| olive oil/vegetable oil | 50 mL | 100 mL | 200 mL |
| salt | 20 g | 40 g | 80 g |
| rigatoni pasta, dry | 2 kg | 4 kg | 8 kg |

**Method**

1 Fill a saucepan with water and bring to the boil.
2 Add oil and salt to water.
3 Plunge pasta into water and stir thoroughly making sure all pasta is separated.
4 Simmer until pasta is firm but tender — 'al dente'.
5 If not used immediately, drain pasta and refresh under cold running water.
6 To re-heat pasta, plunge it into a saucepan of boiling water until pasta is heated through, stirring constantly.
7 Strain and serve.

**Note**

Cooking times will vary depending on the amount and variety of pasta being cooked; careful monitoring is required.

# Char-grilled chicken

| Ingredients | | | 25 | 50 | 100 |
|---|---|---|---|---|---|
|  | chicken, breast/fillet, finely shredded | | 3 kg | 6 kg | 12 kg |
| | olive oil/vegetable oil | | as required | | |

**Method**

1 Pre-heat a flat grill plate or large sauté pan until extremely hot.
2 Toss shredded chicken with a little oil in a container.
3 Cook chicken in small batches agitating continually until all chicken is cooked through.
4 Remove from heat and place to one side until required.
5 Preheat oven to moderate (150–180°C).

# White sauce

| Ingredients | | 25 | 50 | 100 |
|---|---|---|---|---|
|  | butter | 250 g | 500 g | 1 kg |
| | flour, plain | 250 g | 500 g | 1 kg |
| | milk | 3 L | 6 L | 12 L |
| | cream, single | 1 L | 2 L | 4 L |
| | pesto, approx., see following recipe | 300 g | 600 g | 1.2 kg |
| | salt and white pepper | to taste | | |
| | **TO FINISH DISH:** | | | |
| | Cheddar cheese, grated | 400 g | 800 g | 1.6 kg |
| | Parmesan cheese, grated | 100 g | 200 g | 400 g |

**Method**

1 Melt the butter in a saucepan over a moderate heat.
2 Add the flour and mix well with butter using a wooden spoon.
3 Reduce heat. Cook gently for approx. 2–3 minutes without colouring.
4 Gently warm the milk in a separate saucepan.
5 Slowly incorporate the milk in small amounts, making sure each addition has mixed with the roux smoothly.
6 Reduce heat. Cook out gently for approx. 5 minutes stirring regularly.
7 Gently warm the cream in a separate saucepan.
8 Add cream and pesto. Season to taste and mix well.
9 Gently heat the sauce through without boiling.
10 Remove from heat and use as required.

# Walnut pesto sauce

| Ingredients | | 25 | 50 | 100 |
|---|---|---|---|---|
|  | walnuts | 250 g | 500 g | 1 kg |
| | basil, fresh, leaves | 50 g | 100 g | 200 g |
| | garlic, cloves, roughly chopped | 2 | 4 | 8 |
| | olive oil | as required | | |
| | salt and freshly milled black pepper | to taste | | |

continued

<table>
<tr><td>Method</td><td>

1 Place walnuts into a blender with basil, garlic, a little olive oil and blend.
2 Whilst blending, slowly incorporate a little more olive oil until firm but smooth. Season to taste.
3 Use pesto as required.

</td></tr>
</table>

## Then

1 Combine hot sauce in a container with the cooked and refreshed pasta, and the cooked shredded chicken.
2 Add half the grated Cheddar and Parmesan cheeses. Mix well.
3 Place mixture into baking/serving tray/s. Sprinkle evenly with the remaining Cheddar and Parmesan cheeses.
4 Place tray/s into oven. Cook until pasta and sauce are heated through and cheese has melted.
5 Remove from oven and serve.

# Bavette pasta with mushrooms and bacon in a mild mustard sauce

Garnish: finely chopped fresh parsley.

## Bavette pasta

Allow approx. 80 g of dry pasta per person.
Always cook pasta in plenty of lightly salted boiling water to allow for its absorption by the pasta.

**Ingredients**

| | 25 | 50 | 100 |
|---|---|---|---|
| water | 7.5 L | 15 L | 30 L |
| olive oil/vegetable oil | 50 mL | 100 mL | 200 mL |
| salt | 20 g | 40 g | 80 g |
| bavette pasta, dry | 2 kg | 4 kg | 8 kg |

**Method**

1 Fill a saucepan with water and bring to the boil.
2 Add oil and salt to water.
3 Plunge pasta into water and stir thoroughly making sure all pasta is separated.
4 Simmer until pasta is firm but tender — 'al dente'.
5 If not used immediately, drain pasta and refresh under cold running water.
6 To re-heat pasta, plunge it into a saucepan of boiling water until pasta is heated through, stirring constantly.
7 Strain and serve.
8 Pre-heat oven to moderate (150–180°C).

**Note** Cooking times will vary depending on the amount and variety of pasta being cooked; careful monitoring is required.

## Mild mustard sauce

Ingredients

|  | 25 | 50 | 100 |
|---|---|---|---|
| butter | 250 g | 500 g | 1 kg |
| flour, plain | 250 g | 500 g | 1 kg |
| milk | 3 L | 6 L | 12 L |
| cream, single | 1 L | 2 L | 4 L |
| Dijon mustard, to taste, approx. | 150 g | 300 g | 600 g |

**Method**

1 Melt the butter in a saucepan over a moderate heat.
2 Add the flour and mix well with butter using a wooden spoon.
3 Reduce heat and cook gently for approx. 2–3 minutes without colouring.
4 Gently warm the milk in a separate saucepan.
5 Slowly incorporate the milk in small amounts, making sure each addition has mixed with the roux smoothly.
6 Reduce heat and cook out gently for approx. 10 minutes stirring regularly.
7 Thoroughly whisk mustard and cream into sauce in small amounts. Cook for a further 2 minutes until re-heated. Do not re-boil.
8 Remove from heat and keep hot until required. Season to taste.

**Note** It is advisable with this sauce that the mustard be added in small amounts and tasted frequently. This saves the time of preparing a new sauce if too much mustard is added by accident.

## Mushroom and bacon mixture

Ingredients

|  | 25 | 50 | 100 |
|---|---|---|---|
| olive oil/vegetable oil | as required | | |
| garlic, cloves, finely chopped | 3 | 5 | 7 |
| onions, white, finely chopped | 500 g | 1 kg | 2 kg |
| bacon, rind removed, finely chopped | 300 g | 600 g | 1.2 kg |
| mushrooms, button, quartered | 500 g | 1 kg | 2 kg |
| parsley, finely chopped | 25 g | 50 g | 100 g |
| Cheddar cheese, grated | 300 g | 600 g | 1.2 kg |
| Parmesan cheese, grated | 150 g | 300 g | 600 g |

**Method**

1 Place a little oil in a saucepan over a moderate heat and add the garlic and onions. Cook without colour until tender.
2 Add bacon and mushrooms. Cook gently for a further 3–4 minutes. Add parsley and remove from heat.

continued

## Then

1 Combine warm mustard sauce in a container with the cooked and refreshed pasta and the cooked bacon and mushroom mixture.
2 Add half the grated Cheddar cheese and half of the Parmesan cheese. Mix well.
3 Pre-heat oven to moderate (150–180°C).
4 Place mixture into baking/serving tray/s. Sprinkle evenly with the remaining Cheddar and Parmesan cheeses.
5 Place tray/s into oven. Cook until pasta and sauce are heated through and cheese has melted.
6 Remove from oven and serve.

# Penne pasta tossed in a spicy salami, tomato and chilli sauce (arrabbiato)

**G**arnish: julienne of red and green capsicum.

## Penne pasta

**A**llow approx. 80 g of dry pasta per person.
Always cook pasta in plenty of lightly salted boiling water to allow for its absorption by the pasta.

Ingredients

| | 25 | 50 | 100 |
|---|---|---|---|
| water | 7.5 L | 15 L | 30 L |
| olive oil/vegetable oil | 50 mL | 100 mL | 200 mL |
| salt | 20 g | 40 g | 80 g |
| penne pasta, dry | 2 kg | 4 kg | 8 kg |

Method
1 Fill a saucepan with water and bring to the boil.
2 Add oil and salt to water.
3 Plunge pasta into water and stir thoroughly making sure all pasta is separated.
4 Simmer until pasta is firm but tender — 'al dente'.
5 If not used immediately, drain pasta and refresh under cold running water.
6 To re-heat pasta, plunge it into the boiling water until pasta is heated through, stirring constantly.
7 Strain and serve.
8 Pre-heat oven to moderate (150–180°C).

 Cooking times will vary depending on the amount and variety of pasta being cooked; careful monitoring is required.

# Spicy salami, tomato and chilli sauce

| Ingredients | | | 25 | 50 | 100 |
|---|---|---|---|---|---|
|  | olive oil/vegetable oil | | as required | | |
| | onions, white, finely sliced | | 500 g | 1 kg | 2 kg |
| | garlic, cloves, finely chopped | | 4 | 7 | 10 |
| | chillies, small, topped, finely chopped, approx. | | 2–3 | 4–6 | 8–12 |
| | basil, fresh, finely chopped | | 35 g | 70 g | 140 g |
| | sugar, white | | 100 g | 200 g | 400 g |
| | tomatoes, crushed, A10 tin | | 1½ | 3 | 6 |
| | salami, small dice | | 500 g | 1 kg | 2 kg |
| | Parmesan cheese, grated | | 200 g | 400 g | 800 g |
| | salt and freshly milled black pepper | | to lightly season | | |
| | balsamic vinegar | | to taste | | |
| | Cheddar cheese, grated | | 350 g | 700 g | 1.4 kg |
| | Parmesan cheese, grated | | 150 g | 300 g | 600 g |

Method

1 Put a little oil in a saucepan over a moderate heat and then add the onions, garlic and chillies. Cook without colour until soft.
2 Reduce heat and add basil, sugar, tomatoes, salami and the first quantity of Parmesan cheese. Season to taste. Add a little balsamic vinegar to taste. Simmer gently until thickened to the required consistency, stirring regularly.

## Then

1 Combine sauce in a container with the cooked and refreshed penne pasta.
2 Place mixture into baking/serving tray/s. Sprinkle evenly with grated Cheddar and Parmesan cheeses.
3 Place tray/s into oven. Cook until pasta and sauce are heated through and cheese has melted.
4 Remove from oven, garnish and serve.

 Health tip

To reduce the fat content of the dish: use lean ham instead of salami; use low fat cheese.

Note

Parmesan cheese is made from skimmed or partially skimmed cow's milk. Its complex flavour and granular texture are the results of the long ageing process, which can be between 2–4 years. The name comes from Parma in Italy where it was originally made, although it is now made in quite a few countries. The Italian variety is still regarded as the best.

# Baked gnocchi tossed in a creamy pumpkin and sweet potato sauce

Garnish: finely chopped coriander.

## Gnocchi

| | | 25 | 50 | 100 |
|---|---|---|---|---|
| Ingredients | water | 7.5 L | 15 L | 30 L |
| | olive oil/vegetable oil | 50 mL | 100 mL | 200 mL |
| | salt | 20 g | 40 g | 80 g |
| | gnocchi, fresh | 5 kg | 10 kg | 20 kg |

Method
1 Fill a saucepan with water and bring to the boil.
2 Add oil and salt to water.
3 Plunge gnocchi into water and thoroughly stir.
4 As soon as gnocchi floats to the surface remove immediately using a large slotted spoon. Drain thoroughly in a colander.
5 Pre-heat oven to moderate (150–180°C).

 Note

Always cook gnocchi as close to service time as possible. Overcooked gnocchi is tough.

## Pumpkin and sweet potato sauce

| | | 25 | 50 | 100 |
|---|---|---|---|---|
| Ingredients | pumpkin, peeled, seeded, rough dice | 1 kg | 2 kg | 4 kg |
| | sweet potatoes, peeled, rough dice | 1 kg | 2 kg | 4 kg |
| | onions, peeled, roughly chopped | 500 g | 1 kg | 2 kg |
| | stock, chicken | 4 L | 8 L | 16 L |
| | cream, single | 200 mL | 400 mL | 800 mL |
| | salt and freshly milled black pepper | to taste | | |
| | Cheddar cheese, grated | 300 g | 600 g | 1.2 kg |
| | Parmesan cheese, grated | 150 g | 300 g | 600 g |

Method
1 Place pumpkin, sweet potato and onion in a saucepan. Cover with the chicken stock and bring to a gentle simmer, covered with a tight fitting lid. Cook until all ingredients are tender: approx. 45 minutes–1 hour.
2 Add cream. Season to taste. Purée and place to one side. Keep warm.

## Then

1 Combine the hot sauce in a container with the cooked gnocchi.
2 Place mixture into baking/serving tray/s. Sprinkle evenly with the Cheddar and Parmesan cheeses.
3 Place tray/s into oven. Cook until pasta and sauce are heated through and cheese has melted.
4 Remove from oven and serve.

 Health tip

To reduce the fat content, use evaporated milk instead of cream. Use low fat cheese.

# Pappardelle and veal meatballs in a rich tomato sauce

Garnish: chopped parsley.

## Pappardelle pasta

Allow approx. 80 g of dry pasta per person.
Always cook pasta in plenty of lightly salted boiling water to allow for its absorption by the pasta.

Ingredients

| | 25 | 50 | 100 |
|---|---|---|---|
| water | 7.5 L | 15 L | 30 L |
| olive oil/vegetable oil | 50 mL | 100 mL | 200 mL |
| salt | 20 g | 40 g | 80 g |
| pappardelle pasta, dry | 2 kg | 4 kg | 8 kg |

Method

1 Fill a saucepan with water and bring to the boil.
2 Add oil and salt to water.
3 Plunge pasta into water and stir thoroughly making sure all pasta is separated.
4 Simmer until pasta is firm but tender — 'al dente'.
5 If not used immediately, drain pasta and refresh under cold running water.
6 To re-heat pasta, plunge it into the boiling water until pasta is heated through, stirring constantly.
7 Strain and serve.

 Note

Cooking times will vary depending on the amount and variety of pasta being cooked; careful monitoring is required.

## Meatballs and sauce

Ingredients

| | 25 | 50 | 100 |
|---|---|---|---|
| **MEATBALLS:** | | | |
| veal, minced | 5 kg | 10 kg | 20 kg |
| onions, finely minced | 300 g | 600 g | 1.2 kg |
| carrots, peeled, finely grated | 200 g | 400 g | 800 g |
| garlic, cloves, peeled, minced | 5 | 10 | 20 |
| capsicums, red, seeded, minced | 2 | 4 | 8 |
| Parmesan cheese, grated | 200 g | 400 g | 800 g |
| basil, finely chopped | 20 g | 40 g | 80 g |
| eggs | 4 | 8 | 16 |
| salt and freshly milled black pepper | to taste | | |
| breadcrumbs | as required | | |

continued

## SAUCE:

| | | | |
|---|---|---|---|
| tomatoes, crushed, A10 tin | 1½ | 3 | 6 |
| onions, finely chopped | 1 kg | 2 kg | 4 kg |
| basil, finely chopped | 25 g | 50 g | 100 g |
| sugar, white | 100 g | 200 g | 400 g |
| salt and freshly milled black pepper | to taste | | |
| Cheddar cheese | 500 g | 1 kg | 2 kg |
| parsley, fresh, finely chopped | 25 g | 50 g | 100 g |
| Parmesan cheese, grated | 250 g | 500 g | 1 kg |

**Method**

1 Pre-heat oven to moderate (150–180°C).
2 Place all meatball ingredients in a mixing bowl and mix well. Add small amounts of breadcrumbs to produce a firm moulding texture.
3 Mould mixture into the shape of golf balls.
4 Place the meatballs onto lightly greased baking/serving tray/s leaving a small space in between each. Place into oven.
5 Cook for approx. 10–15 minutes or until just cooked. Remove from oven.
6 While meatballs are cooking, place all sauce ingredients into a saucepan and bring to the boil. Reduce heat and simmer gently.
7 Place meatballs onto deep sided baking/serving tray/s.
8 When sauce has reduced by one third, pour into trays containing meatballs.
9 Sprinkle a little Cheddar cheese on top of meatballs followed by chopped parsley and Parmesan cheese.
10 Return trays to oven and cook until cheese is melted.
11 Serve 2–3 meatballs per portion with a little of the sauce on a bed of pappardelle pasta.

# Pipe rigate baked with tuna, continental parsley and fresh lemon

Garnish: fresh lemon wedges.

## Pipe rigate

Allow approx. 80 g of dry pasta per person.
Always cook pasta in plenty of lightly salted boiling water to allow for its absorption by the pasta.

**Ingredients**

| | 25 | 50 | 100 |
|---|---|---|---|
| water | 7.5 L | 15 L | 30 L |
| olive oil/vegetable oil | 50 mL | 100 mL | 200 mL |
| salt | 20 g | 40 g | 80 g |
| pipe rigate pasta, dry | 2 kg | 4 kg | 8 kg |

<table>
<tr><td rowspan="2">Method</td></tr>
</table>

**Method**

1 Fill a saucepan with water and bring to the boil.
2 Add oil and salt to water.
3 Plunge pasta into water and thoroughly stir, making sure all pasta is separated.
4 Simmer until pasta is firm but tender — 'al dente'.
5 If not used immediately, drain pasta and refresh under cold running water.
6 To re-heat pasta, plunge it into a saucepan of boiling water until pasta is heated through, stirring constantly.
7 Strain and serve.

 **Note**   Cooking times will vary depending on the amount and variety of pasta being cooked; careful monitoring is required.

# Cheese sauce

**Ingredients**

| | 25 | 50 | 100 |
|---|---|---|---|
| butter | 200 g | 400 g | 800 g |
| flour, plain | 200 g | 400 g | 800 g |
| milk | 3 L | 6 L | 12 L |
| cheese, Cheddar, grated | 200 g | 400 g | 800 g |
| parsley, finely chopped | 25 g | 50 g | 100 g |
| salt and white pepper | to taste | | |
| tuna, tinned, drained | 1.2 kg | 2.4 kg | 4.8 kg |
| parsley, continental, finely chopped | 30 g | 60 g | 120 g |
| lemon, zest and juice | 2 | 4 | 8 |
| Cheddar cheese, grated | 300 g | 600 g | 1.2 kg |
| Parmesan cheese, grated | 150 g | 300 g | 600 g |

**Method**

1 Pre-heat oven to moderate (150–180°C).
2 Melt the butter in a saucepan over a moderate heat.
3 Add the flour and mix well with butter using a wooden spoon.
4 Reduce heat. Cook gently for approx. 2–3 minutes without colouring.
5 Gently warm the milk in a separate saucepan.
6 Slowly incorporate the milk in small amounts, making sure each addition has mixed with the roux smoothly.
7 Reduce heat. Cook out gently for approx. 10 minutes stirring regularly.
8 Add grated Cheddar cheese, chopped parsley. Season to taste. Mix well.
9 Remove from heat and use as required.

# Then

1 Combine in a container the hot sauce, tuna, parsley, lemon zest and juice with the cooked and refreshed pasta.
2 Place mixture into baking/serving tray/s. Sprinkle evenly with the Cheddar and Parmesan cheeses.

continued

3 Place tray/s into oven. Cook until pasta and sauce are heated through and cheese has melted.

4 Remove from oven and serve.

❤ **Health tip**    To reduce the fat content, use low fat milk and low fat cheese.

# CHAPTER 5

# FISH AND SEAFOOD

# A GUIDE TO THE MOST COMMONLY AVAILABLE FISH AND SEAFOODS

**W**here availability varies no season is given. Please consult your supplier as to the availability of these fish.

These notes are only a general guide and may vary depending on supplier and area.

## Cuts of Fish

| French Term | Meaning |
|---|---|
| filet | a fillet which is free from any bone. |
| tronçon | a section cut from a flat fish with the bone in place. |
| darne | a section cut from a round fish with the bone in place. |
| délice | not a cut but a neatly folded fillet of fish. |
| paupiette | as for délice but spread with a seasoning before being rolled. |
| goujon | a fillet that has been cut into long strips. |

## Fish Species

| Name | Other Names/Methods/Availability | Purchased |
|---|---|---|
| **Barramundi** | | fillets |
| | *Recommended methods of cookery:* all, especially grilling, baking, BBQ. *Available:* all year, usually frozen; fresh October–March. | |
| **Bass** | Freshwater Perch | whole, fillets, steaks and cutlets |
| | *Recommended methods of cookery:* all, especially moist methods. | |
| **Blackfish** | Blacky, Drummer | whole or fillets |
| | *Recommended methods of cookery:* grilling, BBQ, baking, frying. *Available fresh:* all year. | |
| **Blue Grenadier** | | fillets |
| | *Recommended methods of cookery:* grilling, BBQ, baking, frying. *Available:* March–October. | |
| **Boarfish** | | fillets |
| | *Recommended methods of cookery:* all. *Available fresh:* all year. | |
| **Bream** | Tarwhine | whole or fillets |
| | *Recommended methods of cookery:* all. *Available fresh:* all year. | |
| **Carp** | | whole or fillets |
| | *Recommended methods of cookery:* all. *Available fresh:* summer. | |

| Name | Other Names/Methods/Availability | Purchased |
|---|---|---|
| **Catfish** | | whole, fillets, steaks and cutlets |
| | *Recommended methods of cookery:* all. | |
| **Cod** | Codfish | whole, fillets, steaks and cutlets |
| | *Recommended methods of cookery:* all, especially deep frying. | |
| **Coral Trout** | Leopard Cod, Coral Cod | whole or fillets |
| | *Recommended methods of cookery:* grilling, shallow frying, baking, BBQ, poaching. *Available fresh:* all year. | |
| **Dart Fish** | Swallowtail | whole or fillets |
| | *Recommended methods of cookery:* frying, baking, poaching, steaming. *Available fresh:* summer. | |
| **Dhu Fish** | (not related to Jewfish) | whole |
| | *Recommended methods of cookery:* grilling, shallow frying and poaching. *Available fresh:* mainly autumn and winter. | |
| **Dory** | (varieties: John, Mirror, King and Silver Dory) | whole or fillets |
| | *Recommended methods of cookery:* grilling, shallow frying and poaching. *Available fresh:* John Dory — all year; King Dory — all year; Silver Dory — winter and spring; Mirror Dory — winter and spring. | |
| **Eel** | | whole or prepared and portioned when smoked |
| | *Recommended methods of cookery:* BBQ, grilling and baking. *Available:* all year, fresh or smoked. | |
| **Emperor** | (varieties: Red, Sweetlip and Spangled Emperor) | whole or fillets |
| | *Recommended methods of cookery:* all. *Available fresh:* all year. | |
| **Flathead** | (varieties: Sand, Dusky, Tiger, Rock, Bartailed and Marbled Flathead) | whole or fillets |
| | *Recommended methods of cookery:* deep frying, poaching, casseroling or preparing and baking whole. *Available:* all year, mainly autumn. | |
| **Flounder/Sole** | | whole or fillets |
| | *Recommended methods of cookery:* grilling, shallow frying, poaching or preparing and baking whole. *Available fresh:* all year. | |
| **Garfish** | Needlefish | whole or fillets |
| | *Recommended methods of cookery:* grilling, frying, baking, BBQ. *Available fresh:* all year. | |

| Name | Other Names/Methods/Availability | Purchased |
|------|----------------------------------|-----------|
| **Gemfish** | Hake | fillets or cutlets/smoked |
| | *Recommended methods of cookery*: all; grilling, BBQ, and baking. *Available*: fresh during winter; frozen all year. | |
| **Groper** | Grouper | whole, fillets, steaks and cutlets |
| | *Recommended methods of cookery*: grilling, baking, soups and casseroles and all dry methods. | |
| **Hairtail** | | cutlets |
| | *Recommended methods of cookery*: all dry methods. *Available fresh*: autumn and winter. | |
| **Hake** | Gemfish | fillets or cutlets/smoked |
| | *Recommended methods of cookery*: grilling and baking, BBQ. *Available*: fresh during winter; frozen all year. | |
| **Herring** | | whole/smoked |
| | *Recommended methods of cookery*: grilling, frying, baking, BBQ, all dry methods. *Available fresh*: all year. | |
| **Jewfish** | Jewie, Silver, Mulloway and Butterfish Jew | whole or cutlets |
| | *Recommended methods of cookery*: all. *Available fresh*: all year. | |
| **Kingfish** | | whole or cutlets |
| | *Recommended methods of cookery*: all dry methods. *Available fresh*: all year, especially autumn. | |
| **Leather Jacket** | File Fish | whole |
| | *Recommended methods of cookery*: all moist methods. *Available fresh*: all year. | |
| **Ling** | | fillets |
| | *Recommended methods of cookery*: grilling, shallow frying, poaching, steaming, baking, BBQ. *Available fresh*: winter. | |
| **Mackerel** | | whole, steaks and cutlets |
| | *Recommended methods of cookery*: depend on the oil content. If fish is dry use moist methods and if oily use dry methods. *Available fresh*: summer. | |
| **Mullet** | | whole or fillets |
| | *Recommended methods of cookery*: all dry methods. *Available fresh*: autumn and early winter. | |
| **Mullet, Red** | Goatfish | whole or fillets |
| | *Recommended methods of cookery*: all; shallow frying, grilling, baking and BBQ. *Available fresh*: all year. | |

| Name | Other Names/Methods/Availability | Purchased |
|---|---|---|
| **Murray Cod** | | whole or fillets |
| | *Recommended methods of cookery:* all. *Available fresh:* winter. | |
| **Ocean Perch** | | whole or fillets |
| | *Recommended methods of cookery:* all. *Available fresh:* winter. | |
| **Orange Roughy** | Orange Roughie | fillets |
| | *Recommended methods of cookery:* shallow frying and grilling. | |
| **Parrot Fish** | | whole |
| | *Recommended methods of cookery:* all. *Available fresh:* all year, especially winter. | |
| **Perch** | | whole or fillets |
| | *Recommended methods of cookery:* all; can be cooked whole if fish are small. *Available fresh:* all year. | |
| **Pike** | | whole |
| | *Recommended methods of cookery:* all dry methods. *Available fresh:* all year. | |
| **Redfish** | Nannygai | whole or fillets |
| | *Recommended methods of cookery:* shallow frying, deep frying, can be finely chopped and used in fish cakes, all dry methods. *Available fresh:* spring. | |
| **Ribbonfish** | | cutlets |
| | *Recommended methods of cookery:* all dry methods. *Available fresh:* autumn and winter. | |
| **Rock Cod** | | whole or fillets |
| | *Recommended methods of cookery:* all. *Available fresh:* winter. | |
| **Salmon** | | whole, fillets, steaks and cutlets/smoked |
| | *Recommended methods of cookery:* baking, grilling, frying, BBQ and poaching. *Available fresh:* winter, though prepared salmon is widely available all year. | |
| **Sea Bream** | Mor Wong | whole or fillets |
| | *Recommended methods of cookery:* all. *Available fresh:* all year, especially autumn. | |
| **Shark** | | fillets and steaks |
| | *Recommended methods of cookery:* all. *Available fresh:* all year. | |
| **Silver Biddies** | | whole |
| | *Recommended methods of cookery:* grilling, BBQ and frying. *Available fresh:* all year. | |

| Name | Other Names/Methods/Availability | Purchased |
|---|---|---|
| **Silver Warehou** | | fillets |
| | *Recommended methods of cookery:* all. *Available fresh:* winter and spring. | |
| **Skate** | Ray, Roker | wings or flaps |
| | *Recommended methods of cookery:* shallow frying and poaching. *Available fresh:* all year from specialist suppliers. | |
| **Snapper** | Schnapper | whole, fillets, steaks and cutlets |
| | *Recommended methods of cookery:* all. *Available fresh:* all year. | |
| **Snook** | | cutlets |
| | *Recommended methods of cookery:* all dry methods. *Available fresh:* summer. | |
| **Sole/Flounder** | (varieties: Lemon, Black and Dover Sole) | whole or fillets |
| | *Recommended methods of cookery:* grilling, shallow frying and poaching or preparing and baking whole. *Available fresh:* all year. | |
| **Tailor** | Bluefish | whole or fillets |
| | *Recommended methods of cookery:* grilling, baking, BBQ and can also be cooked whole if fish are small; all dry methods. *Available fresh:* summer and autumn. | |
| **Teraglin** | Trag (related to Jewfish) | whole or fillets |
| | *Recommended methods of cookery:* all; can be cooked whole if fish are small. *Available fresh:* spring and summer. | |
| **Trevally** | (varieties: Lowly, Cale, Silver, Blue Golden, Great and Herring Trevally) | whole or fillets |
| | *Recommended methods of cookery:* frying, poaching and casseroles. *Available fresh:* all year. | |
| **Trout** | (varieties: Rainbow Trout) | whole or fillets/ smoked |
| | *Recommended methods of cookery:* poaching and baking. *Available fresh:* all year. | |
| **Trumpeter** | (varieties: Blue Moki, Tasmanian and Striped Trumpeter) | whole or fillets |
| | *Recommended methods of cookery:* shallow frying, grilling, poaching, baking, and BBQ; can also be used in soups and casseroles. *Available fresh:* spring and summer. | |
| **Tuna** | (varieties: Albacore, Bluefin) | fillets, steaks and cutlets |
| | *Recommended methods of cookery:* shallow frying, grilling, baking, BBQ; can also be served raw, usually finely sliced e.g. sashimi. *Available fresh:* all year. | |

| Name | Other Names/Methods/Availability | Purchased |
|---|---|---|
| **Whitebait** | Minnows and Jollytails | whole |
| | *Recommended methods of cookery:* frying, baking. *Available fresh:* all year. | |
| **Whiting** | (varieties: Sand Whiting, King George) | whole or fillets |
| | *Recommended methods of cookery:* all; shallow frying and poaching; can be stuffed and baked whole. *Available fresh:* all year. | |
| **Wrasse** | | whole or fillets |
| | *Recommended methods of cookery:* shallow frying, poaching, steaming, baking and BBQ. *Available fresh:* all year. | |

# Seafood

| Name | Other Names/Methods/Availability | Purchased |
|---|---|---|
| **Abalone** | Sea Ear, Ear Shell, Mutton Fish, Ormer, Paua, Awabi and Bau Yeu (varieties: Greenlip, Blacklip and Tiger) | canned, dried, in shell or shucked |
| | *Recommended methods of cookery:* deep frying in batter, stir-frying, poaching, steaming. *Available fresh:* all year. | |

**Notes**  A mollusc is usually available canned in water or in dried form. Can be obtained fresh but is very expensive. Fresh abalone should be kept in clean salted water. If purchased dead, remove shells and refrigerate immediately. Store in a freezer for up to 10 weeks.

| Name | Other Names/Methods/Availability | Purchased |
|---|---|---|
| **Balmain Bug** | (varieties: Moreton Bay Bug) | alive or dead, cooked or uncooked |
| | *Recommended methods of cookery:* all; grilling, shallow frying, baking, boiling. *Available fresh:* all year. | |

**Notes**  Keep live bugs in a damp hessian bag. Cooked bugs should be wrapped in cling film in an airtight container in a refrigerator for up to 3 days. Store in a freezer for up to 10 weeks. Kill bugs either by drowning or freezing them.
Do not plunge into boiling water as this toughens the flesh.

| Name | Other Names/Methods/Availability | Purchased |
|---|---|---|
| **Calamari** | see Squid | |
| **Cockles** | | in shell or shucked and pickled |
| | *Recommended methods of cookery:* all. *Available fresh:* all year. | |
| **Crab** | (varieties: Blue Swimmer, Coral, Mud, Spanner, Red Spot, King, Tasmanian and Green Shore Crab) | alive or dead, cooked or uncooked |
| | *Recommended methods of cookery:* all; boiling, grilling, baking and stewing. *Available fresh:* all year, especially summer. | |

**Notes**  Keep live crabs in a damp hessian bag. Cooked crabs should be wrapped in cling film in an airtight container in a refrigerator for up to 3 days. Store in a freezer for up to 10 weeks. Kill live crabs by either drowning or freezing them.
Do not plunge into boiling water as this toughens the flesh.

| Name | Other Names/Methods/Availability | Purchased |
|---|---|---|
| **Crayfish** | Yabbie, Yabby, Murray Cray, Marron Cray<br>*2 claws | whole, alive or dead, raw or cooked |

*Recommended methods of cookery: all; boiling, grilling and casseroles. Available fresh: all year.*

**Notes**

When buying whole make sure the claws are intact. Keep live crayfish in a damp hessian bag. Cooked crayfish should be wrapped in cling film in an airtight container in a refrigerator for up to 2 days. Store in a freezer for up to 10 weeks. Kill crayfish by putting a strong knife between the eyes then plunge the blade in quickly and strongly.

Do not plunge into boiling water as this toughens the flesh.

| | | |
|---|---|---|
| **Cuttlefish** | | whole |

*Recommended methods of cookery: all.*
*Available fresh: all year.*

| **Lobster, Rock** | Crawfish (varieties: Flapjack and Spiny Lobster)<br>Spiny lobsters can be referred to as crayfish | alive or dead, cooked or uncooked, flesh or tails or whole |
|---|---|---|

*Recommended methods of cookery: all; boiling and grilling. Available fresh: all year.*

**Notes**

When buying whole make sure the limbs are all intact and that the tail is curled and springs back when straightened. Keep live lobsters in a damp hessian bag. Cooked lobsters should be wrapped in cling film in an airtight container in a refrigerator for up to 3 days. Store in a freezer for up to 10 weeks. Kill lobsters by either drowning, freezing or putting a strong knife between the eyes, then plunge the blade in quickly and strongly pulling the knife down the lobster's back and through the tail.

Do not plunge into boiling water as this toughens the flesh.

Do not purchase dead green lobsters as the flesh will deteriorate rapidly.

| **Mussels** | (varieties: New Zealand Greenlip and Blacklip) alive |
|---|---|

*Recommended methods of cookery: all; grilling, steaming, baking, boiling and BBQ.*
*Available fresh: all year.*

**Note**

Any mussels purchased fresh that have open shells should be discarded. This signifies that the mussel is dead. Store live mussels in a damp hessian bag in a cool place as the coldness of the refrigerator will kill them faster. Mussels have a storage life of between 1–3 days approx. Scrub mussels well under cold running water before use and remove the beard.

| | |
|---|---|
| **Octopus** | whole |

*Recommended methods of cookery: all; grilling, stir-frying and BBQ. Available fresh: all year.*

**Note**

Tenderise prepared octopus using a tenderising mallet or by marinating. Skin can be left on. Slow cooking provides a more tender finished product. Prepared octopus should be wrapped in cling film in an airtight container in a refrigerator for up to 3 days. Store in a freezer for up to 10 weeks.

| Name | Other Names/Methods/Availability | Purchased |
|---|---|---|
| **Oysters** | (varieties: Coral Rock, Blacklip, Pacific, Bluff and Sydney Rock Oysters) | raw, whole, shucked or on the half shell |
| | *Recommended methods of cookery:* all; raw, grilling, poaching, frying. *Available fresh:* all year. | |

 Unopened oysters should be placed in a damp hessian bag. Oysters on the half shell should be stored on ice covered with cling film. Oysters stored correctly should keep for approx. 6–9 days.

| | | |
|---|---|---|
| **Pipis** | | in shell |
| | *Recommended methods of cookery:* all. *Available fresh:* all year. | |
| **Prawns** | Shrimp (varieties: Eastern King, Royal Red Banana, Brown Tiger, Greasyback, Western King and School Prawns) | whole or shelled, cooked or uncooked |
| | *Recommended methods of cookery:* all. *Available fresh:* all year. | |

Note: Prawns should be stored in an airtight container or in a bucket of fresh water in a refrigerator for up to 3 days. Store in a freezer for up to 10 weeks.

| | | |
|---|---|---|
| **Scallops** | (varieties: Saucer and Commercial Scallops) | in shell or meat |
| | *Recommended methods of cookery:* all; shallow frying and poaching. *Available fresh:* all year. | |

Note: Scallops will toughen easily and therefore should be cooked quickly, i.e. frying 30 seconds–1 minute or poaching 2–3 minutes maximum. Whole shells should be intact and closed when purchased. Remove scallops from shells and store the meat in an airtight container in a refrigerator for up to 3 days. Store in a freezer for up to 10 weeks.

| | | |
|---|---|---|
| **Scampi** | Langoustine | whole, dead |
| | *Recommended methods of cookery:* shallow frying, stir-frying, grilling, BBQ; eaten raw in Japan. | |

Notes: Store wrapped in cling film and place into an airtight container in a refrigerator for up to 3 days. Store in a freezer for up to 10 weeks.

Do not plunge into boiling water as this toughens the flesh.

| | | |
|---|---|---|
| **Squid** | (Calamari, varieties: Goulds and Etheridges Squid and Southern Calamari) | whole, tube or rings |
| | *Recommended methods of cookery:* all; shallow frying, deep frying, baking, steaming and BBQ. *Available fresh:* all year. | |

Note: Do not over-cook squid as the flesh will toughen. The tentacles and cleaned hood can be used, the hood either whole or cut into rings. Store wrapped in cling film and place into an airtight container in a refrigerator for up to 3 days. Store in a freezer for up to 10 weeks.

# FISH AND SEAFOOD RECIPES

## Char-grilled cod steaks with a grain mustard and garlic chive butter

Garnish: grain mustard and garlic chive butter.

**Ingredients**

| | 25 | 50 | 100 |
|---|---|---|---|
| **GRAIN MUSTARD AND GARLIC CHIVE BUTTER:** | | | |
| **butter**, room temperature | 1 kg | 2 kg | 4 kg |
| **garlic chives**, finely chopped | 25 g | 50 g | 100 g |
| **mustard**, grain | 50 g | 100 g | 200 g |
| **freshly milled black pepper** | to taste | | |
| | | | |
| **FISH:** | | | |
| **olive oil/vegetable oil** | as required | | |
| **cod steaks**, approx. | | | |
| 180–200 g per portion | 25 | 50 | 100 |

**Method**

1 Pre-heat grill plate/char-grill.
2 Combine all butter ingredients thoroughly. Place along the centre of a sheet of greaseproof paper. Roll into a cylindrical shape approx. 4 cm in diameter totally enclosing butter in greaseproof paper. Place into a freezer until required.
3 Brush cod steaks on all sides with liberal amounts of oil.
4 Lightly brush hot grill plate/char-grill with oil. Cook cod steaks for approx. 5 minutes on either side or until the cod steaks are cooked to the required degree.
5 Place cooked cod steaks neatly onto serving trays. Serve with a generous slice of the frozen butter placed on top as each steak is served.

**Notes**

If the grill plate is small, cod steaks can be seared on each side and placed onto roasting tray/s and put into a pre-heated moderate oven (150–180°C) until cooked to the required degree.

Butter can be pre-sliced and placed into a bowl of iced water near serving station for ease of service.

Adjust ingredients of flavoured butter to suit taste if required.

**♥ Health tip**

To reduce the fat content of this dish, use only **thin** slices of garlic butter.

# Italian-style baked sardines with Parmesan potatoes and sun-dried tomatoes

Garnish: a sprig of basil and a lemon wedge.

| Ingredients | | 25 | 50 | 100 |
|---|---|---|---|---|
| butter | | 125 g | 250 g | 500 g |
| potatoes, peeled, finely sliced on slicer | | 2 kg | 4 kg | 8 kg |
| Parmesan cheese, grated, approx. | | 250 g | 500 g | 1 kg |
| salt and freshly milled black pepper | | to taste | | |
| sardines, cleaned, washed and dried | | 50 | 100 | 200 |
| sun-dried tomatoes, shredded, including oil | | 150 g | 300 g | 600 g |
| crushed tomatoes, A10 tin | | 1/2 | 1 | 2 |
| basil, fresh, finely chopped | | 25 g | 50 g | 100 g |
| onions, white, finely chopped | | 400 g | 800 g | 1.6 kg |
| sugar, white | | 50 g | 100 g | 200 g |

**Method**

1 Pre-heat oven to moderate (150–180°C).
2 Melt butter and liberally brush bottom and sides of a deep sided serving/roasting tray/s.
3 Place a thin layer of potatoes onto bottom of dish.
4 Sprinkle potatoes with a fine layer of Parmesan cheese.
5 Season with a little salt and freshly milled black pepper.
6 Arrange sardines neatly onto potato. Evenly sprinkle sun-dried tomatoes over sardines.
7 Mix tomatoes, basil, onions and sugar and evenly pour over sardines.
8 Lightly season and dust with a little Parmesan cheese.
9 Place a double layer of potatoes over sardines brushing each layer with a little of the melted butter.
10 Season and sprinkle a little Parmesan cheese over potatoes.
11 Cover dish with aluminium foil, making sure it does not touch the sauce or potatoes, and place into oven. Cook for approx. 45 minutes–1 hour or until the sardines are cooked through and the potatoes have turned golden brown.
12 Remove from oven. Serve two sardines per portion with a little of the sauce and potatoes.

**Note**

**Sardines** are a member of the herring family; the name also applies to young pilchards and sprats. These are soft boned salt water fish, silvery in appearance and subject to seasonal availability. The name is believed to have originated from the small pilchards that were caught off the coast of Sardinia.

**Health tip**

To make this dish more suitable for cholesterol-lowering diets, use margarine instead of butter.

# Grilled hake fillets with a fresh tomato sauce and whole roasted garlic cloves

Garnish: whole roasted garlic cloves.

**Ingredients**

| | 25 | 50 | 100 |
|---|---|---|---|
| **TOMATO SAUCE:** | | | |
| olive oil/vegetable oil | as required | | |
| **garlic**, cloves, peeled, finely chopped | 5 | 10 | 20 |
| **onions**, finely sliced | 700 g | 1.4 kg | 2.8 kg |
| **tomatoes**, crushed, A10 tin | 1 | 2 | 4 |
| **basil**, fresh, finely chopped | 30 g | 60 g | 120 g |
| **sugar**, white | 100 g | 200 g | 400 g |
| **tomatoes**, skins removed, 1 cm dice | 2 kg | 4 kg | 8 kg |
| **salt and freshly milled black pepper** | to taste | | |
| | | | |
| **FISH:** | | | |
| **hake fillets**, 180–200 g per portion | 25 | 50 | 100 |
| **salt and freshly milled black pepper** | to taste | | |
| **garlic**, cloves, skin on, roasted | | | |
| (see note) | 50 | 100 | 200 |

**Method**

1 Pre-heat oven to moderate (150–180°C).
2 Heat a little oil in a pan over a moderate heat.
3 Add garlic and onions. Cook without colour until onions are soft.
4 Add crushed tomatoes, basil and sugar. Mix well. Simmer gently until the sauce begins to thicken to required consistency.
5 Add diced tomatoes. Season to taste.
6 Lightly brush serving tray/s with oil. Place fillets onto trays. Brush fillets with a little of the oil and lightly season.
7 Place fillets into oven for approx. 10–15 minutes or until cooked through.
8 Remove cooked fish fillets from oven and serve with a little of the tomato sauce and two roasted garlic cloves if desired.

Roast garlic by placing whole unpeeled bulbs that have been lightly pricked with a fork onto a lightly oiled baking tray. Place into a pre-heated moderate oven (150–180°C) and cook for approx. 20–30 minutes or until cloves are soft to the touch. Remove from oven and serve warm as required. Garlic cloves are roasted, enabling the customer to squeeze the garlic purée from the clove as an accompaniment to their meal. Roasting garlic sweetens its flavour without strong garlic odour.

**Health tip**   Highly recommended for people on cholesterol-lowering and low kilojoule diets.

# Flathead fillets sautéed with a lime, coconut cream and coriander sauce

Garnish: small sprigs of fresh coriander.

Ingredients

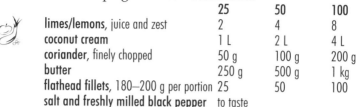

| | | 25 | 50 | 100 |
|---|---|---|---|---|
| limes/lemons, juice and zest | | 2 | 4 | 8 |
| coconut cream | | 1 L | 2 L | 4 L |
| coriander, finely chopped | | 50 g | 100 g | 200 g |
| butter | | 250 g | 500 g | 1 kg |
| flathead fillets, 180–200 g per portion | | 25 | 50 | 100 |
| salt and freshly milled black pepper | | to taste | | |

Method

1 Mix lime/lemon juice and zest, coconut cream and coriander in a mixing bowl. Cover and refrigerate for approx. 1 hour.
2 Place coriander mixture into a saucepan over a moderate heat. Simmer and allow to reduce until the sauce is of the consistency to coat the back of a spoon.
3 Melt required amount of butter on a grill plate or sauté pan over a moderate heat. Gently add fillets.
4 Cook for approx. $1^1/_2$–2 minutes on either side or until fillets are cooked through.
5 Remove from heat and serve hot fillets coated with a little of the warm sauce.

Note

There is often confusion as to the differences between **coconut milk** and **coconut cream**. The difference lies in the ratio of coconut to the liquid. Coconut milk is 1 part liquid to 1 part coconut flesh, whereas coconut cream is 1 part liquid to 4 parts coconut flesh. The liquid is usually water, but milk can be substituted to give an even richer result. The shredded coconut and liquid is simmered, then strained through cheesecloth to give the finished product.

# Bouillabaisse

Garnish: freshly chopped continental parsley.

Ingredients

| | | 25 | 50 | 100 |
|---|---|---|---|---|
| olive oil/vegetable oil | | as required | | |
| prawns, medium, shelled, de-veined, halved lengthways | | 50 | 100 | 200 |
| basil, fresh, finely chopped | | 25 g | 50 g | 100 g |
| garlic, cloves, finely chopped | | 6 | 10 | 15 |
| sugar, white | | 50 g | 100 g | 200 g |
| onions, white, finely chopped | | 300 g | 600 g | 1.2 kg |
| tomatoes, crushed, A10 tin | | $1^1/_2$ | 3 | 6 |

continued

| | | | |
|---|---|---|---|
| **capsicums**, roasted, 2 cm dice | 4 | 8 | 16 |
| **hoki**, fish fillets,or any white fish, cut into 2.5 cm squares | 1.25 kg | 2.5 kg | 5 kg |
| **mussels**, black, bearded, cleaned | 75 | 150 | 300 |
| **salt and freshly milled black pepper** | to taste | | |
| **parsley**, continental, finely chopped | 30 g | 60 g | 120 g |

**Method**

1 Put a little oil in a saucepan over a moderate heat. Add prawns, basil, garlic, sugar and onion. Cook gently until onions are soft, agitating regularly.
2 Add crushed tomato and roasted capsicum. Simmer gently for approx. 10 minutes.
3 Add all other ingredients, season to taste and cook for a further 5 minutes or until hoki fillets and mussels are cooked through.
4 Remove from heat. Stir through chopped parsley and serve.

**Notes**

Roast capsicum by removing stalk and seeds, quartering and roughly chopping. Place capsicum into a deep sided roasting tray tossed with a little olive oil and place into a pre-heated moderate oven (150–180°C) and roast, turning regularly, for approx. 30–45 minutes or until the flesh is soft, and the skin is easily removed.

**Bouillabaisse** is a famous seafood and tomato stew originating from Marseilles, Provence in France. It can be made using most fish and shellfish depending on budget and seasonal availability. To serve a classic bouillabaisse, ladle the seafood stew over thick slices of toasted French bread.

**♥ Health tip**  Highly recommended for people on cholesterol-lowering and low kilojoule diets.

# Whole baby trout baked with almonds, roasted pine nuts and herbed lemon butter

Garnish: pine nuts and herbed lemon butter.

**Ingredients**

| | 25 | 50 | 100 |
|---|---|---|---|
| **butter**, room temperature | 350 g | 700 g | 1.4 kg |
| **lemon**, juice and zest | 1 | 2 | 4 |
| **parsley**, fresh, chopped | 25 g | 50 g | 100 g |
| **basil**, fresh, finely chopped | 25 g | 50 g | 100 g |
| **trout**, baby, whole, gutted and cleaned | 25 | 50 | 100 |
| **almonds**, slivered | 400 g | 800 g | 1.6 kg |
| **pine nuts**, roasted | 400 g | 800 g | 1.6 kg |

| Method | |
|---|---|
| | 1  Pre-heat oven to moderate (150–180°C). |
| | 2  Wash trout thoroughly under cold running water and drain. |
| | 3  Mix butter, lemon juice and zest, parsley, basil, almonds and roasted pine nuts. |
| | 4  Fill each trout with a little of the mixture. |
| | 5  Place trout onto pieces of greased tin foil of a size that can completely enclose a trout. Cover with a little of the remaining butter mixture and enclose fish completely with foil to form a parcel. |
| | 6  Place trout onto baking or serving tray/s and place into oven. Cook for approx. 15–20 minutes or until trout is cooked. |
| | 7  Remove from oven and serve each trout in its parcel. |

 **Note**     This dish is also ideal for the barbecue as an alternative to meat.

❤ **Health tip**     To make more suitable for cholesterol-lowering diets, use margarine instead of butter.

# Baby trout poached in white wine, lemon juice and fresh dill

**G**arnish: finely chopped fresh dill.

| Ingredients | | 25 | 50 | 100 |
|---|---|---|---|---|
| | trout, baby, whole, gutted | 25 | 50 | 100 |
| | onions, Spanish, peeled, finely diced | 500 g | 1 kg | 2 kg |
| | garlic, cloves, peeled, finely chopped | 4 | 6 | 8 |
| | lemons, zest and juice | 3 | 5 | 7 |
| | dill, finely chopped | 30 g | 60 g | 120 g |
| | wine, white | 1 L | 2 L | 4 L |

| Method | |
|---|---|
| | 1  Pre-heat oven to moderate (150–180°C). |
| | 2  Wash trout thoroughly under cold running water and drain well. |
| | 3  Combine all other ingredients and mix well. |
| | 4  Place trout into greased deep sided baking tray/s, one deep. |
| | 5  Pour mixture evenly over trout and seal tray with aluminium foil. |
| | 6  Place tray/s into oven. Cook for approx. 20–30 minutes or until trout is cooked. |
| | 7  Remove from oven and serve each trout with a little of the poaching stock. |

 **Note**     **Trout** is a member of the salmon family and is generally a freshwater fish, although a few species live in salt water. It is a very versatile fish that is suited to most methods of cookery.

❤ **Health tip**     Highly recommended for people on cholesterol-lowering and low kilojoule diets.

# Salmon, continental parsley and Spanish onion fish cakes

Garnish: sprigs of continental parsley and a lemon wedge.

Ingredients

| | 25 | 50 | 100 |
|---|---|---|---|
| potatoes, peeled, cooked | 2.5 kg | 5 kg | 10 kg |
| salmon, tinned | 500 g | 1 kg | 2 kg |
| white fish fillets, cooked, flaked | 2.5 kg | 5 kg | 10 kg |
| eggs | 4 | 8 | 16 |
| parsley, continental, finely chopped | 20 g | 40 g | 80 g |
| lemons, zest and juice | 1 | 2 | 4 |
| onions, Spanish, peeled, finely diced | 1 kg | 2 kg | 4 kg |
| garlic, cloves, peeled, finely diced | 2 | 4 | 8 |
| breadcrumbs | as required | | |
| salt and freshly milled black pepper | to taste | | |
| olive oil/vegetable oil | as required | | |
| flour, plain | as required | | |
| eggs, approx. | 15 | 30 | 60 |
| milk | 250 mL | 500 mL | 1 L |
| breadcrumbs | as required | | |

Method

1 Pre-heat deep fryer to 165°C.
2 Mash potatoes.
3 In a large mixing bowl mix potatoes, salmon, white fish, eggs, parsley, lemon zest and juice.
4 Lightly fry Spanish onions and garlic without colour in a little oil until soft. Drain and add to potato mixture.
5 If mixture is too wet, add small amounts of breadcrumbs mixing well each time until correct consistency is achieved. The texture should be firm yet able to be moulded to the required size and shape.
6 Shape into the required amount of patties allowing two per portion, approx. 130 g each.
7 Coat each fish cake with flour and pass through mixture of beaten egg and milk and evenly coat with breadcrumbs. Carefully place onto trays separating each layer with a sheet of greaseproof paper.
8 Deep fry in small batches until fish cakes are light golden brown.
9 Carefully remove and drain.
10 Serve two per portion.

Note

A little chopped parsley can be mixed with the breadcrumb coating to enhance presentation.

Health tip

To reduce fat content, place fish cakes on a lightly greased oven tray and bake until cooked, or pan-fry in shallow oil.

# Mediterranean seafood frittata topped with herbed mozzarella and Parmesan

Garnish: slices of lemon and orange that have been lightly coated with chopped parsley.

Ingredients

| | 25 | 50 | 100 |
|---|---|---|---|
| eggs | 75 | 150 | 300 |
| milk | 500 mL | 1 L | 2 L |
| cream, single | 100 mL | 200 mL | 400 mL |
| Parmesan cheese, grated | 300 g | 600 g | 1.2 kg |
| parsley, finely chopped | 1 cup | 2 cups | 4 cups |
| basil, roughly chopped | 25 g | 50 g | 100 g |
| salt and freshly milled black pepper | to taste | | |
| olive oil/vegetable oil | as required | | |
| prawns, cooked, peeled, roughly chopped | 750 g | 1.5 kg | 3 kg |
| seafood extender, roughly chopped | 500 g | 1 kg | 2kg |
| white fish fillets, cooked, flaked | 750 g | 1.5 kg | 3 kg |
| mozzarella cheese, grated | 600 g | 1.2 kg | 2.4 kg |

Method

1 Combine eggs, milk, cream, half Parmesan cheese, half parsley and basil and thoroughly whisk. Season to taste.

2 **Either:**

2.1 Pre-heat oven to moderate (150–180°C).

2.2 Lightly grease a deep sided baking dish capable of holding the egg mixture.

2.3 Place mixture into baking dish and evenly add seafood.

2.4 Place mixture into oven and cook until mixture is just set.

2.5 Top with grated mozzarella, parsley, basil and Parmesan cheese.

2.6 Return to oven for a further 2–3 minutes until cheese has melted.

2.7 Remove tray from oven and leave to stand for approx. 2 minutes. Portion and serve immediately.

**Or:**

2.1 Pre-heat salamander to medium.

2.2 Heat a little oil in an omelette pan over a moderate heat and add a ladleful of egg mixture.

2.3 Cook mixture for approx. one minute then lightly mix.

2.4 Cook for a further one to two minutes without colour until mixture can be seen to set.

2.5 Add an even amount of seafood on egg mixture.

2.6 Sprinkle evenly with mozzarella, parsley and a little Parmesan cheese. Place under a salamander until omelette is cooked and cheese starts to brown.

2.7 Gently turn omelette onto plate. Serve immediately.

continued

**Parmesan cheese** is made from skimmed or partially skimmed cow's milk. Its complex flavour and granular texture are the results of the long ageing process, which can be between 2–4 years. The name comes from Parma in Italy where it was originally made, although it is now made in quite a few countries. The Italian variety is still regarded as the best.

**Health tip**

This is unsuitable for low fat diets. To minimise the amount of fat:
- Use reduced fat milk.
- Use mozzarella sparingly.
- Use light sour cream instead of regular cream.

# Jewfish cutlets in a mild curry sauce with spinach served with a Spanish saffron and caraway seed rice

Garnish: julienne of spring onions.

**Ingredients**

| | 25 | 50 | 100 |
|---|---|---|---|
| olive oil/vegetable oil | as required | | |
| **jewfish**, cutlets | 25 | 50 | 100 |
| **onions**, white, finely chopped | 250 g | 500 g | 1 kg |
| **curry powder**, mild, approx. | 75 g | 150 g | 300 g |
| **flour**, plain | 150 g | 300 g | 600 g |
| **stock**, fish, vegetable or chicken, warm | 2 L | 4 L | 8 L |
| **spinach**, washed, trimmed, shredded | 300 g | 600 g | 1.2 kg |
| **sugar**, white | 100 g | 200 g | 400 g |
| **salt and freshly milled black pepper** | to taste | | |

**Method**

1 Pre-heat oven to moderate (150–180°C).
2 Place a little oil in a frying pan or flat grill plate over a moderate heat.
3 Add jewfish cutlets to the oil leaving a little space in between.
4 Cook for approx. 30 seconds on either side.
5 Remove cutlets from the pan and place onto roasting or serving tray/s. Place into oven and cook for approx. 10 minutes or until fish are cooked through. Remove from oven.
6 While fish is cooking heat a little oil in a saucepan. Add onion and cook without colour until tender.
7 Add curry powder and mix well.
8 Add flour and mix well. Cook without colour for approx. one minute.
9 Add warm stock and sugar, stirring continuously until all ingredients are blended together.
10 Simmer sauce until a smooth consistency is reached. Season to taste. Add spinach.

11 Pour a little of the warmed curry sauce over cutlets. Return to oven for a further 1–2 minutes making sure cutlets are heated through.

12 Place a little mound of saffron rice onto each plate and make a hollow in the centre.

13 Place one cutlet into hollow and coat evenly with sauce. Garnish and serve immediately.

## Spanish saffron and caraway seed rice

**Ingredients**

| rice, long grain, uncooked | 1.5 kg | 3 kg | 6 kg |
|---|---|---|---|
| saffron, powdered Spanish | 2 tsps | 4 tsps | 8 tsps |
| salt | 35 g | 70 g | 140 g |
| caraway seeds | 40 g | 80 g | 160 g |

**Method** Bring a saucepan of boiling water to the boil and simmer. Add salt, caraway seeds and saffron and stir. Add rice, mix once and leave to simmer until rice is tender but firm. Remove from heat and drain.

 **Note** Due to the varying size of different varieties of jewfish it is recommended that a portion be between 180–200 g per person.

 **Health tip** Jewfish are low in fat. This dish is particularly recommended for low fat diets.

# Creamy seafood and spring onion vol-au-vents topped with grated Swiss cheese

**G**arnish: small sprigs of fresh dill.

**Ingredients**

| | 25 | 50 | 100 |
|---|---|---|---|
| butter/margarine | 150 g | 300 g | 600 g |
| spring onions, trimmed, finely sliced | 8 | 16 | 32 |
| garlic, cloves, peeled, finely chopped | 3 | 5 | 7 |
| flour, plain | 150 g | 300 g | 600 g |
| milk, warmed | 1 L | 2 L | 4 L |
| cream, single | 200 mL | 400 mL | 800 mL |
| white fish fillets, cooked, flaked | 1.5 kg | 3 kg | 6 kg |
| prawns, cooked, peeled, roughly chopped | 500 g | 1 kg | 2 kg |
| seafood extender, roughly chopped | 750 g | 1.5 kg | 3 kg |
| salt and freshly milled black pepper | to taste | | |
| vol-au-vent cases, 10 cm | 25 | 50 | 100 |
| Swiss cheese, grated | 500 g | 1 kg | 2 kg |
| parsley, finely chopped | as required | | |

continued

**Method**

1 Pre-heat oven to moderate (150–180°C).
2 Melt butter/margarine in a saucepan over a moderate heat.
3 Add spring onions and garlic. Cook without colour for approx. 3–4 minutes.
4 Add flour gradually, mixing well until a smooth paste is achieved.
5 Reduce heat and cook roux without colour for approx. 1–2 minutes stirring continuously.
6 Slowly incorporate warm milk and stir until smooth.
7 Cook slowly for approx. 2–4 minutes stirring constantly.
8 Stir in cream. Gently fold in the fish, prawns and seafood extender. Season to taste and remove pan from the heat.
9 Fill vol-au-vent cases with mixture and top with a little grated cheese and a sprinkle of parsley.
10 Place vol-au-vents onto baking trays and place into oven. Cook until cheese is golden brown.
11 Serve one vol-au-vent per portion.

 **Note**  If the seafood mixture is a little wet add small amounts of breadcrumbs until the required consistency is achieved.

 **Health tip**  Unsuitable for a low fat diet.

# Thai-style fish cakes

**G**arnish: sprigs of fresh coriander.

**Ingredients**

| | 25 | 50 | 100 |
|---|---|---|---|
| **lime leaves**, dried | 6 | 12 | 24 |
| **potatoes**, cooked, mashed | 2.5 kg | 5 kg | 10 kg |
| **white fish fillets**, cooked, flaked | 3 kg | 6 kg | 12 kg |
| **eggs** | 4 | 8 | 16 |
| **coriander**, sprigs, finely chopped | 1 bunch | 2 bunches | 4 bunches |
| **spring onions**, finely sliced | 250 g | 500 g | 1 kg |
| **beans**, green, finely sliced | 500 g | 1 kg | 2 kg |
| **garlic**, cloves, peeled, finely chopped | 5 | 10 | 20 |
| **ginger**, peeled, finely grated | 30 g | 60 g | 120 g |
| **chillies**, seeded, finely chopped | 3 | 6 | 12 |
| **breadcrumbs** | as required | | |
| **salt and freshly milled black pepper** | to taste | | |
| **olive oil/vegetable oil** | as required | | |

1  Pre-heat oven to moderate (150–180°C).
2  Place lime leaves into a bowl and just cover with boiling water. Stand for 2–3 minutes, remove from water and finely chop.
3  Combine lime leaves, potatoes, fish fillets, eggs, coriander, spring onions, green beans, garlic, ginger and chillies. Mix well.
4  Season to taste. Adjust consistency with the addition of small amounts of breadcrumbs if required.
5  Mould into approx. 120 g patties allowing two fish cakes per portion.
6  Heat a little oil in a pan over a moderate heat. Gently cook fish cakes for approx. one minute on each side or until golden brown.
7  Remove from pan and drain well. Place onto a greased baking or serving tray/s and put into oven for approx. 5–10 minutes or until heated through.

If lime leaves are unavailable, substitute zest and juice of lemons or limes.
Ground roasted peanuts can also be added if desired.

# Black mussels poached in white wine, butter, Spanish onions and parsley

Garnish: purple basil sprigs.

Ingredients

| | 25 | 50 | 100 |
|---|---|---|---|
| mussels, black, cleaned | 12.5 kg | 25 kg | 50 kg |
| butter, salted | 500 g | 1 kg | 2 kg |
| onions, Spanish, finely chopped | 1 kg | 2 kg | 4 kg |
| garlic, cloves, peeled, finely chopped | 4 | 8 | 16 |
| wine, white | 1 L | 2 L | 4 L |
| parsley, sprigs, finely chopped | 50 g | 100 g | 200 g |
| freshly milled black pepper | to taste | | |

Method

1  Melt butter and add onions and garlic in a large pan over a moderate heat. Simmer gently until soft.
2  Add white wine, half the parsley, and mussels. Place lid over pan and steam mussels for approx. 5 minutes stirring regularly.
3  Remove from heat. Add remaining parsley and season to taste.
4  Serve with a little of the cooking stock.

This dish is ideally served with some fresh crusty bread or garlic bread.
Avoid mussels with broken shells and discard any that fail to open during cooking.

Highly recommended for people on cholesterol-lowering and low kilojoule diets.
Mussels are a rich source of the minerals iron and zinc.

# Fresh cod fillets deep fried in a traditional beer batter served with fresh aïoli

Garnish: deep fried parsley sprigs and fresh lemon wedges.

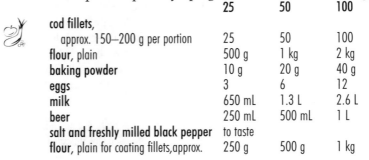

| Ingredients | | 25 | 50 | 100 |
|---|---|---|---|---|
| cod fillets, | | | | |
|    approx. 150–200 g per portion | | 25 | 50 | 100 |
| flour, plain | | 500 g | 1 kg | 2 kg |
| baking powder | | 10 g | 20 g | 40 g |
| eggs | | 3 | 6 | 12 |
| milk | | 650 mL | 1.3 L | 2.6 L |
| beer | | 250 mL | 500 mL | 1 L |
| salt and freshly milled black pepper | | to taste | | |
| flour, plain for coating fillets, approx. | | 250 g | 500 g | 1 kg |

**Method**

1 Pre-heat deep fryer to approx. 160–170°C.
2 Cut fish fillets to required size.
3 Sieve flour and baking flour into a large stainless steel mixing bowl.
4 Add eggs and small amounts of milk and beer gently whisking until smooth. The mixture should coat the back of a spoon. Season to taste.
5 Allow to stand in a cool place for approx. 20 minutes.
6 Ensuring fillets are dry, lightly coat with flour and dip fillets into batter mix making sure all the fillet is coated with the batter. Drain any excess mixture and carefully place fish into hot oil.
7 Cook fillets until they float to the surface of the oil and are golden brown.
8 Remove fish from oil and drain all excess fat before serving with a little aïoli.

**Note**

Batter consistency can be adjusted by the addition of small amounts of milk, beer or flour.

## Aïoli

| Ingredients | | 25 | 50 | 100 |
|---|---|---|---|---|
| mayonnaise | | 1 L | 2 L | 4 L |
| garlic, cloves, peeled and minced | | 6 | 12 | 24 |
| salt and freshly milled black pepper | | to taste | | |

**Method**

1 Combine mayonnaise and minced garlic. Season to taste.
2 Refrigerate until required, allowing one full dessertspoon per portion.

**Note**

When refrigerating aïoli, keep covered so that the garlic aroma does not interfere with other foods.

**Health tip**

Unsuitable for low fat diets.

# Mussels with a tomato, purple basil and chilli sauce

Garnish: sprigs of purple basil.

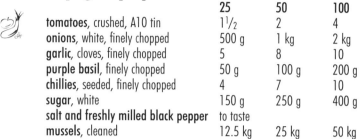

**Ingredients**

| | 25 | 50 | 100 |
|---|---|---|---|
| **tomatoes**, crushed, A10 tin | 1¹/₂ | 2 | 4 |
| **onions**, white, finely chopped | 500 g | 1 kg | 2 kg |
| **garlic**, cloves, finely chopped | 5 | 8 | 10 |
| **purple basil**, finely chopped | 50 g | 100 g | 200 g |
| **chillies**, seeded, finely chopped | 4 | 7 | 10 |
| **sugar**, white | 150 g | 250 g | 400 g |
| **salt and freshly milled black pepper** | to taste | | |
| **mussels**, cleaned | 12.5 kg | 25 kg | 50 kg |

**Method**

1 Place crushed tomatoes, onions, garlic, basil, chillies and sugar in a saucepan. Cover with a tight fitting lid and gently simmer for approx. 1–1¹/₂ hours, stirring occasionally. Season to taste.
2 Add mussels to sauce and place lid over pan. Steam mussels for approx. 5 minutes, stirring regularly.
3 Remove from heat. Season to taste.
4 Serve with a little of the tomato sauce.

**Note**  Mussels have been used as food for over 20 000 years. They are now cultivated in farms to meet the high demand for their flesh. There are many species. The meat is slightly tougher than that of other molluscs but has a distinctive sweet flavour.

Avoid mussels with broken shells and discard any that fail to open during cooking.

**Health tip**  Highly recommended for people on cholesterol-lowering and low kilojoule diets. Mussels are a rich source of the minerals iron and zinc.

# Prawn, leek and fresh Parmesan risotto

Garnish: roughly chopped cooked prawns.

**Ingredients**

| | 25 | 50 | 100 |
|---|---|---|---|
| **olive oil/vegetable oil** | as required | | |
| **garlic**, cloves, finely chopped | 4 | 6 | 8 |
| **onions**, Spanish, finely chopped | 1 kg | 2 kg | 4 kg |
| **leeks**, trimmed, washed, finely sliced | 2 kg | 4 kg | 8 kg |
| **prawns**, cooked, peeled, de-veined, roughly chopped | 1.5 kg | 3 kg | 6 kg |
| **butter** | 250 g | 500 g | 1 kg |
| **rice**, Arborio/long grained | 1.5 kg | 3 kg | 6 kg |
| **stock**, fish, warmed | 4 L | 8 L | 16 L |
| **parsley**, fresh, finely chopped | 100 g | 200 g | 400 g |
| **Parmesan cheese**, shaved | 200 g | 400 g | 800 g |
| **salt and freshly milled black pepper** | to taste | | |

continued

<table>
<tr><td>Method</td><td>

1  Heat a little oil in a saucepan over a moderate heat. Add garlic and onion and cook until onion is soft.
2  Add leeks and prawns. Cook for a further two minutes.
3  Reduce heat and add butter. When butter has melted add rice and stir continually, ensuring all rice is completely coated with butter.
4  Slowly add warmed stock until all has been incorporated, stirring continuously.
5  Place a tight fitting lid over saucepan. Cook slowly, stirring regularly until all stock has been absorbed and the rice is tender.
6  Thoroughly mix in parsley and shaved Parmesan. Cook for a further 2–3 minutes.
7  Season to taste. Remove from heat and serve.

</td></tr>
</table>

**Note**

**Risotto** is a classic Italian dish, usually made with Arborio rice. It is cooked slowly to allow the rice to absorb the many flavours and ingredients that can be used. Arborio rice, with its white core, stays firm while the rest of the grain leaks starch into the liquid, producing a velvety sauce. However, long grained rice can be substituted.

# Flathead fillets in a tempura batter

Garnish: a wedge of lemon.

Ingredients

| | 25 | 50 | 100 |
|---|---|---|---|
| cornflour | 1 kg | 2 kg | 4 kg |
| rice flour | 1 kg | 2 kg | 4 kg |
| vinegar, white | 20 mL | 40 mL | 80 mL |
| water, iced | as required | | |
| salt | to taste | | |
| flour, plain | 1 kg | 2 kg | 4 kg |
| flathead, fillets, approx. 150–200 g per portion | 25 | 50 | 100 |

Method
1  Pre-heat deep fryer to approx. 160–170°C.
2  In a mixing bowl, combine cornflour, rice flour and vinegar. Slowly incorporate iced water until of a consistency that will thickly coat the back of a spoon. Season to taste.
3  Ensuring fillets are dry, lightly coat with flour and dip fillets into batter mix making sure all the fillet is coated in the batter. Drain excess mixture and carefully place fish into hot oil.
4  Cook until fillets float to the surface of the oil and are golden brown.
5  Carefully remove fish from oil and drain all excess fat. Serve one fillet per portion.

**Note**

**Tempura** is a style of cookery developed in Japan that involves deep-frying food in tempura batter. Tempura dishes are generally served with soya sauce. Tempura batter is very light and crisp and a good alternative to conventional batters.

 **Health tip**  Unsuitable for low fat diets.

# Moroccan-style roasted ling fillets

Garnish: sprigs of fresh coriander.

Ingredients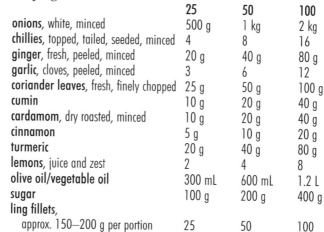

| | 25 | 50 | 100 |
|---|---|---|---|
| onions, white, minced | 500 g | 1 kg | 2 kg |
| chillies, topped, tailed, seeded, minced | 4 | 8 | 16 |
| ginger, fresh, peeled, minced | 20 g | 40 g | 80 g |
| garlic, cloves, peeled, minced | 3 | 6 | 12 |
| coriander leaves, fresh, finely chopped | 25 g | 50 g | 100 g |
| cumin | 10 g | 20 g | 40 g |
| cardamom, dry roasted, minced | 10 g | 20 g | 40 g |
| cinnamon | 5 g | 10 g | 20 g |
| turmeric | 20 g | 40 g | 80 g |
| lemons, juice and zest | 2 | 4 | 8 |
| olive oil/vegetable oil | 300 mL | 600 mL | 1.2 L |
| sugar | 100 g | 200 g | 400 g |
| ling fillets, | | | |
| approx. 150–200 g per portion | 25 | 50 | 100 |

Method
1 Combine all ingredients except ling fillets in a mixing bowl.
2 Place portioned ling fillets into roasting or serving tray/s and coat generously with all the marinade.
3 Cover tray/s with cling wrap and refrigerate for approx. 4–6 hours, turning ling fillets every hour.
4 Remove cling wrap and place tray/s into a pre-heated moderate oven (150–180°C). Cook for approx. 15–20 minutes or until fish is cooked through.
5 Remove from oven and serve.

 Note

**Ginger** is found in tropical and sub-tropical regions of the world. The name 'ginger' is derived from the Sanskrit word for 'horned root'. It is an essential ingredient in Asian cookery and is also valued for its medicinal properties. It has a very distinctive taste and aroma and should be used in moderation as it can have an overpowering effect. Fresh ginger should be used in a little more quantity as its pungency cooks out.

Health tip    Highly recommended for all low fat diets.

# CUTS OF BEEF AND APPROXIMATE WEIGHTS OF THE UNPREPARED PRIMARY CUT

## Approximate cooking times for joints of beef

30 minutes per kilo (2 lb) plus an extra 30 minutes for rare.
45 minutes per kilo (2 lb) plus an extra 45 minutes for medium.
These cooking times may vary depending on the oven used.

### Forequarter

| Cut | French Term | Uses | Approx. Weights |
|---|---|---|---|
| forerib | côte premiere | braising, roasting | 8 kg |
| plate | plat de côte/poitrine | stewing | 9 kg |
| middle rib/rib eye | côte découverte | stewing, braising | 9 kg |
| brisket | poitrine | pickling, boiling | 15 kg |
| chuck rib | côte de collier | stewing, braising | 15 kg |
| blade | – | stewing, braising | 8 kg |
| shank | jambe de devant | soups | 6 kg |

### Hindquarter

| Cut | French Term | Uses | Approx. Weights |
|---|---|---|---|
| shin | jambe | soups, stewing | 7 kg |
| topside | tranche tendre | roasting, braising, stewing | 10 kg |
| silverside | gîte à la noix | boiled, roasted | 13 kg |
| flank | tranche grosse | stewing, braising | 11 kg |
| thin flank | bavette d'aloyau | boiling, stewing | 9 kg |
| rump | culotte | frying, grilling, braising | 10 kg |
| sirloin/striploin/shortloin | aloyau | roasting, grilling, frying | 9 kg |
| fillet/tenderloin } | filet | { roasting, grilling, frying | 2–4 kg |
| backstrap } | | { grilling, frying | 2–3 kg |
| wing ribs | côte d'aloyau | roasting, grilling, frying | 4–5 kg |

### Beef Offal

| Cut | French Term | Uses |
|---|---|---|
| heart | cœur | roasting, braising |
| tongue | langue | boiling, pickling, braising |
| kidney | rognon | soups, stewing |
| liver | foie | frying, braising |
| sweetbread | ris | frying, braising |
| tripe | tripe | boiling |
| bone | os | stock |

♥ **Health tip**   Remove all visible fat from beef.
Order lean beef from the butcher/supplier.

# BEEF RECIPES

## Mexican-style beef nachos with guacamole

Garnish: sliced jalapeño peppers.

Ingredients

| | 25 | 50 | 100 |
|---|---|---|---|
| olive oil/vegetable oil | as required | | |
| **onions**, Spanish, peeled, finely chopped | 1 kg | 2 kg | 4 kg |
| **garlic**, cloves, peeled, finely chopped | 4 | 8 | 16 |
| **red chillies**, seeded, finely chopped | 3–6 | 6–9 | 9–12 |
| **beef**, minced | 3.5 kg | 7 kg | 14 kg |
| **flour**, plain | 150 g | 300 g | 600 g |
| **stock**, beef, warm | 1 L | 2 L | 4 L |
| **tomatoes**, crushed, A10 tin | 1 | 2 | 4 |
| **tomato sauce** | 250 mL | 500 mL | 1 L |
| **kidney beans**, A10 tin, drained | 1/2 | 1 | 2 |
| **nachos chips** | 5 kg | 10 kg | 20 kg |
| **guacamole**, see following recipe | 1.5 kg | 3 kg | 6 kg |
| **sour cream** | 1 kg | 2 kg | 4 kg |
| **Cheddar cheese**, grated | 1 kg | 2 kg | 4 kg |

Method

1. Pre-heat oven to moderate (150–180°C).
2. Heat a little oil in a pan over a moderate heat.
3. Add onions, garlic and chillies. Cook until onions are soft.
4. Add minced beef. Mix well. Cook for approx. 30 minutes stirring occasionally until beef is cooked through.
5. Add flour gradually and mix well.
6. Slowly add warmed beef stock, crushed tomato and tomato sauce. Bring to the boil, then reduce to a gentle simmer. Cook for approx. 30 minutes, or until mixture has reduced and thickened, stirring occasionally.
7. Add drained kidney beans. Mix well. Remove pan from heat.
8. In a serving tray/s add mixture to a depth of approx. 3 cm.
9. Place a thick layer of nachos chips over beef mixture.
10. Spread a thin layer of guacamole over nachos chips and repeat process with sour cream.
11. Generously sprinkle grated Cheddar cheese over sour cream and place tray/s into oven. Cook until cheese is melted and golden brown.
12. Remove from oven, garnish and serve.

Health tip

Unsuitable for low fat diets. To reduce the amount of fat:
- Use light sour cream sparingly or omit.
- Use reduced fat cheese sparingly.

continued

# Guacamole

|  |  | 25 | 50 | 100 |
|---|---|---|---|---|
| Ingredients  | avocado, ripe, peeled, seeded | 1.25 kg | 2.5 kg | 5 kg |
|  | sour cream | 250 g | 500 g | 1 kg |
|  | lemon, juice | 50 mL | 100 mL | 200 mL |
|  | tabasco sauce, optional | to taste |  |  |
|  | salt and freshly milled black pepper | to taste |  |  |

**Method** Combine all ingredients and blend until smooth. Season to taste and serve.

 **Guacamole** is a classic Mexican accompaniment that can be served with a variety of dishes. Ideally made as close to service as possible to avoid discolouration.

**Tabasco sauce** is made from the tabasco pepper. This very hot red pepper has its origins in the Mexican state of Tabasco. The peppers are fermented for approx. three years before being processed with vinegar and salt to produce the famous sauce, which has numerous uses.

 **Health tip** Unsuitable for low fat diets. Use light sour cream or omit altogether.

# Gourmet home-made beefburgers

Garnish: refer to note.

|  |  | 25 | 50 | 100 |
|---|---|---|---|---|
| Ingredients  | olive oil/vegetable oil | as required |  |  |
|  | garlic, cloves, peeled, finely chopped | 4 | 7 | 11 |
|  | onions, Spanish, finely chopped | 1 kg | 2 kg | 4 kg |
|  | beef, minced | 3.75 kg | 7.5 kg | 15 kg |
|  | Worcestershire sauce | 100 mL | 200 mL | 400 mL |
|  | tomato sauce | 150 mL | 300 mL | 600 mL |
|  | eggs | 3 | 6 | 12 |
|  | salt and freshly milled black pepper | to taste |  |  |
|  | breadcrumbs | as required |  |  |
|  | burger buns/focaccia bread | 25 | 50 | 100 |
|  | mayonnaise (see page 214) | as required |  |  |

**Method**
1 Pre-heat oven to moderate (150–180°C).
2 Heat a little oil in a pan over a moderate heat. Add garlic and onions and cook without colour for approx. 4 minutes or until onions are soft. Remove from heat.
3 In a large mixing bowl place onion and garlic mix, beef mince, Worcestershire sauce, tomato sauce, eggs, salt and pepper. Mix well.
4 Gradually add breadcrumbs while mixing until desired texture is achieved.

5 Turn mixture out onto a lightly floured work bench. Shape mixture into patties, approx. 150 g each.
6 Place patties onto tray/s one layer at a time. Place a piece of lightly oiled greaseproof paper between each layer. Refrigerate until required.
7 Heat a sauté pan or grill plate lightly brushed with a little oil. Sear patties on each side until golden brown.
8 Place seared patties onto lightly greased roasting tray/s. Place into oven and cook for approx. 20 minutes or until cooked through.
9 Serve one patty per portion on toasted buns spread with a little mayonnaise.

 **Note** This is only a basic recipe. The burgers can be topped with ingredients such as: crisp bacon, char-grilled pineapple rings, roasted red capsicum, guacamole, Swiss cheese, grilled tomato slices and a sautéed onion and mushroom compote. The only limitation besides your budget is your imagination.

 **Health tip** Use wholemeal buns to increase the fibre.

# Char-grilled sirloin steak served with slow roasted Roma tomatoes and a white onion and wholegrain mustard confit

**G**arnish: suggested confit.

| Ingredients | | 25 | 50 | 100 |
|---|---|---|---|---|
| | olive oil/vegetable oil | as required | | |
| | **Roma tomatoes**, halved | 13 | 25 | 50 |
| | **basil**, fresh, finely chopped | 20 g | 40 g | 80 g |
| | **parsley**, fresh, finely chopped | 20 g | 40 g | 80 g |
| | **salt and freshly milled black pepper** | to taste | | |
| | **sirloin steaks**, approx. 180–200 g each | 25 | 50 | 100 |

**Method**
1 Pre-heat oven to low (130–150°C).
2 Lightly oil baking tray/s with a little oil. Place the tomato halves neatly onto tray/s one layer deep.
3 Sprinkle with a little basil and parsley and lightly season.
4 Place into oven and cook slowly for approx. 30 minutes.
5 Approx. 5–10 minutes before tomatoes are cooked heat a char-grill or flat grill plate brushed with a little oil.
6 Lightly season steaks and cook to the required degree.
7 Place cooked steaks onto serving tray/s. Place half a tomato onto the centre of each steak and a little of the warmed confit on either side.
8 Serve immediately.

continued

**Health tip**  Suitable for low fat diets.
Reduce portion of meat to improve suitability for low kilojoule diets.

# White onion and wholegrain mustard confit

| | 25 | 50 | 100 |
|---|---|---|---|
| olive oil/vegetable oil | as required | | |
| **onions**, white, quartered, finely sliced | 2.5 kg | 5 kg | 10 kg |
| **garlic**, cloves, peeled, finely chopped | 3 | 5 | 7 |
| **mustard**, wholegrain | 250 g | 500 g | 1 kg |
| **salt and freshly milled black pepper** | to taste | | |

**Ingredients**

**Method**
1 Heat a little oil in a pan over a moderate heat.
2 Add onions and garlic. Cook until lightly browned stirring regularly.
3 Reduce heat to low and cover pan with a tight fitting lid. Braise for approx. 45 minutes stirring occasionally.
4 Add mustard and season to taste. Cook for a further 2 minutes.
5 Remove from heat and serve.

**Note**

**Mustards** are produced from the seeds of the mustard plant, which is a member of the cabbage family. The seeds are ground and mixed with spices such as turmeric or liquid such as vinegar, wine or water. The strength of the mustard depends on the variety of mustard seed. Varieties of mustard include: hot English, French Dijon, mild American, German and wholegrain, each with its own distinctive flavour.

# Red Thai-style beef curry

**G**arnish: finely chopped fresh coriander and purple basil.

| | 25 | 50 | 100 |
|---|---|---|---|
| **Thai curry paste**, red | 100 g | 200 g | 400 g |
| **coconut cream**, tinned | 1 L | 2 L | 4 L |
| **cream**, single | 250 mL | 500 mL | 1 L |
| **beef booster**, powdered stock base | to taste | | |
| **olive oil/vegetable oil** | as required | | |
| **blade/chuck steak**, cut into thin strips | 5 kg | 10 kg | 20 kg |

**Ingredients**

**Method**
1 Pre-heat oven to moderate (150–180°C).
2 Cook red curry paste for one minute in a saucepan over a moderate heat, stirring continually.
3 Add cream and coconut cream immediately. Whisk thoroughly until a smooth consistency is reached. Season to taste with beef booster and remove from heat.
4 Heat a large sauté pan or grill plate brushed with a little oil.
5 Gradually add beef pieces; seal and colour on all sides.

6 Remove beef pieces when sealed and place into deep sided roasting tray/s.
7 Pour over sufficient sauce to cover beef pieces. Cover tray/s with aluminium foil.
8 Place tray/s into oven. Cook for approx. $1^1/_2$ hours or until beef is cooked through and tender.
9 Serve beef with its sauce and steamed jasmine rice.

**Notes**

**Red curry paste** is available from most suppliers. Red can also be substituted for green curry paste if a slightly different style of Thai curry is desired.

Additional herbs such as fresh coriander, lemon grass, red basil and kaffir lime leaves can also be added during the cooking process to add extra flavour; these are optional and not necessary to the recipe.

**Health tip**

Not suitable for low fat diets. Reduce coconut cream by half.

# New York-style meatloaf

Garnish: finely sliced tomato and grated Cheddar cheese.

Ingredients

| | 25 | 50 | 100 |
|---|---|---|---|
| olive oil/vegetable oil | as required | | |
| garlic, cloves, peeled, finely chopped | 4 | 7 | 11 |
| onions, Spanish, finely chopped | 1 kg | 2 kg | 4 kg |
| beef, minced | 3.75 kg | 7.5 kg | 15 kg |
| Worcestershire sauce | 100 mL | 200 mL | 400 mL |
| tomato sauce | 150 mL | 300 mL | 600 mL |
| eggs | 3 | 6 | 12 |
| salt and freshly milled black pepper | to taste | | |
| breadcrumbs | as required | | |
| tomatoes, finely sliced | as required | | |
| Cheddar cheese, grated | as required | | |

Method

1 Pre-heat oven to moderate (150–180°C).
2 Heat a little oil in a pan over moderate heat. Add garlic and onions and cook without colour for approx. 4 minutes or until onions are soft. Remove from heat.
3 In a large mixing bowl place onion and garlic mix, beef mince, Worcestershire sauce, tomato sauce, eggs, salt and pepper. Mix well.
4 Gradually add breadcrumbs whilst mixing until desired texture is achieved.
5 Lightly grease large pieces of aluminium foil. Place meat mixture evenly along centre in a cylindrical shape.
6 Fold foil around mixture until all meat mixture has been enclosed.

continued

7 Place onto lightly oiled roasting tray/s and place into oven. Cook for approx. 45 minutes–1 hour or until meatloaf is cooked through.
8 Remove from oven and remove foil.
9 Place sliced tomatoes along the centre of the meatloaf and sprinkle liberally with grated cheese.
10 Return to oven and cook until cheese is melted and golden brown.
11 Remove from oven. Cool slightly.
12 Slice into required portions. Serve hot or cold.

**Note** Allow meatloaf to rest for approx. 2–4 minutes after cooking before slicing carefully with a sharp serrated knife.

**❤ Health tip** Omit cheese to make suitable for low fat diets.

# Savoury minced beef

Garnish: freshly chopped parsley.

| Ingredients | | 25 | 50 | 100 |
|---|---|---|---|---|
| olive oil/vegetable oil | | as required | | |
| garlic, cloves, peeled, finely chopped | | 5 | 8 | 11 |
| onions, finely chopped | | 1 kg | 2 kg | 4 kg |
| beef, mince | | 5 kg | 10 kg | 20 kg |
| tomato paste | | 300 g | 600 g | 1.2 kg |
| tomatoes, crushed, A10 tin | | 1/2 | 1 | 2 |
| stock, beef | | 1 L | 2 L | 4 L |
| salt and freshly milled black pepper | | to taste | | |

**Method**
1 Heat a little oil in a pan over a moderate heat.
2 Add garlic and onions and cook without colour until soft.
3 Add beef and mix well. Cook, stirring occasionally until meat is lightly browned.
4 Add tomato paste, crushed tomato and beef stock. Mix well. Simmer gently and reduce until it has thickened.
5 Season to taste and serve.

**Note** Variations:
This basic recipe can be used in more complex dishes such as lasagne, beef moussaka, cottage pie, bolognese sauce and as a beef cannelloni filling.

# Sautéed leek, beef and potato lasagne

Garnish: crispy julienne of leeks.

| Ingredients | | 25 | 50 | 100 |
|---|---|---|---|---|
| potatoes, peeled | | 3 kg | 6 kg | 12 kg |
| butter | | as required | | |
| leeks, trimmed, washed, finely sliced | | 4 kg | 8 kg | 16 kg |
| olive oil/vegetable oil | | as required | | |
| garlic, cloves, peeled, finely chopped | | 5 | 8 | 11 |
| onions, finely sliced | | 500 g | 1 kg | 2 kg |
| beef, mince | | 3 kg | 6 kg | 12 kg |
| tomato paste | | 300 g | 600 g | 1.2 kg |
| tomatoes, crushed, A10 tin | | ½ | 1 | 2 |
| stock, beef | | 1 L | 2 L | 4 L |
| salt and freshly milled black pepper | | to taste | | |

Method

1 Pre-heat oven to moderate (150–180°C).
2 Slice potatoes as finely as possible on a slicing machine.
3 Place sliced potatoes into a pan, cover with cold water and bring to the boil.
4 As soon as water boils remove from heat. Refresh potatoes under cold running water; when cooled drain well.
5 Melt a little butter in a pan over a moderate heat. Add leeks and cook until soft. Remove from heat.
6 Heat a little oil in a pan over a moderate heat.
7 Add garlic and onions and cook without colour for approx. 4 minutes or until soft.
8 Add beef and mix well. Cook, stirring occasionally, until meat is lightly browned.
9 Add tomato paste, crushed tomato and beef stock. Mix well. Simmer gently and reduce until it has thickened.
10 Season to taste.
11 In a serving tray/s place a 2 cm layer of cooked meat mixture.
12 Cover this with a layer of potato, then spread a thin layer of sautéed leeks over potatoes.
13 Repeat process with one more layer of mince, potato and leek.
14 Brush top layer of potatoes with a little melted butter. Place trays into oven and cook for approx. 30–45 minutes.
15 Remove from oven, garnish and serve.

Note

To produce a crispy julienne of leeks, top and tail, remove any green and cut into a fine julienne. Heat deep frying oil to approx. 170°C and fry julienne of leeks until crisp and golden. Remove from oil and drain on kitchen paper to absorb any excess oil. Use as a garnish.

# Winter beef and vegetable cottage pie

Garnish: freshly chopped parsley.

| Ingredients | | | 25 | 50 | 100 |
|---|---|---|---|---|---|
|  | olive oil/vegetable oil | | as required | | |
| | garlic, cloves, peeled, finely chopped | | 5 | 8 | 11 |
| | onions, finely sliced | | 500 g | 1 kg | 2 kg |
| | beef, mince | | 3 kg | 6 kg | 12 kg |
| | tomato paste | | 300 g | 600 g | 1.2 kg |
| | tomatoes, crushed, A10 tin | | $\frac{1}{2}$ | 1 | 2 |
| | stock, beef | | 1 L | 2 L | 4 L |
| | salt and freshly milled pepper | | to taste | | |
| | pumpkin, peeled, seeded, diced | | 2 kg | 4 kg | 8 kg |
| | parsnips, peeled, diced | | 1 kg | 2 kg | 4 kg |
| | potatoes, peeled, diced | | 3 kg | 6 kg | 12 kg |
| | leeks, trimmed, washed, finely sliced | | 1 kg | 2 kg | 4 kg |
| | butter | | as required | | |

Method

1 Pre-heat oven to moderate (150–180°C).
2 Heat a little oil in a pan over a moderate heat.
3 Add garlic and onions and cook without colour for approx. 4 minutes or until soft.
4 Add beef and mix well. Cook, stirring occasionally, until meat is slighty browned.
5 Add tomato paste, crushed tomato and beef stock. Mix well. Simmer gently and reduce until thickened.
6 Season to taste. Remove from heat.
7 In serving tray/s pour meat mixture to a depth of approx. 3.5 cm and place to one side.
8 Place pumpkin, parsnips and potatoes onto separate steamer trays. Steam until very tender. While vegetables are cooking, sweat leeks in a little butter until soft and remove from heat.
9 Remove vegetables from steamer. Place into a commercial mixer with leeks and a little melted butter and mash. Season to taste.
10 Spoon mashed vegetables evenly over beef mixture and score with a fork. Brush lightly with a little melted butter and place tray/s into oven for approx. 20–25 minutes or until heated through and light golden brown.
11 Remove from oven, portion, garnish and serve.

Note

The vegetable topping can be varied depending on seasonal availability and budget.

Health tip

A highly nutritious dish with vegetables included. High in fibre.

# Braised beef in red wine, seeded mustard, Spanish onions and garlic

Garnish: finely chopped fresh basil.

**Ingredients**

| | 25 | 50 | 100 |
|---|---|---|---|
| olive oil/vegetable oil | as required | | |
| onions, Spanish, peeled, sliced | 1.5 kg | 3 kg | 6 kg |
| garlic, cloves, peeled, chopped | 3 | 5 | 8 |
| beef, blade, trimmed, diced | 5 kg | 10 kg | 20 kg |
| wine, red | 300 mL | 600 mL | 1.2 L |
| mustard, seeded | 200 g | 400 g | 800 g |
| flour, plain | 150 g | 300 g | 600 g |
| stock, beef, warm | 1.75 L | 3.5 L | 7 L |
| **salt and freshly milled black pepper** | to taste | | |

**Method**

1 Pre-heat oven to moderate (150–180°C).
2 Over a moderate heat place a little oil in a pan.
3 Add onions and garlic and cook without colour until onions are soft.
4 Add beef and stir until all beef is lightly browned.
5 Add wine and cook, stirring occasionally until most of the wine has evaporated.
6 Mix in mustard and add flour. Mix well.
7 Gradually add warmed stock, stirring continuously until of the required consistency.
8 Pour mixture into roasting or serving tray/s and cover with aluminium foil. Place into oven and cook for approx. 1–1$^1/_2$ hours or until meat is tender.
9 Remove from oven, season to taste, garnish and serve.

**Note**

**Braising** is one of the most nutritious methods of cookery because all the nutrients of the food are retained in the dish, also helping to enhance the overall flavour. It is a method of cookery by which food is first browned, covered and then cooked with liquid at a low temperature for a long period of time. This slow method of cookery allows flavour from all the ingredients to develop and tenderises the meat by breaking down the connective tissues.

# Spanish meatballs in a rich herbed tomato sauce

Garnish: melted mozzarella cheese and chopped parsley.

Ingredients

|  | 25 | 50 | 100 |
|---|---|---|---|
| **MEATBALLS:** | | | |
| **beef**, minced | 5 kg | 10 kg | 20 kg |
| **onions**, Spanish, finely minced | 300 g | 600 g | 1.2 kg |
| **carrots**, peeled, minced | 200 g | 400 g | 800 g |
| **garlic**, cloves, peeled, minced | 5 | 10 | 20 |
| **capsicums**, red, seeded, minced | 2 | 4 | 8 |
| **Parmesan cheese**, grated | 200 g | 400 g | 800 g |
| **chillies**, seeded, minced | 2 | 4 | 8 |
| **basil**, finely chopped | 20 g | 40 g | 80 g |
| **eggs** | 3 | 6 | 12 |
| **salt and freshly milled black pepper** | to taste | | |
| | | | |
| **SAUCE:** | | | |
| **tomatoes**, crushed, A10 tin | 1½ | 3 | 6 |
| **onions**, Spanish, finely chopped | 1 kg | 2 kg | 4 kg |
| **mint**, leaves, chopped | 15 g | 30 g | 60 g |
| **basil**, finely chopped | 25 g | 50 g | 100 g |
| **sugar**, white | 100 g | 200 g | 400 g |
| **salt and freshly milled black pepper** | to taste | | |
| **mozzarella cheese**, finely sliced, approx. | 400 g | 800 g | 1.6 kg |
| **parsley**, fresh, finely chopped | 25 g | 50 g | 100 g |
| **Parmesan cheese**, grated | 250 g | 500 g | 1 kg |

Method

1 Pre-heat oven to moderate (150–180°C).
2 Place all meatball ingredients in a mixing bowl and mix well.
3 Mould all mixture into the approximate shape of golf balls.
4 Place the meatballs onto lightly greased roasting tray/s leaving a small space in between. Place into oven.
5 Cook for approx. 10–15 minutes or until just cooked. Remove from oven.
6 While meatballs are cooking, place all sauce ingredients into a saucepan and bring to the boil. Reduce heat and simmer gently, reducing to one third.
7 Place meatballs into deep sided serving tray/s.
8 Pour sauce over meatballs, covering by two thirds.
9 Place a little mozzarella cheese on top of each meatball, then liberally sprinkle whole dish with Parmesan cheese.
10 Return trays to oven and cook until cheese has melted and is golden brown.
11 Serve with a little of the sauce allowing 2–3 meatballs per portion. Garnish with chopped parsley.

**Notes**

The melted mozzarella cheese and chopped parsley are essential for the final taste and presentation.

Grated Cheddar cheese can be substituted for Mozzarella cheese.

**Health tip**

To make more suitable for low fat diets, use less cheese.

# Braised steak, onions and pink-eyed potatoes bound in a rich jus topped with golden puff pastry

Garnish: finely chopped parsley.

**Ingredients**

| | 25 | 50 | 100 |
|---|---|---|---|
| olive oil/vegetable oil | as required | | |
| onions, peeled, finely sliced | 1.5 kg | 3 kg | 6 kg |
| beef, blade/chuck, fat trimmed, diced | 3.5 kg | 7 kg | 14 kg |
| mixed herbs, dried | 100 g | 200 g | 400 g |
| tomato purée | 200 g | 400 g | 800 g |
| flour, plain | 125 g | 250 g | 500 g |
| stock, beef, warm | 2 L | 4 L | 8 L |
| salt and freshly milled black pepper | to taste | | |
| potatoes, pink-eyed, peeled, 1 cm dice, cooked | 500 g | 1 kg | 2 kg |
| pastry, puff | as required | | |
| eggs | 2 | 4 | 8 |
| milk | 100 mL | 200 mL | 400 mL |

**Method**

1 Pre-heat oven to moderate (150–180°C).
2 Put a little oil in a suitably sized pan, over a moderate heat.
3 Add onions and cook without colour until soft.
4 Add steak and herbs and cook until lightly browned.
5 Add tomato purée and mix well.
6 Add flour and mix well. Cook gently for 2–3 minutes mixing continuously.
7 While stirring, gradually add small amounts of warmed stock.
8 Season and simmer gently for approx. 1–1$^1/_2$ hours or until meat is tender, stirring occasionally. When meat is cooked, gently mix in cooked potatoes.
9 Place mixture in deep sided roasting or serving tray/s and cool for 10–15 minutes.
10 Roll out puff pastry to required size and cover trays, pressing down firmly at the edges.
11 Score pastry lightly with a knife to determine portion sizes.
12 Mix eggs with the milk and brush evenly over pastry.

continued

13  Place trays into oven and cook until pastry is golden brown.
14  Remove from oven, pre-portion and serve.

Puff pastry is high in fat, making this dish not really suitable for low fat diets.
If possible, use filo pastry to reduce fat content.

# Gougons of beef wrapped in golden wholegrain breadcrumbs and served with a mild American mustard sauce

Garnish: a sprig of fresh continental parsley.

Ingredients

| | 25 | 50 | 100 |
|---|---|---|---|
| flour, plain | as required | | |
| salt and freshly milled black pepper | as required to highly season | | |
| paprika, sweet | 30 g | 60 g | 120 g |
| eggs, approx. | 8 | 16 | 32 |
| milk | 250 mL | 500 mL | 1 L |
| breadcrumbs, wholegrain | as required | | |
| beef schnitzels, cut into 10 cm by 2 cm strips | 5 kg | 10 kg | 20 kg |
| butter | 200 g | 400 g | 800 g |
| flour, plain | 200 g | 400 g | 800 g |
| milk, warm | 1.5 L | 3 L | 6 L |
| cream, single | 500 mL | 1 L | 2 L |
| mustard, American, approx. | 150 g | 300 g | 600 g |
| parsley, finely chopped | 30 g | 60 g | 120 g |

Method

1  Pre-heat deep fryer to 170°C.
2  Sieve flour, salt, pepper and paprika together into a mixing bowl.
3  Using a mixing bowl, whisk eggs and milk together thoroughly.
4  Place breadcrumbs into a mixing bowl.
5  Pass beef strips through flour, egg mixture and breadcrumbs making sure beef is evenly coated at each stage. Place onto large baking trays, one layer only, then cover with cling film and place in refrigerator until required.
6  Melt butter in a pan over a moderate heat.
7  Using a wooden spoon, mix in flour. Cook out without colour for approx. 2 minutes.
8  Add small amounts of warm milk to mixture stirring constantly. When sauce thickens add more milk until all the milk has been incorporated into mixture; the consistency should coat the back of a spoon. Reduce the heat to low.
9  Mix in cream and small amounts of mustard to the sauce until a strong but not overpowering taste is achieved.

10 Add parsley and season to taste. Keep sauce warm.
11 Place small amounts of beef into hot fat.
12 Cook for approx. 1–2 minutes or until meat is just cooked and light golden brown. Remove from oil and drain any excess oil.
Repeat process until all beef is cooked, keeping cooked beef hot if further batches are to be cooked.
13 Serve placing approx. five pieces of meat onto each plate with a little of the mustard sauce.

 **Note**  Wholegrain breadcrumbs can be made from any left over grain breads or rolls that have been properly dried before being ground into breadcrumbs.

 **Health tip**  Unsuitable for low fat diets.

# Italian-style braised steak with a tomato, basil and black olive sauce

Garnish: sprigs of fresh basil.

| Ingredients | | 25 | 50 | 100 |
|---|---|---|---|---|
|  blade steaks, | | | | |
| 180–200 g steak per portion | | 25 | 50 | 100 |
| olive oil/vegetable oil | | as required | | |
| onions, white, peeled, finely sliced | | 500 g | 1 kg | 2 kg |
| olives, black, stoned, halved | | 300 g | 600 g | 1.2 kg |
| tomatoes, medium dice | | 200 g | 400 g | 800 g |
| basil, fresh, finely chopped | | 35 g | 70 g | 140 g |
| sugar, white | | 100 g | 200 g | 400 g |
| salt and freshly milled black pepper | | to taste | | |
| tomatoes, crushed, A10 tins | | 1 1/2 | 3 | 6 |
| Parmesan cheese, grated | | 200 g | 400 g | 800 g |

**Method**
1 Pre-heat oven to moderate (150–180°C).
2 Lightly beat out steaks with a meat tenderiser.
3 Over a moderate heat, place a little oil in a frypan or on a flat grill plate.
4 Lightly cook steaks on either side until lightly browned.
5 Drain steaks and place into deep sided roasting or serving tray/s.
6 Layer the steaks evenly with the onions, olives, diced tomatoes, chopped basil and sugar, which have all been combined and seasoned to taste.
7 Cover all ingredients with crushed tomatoes and sprinkle with Parmesan cheese.
8 Cover baking tray/s with aluminium foil and place into oven.
Cook for approx. 1–1 1/2 hours or until steak is cooked and tender.
9 Remove steaks from oven and serve one steak per portion with a little of the braising sauce.

continued

**Braising** is one of the most nutritious methods of cookery because all the nutrients of the food are retained in the dish, also helping to enhance the overall flavour. It is a method of cookery by which food is first browned, covered and then cooked with liquid at a low temperature for a long period of time. This slow method of cookery allows flavour from all the ingredients to develop and tenderises the meat by breaking down the connective tissues.

# Stir-fried chilli beef with spinach, coriander and buttered Chinese egg noodles

Garnish: sprigs of fresh coriander.

**Ingredients**

| | 25 | 50 | 100 |
|---|---|---|---|
| **oil**, sesame | 40 mL | 80 mL | 160 mL |
| **onions**, finely sliced | 500 g | 1 kg | 2 kg |
| **spring onions**, topped, tailed, sliced diagonally | 500 g | 1 kg | 2 kg |
| **chillies**, seeded, finely chopped | 2 | 4 | 8 |
| **beef schnitzel**, cut into 1 cm by 6 cm strips | 4.5 kg | 9 kg | 18 kg |
| **sweet chilli sauce** | 150 mL | 300 mL | 600 mL |
| **capsicums**, red, seeded, finely sliced, blanched, refreshed | 3 | 6 | 12 |
| **capsicums**, green, seeded, finely sliced, blanched, refreshed | 3 | 6 | 12 |
| **coriander**, fresh, roughly chopped | 30 g | 60 g | 120 g |
| **spinach**, trimmed, blanched, finely sliced | 1 kg | 2 kg | 4 kg |
| **cornflour** | 60 g | 120 g | 240 g |
| **Chinese egg noodles**, see following recipe | | | |

**Method**

1 Heat oil in a saucepan over a high heat. Add onions, spring onions and chillies and cook until onions are soft.
2 Add beef and stir-fry until just cooked.
3 Add sweet chilli sauce, capsicums, coriander and spinach, mix through other ingredients and cook until all ingredients are heated through.
4 Mix cornflour with a little water and add to beef and vegetable mixture. Cook out for 1 minute while constantly stir-frying.
5 Remove beef mixture from heat and serve on a small bed of buttered noodles.

## Chinese egg noodles

| Ingredients |  | | 25 | 50 | 100 |
|---|---|---|---|---|---|
| | | olive oil/vegetable oil | 50 mL | 100 mL | 200 mL |
| | | Chinese egg noodles, thick | 1.5 kg | 3 kg | 6 kg |
| | | butter, approx. | 250 g | 500 g | 1 kg |
| | | salt and freshly milled black pepper | to taste | | |

**Method**

1 Plunge noodles into boiling water that has had a little oil added. Simmer until cooked but firm, strain and place to one side.
2 Melt butter in a separate pan over a moderate heat. Add noodles, salt and pepper to taste. Mix well, then turn heat to low and cover with a lid for approx. two minutes and serve.

 **Note** **Egg noodles** are produced from a dough of wheat flour and eggs. They come in a variety of strands. Egg noodles are golden brown in colour and taste similar to Italian spaghetti which is produced from a similar style of dough. Egg noodles were originally produced four hundred years ago in south-eastern China.

 **Health tip** To make suitable for low fat diets, reduce quantity of butter used over the noodles.

# Indian kofta curry

Garnish: dry roasted sliced almonds.

| Ingredients |  | | 25 | 50 | 100 |
|---|---|---|---|---|---|
| | | **CURRIED MEATBALLS:** | | | |
| | | beef, minced | 5 kg | 10 kg | 20 kg |
| | | garlic, cloves, finely chopped | 4 | 6 | 8 |
| | | curry powder, mild | 50 g | 100 g | 200 g |
| | | onions, peeled, finely chopped | 500 g | 1 kg | 2 kg |
| | | parsley, finely chopped | 25 g | 50 g | 100 g |
| | | eggs | 3 | 5 | 8 |
| | | breadcrumbs | as required | | |
| | | salt and freshly milled black pepper | to taste | | |
| | | | | | |
| | | **SAUCE:** | | | |
| | | olive oil/vegetable oil | as required | | |
| | | onions, peeled, finely sliced | 500 g | 1 kg | 2 kg |
| | | tomato paste | 100 g | 200 g | 400 g |
| | | curry powder, mild, approx. | 75 g | 150 g | 300 g |
| | | sugar, white | 50 g | 100 g | 200 g |
| | | flour, plain | 150 g | 300 g | 600 g |
| | | stock, chicken | 2 L | 4 L | 8 L |
| | | salt and freshly milled black pepper | to taste | | |

continued

**Method**

1 Pre-heat oven to moderate (150–180°C).
2 Mix all meatball ingredients together, except for the breadcrumbs. Gradually add breadcrumbs in small amounts until desired consistency is achieved.
3 Gently fry onions in a little oil over a moderate heat until tender.
4 Mix tomato paste, curry powder and sugar.
5 Add flour and mix well.
6 Mix in small amounts of warmed stock until all is incorporated.
7 Cook slowly until it starts to thicken.
8 Once the sauce has reached the correct consistency, season to taste and keep warm.
9 Mould meat mixture into balls (approx. 45–50 g per meatball allowing three to four per portion) and place onto lightly greased roasting or serving tray/s one deep.
10 Place into oven and cook for approx. 20–30 minutes or until just cooked through.
11 Remove meatballs from oven and place onto a clean serving tray/s and barely cover with sauce.
12 Return meatballs to oven and cook for a further 10–15 minutes. Serve immediately on a bed of cooked rice with a little of the curry sauce.

**Note**

**Curry powder** is widely used in Indian cookery and can vary in flavour and strength depending on the region where it is produced. Curry powder is made from a ground blend of approx. eighteen herbs, seeds and spices, predominantly: cardamom, chillies, cinnamon, cloves, coriander, cumin, fennel seeds, saffron, tamarind, turmeric and garlic.

# Whole roasted sirloin studded with garlic and served with a puréed leek sauce

Garnish: crisp julienne of leek.

**Ingredients**

| | 25 | 50 | 100 |
|---|---|---|---|
| sirloin, whole, trimmed of fat and sinew | 5 kg | 10 kg | 20 kg |
| garlic, cloves, peeled, quartered | 5 | 10 | 20 |
| olive oil/vegetable oil | as required | | |
| salt and freshly milled black pepper | to taste | | |
| **SAUCE:** | | | |
| onions, peeled, finely chopped | 250 g | 500 g | 1 kg |
| garlic, cloves, peeled, slivered | 3 | 6 | 12 |
| leeks, trimmed, washed, finely sliced, whites only | 2 kg | 4 kg | 8 kg |
| sherry, dry | 150 mL | 300 mL | 600 mL |
| potato, peeled, finely diced | 200 g | 400 g | 800 g |
| stock, chicken | 1.2 L | 2.4 L | 4.8 L |
| salt and freshly milled black pepper | to taste | | |

**Method**

1 Pre-heat oven to hot (180–200°C).
2 Using butcher's twine, secure sirloin/s into a tight roll.
3 At regular intervals along the sirloin make small incisions approx. 3 cm apart, deep enough to hold one sliver of garlic using a knife. Place one sliver of a garlic clove firmly into each incision.
4 Brush sirloin lightly with oil and season with salt and freshly milled black pepper.
5 Place sirloin onto a lightly oiled roasting tray and place in oven. When sealed and lightly browned reduce heat to moderate (150–180°C) and cook to the required degree.
6 While sirloin is roasting, place a little oil into a pan over a moderate heat.
7 Add onions, garlic, and leeks and cook without colour until onions are soft.
8 Add sherry and reduce completely.
9 Add potato and stock. Gently simmer until potatoes break down and sauce starts to thicken.
10 Purée sauce. Season to taste and keep warm until service.
11 Remove sirloin from oven and allow to rest for approx. 5 minutes covered with aluminium foil. Carve thinly allowing two or three slices per portion.
12 Serve a little of the warm sauce with the sliced sirloin garnished with julienne of leek.

**Note**

To produce a crispy julienne of leeks, top and tail, remove any green and cut into a fine julienne. Heat deep frying oil to approx. 170°C and fry julienne of leeks until crisp and golden. Remove from oil and drain on kitchen paper to absorb any excess oil. Use as a garnish.

# Stir-fried beef with broccoli, oyster mushrooms and cashew nuts

Garnish: fine julienne of blanched and refreshed red capsicum.

**Ingredients**

|  | 25 | 50 | 100 |
| --- | --- | --- | --- |
| beef, rump | 3.5 kg | 7 kg | 14 kg |
| broccoli, small florets leaving a long stalk | 2.5 kg | 5 kg | 10 kg |
| mushrooms, oyster | 500 g | 1 kg | 2 kg |
| oil, sesame | as required | | |
| ginger, peeled and minced | 20 g | 40 g | 80 g |
| cashew nuts | 500 g | 1 kg | 2 kg |
| honey | 100 mL | 200 mL | 400 mL |
| oyster sauce | 100 mL | 200 mL | 400 mL |
| soya sauce | 50 mL | 100 mL | 200 mL |
| cornflour | 75 g | 150 g | 300 g |
| salt and freshly milled black pepper | to taste | | |

continued

**Method**
1 Finely slice beef into thin strips approx. 1 cm x 3 cm.
2 Place broccoli florets into a pan of boiling water for at least 10 seconds remove and refresh under cold running water. Drain.
3 Tear any large oyster mushrooms in half.
4 Heat a grill plate until it is very hot and add a liberal amount of sesame oil. Add ginger and beef strips when oil is hot and stir-fry until beef is golden brown and just cooked.
5 Add mushrooms and stir-fry for approx. 2 minutes.
6 Add cashew nuts, honey, oyster sauce and soya sauce. Mix well.
7 Mix a little water with cornflour until thoroughly combined. Add to stir-fry mix, incorporating thoroughly, and cook for a further 1 minute stirring continually.
8 Season to taste and remove from heat.
9 Serve on a bed of steamed rice.

 **Soya sauce** is an essential ingredient in Asian cuisine. It is produced by fermenting boiled soya beans and roasted wheat or barley.

 **Health tip**   A very nutritious dish, which uses small portions of meat.

# Beef Stroganoff with button mushrooms and baby gherkins

**G**arnish: sour cream and freshly chopped parsley.

**Ingredients**

| | 25 | 50 | 100 |
|---|---|---|---|
| olive oil/vegetable oil | as required | | |
| **onions**, finely sliced | 400 g | 800 g | 1.6 kg |
| **garlic**, cloves, finely chopped | 3 | 5 | 7 |
| **beef**, blade/chuck, diced | 5 kg | 10 kg | 20 kg |
| **spring onions**, trimmed, finely sliced | 150 g | 300 g | 600 g |
| **flour**, plain | 150 g | 300 g | 600 g |
| **stock**, chicken, warm | 2.5 L | 5 L | 10 L |
| **mushrooms**, button, quartered, washed | 250 g | 500 g | 1 kg |
| **gherkins**, baby, roughly chopped | 250 g | 500 g | 1 kg |
| **sour cream** | 400 g | 800 g | 1.6 kg |
| **parsley**, fresh, finely chopped | 50 g | 100 g | 200 g |
| **salt and freshly milled black pepper** | to taste | | |

**Method**

1 Heat oil in a saucepan over a moderate heat. Add onions and garlic and allow to cook until onions are soft. Add beef and spring onions and cook over a high heat until beef is lightly browned.
2 Reduce heat and add flour. Mix well.
3 Mix in small amounts of warmed stock until all has been incorporated. Add mushrooms and cover pan with a tight fitting lid and simmer gently for $1-1^1/_2$ hours or until meat is soft and tender, stirring occasionally.
4 Add gherkins, sour cream and parsley. Season to taste.
5 Remove from heat and serve on a bed of cooked rice or buttered noodles.

 **Beef Stroganoff** is a classic Russian dish named after Count Paul Stroganoff, who was a well known 19th century Russian diplomat.

**Health tip** Unsuitable for low fat diets unless you use light sour cream.

# CUTS OF VEAL AND APPROXIMATE WEIGHTS OF THE UNPREPARED PRIMARY CUT

## Approximate cooking time for joints of veal
50 minutes per kilo (2 lb) plus an extra 50 minutes.
These cooking times may vary depending on the oven used.

## Veal Cuts

| Cut | French Term | Uses | Approx. Weights |
|---|---|---|---|
| knuckle/shin/shank | jarret | osso buco, stewing | 2 kg |
| leg | cuisseau/cuissot | frying, roasting, braising | 5 kg |
| breast | poitrine | roasting, stewing | 2–3 kg |
| loin | longe | frying, roasting, grilling | 3.5 kg |
| best end/rack | carré | frying, roasting, grilling | 3 kg |
| fillet | filet | roasting, grilling, frying | 2–3 kg |
| backstrap | | grilling, frying | 1.5–2.5 kg |
| shoulder | épaule | stewing, braising | 5 kg |
| neck end | côté découverte/cou | frying, stewing | 2–3 kg |
| scrag | cou | stewing | 1–2 kg |

## Veal Leg
Leg of veal can be divided into 3 sections, which can be cut into escalopes:

| Cut | French Term | Uses | Approx. Weights |
|---|---|---|---|
| cushion | noix | frying, roasting, braising | 2.5–3 kg |
| under cushion | sous noix | frying, roasting, braising | 3 kg |
| thick flank | noix patissiere | frying, roasting, braising | 2.5–3 kg |

## Veal Offal

| Cut | French Term | Uses |
|---|---|---|
| kidneys | rognons | frying, soups, stewing |
| liver | foie | frying, braising |
| head | tête | soup |
| sweetbread | ris | frying, braising |
| brains | cervelle | frying, boiling |
| bones | os | stock |

♥ **Health tip** Remove all visible fat from veal. Order lean veal from the butcher/supplier.

# VEAL RECIPES
## Veal Parmigiana

**G**arnish: a little finely chopped fresh parsley.

Ingredients

| | 25 | 50 | 100 |
|---|---|---|---|
| **VEAL:** | | | |
| flour, plain | as required | | |
| paprika | 25 g | 50 g | 100 g |
| eggs | 10 | 20 | 40 |
| milk | 300 mL | 600 mL | 1.2 L |
| breadcrumbs | as required | | |
| veal schnitzel steaks, approx. 150 g | 25 | 50 | 100 |
| Parmesan cheese, finely grated | 100 g | 200 g | 400 g |
| parsley, fresh, finely chopped | 15 g | 30 g | 60 g |
| **SAUCE:** | | | |
| tomatoes, crushed, A10 tin | 1¹/₂ | 3 | 6 |
| tomatoes, roughly chopped | 1 kg | 2 kg | 4 kg |
| basil, chopped | 20 g | 40 g | 80 g |
| garlic, cloves, finely chopped | 3 | 5 | 9 |
| onions, white, finely chopped | 350 g | 700 g | 1.4 kg |
| sugar, white | 100 g | 200 g | 400 g |
| stock, chicken/veal | 200 mL | 400 mL | 800 mL |
| salt and freshly milled black pepper | to taste | | |
| Parmesan cheese, grated | 200 g | 400 g | 800 g |
| mozzarella cheese, finely sliced | 1 kg | 2 kg | 4 kg |

Method

1 Pre-heat deep fryer to 160–170°C.
2 Place flour and paprika into a mixing bowl and mix well. Place the eggs, which have been beaten together with the milk, into a second bowl. Place the breadcrumbs, which have been mixed with the Parmesan cheese and parsley, into a third bowl.
3 Dredge veal schnitzel steaks through flour, egg mixture and breadcrumbs. Gently shake off any excess breadcrumbs. Place schnitzels onto tray/s one layer deep, separating each layer with greaseproof paper, and refrigerate until required.
4 Place tomatoes, basil, garlic, onions, sugar and chicken/veal stock into a pan over a moderate heat and simmer.
5 When the sauce has reduced and thickened, season and remove from heat; keep warm. Pre-heat oven to moderate (150–180°C).
6 Gently place schnitzels into fat in small batches and cook to a light golden brown. Remove from oil and drain any excess fat.
7 Place schnitzels onto roasting tray/s, and put into oven. Cook for approx. 3–5 minutes or until cooked through. Remove from oven and spoon over a generous amount of the sauce. Sprinkle with a little of the Parmesan and mozzarella cheese and return tray/s to oven until cheese turns golden brown.
8 Serve allowing one schnitzel per portion.

continued

# Veal minute steaks topped with smoked ham, mild Cheddar cheese and Parmesan

**G**arnish: sprigs of fresh basil.

**Ingredients**

| | 25 | 50 | 100 |
|---|---|---|---|
| veal schnitzel steaks, approx. 150 g each | 25 | 50 | 100 |
| flour, plain | 500 g | 1 kg | 2 kg |
| paprika | 20 g | 40 g | 80 g |
| salt and freshly milled black pepper | to taste | | |
| olive oil/vegetable oil | as required | | |
| ham, smoked, shaved | 1.5 kg | 3 kg | 6 kg |
| Cheddar cheese, shredded | 500 g | 1 kg | 2 kg |
| Parmesan cheese, grated | 100 g | 200 g | 400 g |
| parsley, fresh, finely chopped | 20 g | 40 g | 80 g |
| capsicums, red, finely sliced | 200 g | 400 g | 800 g |

**Method**

1 Pre-heat oven to moderate (150–180°C).
2 Heat a little oil over a moderate heat in a sauté pan or flat grill.
3 Lightly coat schnitzel steaks with flour seasoned with paprika, salt and pepper. Place into oil and cook in small batches.
4 Cook gently for approx. 1 minute on either side.
5 Remove from pan and place onto lightly oiled roasting or serving tray/s leaving a space in between each steak.
6 Place a small mound of ham along the centre of each steak.
7 Cover with a little grated Cheddar cheese.
8 Sprinkle with chopped parsley and place two strips of capsicum criss-cross on the top.
9 Sprinkle with Parmesan cheese and place into oven until cheese is melted and steaks are cooked through.

**Note**    **Parsley** is one of the most popular and widely available fresh herbs. Most commonly used is the curly leaf parsley and the Italian flat leaf continental variety. There are at least another twenty-five varieties to be found. Parsley has been known for thousands of years and is mentioned in Greek mythology. It is an excellent source of vitamins A and C.

♥ **Health tip**    Unsuitable for low fat diets.

# Creamy veal Louise

Garnish: chives cut at 2 cm intervals.

Ingredients

| | 25 | 50 | 100 |
|---|---|---|---|
| olive oil/vegetable oil | as required | | |
| onions, white, finely sliced | 250 g | 500 g | 1 kg |
| garlic, cloves, finely chopped | 2 | 4 | 7 |
| veal, topside, 2 cm dice | 5.5 kg | 11 kg | 22 kg |
| flour, plain | 150 g | 300 g | 600 g |
| stock, chicken, warmed | 2.5 L | 5 L | 10 L |
| walnuts, crushed | 250 g | 500 g | 1 kg |
| sultanas | 100 g | 200 g | 400 g |
| sour cream | 150 g | 300 g | 600 g |
| cream, single | 200 mL | 400 mL | 800 mL |
| salt and freshly milled black pepper | to taste | | |

Method

1. Heat a little oil over a moderate heat in a saucepan.
2. Add onions and garlic and cook until onions are soft.
3. Add veal and cook until sealed and golden brown.
4. Add flour, mix well, cook for approx. 2–3 minutes.
5. Add warmed stock slowly, stirring continuously until all stock has been incorporated.
6. Simmer gently covered with a tight fitting lid, stirring regularly, until veal is cooked through and tender.
7. When sauce is of the consistency to smoothly coat the back of a spoon add walnuts, sultanas, sour cream and cream. Season to taste and mix well. Re-heat, making sure sauce does not boil and serve immediately on a bed of steamed rice.

**Sultanas** were originally preserved in Turkey and the Mediterranean by lightly drying the grapes on racks in the sun. Sultanas are now commercially produced around the world.

Unsuitable for low fat diets.

# Fragrant lemon, sage and oregano veal schnitzel

Garnish: sprigs of fresh continental parsley.

Ingredients

| | 25 | 50 | 100 |
|---|---|---|---|
| veal schnitzel steaks, approx. 150 g each | 25 | 50 | 100 |
| flour, plain | 500 g | 1 kg | 2 kg |
| paprika | 20 g | 40 g | 80g |
| eggs | 10 | 20 | 40 |
| milk | 300 mL | 600 mL | 1.2 L |
| breadcrumbs | as required | | |
| lemon, zest | 2 | 4 | 8 |
| sage, dried | 20 g | 40 g | 80 g |
| oregano, dried | 20 g | 40 g | 80 g |
| salt and freshly milled black pepper | to taste | | |

Method

1 Pre-heat deep fryer to 160–170°C.
2 Place flour and paprika into a bowl. Place eggs, which have been beaten together with the milk, into a second bowl. Place the breadcrumbs, which have been mixed with all the other ingredients, into a third bowl.
3 Dredge schnitzels through flour, egg mixture and breadcrumbs. Gently shake off any excess breadcrumbs. Pre-heat oven to moderate (150–180°C).
4 Gently place schnitzels into fat in small batches and cook to a light golden brown. Remove from oil and drain any excess fat.
5 Place schnitzels onto roasting or serving tray/s then into oven. Cook for approx. 5 minutes or until cooked through.
6 Serve allowing one schnitzel per portion.

**Notes**

When zesting citrus fruit ensure only the rind is removed, as this contains the concentrated aromatic oils which add to the flavour of the food.

**Paprika** is produced by grinding certain sweet red capsicum pods to produce a powder. The flavour of paprika can vary from mild to hot and the colour from a dull red to a deep blood red, depending on the variety of capsicum used. The Hungarian varieties of paprika are considered to be the best and have been an essential ingredient in Hungarian cuisine. Paprika has excellent flavour and is also useful for garnishing.

♥ **Health tip**   Unsuitable for a low fat diet.

# Chunky veal, onion and seasonal vegetables topped with golden puff pastry

Garnish: finely chopped parsley.

**Ingredients**

| | 25 | 50 | 100 |
|---|---|---|---|
| olive oil/vegetable oil | as required | | |
| onions, white, finely sliced | 1.5 kg | 3 kg | 6 kg |
| veal, shoulder, 2 cm dice | 3.5 kg | 7 kg | 14 kg |
| vegetables, assorted, cut into 2 cm dice, e.g. carrots, parsnips, potatoes, mushrooms, celery | 500 g | 1 kg | 2 kg |
| mixed herbs | 30 g | 60 g | 120 g |
| flour, plain | 150 g | 300 g | 600 g |
| stock, chicken/veal, warm | 2 L | 4 L | 8 L |
| salt and freshly milled black pepper | to taste | | |
| pastry, puff | as required | | |
| eggs | 2 | 4 | 8 |
| milk | 100 mL | 200 mL | 400 mL |

**Method**

1 Pre-heat oven to moderate (150–180°C).
2 Place a little oil in a pan over a moderate heat.
3 Add onions and cook without colour until soft.
4 Add veal and vegetables and cook until lightly browned.
5 Add flour and mix well. Cook gently for 2–3 minutes mixing continuously.
6 Gradually mix in warmed stock in small amounts, stirring continuously.
7 Season and simmer gently, stirring occasionally, for approx. 1–1¹/₂ hours or until meat is tender. Remove from heat.
8 Place mixture in deep sided serving tray/s and cool for 10–15 minutes.
9 Roll out puff pastry to required size and cover baking trays, pressing down firmly at the edges.
10 Score pastry lightly with a knife to determine portion sizes.
11 Mix eggs with the milk and brush evenly over pastry.
12 Place trays into oven and cook until pastry is golden brown.
13 Remove from oven, pre-portion and serve.

**Note**

**Pepper,** although now plentiful and inexpensive, was once a rare commodity used in place of currency. Pepper is generally found in three forms:
• Black, which is picked when the berry is unripened, then dried, and either left whole or ground;
• White, which is picked when ripened, has the skin removed and is then dried and usually ground; and
• Green, which is the picked soft unripened berry that is usually preserved whole.

**Health tip** To reduce fat content of this dish, use filo pastry instead of puff pastry.

# Roasted shortloin of veal stuffed with home-made pesto

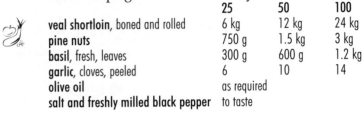

Garnish: small sprigs of fresh rosemary.

| Ingredients | | 25 | 50 | 100 |
|---|---|---|---|---|
| veal shortloin, boned and rolled | | 6 kg | 12 kg | 24 kg |
| pine nuts | | 750 g | 1.5 kg | 3 kg |
| basil, fresh, leaves | | 300 g | 600 g | 1.2 kg |
| garlic, cloves, peeled | | 6 | 10 | 14 |
| olive oil | | as required | | |
| salt and freshly milled black pepper | | to taste | | |

**Method**

1 Pre-heat oven to moderate (150–180°C).
2 Roast pine nuts until light golden brown. Place into a blender with basil, garlic and a little olive oil and blend.
3 While blending, slowly incorporate olive oil until a firm but smooth paste is achieved. Season to taste.
4 Using a clean steel, push into centre of joint from either end creating a small cavity the length of the shortloin.
5 Half fill a piping bag, fitted with a large nozzle, with pesto. Pipe small amounts into the cavity, pushing pesto into the centre with the handle of a large wooden spoon. Continue process until cavity is completely filled. Secure each end with a metal skewer.
6 Place joints onto lightly oiled roasting tray/s. Brush with a little oil and season. Place into oven and cook for approx. $1^1/_2$–2 hours or until cooked to the required degree. Remove from oven and stand for 10–15 minutes before serving, covered with aluminium foil.

**Note** Always let cooked joints of meat that have just been removed from the oven stand about 10 minutes before carving. This allows the connective tissues of the meat to relax as the temperature drops and permits easier carving, better portion control and tenderer meat.

# Char-grilled veal cutlets served with a lemon and roasted garlic butter

Garnish: lemon and roasted garlic butter.

| Ingredients | | 25 | 50 | 100 |
|---|---|---|---|---|
| **LEMON AND ROASTED GARLIC BUTTER:** | | | | |
| butter, room temperature | | 1 kg | 2 kg | 4 kg |
| lemons, juice and zest | | 1 | 2 | 4 |
| garlic bulbs, roasted, see note below | | 1 | 2 | 4 |

**VEAL:**

| | 25 | 50 | 100 |
|---|---|---|---|
| **veal**, cutlets, allow one per portion | 25 | 50 | 100 |
| **olive oil/vegetable oil** | as required | | |
| **salt and freshly milled black pepper** | to taste | | |

**Method**

1 Combine all butter ingredients thoroughly and place along the centre of a lightly oiled sheet of greaseproof paper. Roll into a cylindrical shape approx. 4 cm in diameter totally enclosing butter in greaseproof paper. Place into a freezer until required.
2 Brush cutlets on all sides with a little oil.
3 Lightly brush a hot pre-heated sauté pan or grill plate with oil and seal cutlets on either side. Cook to the required degree.
4 Place cooked cutlets neatly onto serving tray/s. Serve with a generous slice of the frozen butter placed on top as each cutlet is served.

 **Notes**

If the grill is small or unavailable, the cutlets can be seared on both sides and then placed onto roasting tray/s in a pre-heated moderate oven (150–180°C) until cooked to the required degree.

Butter can be pre-sliced and placed into a bowl of iced water near the serving station for convenience during long service periods.

To roast garlic, take whole bulbs and lightly prick cloves. Place onto a roasting tray and put into a pre-heated moderate oven (150–180°C) for approx. 20–30 minutes or until garlic cloves are soft to the touch. Remove from oven and cool completely. To extract roasted garlic purée, trim the base of the bulb and squeeze out the purée. The reason garlic is sometimes roasted is that it gives a milder, richer flavour.

 **Health tip**    To lower the fat content of this dish, serve only very **thin** slices of the garlic butter.

# Veal braised in white wine, Dijon mustard and roasted garlic

**G**arnish: finely chopped fresh basil.

**Ingredients**

| | 25 | 50 | 100 |
|---|---|---|---|
| **olive oil/vegetable oil** | as required | | |
| **onions**, white, finely sliced | 1.5 kg | 3 kg | 6 kg |
| **garlic**, bulbs, roasted, see note below | 2 | 4 | 8 |
| **veal**, shoulder, 2 cm dice | 5 kg | 10 kg | 20 kg |
| **wine**, white | 300 mL | 600 mL | 1.2 L |
| **mustard**, Dijon | 200 g | 400 g | 800 g |
| **flour**, plain | 150 g | 300 g | 600 g |
| **stock**, chicken, warm | 2.5 L | 5 L | 10 L |
| **salt and freshly milled black pepper** | to taste | | |

continued

**Method**
1 Pre-heat oven to moderate (150–180°C).
2 Heat a little oil in a pan.
3 Add onions and garlic and cook without colour until soft.
4 Add veal and stir until lightly browned.
5 Add wine and cook, stirring occasionally until most of the wine has evaporated.
6 Mix in mustard, add flour and mix well.
7 Gradually add warmed stock, stirring continuously.
8 Pour mixture into serving tray/s and cover with aluminium foil. Place into oven and cook for approx. $1-1^1/_2$ hours or until meat is tender.
9 Remove from oven. Season to taste, garnish and serve.

**Notes**

**Braising** is one of the most nutritious methods of cookery because all the nutrients of the food are retained in the dish, also helping to enhance the overall flavour. It is a method of cookery by which food is first browned, covered and then cooked with liquid at a low temperature for a long period of time. This slow method of cookery allows flavour from all the ingredients to develop and tenderises the meat by breaking down the connective tissues.

To roast garlic, take whole bulbs and lightly prick cloves. Place onto a roasting tray and put into a pre-heated moderate oven (150–180°C) for approx. 20–30 minutes or until garlic cloves are soft to the touch. Remove from oven and cool completely. To extract roasted garlic purée, trim the base of the bulb and squeeze out the purée. The reason garlic is sometimes roasted is that it gives a milder, richer flavour.

**Health tip**

Veal is a low fat meat. This dish is suitable for low fat diets.

# CUTS OF LAMB AND APPROXIMATE WEIGHTS OF THE UNPREPARED PRIMARY CUT

## Approximate cooking time for joints of lamb
40 minutes per kilo (2 lb) plus an extra 40 minutes.
These cooking times may vary depending on the oven used.

### Lamb Cuts

| Cut | French Term | Uses | Approx. Weights |
|---|---|---|---|
| leg | gigot | roasting, stewing | 3.5–4 kg |
| shoulder | épaule | roasting | 3 kg |
| breast | poitrine | roasting, stewing | 1.5–2 kg |
| scrag end | cou | stewing | 750 g |
| saddle/shortloin | selle | frying, roasting, grilling | 2.5–3.5 kg |
| best end/loin/rack | carré | frying, roasting, grilling | 2 kg |
| middle neck | côte découverte/cou | stewing | 2 kg |

### Lamb Offal

| Cut | French Term | Uses |
|---|---|---|
| heart | cœur | braising |
| kidney | rognon | frying, braising, grilling |
| liver | foie | frying |
| tongue | langue | braising, boiling |
| sweetbread | ris | frying, braising |

 **Health tip** — Remove all visible fat from lamb.
Order lean lamb from the butcher/supplier.

# LAMB RECIPES

## Marinated lamb, Spanish onion and apricot kebabs

Garnish: finely chopped continental parsley.
Yields: 2 kebabs/person.

Ingredients

|  | 25 | 50 | 100 |
|---|---|---|---|
| **onions**, Spanish, 2 cm square dice | 3 kg | 6 kg | 12 kg |
| **lamb**, leg, 2 cm x 2 cm dice | 5 kg | 10 kg | 20 kg |
| **apricots**, dried | 2½ kg | 5 kg | 10 kg |
| **MEDITERRANEAN MARINADE:** | | | |
| olive oil | 200 mL | 400 mL | 800 mL |
| **lemons**, juice and zest | 2 | 4 | 8 |
| **parsley**, continental, leaves, finely chopped | 20 g | 40 g | 80 g |
| **wine**, white | 200 mL | 400 mL | 800 mL |
| **olive oil/vegetable oil** | as required | | |
| **salt and freshly milled black pepper** | to taste | | |

Method

1 Soak bamboo skewers in cold water for approx. 30 minutes.
2 Heat deep fryer oil to 170°C.
3 Place onions into fryer baskets and cook in the hot oil for 10 seconds, agitating baskets constantly. Remove from oil and drain well.
4 Place pieces of lamb alternately with onions and apricots that have been folded in half onto bamboo skewers. Repeat process until skewers are full of ingredients pushed firmly together.
5 Place all kebabs into roasting or serving tray/s and put to one side.
6 Combine all marinade ingredients in a bowl, reserving a little of the chopped parsley for garnish.
7 Liberally brush each kebab on all sides with marinade. Pour remaining marinade over kebabs.
8 Cover trays with plastic wrap and refrigerate for 4–6 hours turning kebabs every two hours. Pre-heat oven to moderate (150–180°C).
9 Heat a sauté pan or salamander and brush with a little oil.
10 Place kebabs onto sauté pan or onto grill plate and cook to a light brown on all sides.
11 Return kebabs to roasting or serving tray/s. Pour over any remaining marinade and place tray/s into oven for approx. 15–20 minutes or until lamb is cooked through.
12 Serve two kebabs per portion.

Note

Soak bamboo skewers in water before use for approx. 30 minutes to stop skewers burning during cooking.

# Marinated tandoori lamb cutlets served with a minted lemon yoghurt

Garnish: finely chopped fresh mint leaves.

Ingredients

| | 25 | 50 | 100 |
|---|---|---|---|
| yoghurt, natural | 1 kg | 2 kg | 4 kg |
| lemons, zest and juice | 2 | 4 | 8 |
| sugar, castor | 100 g | 200 g | 400 g |
| tandoori paste | 250 g | 500 g | 1 kg |
| lamb, cutlets | 75 | 150 | 300 |

Method

1 Pre-heat oven to moderate (150–180°C).
2 In a large bowl combine all ingredients except lamb cutlets and whisk to a smooth consistency.
3 Completely coat lamb cutlets in the marinade.
4 Refrigerate lamb cutlets for approx. 6–8 hours turning cutlets every 2 hours.
5 Place lamb cutlets into roasting tray/s one deep and put into oven. Cook for approx. 15–20 minutes or until cooked through.
6 Serve three lamb cutlets per portion on a bed of steamed rice and a little minted lemon yoghurt.

## Minted lemon yoghurt

Ingredients

| | 25 | 50 | 100 |
|---|---|---|---|
| yoghurt, natural | 1 kg | 2 kg | 4 kg |
| mint, fresh leaves | 50 g | 100 g | 200 g |
| lemon, juice | 75 mL | 150 mL | 300 mL |
| sugar, castor | 200 g | 400 g | 800 g |

Method

1 Place all ingredients in a blender and bring to a smooth consistency.
2 Refrigerate for 2 hours before service.

 Note

Minted lemon yoghurt is an ideal accompaniment to spiced meats and Asian style dishes.

♥ Health tip

To reduce fat content:
• remove visible fat from meat
• use low fat yoghurt.

# Country-style lamb pie topped with cheese and chive potatoes

Garnish: grated Cheddar cheese and finely sliced chives.

Ingredients

| | 25 | 50 | 100 |
|---|---|---|---|
| olive oil/vegetable oil | as required | | |
| onions, Spanish, peeled, large dice | 1 kg | 2 kg | 4 kg |
| garlic, cloves, peeled, minced | 4 | 8 | 16 |
| thyme, dried | 10 g | 20 g | 40 g |
| rosemary, dried | 10 g | 20 g | 40 g |
| lamb, leg, finely diced | 5 kg | 10 kg | 20 kg |
| flour, plain | 150 g | 300 g | 600 g |
| tomato purée | 150 g | 300 g | 600 g |
| stock, beef/lamb, warm | 1.5 L | 3 L | 6 L |
| tomatoes, crushed, A10 tin | 1 L | 2 L | 4 L |
| parsnips, peeled, small dice | 300 g | 600 g | 1.2 kg |
| carrots, peeled, small dice | 300 g | 600 g | 1.2 kg |
| salt and freshly milled black pepper | to taste | | |
| potatoes, peeled, finely sliced | 3 kg | 6 kg | 12 kg |
| butter | 200 g | 400 g | 800 g |
| Cheddar cheese, grated | 500 g | 1 kg | 2 kg |
| chives, finely chopped | 20 g | 40 g | 80 g |

Method

1 Pre-heat oven to moderate (150–180°C).
2 Put a little oil in a pan and gently cook onions, garlic, thyme and rosemary until onions are soft.
3 Add lamb and cook until lightly browned.
4 Thoroughly mix in flour and then mix in tomato purée. Cook gently for approx. 3–4 minutes.
5 Slowly add warmed stock until all has been incorporated.
6 Mix in crushed tomatoes, parsnips and carrots and simmer gently for approx. one hour or until lamb is tender.
7 Season to taste. Remove from heat and cool.
8 Using baking/serving tray/s, three-quarters fill with braised lamb and cover this neatly with sliced potatoes. Brush liberally with melted butter.
9 Place trays into oven and cook until potatoes are golden brown.
10 Remove from oven and sprinkle with grated cheese that has been mixed with the chives. Return to oven until cheese is melted and light golden brown.
11 Remove from oven, pre-portion and serve.

Note

The vegetables in this dish can be varied according to seasonal availability.

Health tip

To reduce fat, omit cheese from the top or use low fat cheese.
To make suitable for cholesterol-lowering diet use margarine, not butter.

# Mediterranean-style braised leg of lamb

Garnish: roughly chopped continental parsley leaves.

| Ingredients | 25 | 50 | 100 |
|---|---|---|---|
| olive oil/vegetable oil | as required | | |
| lamb, leg, 2 cm x 2 cm dice | 5 kg | 10 kg | 20 kg |
| onions, Spanish, peeled, finely sliced | 2 kg | 4 kg | 8 kg |
| garlic, cloves, peeled, finely chopped | 4 | 7 | 10 |
| capsicums, roasted red, medium dice | 3 | 6 | 12 |
| tomatoes, crushed, A10 tin | 1 | 2 | 4 |
| stock, lamb/beef, warmed | 250 mL | 500 mL | 1 L |
| olives, Kalamata, stoned, roughly chopped | 100 g | 200 g | 400 g |
| bay-leaves | 2 | 4 | 8 |
| salt and freshly milled black pepper | to taste | | |

**Method**

1 Pre-heat oven to moderate (150–180°C).
2 Heat a large sauté pan or grill plate and brush with a little oil. Seal diced lamb on all sides, remove and place into deep sided roasting or serving tray/s.
3 Heat a little oil in a saucepan over a moderate heat.
4 Add onions and garlic and cook without colour until tender.
5 Add roasted red capsicums, crushed tomatoes, lamb/beef stock, olives, bay-leaves. Season to taste.
6 Simmer gently for 5 minutes stirring occasionally.
7 Pour over sufficient sauce to cover lamb and cover tray/s with aluminium foil. Place tray/s into oven and braise for approx. $1^1/_2$ hours or until lamb is cooked through and tender.
8 Remove foil from tray/s for the last 15–20 minutes of cooking to allow sauce reduction.
9 Remove from oven and serve.

**Note**

Roast capsicum by removing stalk and seeds, quartering and roughly chopping. Place capsicum into a deep sided roasting tray tossed with a little olive oil and place into a pre-heated moderate oven (150–180°C) and roast, turning regularly, for approx. 30–45 minutes or until the flesh is soft, and the skin is easily removed.

**Health tip**

Mediterranean-style cooking is recommended for prevention of heart disease.

# Lemon, rosemary and Parmesan lamb cutlets

Garnish: finely chopped fresh mint.

| Ingredients | | 25 | 50 | 100 |
|---|---|---|---|---|
| lamb cutlets | | 50 | 100 | 200 |
| flour, plain | | as required | | |
| salt and freshly milled black pepper | | to taste | | |
| eggs | | 10 | 20 | 40 |
| milk | | 300 mL | 600 mL | 1.2 L |
| breadcrumbs | | as required | | |
| lemons, zest | | 2 | 4 | 8 |
| rosemary, fresh, leaves, finely chopped | | 20 g | 40 g | 80 g |
| Parmesan cheese, freshly grated | | 100 g | 200 g | 400 g |

**Method**

1 Pre-heat deep fryer to 160–170°C.
2 Lay lamb cutlets onto a chopping board and gently tenderise with a meat mallet.
3 Place flour, which has been lightly seasoned, into a bowl and the eggs, which have been beaten together with the milk, into a second bowl. Place the breadcrumbs, which have been mixed with all the other ingredients, into a third bowl.
4 Dredge lamb cutlets through flour, egg mixture and breadcrumbs and gently shake off any excess breadcrumbs. Place cutlets one layer deep onto tray/s separating each layer with a sheet of greaseproof paper. Pre-heat oven to moderate (150–180°C).
5 Gently place cutlets into deep fryer in small batches and cook to a light golden brown. Remove from oil and drain any excess fat.
6 Place cutlets into roasting or serving tray/s and put into oven. Cook for approx. 5 minutes or until cooked through.
7 Remove from oven and serve.

 **Note**

Rosemary has been widely used since 500 BC and is native to the Mediterranean. Rosemary is now widely cultivated around the world. A member of the mint family, it has a distinctive aroma that is associated with many lamb dishes.

**Health tip**

To lower fat content:
• remove visible fat from meat
• pan-fry or bake instead of deep frying.

# Roasted leg of lamb stuffed with spinach, apricots, garlic and bacon

Garnish: small sprigs of fresh rosemary.

**Ingredients**

| | 25 | 50 | 100 |
|---|---|---|---|
| lamb, legs, boned, trimmed | 4 | 8 | 16 |
| mint jelly | 300 g | 600 g | 1.2 kg |
| spinach, trimmed and washed | 1 kg | 2 kg | 4 kg |
| olive oil/vegetable oil | as required | | |
| onions, peeled, finely diced | 500 g | 1 kg | 2 kg |
| garlic, cloves, peeled, finely diced | 2 | 3 | 5 |
| bacon, trimmed, finely diced | 150 g | 300 g | 600 g |
| apricots, dried, finely chopped | 200 g | 400 g | 800 g |
| eggs | 3 | 5 | 7 |
| salt and freslhy milled black pepper | to taste | | |

**Method**

1 Pre-heat oven to moderate (150–180°C).
2 Place lamb legs onto chopping board and remove any string or netting. Open flat on work surface or chopping board and brush all sides with liberal amounts of mint jelly. Cover and leave to one side.
3 Place a pan of salted water onto the stove and bring to a simmer.
4 Add spinach and cook for approx. 40 seconds.
5 Remove spinach, refresh and drain, squeezing out as much liquid as possible. Finely chop and place into a large mixing bowl.
6 Place a little oil into a pan over a moderate heat.
7 Add onions, garlic and bacon and cook without colour until onions are tender.
8 Add this mixture with apricots to spinach.
9 Add eggs and combine all ingredients together. Season to taste.
10 With the lamb fat side down place liberal amounts of stuffing mixture along the centre of the joint of lamb.
11 Fold lamb over stuffing so it is completely encased; re-tie or place back into netting.
12 Place lamb onto a roasting tray and put into oven. Cook for approx. 1¹/₂–2 hours or until cooked to the required degree.
13 Remove from oven, stand meat for 10 mins. Serve.

**Note**

Always let cooked joints of meat that have just been removed from the oven stand about 10 minutes before carving. This allows the connective tissues of the meat to relax as the temperature drops and permits easier carving, better portion control and tenderer meat.

# Leg of lamb roasted and stuffed with roasted onions, red capsicums, Kalamata olives and fresh rosemary

Garnish: small sprigs of fresh rosemary.

Ingredients

| | 25 | 50 | 100 |
|---|---|---|---|
| **lamb**, legs, boned, trimmed | 4 | 8 | 16 |
| **onions**, peeled, roughly chopped | 1 kg | 2 kg | 4 kg |
| **olive oil/vegetable oil** | as required | | |
| **red capsicums**, roasted | 500 g | 1 kg | 2 kg |
| **olives**, Kalamata, stoned, roughly chopped | 200 g | 400 g | 800 g |
| **rosemary**, fresh, leaves, finely chopped | 25 g | 50 g | 100 g |
| **garlic**, cloves, peeled, chopped | 4 | 8 | 16 |
| **salt and freshly milled black pepper** | to taste | | |

Method

1 Pre-heat oven to moderate (150–180°C).
2 Place lamb legs onto chopping board and remove any string or netting. Open flat on work surface or chopping board, cover and leave to one side.
3 Place onions into a roasting tray and mix with a little oil.
4 Place roasting tray into oven and cook until onions are soft and lightly browned, remove from oven and allow to cool.
5 Roughly chop roasted red capsicums and place into bowl. Add olives, rosemary and garlic and then add cooled onions. Mix well and season to taste.
6 With the lamb fat side down, place liberal amounts of stuffing mixture along the centre of the joint.
7 Fold lamb over stuffing so it is completely encased and re-tie or place back into netting.
8 Place lamb onto a roasting tray and into oven. Cook for approx. $1^1/_2$–2 hours or until cooked to the required degree.
9 Remove from oven, stand for 20 minutes and serve.

Notes

Roast capsicum by removing stalk and seeds, quartering and roughly chopping. Place capsicum into a deep sided roasting tray tossed with a little olive oil and place into a pre-heated moderate oven (150–180°C) and roast, turning regularly, for approx. 30–45 minutes or until the flesh is soft, and the skin is easily removed.

Always let cooked joints of meat that have just been removed from the oven stand about 10 minutes before carving. This allows the connective tissues of the meat to relax as the temperature drops and permits easier carving, better portion control and tenderer meat.

# Greek moussaka

Garnish: freshly chopped parsley.

| Ingredients | | 25 | 50 | 100 |
|---|---|---|---|---|
| olive oil/vegetable oil | | as required | | |
| garlic, cloves, peeled, finely chopped | | 5 | 8 | 11 |
| onions, finely sliced | | 500 g | 1 kg | 2 kg |
| lamb/beef mince | | 5 kg | 10 kg | 20 kg |
| tomato paste | | 300 g | 600 g | 1.2 kg |
| tomatoes, crushed, A10 tin | | $^{1}/_{2}$ | 1 | 2 |
| stock, beef | | 1 L | 2 L | 4 L |
| salt and freshly milled black pepper | | to taste | | |

**WHITE SAUCE/BÉCHAMEL:**

| | 25 | 50 | 100 |
|---|---|---|---|
| butter/margarine | 300 g | 600 g | 1.2 kg |
| flour, plain | 300 g | 600 g | 1.2 kg |
| milk, warm | 3 L | 6 L | 12 L |
| salt and freshly milled black pepper | to taste | | |
| eggplants, whole, topped, tailed, thin slices | 8 | 16 | 32 |
| Cheddar cheese, grated | 500 g | 1 kg | 2 kg |

**Method**

1 Pre-heat oven to moderate (150–180°C).
2 Heat a little oil in a saucepan over a moderate heat.
3 Add garlic and onions and cook without colour for 2 minutes.
4 Add lamb/beef mince and mix with garlic and onion. Cook, stirring occasionally until meat is lightly browned.
5 Add tomato paste, crushed tomatoes and beef stock and mix well. Simmer gently and reduce until sauce has thickened. Season to taste and remove from heat.
6 In a saucepan over a moderate heat, melt butter/margarine; then add flour, mixing thoroughly. Reduce heat and allow roux to cook out for approx. 2–3 minutes without colour.
7 Slowly add warmed milk stirring continuously until all milk has been incorporated. Simmer for approx. 5 minutes stirring regularly. Remove from heat.
8 Place a layer of the mince mixture evenly onto the bottom of a serving tray and cover the mixture with a layer of sliced eggplant.
9 Coat eggplant with a thin layer of white sauce/béchamel. Repeat this process until all ingredients are used.
10 Generously cover with grated Cheddar cheese and wipe edges clean of any spills.
11 Place tray/s into oven and cook for approx. 45 minutes–1 hour or until moussaka is heated through and the cheese has turned golden brown.
12 Remove from oven, pre-portion and serve.

**Notes** This famous dish originated in Greece and is also popular throughout the Near East. It is traditionally made with eggplant and minced lamb or beef but now has endless variations, the most popular being the addition of white sauce/béchamel.

When making a white sauce/béchamel it is always advisable to use butter rather than margarine as it will give a slightly richer flavour. Nonetheless margarine will give a good finished product.

**Health tip** To reduce fat content:
- use low fat milk
- use low fat cheese
- use very lean mince.

# Navarin of lamb

**G**arnish: small sprigs of fresh rosemary.

**Ingredients**

| | 25 | 50 | 100 |
|---|---|---|---|
| olive oil/vegetable oil | as required | | |
| **onions**, peeled, large dice | 1 kg | 2 kg | 4 kg |
| **garlic**, cloves, peeled, minced | 4 | 8 | 16 |
| **rosemary**, fresh, leaves, finely chopped | 20 g | 40 g | 80 g |
| **lamb**, leg, finely diced | 4.5 kg | 9 kg | 18 kg |
| **flour**, plain | 150 g | 300 g | 600 g |
| **tomato purée** | 150 g | 300 g | 600 g |
| **stock**, beef/lamb, warm | 1.5 L | 3 L | 6 L |
| **tomatoes**, crushed, A10 tin | 1/2 | 1 | 2 |
| **carrots**, peeled, small dice | 500 g | 1 kg | 2 kg |
| **wine**, red | 200 mL | 400 mL | 800 mL |
| **salt and freshly milled black pepper** | to taste | | |

**Method**

1 Gently cook the onions, garlic and rosemary in a pan over a moderate heat in a little oil until onions are soft.
2 Add lamb and cook until lightly browned.
3 Thoroughly mix in flour and then add in tomato purée. Cook gently for approx. 3–4 minutes.
4 Slowly add warmed stock until all has been incorporated.
5 Mix in crushed tomatoes, carrots, and red wine. Simmer gently for approx. one hour or until lamb is tender.
6 Season to taste, remove from heat and serve.

**Note** **Navarin**, the term used for this classic French dish, translates as 'brown stew'. Navarin is commonly associated with lamb. It was traditionally made using mutton and whole baby onions. **Printanier** is another form of navarin that uses large diced spring vegetables.

# Tuscan lamb pie topped with golden puff pastry

Garnish: poppy seeds.

Ingredients

| | | 25 | 50 | 100 |
|---|---|---|---|---|
| olive oil/vegetable oil | | as required | | |
| onions, white, roughly chopped | | 1 kg | 2 kg | 4 kg |
| garlic, cloves, peeled, finely chopped | | 4 | 7 | 10 |
| lamb, leg, 2 cm x 2 cm dice | | 5 kg | 10 kg | 20 kg |
| red capsicums, roasted, roughly diced | | 3 | 6 | 12 |
| tomatoes, crushed, A10 tin | | 1 | 2 | 4 |
| stock, beef, warm | | 250 mL | 500 mL | 1 L |
| olives, black, stoned, roughly chopped | | 200 g | 400 g | 800 g |
| rosemary, fresh, leaves, finely chopped | | 20 g | 40 g | 80 g |
| freshly milled black pepper | | to taste | | |
| pastry, puff | | as required | | |
| eggs | | 2 | 4 | 8 |
| milk | | 100 mL | 200 mL | 400 mL |
| poppy seeds | | as required | | |

Method

1 Pre-heat oven to moderate (150–180°C).
2 Place a little oil in a saucepan over a moderate heat.
3 Add onions and garlic and cook without colour until tender.
4 Add diced lamb and cook until lightly browned on all sides.
5 Add roasted red capsicums, crushed tomatoes, beef stock, black olives, and rosemary. Season to taste.
6 Simmer gently for approx. 1 hour or until lamb is tender, stirring regularly.
7 Place mixture in deep sided baking or serving trays and allow to cool.
8 Roll out puff pastry to required size and cover baking or serving trays, pressing down firmly at the edges.
9 Score pastry lightly with a knife to determine portion sizes.
10 Mix eggs with the milk and brush evenly over pastry. Sprinkle lightly with poppy seeds.
11 Place trays into oven and cook until pastry is golden brown.
12 Remove from oven, pre-portion and serve.

Note

Roast capsicum by removing stalk and seeds, quartering and roughly chopping.
Place capsicum into a deep sided roasting tray tossed with a little olive oil and place
into a pre-heated moderate oven (150–180°C) and roast, turning regularly, for
approx. 30–45 minutes or until the flesh is soft, and the skin is easily removed.

Health tip To reduce fat content use filo pastry instead of puff pastry.

# Baby racks of lamb marinated in lemon, fresh rosemary, red wine and roasted garlic

Garnish: roughly chopped continental parsley.

Ingredients

| | | 25 | 50 | 100 |
|---|---|---|---|---|
| lamb, baby racks (three cutlets) | | 25 | 50 | 100 |
| **MARINADE:** | | | | |
| lemons, zest and juice | | 2 | 4 | 8 |
| rosemary, fresh, leaves, finely chopped | | 30 g | 60 g | 120 g |
| wine, red | | 500 mL | 1 L | 2 L |
| garlic, bulbs, roasted, see note below | | 1 | 2 | 4 |
| olive oil | | 100 mL | 200 mL | 400 mL |

Method

1 Combine all marinade ingredients in mixing bowl.
2 Dip each rack of lamb into the marinade and place onto a baking tray. Pour a little of the remaining marinade over each rack of lamb.
3 Cover tray/s with cling film and refrigerate for 24 hours.
4 Remove cling film and place tray/s into a pre-heated moderate oven (150–180°C). Cook for approx. 20–40 minutes or until cooked to the required degree.
5 Remove from oven and serve, allowing one rack per portion.

To roast garlic, take whole bulbs and lightly prick cloves. Place onto a roasting tray and put into a pre-heated moderate oven (150–180°C) for approx. 20–30 minutes or until garlic cloves are soft to the touch. Remove from oven and cool completely. To extract roasted garlic purée, trim the base of the bulb and squeeze out the purée. The reason garlic is sometimes roasted is that it gives a milder, richer flavour.

**Rosemary** has been widely used since 500 BC and is native to the Mediterranean. Rosemary is now widely cultivated around the world. A member of the mint family, it has a distinctive aroma that is associated with many lamb dishes.

This dish can also be char-grilled.

 Health tip

To reduce fat, remove visible fat from lamb.

# Traditional Greek-style roasted lamb legs served with tzatziki sauce

Garnish: home-made tzatziki sauce.

**Ingredients**

| | 25 | 50 | 100 |
|---|---|---|---|
| tomatoes, crushed, A10 tin | 1 | 2 | 4 |
| lemons, zest and juice | 2 | 4 | 8 |
| garlic, cloves, peeled, minced | 4 | 8 | 16 |
| rosemary, fresh, leaves, finely chopped | 20 g | 40 g | 80 g |
| lamb, legs, boned and rolled | 4 | 8 | 16 |
| garlic, cloves, peeled, quartered lengthways | 8 | 16 | 32 |

**Method**

1 Combine tomatoes, lemons, garlic and rosemary and mix well.
2 At regular intervals around lamb legs, make a small incision with a vegetable knife and place a sliver of garlic into each.
3 Place lamb legs into roasting tray/s and pour over the marinade. Cover with cling film and refrigerate for approx. 12 hours, basting marinade over lamb legs every 2 hours.
4 Place lamb into clean roasting tray/s, retaining marinade. Place into a pre-heated moderate oven (150–180°C) for approx. 1–1¹/₂ hours.
5 30 minutes before lamb is cooked to the required degree, pour marinade into the base of the roasting tray/s and allow to reduce with the meat juices.
6 Remove tray/s from oven and place lamb legs onto a clean tray. Cover with aluminium foil and rest for approx. ten minutes, keeping the reduced marinade warm.
7 Carve, allowing two to three slices per portion. Serve with a little of the reduced marinade and a little tzatziki sauce on the side.

## Tzatziki sauce

**Ingredients**

| | 25 | 50 | 100 |
|---|---|---|---|
| yoghurt, natural | 500 g | 1 kg | 2 kg |
| garlic, cloves, peeled, minced | 2 | 4 | 8 |
| cucumbers, peeled, seeded, minced | 250 g | 500 g | 1 kg |
| lemons, zest and juice | 1 | 2 | 4 |
| mint, fresh, leaves, finely chopped | 15 g | 30 g | 60 g |

**Method**

Combine all ingredients. Cover with cling film and refrigerate for at least one hour before use.

 **Note** Always let cooked joints of meat that have just been removed from the oven stand about 10 minutes before carving. This allows the connective tissues of the meat to relax as the temperature drops and permits easier carving, better portion control and tenderer meat.

 **Health tip** Use reduced or low fat yoghurt.

# Lamb korma curry served with crispy lentil pappadams

Garnish: fresh sprigs of mint.

Ingredients

| | | 25 | 50 | 100 |
|---|---|---|---|---|
| olive oil/vegetable oil | | as required | | |
| onions, peeled, large dice | | 1 kg | 2 kg | 4 kg |
| garlic, cloves, peeled, minced | | 4 | 8 | 16 |
| lamb, leg, finely diced | | 4.5 kg | 9 kg | 18 kg |
| curry powder, mild, approx. to taste | | 100 g | 200 g | 400 g |

### SAUCE:

| | 25 | 50 | 100 |
|---|---|---|---|
| flour, plain | 150 g | 300 g | 600 g |
| tomato purée | 150 g | 300 g | 600 g |
| stock, beef/lamb, warm | 1.5 L | 3 L | 6 L |
| tomatoes, crushed, A10 tin | 1 L | 2 L | 4 L |
| carrots, peeled, small dice | 500 g | 1 kg | 2 kg |
| cream, single | 250 mL | 500 mL | 1 L |
| salt and freshly milled black pepper | to taste | | |

Method

1 Gently cook onions and garlic in a little oil in a saucepan over a moderate heat until onions are soft.
2 Add lamb and cook until lightly browned. Add curry powder and cook for a further 1–2 minutes.
3 Thoroughly mix in flour and tomato purée and cook gently for approx. 3–4 minutes.
4 Slowly add warmed stock until all has been incorporated.
5 Mix in crushed tomatoes and carrots. Simmer gently for approx. one hour or until lamb is tender.
6 Add cream, mixing thoroughly. Season to taste.
7 Remove from heat and serve with steamed rice and crispy lentil pappadams.

 **Note**  Korma is a spicy curry dish popular in India and Pakistan. It is usually made with lamb, mutton or chicken with the addition of onions and various vegetables.

 **Health tip**  For low fat diets, omit the cream. Stir in low fat natural yoghurt at Stage 6.

# Lamb's liver braised with bacon, balsamic vinegar and Spanish onions

Garnish: finely chopped parsley.

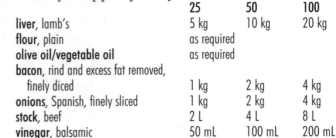

| Ingredients | | 25 | 50 | 100 |
|---|---|---|---|---|
| liver, lamb's | | 5 kg | 10 kg | 20 kg |
| flour, plain | | as required | | |
| olive oil/vegetable oil | | as required | | |
| bacon, rind and excess fat removed, finely diced | | 1 kg | 2 kg | 4 kg |
| onions, Spanish, finely sliced | | 1 kg | 2 kg | 4 kg |
| stock, beef | | 2 L | 4 L | 8 L |
| vinegar, balsamic | | 50 mL | 100 mL | 200 mL |

**Method**

1 Pre-heat oven to moderate (150–180°C).
2 Wash lamb's liver under cold running water and drain. Cut into even sized pieces.
3 Dredge lamb's liver through flour, shaking off any excess flour.
4 Heat a sauté pan or grill plate and brush liberally with oil and cook liver in batches until lightly browned on all sides and place into roasting tray/s with the bacon and onions.
5 Combine beef stock and balsamic vinegar and pour over liver until just covered. Cover tray/s with aluminium foil.
6 Place tray/s into an oven and cook for approx. 1–1$^1$/$_2$ hours or until liver is cooked through and sauce has thickened.
7 Remove from oven and serve the liver with a little of the thickened stock.

**Note**

'Vinegar' is derived from the French term *vin aigre* which means 'sour wine'. Vinegar is made by bacterial activity which converts fermented liquids such as beer, cider and wine into a weak solution of acetic acid. This is what gives vinegar its sour taste. Vinegar has been used for hundreds of years to make beverages, as a preservative and as a flavour enhancer and it was also believed to have medicinal properties. Many countries around the world have developed their own varieties of vinegar, such as the English malt vinegar, French wine and herb vinegars, Italian balsamic vinegars, and Chinese and Japanese rice vinegars.

**Health tip**

Livers are a rich source of the minerals iron and zinc. Many people would benefit from eating livers more often.

# Hearty Irish stew

Garnish: freshly chopped parsley.

Ingredients

| | 25 | 50 | 100 |
|---|---|---|---|
| **lamb**, forequarter, diced | 3 kg | 6 kg | 12 kg |
| **onions**, white, roughly chopped | 1 kg | 2 kg | 4 kg |
| **carrots**, peeled, 2 cm dice | 1 kg | 2 kg | 4 kg |
| **potatoes**, peeled, 2 cm dice | 4 kg | 8 kg | 16 kg |
| **stock**, chicken | 5 L | 10 L | 20 L |
| **salt and freshly milled black pepper** | to taste | | |

Method

1 Place all ingredients into a saucepan and bring to the boil. Reduce to a gentle simmer and cover with a tight fitting lid.
2 Simmer gently for approx. $1^1/_2$–2 hours or until lamb and vegetables are cooked through and tender, and the sauce has thickened; skim surface regularly to remove any scum that forms.
3 Remove from heat and serve.

**Note** This stew is thickened with the broken down potato. Extra stock can be added during the cooking process should the stew become too thick.

# Fresh herb, lemon and paprika lamb schnitzels

Garnish: fresh lemon wedges.

Ingredients

| | 25 | 50 | 100 |
|---|---|---|---|
| **flour**, plain | as required | | |
| **eggs**, approx. | 10 | 20 | 40 |
| **milk** | 300 mL | 600 mL | 1.2 L |
| **breadcrumbs** | as required | | |
| **paprika** | 50 g | 100 g | 200 g |
| **rosemary**, fresh, leaves, finely chopped | 15 g | 30 g | 60 g |
| **lemon**, zest only | 1 | 2 | 4 |
| **pepper**, black, ground | 20 g | 40 g | 80 g |
| **parsley**, fresh, finely chopped | 20 g | 40 g | 80 g |
| **lamb**, topside schnitzel, approx. 170 g | 25 | 50 | 100 |

Method

1 Pre-heat deep fryer to 160–170°C.
2 Place flour into a bowl and the eggs, which have been beaten together with the milk, into a second bowl. Place the breadcrumbs, which have been mixed with all the other ingredients, into a separate bowl.

continued

3 Dredge lamb schnitzels through flour, egg mixture and breadcrumbs. Gently shake off any excess breadcrumbs. Place schnitzels one layer deep onto tray/s separating each layer with a sheet of greaseproof paper. Pre-heat oven to moderate (150–180°C).
4 Place schnitzels into fat in small batches and cook to a light golden brown. Remove from oil and drain any excess fat.
5 Place schnitzels onto roasting tray/s and put into oven. Cook for approx. 5 minutes or until cooked through.
6 Remove from oven and serve one schnitzel per portion with a lemon wedge.

**Note**

**Paprika** is produced by grinding certain sweet red capsicum pods to produce a powder. The flavour of paprika can vary from mild to hot and the colour from a dull red to a deep blood red, depending on the variety of capsicum used. The Hungarian varieties of paprika are considered to be the best and have been an essential ingredient in Hungarian cuisine. Paprika has excellent flavour and is also useful for garnishing.

**♥ Health tip**

Unsuitable for low fat diets.
In lieu of deep frying, bake on a roasting tray.

# Tender lamb chops slow cooked in a Lyonnaise-style jus with a hint of fresh mint

**G**arnish: finely chopped fresh mint.
Yields: 2 chops/person.

**Ingredients**

| | 25 | 50 | 100 |
|---|---|---|---|
| **lamb**, chops, fat trimmed | 50 | 100 | 200 |
| **flour**, plain | as required | | |
| **olive oil/vegetable oil** | as required | | |
| **onions**, white, finely sliced | 1 kg | 2 kg | 4 kg |
| **mint**, fresh, finely chopped | 20 g | 40 g | 80 g |
| **salt and freshly milled black pepper** | to taste | | |
| **stock**, beef/lamb | 2 L | 4 L | 8 L |

**Method**

1 Pre-heat oven to moderate (150–180°C).
2 Dredge lamb chops through flour, shaking off any excess flour.
3 Heat a sauté pan or grill plate and brush liberally with oil. Seal lamb chops on both sides until light golden brown. Layer the chops in roasting or serving tray/s with onions and mint. Season to taste between layers.
4 Pour beef/lamb stock over lamb chops so they are just covered. Cover tray/s with aluminium foil.
5 Place tray/s into oven. Cook for approx. 1–1$^1$/$_2$ hours or until lamb chops are cooked through and sauce has thickened.
6 Remove from oven and serve the chops with a little of the thickened stock.

# Char-grilled lamb topside steaks served with lemon, rosemary and roasted garlic butter

Garnish: lemon, rosemary and roasted garlic butter.

**Ingredients**

| | 25 | 50 | 100 |
|---|---|---|---|
| **LEMON, ROSEMARY AND ROASTED GARLIC BUTTER:** | | | |
| **butter**, room temperature | 1 kg | 2 kg | 4 kg |
| **lemons**, juice and zest | 1 | 2 | 4 |
| **rosemary**, fresh, leaves, finely chopped | 20 g | 40 g | 80 g |
| **garlic bulbs**, roasted, see note below | 1 | 2 | 4 |
| | | | |
| **LAMB:** | | | |
| **lamb**, topside steaks, 200 g per portion | 25 kg | 50 kg | 100 kg |
| **olive oil/vegetable oil** | as required | | |
| **salt and freshly milled black pepper** | to taste | | |

**Method**

1. Combine all butter ingredients thoroughly and place along the centre of a sheet of greaseproof paper. Roll into a cylindrical shape approx. 4 cm in diameter. Totally enclose butter in greaseproof paper and place into a freezer until required.
2. Brush steaks on all sides with a little of the oil and season.
3. Lightly brush a pre-heated sauté pan or grill plate with oil. Seal steaks on either side and cook to the required degree.
4. Place cooked steaks neatly into serving trays. Serve with a generous slice of the frozen butter placed on top as each steak is served.

 **Notes**

If the grill plate is small or unavailable, the steaks can be seared on both sides and then placed onto roasting tray/s. Cook in a pre-heated moderate oven (150–180°C) until the required degree.

Butter can be pre-sliced and placed into a bowl of iced water for convenience during long service periods.

To roast garlic, take whole bulbs and lightly prick cloves. Place onto a roasting tray and put into a pre-heated moderate oven (150–180°C) for approx. 20–30 minutes or until garlic cloves are soft to the touch. Remove from oven and cool completely. To extract roasted garlic purée, trim the base of the bulb and squeeze out the purée. The reason garlic is sometimes roasted is that it gives a milder, richer flavour.

**♥ Health tip**

To reduce the fat content, serve only very thin slices of garlic butter on the steak.

# CHAPTER 9

# CHICKEN

# CUTS OF POULTRY AND APPROXIMATE WEIGHTS OF THE UNPREPARED PRIMARY CUT

## Approximate cooking times for poultry
50 minutes per kilo (2 lb) plus an extra 50 minutes.

| Chicken Cut | French Term | Uses |
|---|---|---|
| leg | cuisse | sauté, casserole, BBQ |
| drumstick | pilon de cuisse | sauté, casserole, BBQ |
| thigh | gras de cuisse | sauté, casserole, BBQ |
| winglet | aileron | sauté, casserole, BBQ |
| wing | aile | sauté, casserole, BBQ |
| breast | blanc | sauté, casserole, BBQ |
| carcass | carcasse | stocks |

| English Term | French Term | Uses | Approx. Weights and Portions |
|---|---|---|---|
| baby chicken<br>Age: approx. 5 weeks | single poussin | grilling, roasting | 300–500 g<br>1 portion |
| double baby chicken | double poussin | grilling, roasting | 500–750 g<br>2 portions |
| small roaster<br>Age: approx. 4 months | poulet de grain | roasting, grilling, most moist methods | 750 g–1 kg<br>4 portions |
| medium roaster<br>Age: at prime | poulet reine | roasting, grilling, frying, most moist methods | 1–2 kg<br>5–6 portions |
| large roaster (boiling chicken)<br>Age: fully grown | poularde | roasting, boiling, most moist methods | 2–3 kg<br>8 portions |
| capon | chapon | roasting | 3–4 kg<br>10 portions |
| boiling fowl<br>Age: old hen that has finished laying | poule | soups and stocks | 2.5–4 kg |
| turkey | dinde | roasting, most moist methods | 4–20 kg<br>8–12 portions |

 No blood should be present in the meat.

 **Health tip** Remove skin from chicken before cooking. Order skinless chicken from the supplier.

# CHICKEN RECIPES
## Mediterranean-style braised chicken with fresh herb polenta

Garnish: roughly chopped continental parsley leaves.

**Ingredients**

| | 25 | 50 | 100 |
|---|---|---|---|
| **chicken**, thigh fillets | 5 kg | 10 kg | 20 kg |
| **olive oil/vegetable oil** | as required | | |
| **onions**, Spanish, peeled, finely sliced | 1 kg | 2 kg | 4 kg |
| **garlic**, cloves, peeled, finely chopped | 4 | 7 | 10 |
| **red capsicums**, roasted, medium dice | 3 | 6 | 12 |
| **tomatoes**, crushed, A10 tin | $1^1/_2$ | 3 | 6 |
| **stock**, chicken | 250 mL | 500 mL | 1 L |
| **Kalamata olives**, stoned, roughly chopped | 100 g | 200 g | 400 g |
| **bay-leaves** | 2 | 4 | 8 |
| **salt and freshly milled black pepper** | to taste | | |

**Method**

1 Pre-heat oven to moderate (150–180°).
2 Cut each thigh fillet into two even sized pieces.
3 Heat a large sauté pan or grill plate and brush with a little oil. Seal chicken on all sides. Remove and place in deep sided roasting or serving tray/s.
4 Put a little oil in a saucepan over a moderate heat.
5 Add onions and garlic and cook without colour until tender.
6 Add capsicums, tomatoes, stock, olives and bay-leaves. Season.
7 Simmer gently for 5 minutes stirring occasionally.
8 Pour over sufficient sauce to cover chicken and cover tray/s with aluminium foil. Place tray/s into oven and braise for approx. $1^1/_2$ hours or until cooked through and tender.
9 Remove foil from tray/s for the last twenty minutes of cooking to allow the sauce to reduce and thicken.
10 Remove from oven and serve the chicken with herb polenta.

**Note** Roast capsicum by removing stalk and seeds, quartering and roughly chopping. Place capsicum into a deep sided roasting tray tossed with a little olive oil and place into a pre-heated moderate oven (150–180°C) and roast, turning regularly, for approx. 30–45 minutes or until the flesh is soft, and the skin is easily removed.

## Fresh herb polenta

**Ingredients**

| | 25 | 50 | 100 |
|---|---|---|---|
| **water** | 2.3 L | 4.6 L | 9.2 L |
| **chives**, finely chopped | 10 g | 20 g | 40 g |
| **basil**, finely chopped | 10 g | 20 g | 40 g |
| **parsley**, finely chopped | 10 g | 20 g | 40 g |
| **polenta** | 660 g | 1.3 kg | 2.6 kg |
| **salt and freshly milled black pepper** | to taste | | |

continued

| Method | |
|---|---|
| | 1 Bring a pan of water to a simmer. |
| | 2 Add herbs and simmer for approx. 2 minutes allowing herbs to infuse. |
| | 3 Add polenta and stir continuously until polenta absorbs all liquid and thickens. Stir for approx. 1 minute to cook out. Remove from heat. |
| | 4 Season to taste. Serve with braised chicken. |

 **Note** **Polenta** is a coarse granular flour made from corn or maize. It is a staple food widely used in many ethnic cuisines.

 **Health tip** To reduce the fat content, remove skin from chicken.

# Chicken legs cooked with sun-dried tomatoes, balsamic vinegar and roasted eggplant

Garnish: finely chopped fresh basil.

**Ingredients**

| | 25 | 50 | 100 |
|---|---|---|---|
| eggplants, topped and tailed | 2 kg | 4 kg | 8 kg |
| olive oil/vegetable oil | as required | | |
| chicken, legs | 25 | 50 | 100 |
| onions, white, finely chopped | 500 g | 1 kg | 2 kg |
| garlic, cloves, finely chopped | 3 | 6 | 12 |
| tomatoes, crushed, A10 tin | 1½ | 3 | 6 |
| stock, chicken | 250 mL | 500 mL | 1 L |
| sun-dried tomatoes, finely shredded | 250 g | 500 g | 1 kg |
| balsamic vinegar | 50 mL | 100 mL | 200 mL |
| salt and freshly milled black pepper | to taste | | |

Method

1 Pre-heat oven to moderate (150–180°C).
2 Cut eggplant into small dice and sauté in a little oil over a high heat until lightly browned. Remove from heat.
3 Place eggplant onto lightly oiled roasting tray/s and place into oven. Roast for approx. 10–15 minutes.
4 Cut chicken legs into two pieces and lightly brown all sides over a high heat in a lightly oiled sauté pan or grill plate. Place chicken legs into roasting or serving tray/s and cover evenly with eggplant.
5 Put a little oil in a saucepan over a moderate heat. Add onions and garlic and cook without colour until soft.
6 Reduce heat. Add all other ingredients and simmer gently for 5 minutes. Season to taste. Remove from heat and pour evenly over chicken legs and eggplant.
7 Cover roasting tray/s with aluminium foil and place into oven for 1–1½ hours or until chicken is cooked through and tender.
8 Serve chicken with a little of the sauce.

**Note**    **Balsamic vinegar** is a dark vinegar produced in Modena, Italy. It is made from the white Trebbiano grape that develops its flavour, colour and sweetness through ageing in barrels of different woods such as oak, chestnut, mulberry, juniper and cherrywood, each imparting its own flavour. The vinegar is aged for at least twenty years before it is bottled for sale.

**Health tip**    To reduce fat content, remove skin from chicken.

# Marinated tandoori chicken served with minted lemon yoghurt

Garnish: crisp lentil pappadams.

**Ingredients**

| | 25 | 50 | 100 |
|---|---|---|---|
| **chickens**, whole, no. 12 | 10 | 20 | 40 |
| **yoghurt**, natural | 1 kg | 2 kg | 4 kg |
| **lemons**, zest and juice | 2 | 4 | 8 |
| **sugar**, castor | 200 g | 400 g | 800 g |
| **tandoori paste** | 250 g | 500 g | 1 kg |

**Method**

1 Cut chickens into eight pieces, removing all skin and retaining carcasses for stock.
2 Combine all other ingredients in a large bowl and whisk to a smooth consistency.
3 Add chicken pieces with the tandoori marinade, mix well and cover with cling wrap.
4 Refrigerate chicken pieces for approx. six to eight hours, turning mixture every two hours if possible.
5 Place chicken pieces into roasting tray/s one deep. Place into a pre-heated moderate oven (150–180°C) and cook for approx. 20–30 minutes or until cooked through.
6 Serve three pieces of chicken per portion on a bed of steamed rice with a crisp lentil pappadam and a little minted lemon yoghurt.

## Minted lemon yoghurt

**Ingredients**

| | 25 | 50 | 100 |
|---|---|---|---|
| **yoghurt**, natural | 1 kg | 2 kg | 4 kg |
| **mint**, fresh, leaves | 50 g | 100 g | 200 g |
| **lemon juice** | 75 ml | 150 mL | 300 mL |
| **sugar**, castor | 200 g | 400 g | 800 g |

**Method**

1 Place all ingredients in a blender and bring to a smooth consistency.
2 Refrigerate for 2 hours before service.

continued

# Shredded tandoori chicken and cashew nuts braised in coconut cream

**G**arnish: shredded fresh coriander leaves.

**Ingredients**

|  | 25 | 50 | 100 |
|---|---|---|---|
| **chicken**, thigh fillets | 5 kg | 10 kg | 20 kg |
| **yoghurt**, natural | 500 g | 1 kg | 2 kg |
| **tandoori paste** | 200 g | 400 g | 800 g |
| **curry powder** | 20 g | 40 g | 80 g |
| **cashew nuts**, roughly chopped | 250 g | 500 g | 1 kg |
| **coconut cream**, tinned | 1 L | 2 L | 4 L |
| **cream**, single | 250 mL | 500 mL | 1 L |
| **chicken booster**, powdered stock base | to taste | | |

**Method**

1 Shred thigh fillets and place to one side.
2 Mix yoghurt, tandoori paste and curry powder in a bowl to a smooth consistency. Add chicken, mixing well.
3 Refrigerate for 4–6 hours, turning every 2 hours.
4 Pre-heat oven to moderate (150–180°C). Heat a large sauté pan and brush with a little oil. Add chicken and cook until lightly browned. Add cashew nuts, coconut cream and cream.
5 Bring mixture to a simmer and add chicken stock booster. Remove from heat.
6 Place mixture into roasting or serving tray/s and cover with aluminium foil. Place into oven and cook for approx. 45 minutes–1 hour or until cooked through.
7 Remove from oven. Serve on a bed of steamed saffron rice.

# Curry crusted chicken served with minted lemon yoghurt

Garnish: minted lemon yoghurt.

**Ingredients**

| | 25 | 50 | 100 |
|---|---|---|---|
| chickens, no. 12 | 10 | 19 | 39 |
| curry powder, mild, approx. | 250 g | 500 g | 1 kg |
| chicken booster, powdered stock base | to taste | | |
| olive oil/vegetable oil | as required | | |

**Method**

1 Pre-heat oven to moderate (150–180°C).
2 Cut each chicken into eight pieces, retaining carcass for stock.
3 Place curry powder and a little chicken booster into a bowl.
4 Dredge all chicken pieces through curry powder mix, coating all of chicken.
5 Heat a sauté pan or grill plate brushed liberally with oil.
6 Add chicken pieces and sear on all sides.
7 Place seared chicken pieces into roasting tray/s and place into oven for approx. 20–30 minutes or until chicken is cooked through.
8 Serve chicken, allowing three pieces per portion on a bed of steamed rice with a little minted yoghurt.

**Note** Curry powder is widely used in Indian cookery and can vary in flavour and strength depending on the region where it is produced. Curry powder is made from a ground blend of approx. eighteen herbs, seeds and spices, predominantly: cardamom, chillies, cinnamon, cloves, coriander, cumin, fennel seeds, saffron, tamarind, turmeric and garlic.

## Minted lemon yoghurt

**Ingredients**

| | 25 | 50 | 100 |
|---|---|---|---|
| yoghurt, natural | 1 kg | 2 kg | 4 kg |
| mint, fresh leaves | 50 g | 100 g | 200 g |
| lemon juice | 75 mL | 150 mL | 300 mL |
| sugar, castor | 200 g | 400 g | 800 g |

**Method**

1 Place all ingredients into a blender and blend to a smooth consistency.
2 Refrigerate for two hours before use.

**Note** Minted lemon yoghurt is an ideal accompaniment to spiced meats and Asian-style dishes.

**Health tip** To reduce fat content, remove skin from chicken, use low fat yoghurt.

# Tex-Mex chicken

Garnish: home-made coleslaw.

| Ingredients  | 25 | 50 | 100 |
|---|---|---|---|
| tomato sauce, commercial | 2.25 L | 4.5 L | 9 L |
| Worcestershire sauce | 250 mL | 500 mL | 1 L |
| mustard, English | 125 g | 250 g | 500 g |
| sugar, brown, soft | 500 g | 1 kg | 2 kg |
| chickens, no. 12 | 10 | 19 | 39 |

**Method**

1 Pre-heat oven to moderate (150–180°C).
2 Combine tomato sauce, Worcestershire sauce, mustard and sugar in a saucepan over a low heat.
3 Stir continuously until all ingredients are combined and thickened. Remove from heat and cool.
4 Cut chickens into eight pieces, retaining carcass for stock.
5 Mix chicken pieces with approx. one-third of the sauce.
6 Place chicken pieces one deep into roasting tray/s.
7 Place tray/s into oven for approx. 20–30 minutes or until chicken is cooked through.
8 Serve, allowing three chicken pieces per portion, with a little of the remaining warmed sauce and home-made coleslaw.

 **Note**

The popular **Worcestershire sauce** was originally developed by the British in India but was first bottled in Worcester, England. Its main ingredients are soya sauce, tamarind, garlic, onions, molasses, anchovies, vinegar and limes.

 **Health tip**

To reduce the fat content, remove skin from chicken.

# Spicy deep fried Southern-style chicken

Garnish: home-made tomato and balsamic vinegar salsa.

| Ingredients  | 25 | 50 | 100 |
|---|---|---|---|
| chickens, whole, no. 12 | 10 | 19 | 39 |
| flour, plain | as required | | |
| eggs, approx. | 10 | 20 | 40 |
| milk | 300 mL | 600 mL | 1.2 L |
| breadcrumbs | as required | | |
| paprika | 25 g | 50 g | 100 g |
| chicken booster, powdered stock base | 50 g | 100 g | 200 g |
| pepper, black, ground | 20 g | 40 g | 80 g |
| parsley, fresh, finely chopped | 20 g | 40 g | 80 g |

**Method**

1 Heat deep fryer to 160–170°C.
2 Cut chickens into eight pieces, retaining carcasses for stock.
3 Place all chicken pieces into a pan and cover with water. Place over a moderate heat and simmer until chicken pieces are cooked through; do not over-cook.
4 When chicken pieces are cooked, place into a strainer and drain all liquid. Keep stock for future use.
5 Once chicken pieces have cooled sufficiently, place flour; eggs and milk which have been beaten together; and breadcrumbs mixed with all other ingredients into three separate mixing bowls.
6 Dredge chicken pieces through flour and then the egg mixture followed by the breadcrumb mixture, shaking off any excess crumbs.
7 Place one layer of chicken pieces into deep frying baskets and cook until golden brown. Drain chicken thoroughly, repeating process as chicken pieces are required.
8 Serve chicken, allowing three pieces per portion, served with a tablespoon of home-made tomato and balsamic vinegar salsa.

**Notes** Chicken can be steamed or roasted prior to breadcrumbing and deep frying.

If chicken pieces are poached, the cooking liquor should be turned into chicken stock by mixing it with the roughly chopped carcasses, roughly chopped onions, carrots, parsley stalks and bay-leaves and allow it to gently simmer. Refer to chicken stock recipe in the stocks and sauces chapter, page 4.

**Health tip** Bake chicken instead of deep frying.

# Tomato and balsamic vinegar salsa

| Ingredients | | 25 | 50 | 100 |
|---|---|---|---|---|
| tomatoes | | 13 | 25 | 50 |
| chillies, red, small | | 4 | 8 | 16 |
| onions, Spanish, finely diced | | 3 | 6 | 12 |
| garlic, cloves, peeled, finely diced | | 4 | 7 | 10 |
| olive oil | | 50 mL | 100 mL | 200 mL |
| lemons/limes, juice of | | 2 | 4 | 8 |
| balsamic vinegar | | to taste | | |
| salt and freshly milled black pepper | | to taste | | |

**Method**

1 Score bottoms of tomatoes and place into a pan of boiling water for approx. 20 seconds or until skin separates from tomato.
2 Refresh tomatoes immediately under cold running water. Remove skin and drain.
3 Quarter tomatoes and remove seeds. Core and finely dice the flesh.
4 Top and tail chillies, remove seeds and finely dice the flesh. Mix with tomatoes in a bowl.
5 Add Spanish onion and garlic to tomatoes and combine.

continued

6 Add olive oil, lemon/lime juice, balsamic vinegar and salt and pepper. Combine.

7 Cover with cling wrap and refrigerate for at least 2–3 hours before serving.

**Note** **Salsa** is the Mexican word for sauce; it can be applied to cooked or uncooked mixtures. It is classically made up of tomatoes, chillies and onions and can be used as an accompaniment to a wide variety of dishes.

# Fragrant lemon and Parmesan chicken breast schnitzels

**G**arnish: home-made preserved lemon.
Yields: 1 schnitzel/person.

**Ingredients**

| | 25 | 50 | 100 |
|---|---|---|---|
| **chicken**, fillets, large | 13 | 25 | 50 |
| **flour**, plain | as required | | |
| **eggs** | 10 | 20 | 40 |
| **milk** | 300 mL | 600 mL | 1.2 L |
| **breadcrumbs** | as required | | |
| **lemons**, zest | 2 | 4 | 8 |
| **Parmesan cheese**, freshly grated | 100 g | 200 g | 400 g |
| **salt and freshly milled black pepper** | to taste | | |

**Method**

1 Pre-heat deep fryer to 160–170°C.

2 Lay chicken fillets flat onto a chopping board. Using a sharp knife, cut fillets in half holding the knife horizontal to the chopping board.

3 Using the flat side of a tenderiser, gently flatten fillets.

4 Place flour into a bowl. Place the eggs, which have been beaten together with the milk, into a second bowl. Place the breadcrumbs, which have been mixed with all the other ingredients, into a third bowl.

5 Dredge all chicken fillets through flour, egg mixture and breadcrumbs and gently shake off any excess breadcrumbs. Pre-heat oven to moderate (150–180°C).

6 Place schnitzels into fat in small batches and cook to a light golden brown. Remove from oil and drain any excess fat.

7 Place schnitzels onto roasting tray/s and put into an oven. Cook for approx. 5 minutes or until cooked through.

8 Serve, allowing one schnitzel per portion, garnished with a little preserved lemon.

 **Health tip** Unsuitable for low fat diets. Bake the chicken instead of deep frying.

## Preserved lemons

Ingredients

| | 25 | 50 | 100 |
|---|---|---|---|
| lemons | 6 | 12 | 24 |
| salt | 3 tbsp | 6 tbsp | 12 tbsp |
| coriander seeds | 1 tsp | 2 tsp | 4 tsp |
| cinnamon sticks | 2 | 4 | 8 |
| cloves | 1 tsp | 2 tsp | 4 tsp |
| peppercorns, black | 1 tsp | 2 tsp | 4 tsp |
| bay-leaves | 2 | 4 | 8 |
| lemon juice, fresh | as required | | |

Method

1 Stand each lemon on end and cut into quarters to 5 mm from bottom.
2 Gently pull segments apart so that salt can be sprinkled inside, then re-form the lemon.
3 In sterilised preserving jar/s make one layer of lemons, then sprinkle a little of all ingredients except lemon juice over them. Repeat until jar/s are full.
4 Press lemons down firmly to release a little of their own juice. Cover with lemon juice and seal the jar/s.
5 Shake the jar/s each day for 3–4 weeks.
6 Before serving the lemons remove the flesh, as the skin is the only part used. Wash under cold running water and pat dry.
7 Cut preserved lemon quarters into small strips and use as an edible garnish.

 Note

This dish has its origins in North Africa. It was used to preserve lemons for future use as a flavour enhancer and garnish. It creates a distinct flavour in certain foods such as lamb tagine and smoked fish. It is worth making when time allows.

 Health tip

Unsuitable for low fat diets.

# Chicken cacciatore

Garnish: small bunches of fresh basil.

Ingredients

| | 25 | 50 | 100 |
|---|---|---|---|
| chickens, whole, no. 12 | 7 | 13 | 26 |
| olive oil/vegetable oil | as required | | |
| garlic, cloves, peeled, finely chopped | 5 | 10 | 15 |
| chillies, medium size, seeded, finely sliced | 3 | 6 | 12 |
| onions, finely sliced | 700 g | 1.4 kg | 2.8 kg |
| tomatoes, crushed, A10 tin | 2 | 4 | 8 |
| basil, fresh, finely chopped | 30 g | 60 g | 120 g |
| tomatoes, 1 cm dice | 1 kg | 2 kg | 4 kg |
| mushrooms, button, washed, quartered | 1 kg | 2 kg | 4 kg |
| salt and freshly milled black pepper | to taste | | |

continued

| | | |
|---|---|---|
| **Method** | 1 | Pre-heat oven to moderate (150–180°C). |
| | 2 | Cut chickens into four pieces, retaining carcasses for stock. Place onto baking tray/s and brush with a little oil. Place into oven for approx. 20–30 minutes or until chicken is cooked through. Remove from oven and place to one side. |
| | 3 | Heat a little oil in a pan over a moderate heat. |
| | 4 | Add garlic, chillies and onions and cook without colour until onions are soft. |
| | 5 | Add crushed tomatoes and basil. Mix well. Simmer for approx. 15 minutes. |
| | 6 | Add diced tomatoes and mushrooms. Season to taste. |
| | 7 | Cook sauce for a further 5 minutes, gently simmering. |
| | 8 | Place chicken pieces into deep sided roasting or serving tray/s one deep and cover with sauce. |
| | 9 | Return to oven and cook for a further 15 minutes. Remove from oven. |
| | 10 | Serve with a little of the mushroom and tomato sauce. |

 **Cacciatore** is an Italian term for 'hunter'.

 **Health tip**   To reduce the fat content, remove skin from chicken.

# Gourmet home-made chicken burgers

**G**arnish: refer to note.

| Ingredients | | 25 | 50 | 100 |
|---|---|---|---|---|
| | olive oil/vegetable oil | as required | | |
| | garlic, cloves, peeled, finely chopped | 4 | 7 | 11 |
| | onions, Spanish, finely chopped | 1 kg | 2 kg | 4 kg |
| | chicken, mince | 3.75 kg | 7.5 kg | 15 kg |
| | Worcestershire sauce | 100 mL | 200 mL | 400 mL |
| | tomato sauce | 150 mL | 300 mL | 600 mL |
| | eggs | 3 | 6 | 12 |
| | chicken booster, powdered stock base | 10 g | 20 g | 40 g |
| | freshly milled black pepper | to taste | | |
| | breadcrumbs | as required | | |
| | burger buns/focaccia bread | | | |
| | as required | 25 | 50 | 100 |

| | | |
|---|---|---|
| **Method** | 1 | Heat a little oil in a pan over a moderate heat. Add garlic and onions and cook without colour until soft. Remove from heat. |
| | 2 | In a large bowl place onion and garlic mix, chicken mince, Worcestershire sauce, tomato sauce, eggs, chicken booster and pepper. Mix well. |
| | 3 | Gradually add breadcrumbs while mixing until desired texture is achieved. |

4 Turn mixture out onto a lightly floured work bench and shape mixture into patties (approx. 150 g each).

5 Place patties onto tray/s one layer at a time and place a piece of lightly oiled greaseproof paper between each layer. Refrigerate until required. Pre-heat oven to moderate (150–180°C).

6 Heat a sauté pan or grill plate lightly brushed with a little oil. Sear patties on each side until golden brown.

7 Place seared patties onto lightly greased roasting tray/s and put into oven. Cook for approx. 20 minutes or until cooked through.

8 Serve one patty per portion on a toasted sesame seed bun or a small piece of toasted foccacia spread with a little mayonnaise.

**Note** This is only a basic recipe. Other ingredients such as crisp bacon, char-grilled pineapple rings, roasted red capsicum, guacamole, Swiss cheese, grilled tomato slices or a sautéed onion and mushroom compote can be used as a topping. The only limitation besides your budget is your imagination.

# Chicken stir-fried with bok choy, oyster mushrooms and almonds

Garnish: fine julienne of red capsicum, blanched and refreshed.

Ingredients

| | 25 | 50 | 100 |
|---|---|---|---|
| chicken, thigh fillets | 4 kg | 8 kg | 16 kg |
| bok choy | 3.5 kg | 7 kg | 14 kg |
| mushrooms, oyster | 500 g | 1 kg | 2 kg |
| oil, sesame | as required | | |
| ginger, peeled and minced | 20 g | 40 g | 80 g |
| almonds, slivered | 500 g | 1 kg | 2 kg |
| honey | 100 mL | 200 mL | 400 mL |
| oyster sauce | 100 mL | 200 mL | 400 mL |
| soya sauce | 50 mL | 100 mL | 200 mL |
| cornflour | 75 g | 150 g | 300 g |
| salt and freshly milled black pepper | to taste | | |

Method

1 Finely slice all chicken thighs into thin strips.

2 Remove 1 cm from bottoms of whole bok choys and discard outer leaves. Separate all remaining leaves, tearing in half any that are very large. Blanch in a pan of boiling water for at least 10 seconds. Remove and refresh under cold running water and drain completely.

3 Tear any large oyster mushrooms into halves or quarters.

continued

4 Heat a grill plate until it is very hot and add a liberal amount of sesame oil. Add ginger and chicken when oil is extremely hot and stir-fry until chicken is golden brown and just cooked.

5 Add mushrooms and bok choy. Stir-fry for approx. 2 minutes.

6 Add almonds, honey, oyster sauce and soya sauce. Mix well.

7 Mix a little water with cornflour until thoroughly combined. Add to stir-fry mixing well. Cook for a further 1 minute, stirring continually.

8 Season to taste and remove from heat.

9 Serve garnished on a bed of steamed rice.

**Soya sauce** is an essential ingredient in Asian cuisine. It is produced by fermenting boiled soya beans and roasted wheat or barley.

**Bok choy** is a vegetable that is widely used in Asia and has become very popular in modern Australian cuisine. It has a crunchy stalk and dark green leaves and is ideal raw in salads, cooked as a vegetable or as part of a stir-fry.

**Health tip**    Suitable for cholesterol-lowering diets.

# Roasted chicken with a sage, onion and garlic crust

Garnish: freshly chopped parsley.

**Ingredients**

| | 25 | 50 | 100 |
|---|---|---|---|
| chickens, whole, no. 12 | 7 | 13 | 25 |
| olive oil/vegetable oil | as required | | |
| onions, Spanish, finely diced | 1 kg | 2 kg | 4 kg |
| garlic, cloves, peeled, finely diced | 4 | 6 | 8 |
| sage, dried | 10 g | 20 g | 40 g |
| eggs | 8 | 16 | 32 |
| breadcrumbs | 2 kg | 4 kg | 8 kg |
| stock, chicken | as required | | |
| salt and freshly milled black pepper | to taste | | |
| chicken stock | as required | | |

**Method**

1 Pre-heat oven to moderate (150–180°C).

2 Cut chickens into four pieces, retaining carcasses for stock.

3 Place chicken quarters into a lightly oiled roasting tray/s one layer deep. Place into oven and cook for 20 minutes. Remove from oven immediately.

4 While chickens are cooking heat a little oil in a sauté pan over a moderate heat and fry onions, garlic and sage until onions are soft.

5 Remove onion mix from heat and place into a mixing bowl. Allow to cool for 5 minutes.

6 Add eggs and breadcrumbs, season and mix thoroughly until a thick mixture is reached.

7 Add small amounts of chicken stock until a moist consistency is achieved that will allow moulding.
8 Place small amounts of stuffing onto each chicken quarter and press down firmly.
9 Return trays to oven and cook for approx. 10–15 minutes or until chicken is cooked through, ensuring the crust does not burn.
10 Remove from oven and serve one piece of chicken per portion.

 **Note** This stuffing can be changed according to taste using suitable herbs, spices and seasonings.

 **Health tip** To reduce the fat content, remove skin from chicken.

# Chicken, leek and thyme topped with puff pastry

Garnish: poppy seeds.

| Ingredients | | 25 | 50 | 100 |
|---|---|---|---|---|
| butter/margarine | | 200 g | 400 g | 800 g |
| garlic, cloves, peeled, chopped | | 3 | 6 | 12 |
| leeks, trimmed, finely sliced, washed | | 1 kg | 2 kg | 4 kg |
| flour, plain | | 200 g | 400 g | 800 g |
| stock, chicken, warm | | 1 L | 2 L | 4 L |
| milk, warm | | 750 mL | 1.5 L | 3 L |
| cream, single | | 250 mL | 500 mL | 1 L |
| thyme, dried, approx. | | 10 g | 20 g | 40 g |
| salt and freshly milled black pepper | | to taste | | |
| chicken meat, cooked, free of bone and skin | | 3.75 kg | 7.5 kg | 15 kg |
| pastry, puff | | as required | | |
| eggs | | 2 | 4 | 8 |
| milk | | 50 ml | 100 mL | 200 mL |
| poppy seeds | | as required | | |

Method
1 Pre-heat oven to moderate (150–180°C).
2 Melt the butter/margarine in a pan over a moderate heat.
3 Add garlic and leeks and cook without colour until soft.
4 Add flour and mix well until all ingredients are combined. Cook gently for a further 2–4 minutes stirring continuously.
5 Add small amounts of warmed chicken stock until all stock has been incorporated. Repeat process with warmed milk and simmer gently for approx. 5 minutes.

continued

6  Whisk in cream and thyme. Season to taste. Remove sauce from heat.
7  Add chicken meat to sauce and mix well.
8  Place chicken mixture into serving trays or dishes to an approx. depth of 4 cm. Allow to cool for 20–25 minutes.
9  Roll out puff pastry to required size and cover baking trays/dishes pressing down firmly at the edges.
10  Score pastry lightly with a knife to determine portion sizes.
11  Mix eggs with the milk and brush evenly over pastry. Sprinkle liberally with poppy seeds.
12  Place trays/dishes into oven and cook until pastry is golden brown.
13  Remove from oven, pre-portion and serve.

**Garlic** is one of the most widely used ingredients in the world. It is a member of the lily family and related to leeks, chives and onions. The edible bulb containing the cloves grows underground. Fresh garlic properly stored, in a cool dark place, will keep for up to eight weeks.

 **Health tip**

To reduce fat in recipe:
• use evaporated milk instead of cream
• use low fat milk
• use filo pastry instead of puff pastry.

# Chicken, red wine, basil and Roma tomatoes topped with puff pastry

**G**arnish: finely chopped black olives.

**Ingredients**

| | 25 | 50 | 100 |
|---|---|---|---|
| olive oil/vegetable oil | as required | | |
| onions, Spanish, peeled, finely chopped | 1 kg | 2 kg | 4 kg |
| garlic, cloves, peeled, finely chopped | 4 | 8 | 16 |
| basil, fresh, finely chopped | 25 g | 50 g | 100 g |
| wine, red | 250 mL | 500 mL | 1 L |
| balsamic vinegar | to taste | | |
| Roma tomatoes, A10 tin | 1 | 2 | 4 |
| salt and freshly milled black pepper | to taste | | |
| chicken meat, cooked, free of bone and skin | 3.75 kg | 7.5 kg | 15 kg |
| pastry, puff | as required | | |
| eggs | 2 | 4 | 8 |
| milk | 50 mL | 100 mL | 200 mL |

| Method | |
|---|---|
| | 1 Heat oil in a pan over a moderate heat. |
| | 2 Add onions and garlic and cook without colour until onions are soft. |
| | 3 Add basil, red wine and balsamic vinegar to taste. |
| | 4 Add tomatoes that have been roughly chopped and all juices. |
| | 5 Simmer gently and reduce until sauce has thickened. |
| | 6 Season to taste and remove from heat. |
| | 7 Add chicken to sauce and mix well. Pre-heat oven to moderate (150–180°C). |
| | 8 Place chicken mixture into serving trays or dishes to an approx. depth of 4 cm. Allow to cool for 20–25 minutes. |
| | 9 Roll out puff pastry to required size and cover serving trays/dishes, pressing down firmly at the edges. |
| | 10 Score pastry lightly with a knife to determine portion sizes. |
| | 11 Mix eggs with the milk and brush evenly over pastry. |
| | 12 Place trays/dishes into oven and cook until pastry is golden brown. |
| | 13 Remove from oven, pre-portion and serve. |

**Note** Olive oil is obtained by pressing tree ripened olives. It is graded in accordance with its degree of acidity. The best is extra virgin olive oil, which is extracted from the olives by gentle pressure as they are rolled between two boards. Lesser quality olive oils are extracted after this first pressing. Olive oil is a monounsaturated oil which is cholesterol free. It is a very versatile oil that can be used for cooking, marinades, dressings, and flavouring food.

 **Health tip** To reduce fat content, use filo pastry instead of puff pastry.

# Chicken breast stuffed with spinach, bacon, garlic and roasted red capsicum

Garnish: finely chopped continental parsley.

| Ingredients | | 25 | 50 | 100 |
|---|---|---|---|---|
|  | olive oil/vegetable oil | as required | | |
| | **onions**, Spanish, roughly chopped | 750 g | 1.5 kg | 3 kg |
| | **garlic**, cloves, peeled | 3 | 6 | 12 |
| | **bacon**, finely diced | 250 g | 500 g | 1 kg |
| | **red capsicums**, roasted, finely diced | 250 g | 500 g | 1 kg |
| | **spinach**, trimmed, washed, finely shredded | 1 kg | 2 kg | 4 kg |
| | **salt and freshly milled black pepper** | to taste | | |
| | **chicken**, breast | 25 | 50 | 100 |

continued

| | | | |
|---|---|---|---|
| **Method** | 1 | Pre-heat oven to moderate (150–180°C). | |

**Method**

1 Pre-heat oven to moderate (150–180°C).
2 Heat a little oil in a pan over a moderate heat.
3 Add onions, garlic and bacon. Cook until onions are soft.
4 Add roasted red capsicums. Mix well. Remove from heat.
5 Blanch and refresh spinach, squeezing out excess water.
6 Place spinach and onion mix into a food processor; lightly season. Process until smooth but not puréed.
7 Using a knife with a narrow blade, make an incision three-quarters the length of the breast into the neck end of the fillet.
8 Fit a piping bag with a small round nozzle and half fill with stuffing mixture.
9 Insert nozzle into incision and pipe in sufficient stuffing to fill cavity. Repeat process with all chicken breasts.
10 Heat a sauté pan or grill plate and brush with a little oil. Brown chicken breasts on either side, then place them into lightly oiled roasting or serving tray/s one layer deep.
11 Place tray/s into oven. Cook for approx. 15–20 minutes or until cooked through.
12 Remove from oven and serve, allowing one breast per portion.

**Note**

Roast capsicum by removing stalk and seeds, quartering and roughly chopping. Place capsicum into a deep sided roasting tray tossed with a little olive oil and place into a pre-heated moderate oven (150–180°C) and roast, turning regularly, for approx. 30–45 minutes or until the flesh is soft, and the skin is easily removed.

# Chicken, leek and fresh Parmesan risotto

**G**arnish: finely diced tomato concassé mixed with freshly chopped parsley.

**Ingredients**

| | 25 | 50 | 100 |
|---|---|---|---|
| olive oil/vegetable oil | as required | | |
| garlic, cloves, finely chopped | 4 | 8 | 16 |
| onions, Spanish, finely chopped | 1 kg | 2 kg | 4 kg |
| leeks, trimmed, washed, finely sliced | 2 kg | 4 kg | 8 kg |
| butter | 250 g | 500 g | 1 kg |
| rice, Arborio/long grain | 1.5 kg | 3 kg | 6 kg |
| stock, chicken, warm | 4 L | 8 L | 16 L |
| parsley, fresh, finely chopped | 50 g | 100 g | 200 g |
| chicken, meat, free from skin and bone, cooked, shredded | 1.5 kg | 3 kg | 6 kg |
| Parmesan cheese, shaved or grated | 100 g | 200 g | 400 g |
| salt and freshly milled black pepper | to taste | | |

**Method**

1 Heat a little oil in a saucepan over a moderate heat. Add garlic and onions and cook until onions are soft.
2 Add leeks and cook for a further two minutes.
3 Reduce heat and add butter. When butter has melted, add rice and stir continually, ensuring all rice is completely coated with butter.
4 Slowly add warmed stock until all has been incorporated, stirring continually.
5 Place a tight fitting lid over saucepan. Cook slowly, stirring regularly until all stock has been absorbed and the rice is tender.
6 Mix in parsley, chicken and Parmesan. Cook for a further five minutes (stir regularly to ensure rice does not stick and burn to the bottom of the pan).
7 Season to taste. Remove from heat and serve.

**Note**

**Risotto** is a classic Italian dish, usually made with Arborio rice. It is cooked slowly to allow the rice to absorb the many flavours and ingredients that can be used. Arborio rice, with its white core, stays firm while the rest of the grain leaks starch into the liquid, producing a velvety sauce. However, long grained rice can be substituted.

# Braised Malaysian curried chicken pieces

Garnish: roasted sliced almonds.

**Ingredients**

| | 25 | 50 | 100 |
|---|---|---|---|
| chickens, whole, no. 12 | 7 | 13 | 25 |
| stock, chicken | 3 L | 6 L | 12 L |
| lime leaves | 6 | 10 | 18 |
| curry paste (Malaysian-style) | 100 g | 200 g | 400 g |
| lemon, juice and zest | 1 | 2 | 4 |
| chillies, seeded, finely chopped | 3 | 5 | 7 |
| sugar, white | 150 g | 300 g | 600 g |
| coconut cream, 375 mL tin | 2 | 4 | 6 |
| cornflour | 50 g | 100 g | 200 g |
| red capsicums, roasted, finely chopped | 6 | 12 | 24 |
| salt | to taste | | |

**Method**

1 Pre-heat oven to moderate (150–180°C).
2 Cut chickens into eight pieces, retaining carcasses for stock. Place chicken pieces into lightly oiled roasting tray/s.
3 Place stock into a pan and over a moderate heat. Bring to the boil, reduce heat and simmer gently.
4 Break lime leaves into stock and simmer approx. 5 minutes.
5 Add curry paste. Whisking thoroughly, add lemon juice and zest, chillies, sugar and coconut cream and return to a gentle simmer.

continued

6 Mix cornflour with a little cold water to a smooth paste. Add to chicken stock mixture, whisking thoroughly. Allow sauce to thicken and cook for a further 2 minutes. Add roughly chopped roasted red capsicum. Season to taste and remove from heat.

7 Pour sufficient sauce over chicken pieces to cover. Seal trays with aluminium foil and place into oven and cook for approx. 1 hour or until chicken is cooked through.

8 Remove chicken from oven and serve two pieces per portion with a little of the sauce on a bed of steamed jasmine rice.

**Notes**

Roast capsicum by removing stalk and seeds, quartering and roughly chopping. Place capsicum into a deep sided roasting tray tossed with a little olive oil and place into a pre-heated moderate oven (150–180°C) and roast, turning regularly, for approx. 30–45 minutes or until the flesh is soft, and the skin is easily removed.

**Jasmine rice** is a long grained rice originally grown and used in Asian cuisine. It has a distinctive fragrant aroma and flavour; also known as Thai rice.

 **Health tip**

Unsuitable for low fat and cholesterol-lowering diets.

# Thai chicken green curry

**G**arnish: finely chopped fresh coriander and red basil.

**Ingredients**

| | | 25 | 50 | 100 |
|---|---|---|---|---|
| **chicken**, thigh fillets | | 5 kg | 10 kg | 20 kg |
| **Thai curry paste**, green | | 100 g | 200 g | 400 g |
| **coconut cream**, tinned | | 1 L | 2 L | 4 L |
| **cream**, single | | 250 mL | 500 mL | 1 L |
| **chicken booster**, powdered stock base | | to taste | | |

**Method**

1 Pre-heat oven to moderate (150–180°C).

2 Cut each thigh fillet into two even sized pieces.

3 Cook green curry paste in a saucepan over a moderate heat for one minute, stirring continually.

4 Immediately add coconut cream and cream. Whisk thoroughly until a smooth consistency is reached. Season to taste with chicken booster and remove from heat.

5 Heat a large sauté pan or grill plate and brush with a little oil.

6 Gradually add chicken pieces and seal and colour on all sides.

7 Remove chicken pieces when sealed and place into deep sided roasting or serving tray/s.

8 Pour over sufficient sauce to cover chicken pieces and cover tray/s with aluminium foil.

9 Place tray/s into oven. Cook for approx. $1^1/_2$ hours or until chicken is cooked through and tender.

10 Serve chicken with its sauce and steamed jasmine rice.

**Notes**

**Green curry paste** is available from most suppliers and can also be substituted for red. Use red curry paste if a slightly different style of curry is desired, in a Thai style.

Additional herbs such as fresh coriander, lemon grass, red basil and kaffir lime leaves can also be added during the cooking process to add extra flavour. This is optional and is not essential to the recipe.

**Health tip**    Unsuitable for low fat and cholesterol-lowering diets.

# CHAPTER 10

# CUTS OF PORK AND APPROXIMATE WEIGHTS OF THE UNPREPARED PRIMARY CUT

## Approximate cooking times for pork
50 minutes per kilo (2 lb) plus an extra 50 minutes.

### Pork Cuts

| Leg (Cuissot) and Rump | French Term | Uses | Approx. Weights |
| --- | --- | --- | --- |
| hock | – | braising | 650 g |
| leg | – | roasting, sauté, braising | 7.120 kg |
| topside | – | roasting, sauté, braising | 1.10 kg |
| round | – | roasting, sauté, braising | 780 g |
| rump | – | roasting, sauté, braising | 840 g |
| silverside | – | roasting, braising | 1.40 kg |
| butt fillet | – | grilling, sauté | 150 g |

| Full Loin (Longe) and Spring | French Term | Uses | Approx. Weights |
| --- | --- | --- | --- |
| midloin | carré | sauté, roasting, grilling, braising | 2.160 kg |
| fillet | filet | sauté, roasting, grilling, braising | 260 g |
| spring/belly | poitrine | roasting, braising, poaching, frying | 2.740 kg |
| spare ribs | basse-côte/ echine | roasting, braising, grilling, frying | 450 g |

| Forequarter | French Term | Uses | Approx. Weights |
| --- | --- | --- | --- |
| hock | – | braising | 580 g |
| foreloin (boneless, trussed) | – | roasting, sauté, braising | 1.670 kg |
| shoulder (boneless) | épaule | roasting, braising, steaming | 1.850 kg |
| breast | – | roasting, sauté, braising | 2.200 kg |
| spare ribs | – | roasting, braising, grilling, frying | 610 g |

 **Note** No blood should be present in the meat.

# PORK RECIPES
## Char-grilled pork ribs with a tangy plum sauce

Garnish: finely chopped fresh parsley.

Ingredients

| | 25 | 50 | 100 |
|---|---|---|---|
| **jam**, plum | 2 kg | 4 kg | 8 kg |
| **water**, boiling | as required | | |
| **cayenne pepper** | to taste | | |
| **pork**, spare ribs | 7.5 kg | 15 kg | 30 kg |

Method

1 Place plum jam into a mixing bowl and whisk in small amounts of boiling water until thick enough to be brushed onto ribs. Add small amounts of cayenne pepper until it gives a slightly hot taste.

2 Liberally brush ribs on all sides and place into the refrigerator for a minimum of 2 hours (overnight is preferable).

3 Pre-heat a char-grill or flat grill plate, brushed with a little oil, and cook ribs for approx. 2 minutes on either side. Pre-heat oven to moderate (150–180°C).

4 Lay single rows of char-grilled ribs into roasting trays, brush with any remaining marinade. Place into oven and cook for approx. 20–30 minutes or until ribs are cooked through. Care should be taken not to burn marinade; adjust oven accordingly. If any marinade remains, baste ribs every 10 minutes.

5 Serve immediately.

♥ Health tip To make suitable for low fat diets, remove visible fat from pork ribs.

## Creamy pork, apple and walnut casserole

Garnish: chives cut at 2 cm intervals.

Ingredients

| | 25 | 50 | 100 |
|---|---|---|---|
| **olive oil/vegetable oil** | as required | | |
| **onions**, white, peeled, dice | 500 g | 1 kg | 2 kg |
| **sage**, dried | 15 g | 30 g | 60 g |
| **pork**, leg, trimmed, diced | 4.5 kg | 9 kg | 18 kg |
| **flour**, plain | 150 g | 300 g | 600 g |
| **stock**, chicken, warm | 2 L | 4 L | 8 L |
| **apple juice** | 1 L | 2 L | 4 L |
| **walnuts**, roughly chopped | 250 g | 500 g | 1 kg |
| **apples**, red, cored, 2 cm dice | 1 kg | 2 kg | 4 kg |
| **sour cream** | 150 g | 300 g | 600 g |
| **cream**, single | 200 mL | 400 mL | 800 mL |
| **salt and freshly milled black pepper** | to taste | | |

continued

| Method | 1 Heat a little oil over a moderate heat in a pan. |
|---|---|
| | 2 Add onions and sage and cook without colour until onions are soft. |
| | 3 Add pork and cook until sealed and lightly browned. |
| | 4 Add flour. Mix well and cook for approx. 2–3 minutes. |
| | 5 Add warmed chicken stock and apple juice slowly. Mix in walnuts. |
| | 6 Gently bring sauce to a simmer until sauce reduces and starts to thicken: approx. 30–45 minutes. |
| | 7 When sauce is of the consistency to thickly coat the back of a spoon, add apples, mixing gently. |
| | 8 Cook for a few minutes and correct the consistency, if required, by the addition of small amounts of warmed stock. |
| | 9 Add cream and sour cream. Re-heat. Season to taste, and serve on a bed of steamed rice or noodles. |

 **Health tip**  To make suitable for low fat diets, omit the cream and sour cream.

# Sweet-and-sour pork chops

Garnish: crisp stir-fried julienne of seasonal vegetables.

| Ingredients | | 25 | 50 | 100 |
|---|---|---|---|---|
| olive oil/vegetable oil | | as required | | |
| onions, finely chopped | | 500 g | 1 kg | 2 kg |
| garlic, cloves, finely chopped | | 5 | 10 | 20 |
| ginger, fresh, peeled, minced | | 10 g | 20 g | 40 g |
| vinegar, white | | 250 mL | 500 mL | 1 L |
| soya sauce | | 50 mL | 100 mL | 200 mL |
| pineapples, rings and juice, A10 tin | | 1 | 2 | 4 |
| tomato purée | | 200 g | 400 g | 800 g |
| sugar, white | | to taste | | |
| cornflour | | as required | | |
| water | | as required | | |
| pork chops, large, trimmed of excess fat | | 25 | 50 | 100 |

| Method | 1 Put a little oil in a saucepan over a moderate heat. Gently fry onions, garlic and ginger until onions are softened. |
|---|---|
| | 2 Add vinegar, soya sauce, pineapple rings that have been finely minced, pineapple juice, tomato purée and sugar. Whisk together thoroughly. |
| | 3 Simmer gently for approx. 10 minutes. |
| | 4 Mix small amounts of cornflour with small amounts of water to a smooth paste. Whisk into sauce until the sauce lightly coats the back of the spoon. |
| | 5 Remove from heat and place to one side. |
| | 6 Heat a grill plate or char-grill and brush with a little oil. |

7 Cook pork chops for approx. 3–4 minutes on either side or until cooked through.
8 Serve one pork chop per portion with a little of the hot sweet-and-sour sauce on a bed of stir-fried vegetables of your choice.

 **Health tip**   To make suitable for low fat diets, remove visible fat from pork chops prior to cooking.

# Spanish-style braised leg of pork

Garnish: roughly chopped continental parsley leaves.

| Ingredients | | 25 | 50 | 100 |
|---|---|---|---|---|
| olive oil/vegetable oil | | as required | | |
| onions, Spanish, peeled, finely sliced | | 500 g | 1 kg | 2 kg |
| garlic cloves, peeled, finely chopped | | 4 | 8 | 16 |
| lemon thyme, leaves, roughly chopped | | 10 g | 20 g | 40 g |
| carrots, peeled, finely diced | | 500 g | 1 kg | 2 kg |
| celery, finely diced | | 500 g | 1 kg | 2 kg |
| pork, leg/shoulder, 2 cm dice | | 4.5 kg | 9 kg | 18 kg |
| tomatoes, crushed, A10 tin | | 1 | 2 | 4 |
| stock, chicken | | 250 mL | 500 mL | 1 L |
| Kalamata olives, stoned, roughly chopped | | 100 g | 200 g | 400 g |
| red capsicums, roasted, medium dice | | 3 | 6 | 12 |
| bay-leaves | | 2 | 4 | 8 |
| salt and freshly milled black pepper | | to taste | | |

**Method**
1 Put a little oil in a saucepan over a moderate heat.
2 Add onions, garlic and thyme and cook without colour until onions are soft.
3 Add carrots, celery and pork and cook gently for approx. 5–10 minutes.
4 Add crushed tomato, chicken stock, olives, capsicum and bay-leaves. Mix well. Simmer gently for 45–60 minutes stirring occasionally until the pork is cooked through and the sauce has reduced and thickened.
5 Season to taste and serve.

**Note**   Roast capsicum by removing stalk and seeds, quartering and roughly chopping. Place capsicum into a deep sided roasting tray tossed with a little olive oil and place into a pre-heated moderate oven (150–180°C) and roast, turning regularly, for approx. 30–45 minutes or until the flesh is soft, and the skin is easily removed.

 **Health tip**   Suitable for low fat diets.

# Breaded pork schnitzel steaks with a turmeric and mustard sauce

Garnish: chopped parsley mixed with finely diced red capsicum.

Ingredients

| | | 25 | 50 | 100 |
|---|---|---|---|---|
| flour, plain | | as required | | |
| paprika | | 25 g | 50 g | 100 g |
| eggs | | 10 | 20 | 40 |
| milk | | 300 mL | 600 mL | 1.2 L |
| breadcrumbs | | as required | | |
| pork schnitzel steaks, approx. 150 g each | | 25 | 50 | 100 |
| parsley, fresh, finely chopped | | 15 g | 30 g | 60 g |
| | | | | |
| **SAUCE:** | | | | |
| butter | | 150 g | 300 g | 600 g |
| flour, plain | | 150 g | 300 g | 600 g |
| milk | | 2 L | 4 L | 8 L |
| If a hot mustard is used such as **English mustard**, use approx. | | 100 g | 200 g | 400 g |
| If a mild mustard is used such as **grain mustard**, use approx. | | 150 g | 300 g | 600 g |
| turmeric | | as required to colour sauce | | |

Method

1 Place flour and paprika into a bowl and mix well. Place the eggs, which have been beaten together with the milk, into a second bowl and place the breadcrumbs into a third bowl.

2 Dredge all pork schnitzel steaks through flour, egg mixture and breadcrumbs. Shake off any excess breadcrumbs. Layer schnitzels onto tray/s between sheets of greaseproof paper and refrigerate until required.

3 Melt the butter in a saucepan over a moderate heat.

4 Add the flour and mix with butter using a wooden spoon.

5 Reduce heat and cook gently for approx. 2–3 minutes without colouring.

6 Gently warm the milk in a separate saucepan.

7 Slowly incorporate the milk in small amounts making sure each addition has mixed with the roux smoothly.

8 Reduce heat and cook out gently for approx. 10 minutes stirring regularly. Pre-heat deep fryer to 160–170°C.

9 Thoroughly whisk mustard into sauce in small amounts and cook for a further 1–2 minutes.

10 Add small amounts of turmeric until a deep yellow colour is reached.

11 Remove sauce from heat and keep warm. Pre-heat oven to moderate (150–180°C).

12 Place schnitzels into fat in small batches and cook to a light golden brown. Remove from oil and drain any excess fat.
13 Place schnitzels onto roasting tray/s. Place into oven and cook for approx. 3–5 minutes or until cooked through.
14 Serve one schnitzel per portion coated with a little of the sauce.

 **Note**  It is advisable with this sauce that the mustard be added in small amounts and tasted frequently. This saves waste, and the time of preparing a new sauce if too much mustard is added by accident.

 **Health tip**  Unsuitable for low fat diets.

# Garlic studded roasted shoulder of pork with cinnamon baked apple

Garnish: small sprigs of fresh thyme.

**Ingredients**

| | 25 | 50 | 100 |
|---|---|---|---|
| **pork**, shoulder/s, boned and rolled | 6 kg | 12 kg | 24 kg |
| **garlic**, cloves, sliced and quartered lengthways | 6 | 10 | 14 |
| **olive oil** | as required | | |
| **salt and freshly milled black pepper** | to taste | | |
| **apples**, cored, quartered | 7 | 13 | 25 |
| **cinnamon** | as required | | |

**Method**

1 Pre-heat oven to moderate (150–180°C).
2 Place joints onto lightly oiled roasting tray/s, brush with a little oil and season.
3 Using a small, narrow-bladed knife make small incisions at regular intervals. Insert a quarter of garlic into each incision.
4 Place pork into oven and cook for approx. $1^1/_2$–2 hours or until cooked through. Remove from oven and allow to stand 10–15 minutes.
5 Whilst the pork is cooking, place quartered apples onto a lightly greased roasting tray/s. Sprinkle with a little oil and lightly dust with cinnamon.
6 Place roasting tray/s into a pre-heated low oven (130–150°C) and cook apples until they become tender. Remove from oven and keep warm, covered with aluminium foil.
7 Serve sliced roasted pork with a piece of the pork crackling, one piece of baked apple and gravy.

continued

## Sage and onion gravy

Ingredients

| | 25 | 50 | 100 |
|---|---|---|---|
| butter | 150 g | 300 g | 600 g |
| sage, dried | 20 g | 40 g | 80 g |
| onions, finely sliced | 250 g | 500 g | 1 kg |
| flour, plain | 150 g | 300 g | 600 g |
| stock, beef, veal, chicken or vegetable | 2 L | 4 L | 8 L |
| parisienne essence | to colour as required | | |
| salt and freshly milled black pepper | to taste | | |

Method

1 Melt the butter in a saucepan over a moderate heat.
2 Add onions and sage and cook without colour until onions are tender.
3 Add the flour and thoroughly incorporate with butter using a wooden spoon.
4 Reduce heat. Cook gently until the roux turns brown in colour.
5 Gently warm the stock in a separate saucepan.
6 Slowly incorporate the stock in small amounts making sure each addition has mixed with the roux smoothly.
7 Whisk in parisienne essence until the required colour is achieved.
8 Reduce heat and cook out gently for approx. 10 minutes, stirring regularly.
9 Season to taste.
10 Remove from heat and serve.

Health tip  For low fat diets, do not serve the pork with crackling.

# Thick pork sausages filled with tomato, Spanish onion and Cheddar cheese

Garnish: a light dusting of paprika.

Ingredients

| | 25 | 50 | 100 |
|---|---|---|---|
| sausages, pork, thick, blanched | 50 | 100 | 200 |
| tomatoes, cored, finely diced | 600 g | 1.2 kg | 2.4 kg |
| onions, Spanish, finely diced | 600 g | 1.2 kg | 2.4 kg |
| parsley, finely chopped | 20 g | 40 g | 80 g |
| cheese, Cheddar, grated | 2 kg | 4 kg | 8 kg |

Method

1 Pre-heat oven to moderate (150–180°C).
2 Slit sausages halfway through lengthways and place onto baking tray/s one layer deep.
3 Mix tomato, onion, parsley and a little cheese together in a bowl.
4 Place a little of this mixture evenly into slits in the sausages.

5 Sprinkle remaining cheese over sausages and place tray/s into oven. Cook until sausages are heated through and lightly browned and cheese is melted and golden brown.

6 Remove trays from oven and serve two sausages per portion.

 **Health tip**   Unsuitable for low fat diets.

# Bacon, egg and spinach pie

**G**arnish: finely sliced chives.

| Ingredients | | | 25 | 50 | 100 |
|---|---|---|---|---|---|
|  | eggs | | 25 | 50 | 100 |
| | milk | | 2 L | 4 L | 8 L |
| | sour cream | | 500 g | 1 kg | 2 kg |
| | salt and freshly milled black pepper | | to taste | | |
| | spinach, stalks removed, blanched, refreshed, drained, finely shredded, squeezed of any excess moisture | | 4 kg | 8 kg | 16 kg |
| | bacon, finely diced, cooked | | 500 g | 1 kg | 2 kg |
| | parsley, chopped | | 20 g | 40 g | 80 g |
| | butter, melted | | as required | | |
| | pastry, filo | | as required, depending on size of filo pastry sheets used | | |

**Method**

1 Pre-heat oven to moderate (150–180°C).

2 In a mixing bowl whisk eggs, milk and sour cream together. Season to taste.

3 Lightly brush serving tray/s with melted butter and line the bottom and sides with sheets of filo pastry. Make sure each piece overlaps by at least 3 cm.

4 Lightly brush the top of the filo pastry with melted butter; repeat this process until filo pastry is four layers thick.

5 In another mixing bowl, mix spinach, bacon and parsley. Pour this mixture evenly into the bottom of the serving tray/s.

6 Pour egg mixture into tray/s keeping mixture approx. 2 cm from the rim of the tray.

7 Carefully place tray/s into oven and cook gently until egg mix is firm to the touch. Remove from the oven.

8 Line the top of the egg mix with a layer of filo pastry making sure each piece overlaps by at least 3 cm. Lightly brush the pastry with melted butter. Repeat this process until filo pastry is four layers thick.

9 Return tray/s to oven and cook until filo pastry turns golden brown.

10 Remove from oven and cool for approx. 4–5 minutes.

11 Pre-portion and serve.

**Health tip**   Unsuitable for low fat diets.

# CHAPTER 11

# VEGETARIAN AND VEGAN

This chapter includes a selection of vegetarian recipes, some of which are suitable for vegan diets. These recipes are marked accordingly. For further information on vegetarian and vegan diets, refer to the section on specialised dietary requirements in Chapter 17.

The chapter on pasta dishes (4) also includes some vegetarian recipes. Also see the chapters on soups, entrées and potatoes (2, 3 and 13).

# Green Thai-style vegetable curry with steamed jasmine rice

This dish is suitable for a vegan diet.
Garnish: fresh coriander sprigs or finely chopped purple basil.

**Ingredients**

| | 25 | 50 | 100 |
|---|---|---|---|
| **potatoes**, peeled, 2 cm dice | 2 kg | 4 kg | 8 kg |
| **carrots**, peeled, halved lengthways, sliced at 45° | 500 g | 1 kg | 2 kg |
| **celery**, washed, trimmed, sliced at 45° | 500 g | 1 kg | 2 kg |
| **cauliflower**, small florets | 500 g | 1 kg | 2 kg |
| **beans**, green, topped, tailed, 3 cm pieces | 500 g | 1 kg | 2 kg |
| **garden peas** | 250 g | 500 g | 1 kg |
| **broccoli**, small florets | 500 g | 1 kg | 2 kg |
| **capsicums**, red and yellow, 3 cm strips | 250 g | 500 g | 1 kg |
| **beansprouts** | 500 g | 1 kg | 2 kg |

N.B. The required weights for any combination of the above vegetables are:

| | 25 | 50 | 100 |
|---|---|---|---|
| | 5.5 kg | 11 kg | 22 kg |

## GREEN CURRY SAUCE:

| | 25 | 50 | 100 |
|---|---|---|---|
| **olive oil/vegetable oil** | as required | | |
| **onions**, finely chopped | 350 g | 700 g | 1.4 kg |
| **Thai curry paste**, green | 100 g | 200 g | 400 g |
| **coconut cream** | 1.5 L | 3 L | 6 L |
| **stock**, vegetable (see Chapter 1, Stocks and Sauces) | 500 mL | 1 L | 2 L |
| **coriander leaves**, roughly chopped | 20 g | 40 g | 80 g |
| **soya sauce** | to taste | | |
| **cornflour** | 100 g | 200 g | 400 g |
| **salt and freshly milled black pepper** | to taste | | |

**Method**

1 Boil or steam potatoes until just cooked. Refresh in cold water and drain well.
2 Bring a pan half filled with water to the boil.
3 Keeping spider close by place the carrots into the boiling water and cook for 1 minute. Add celery and cauliflower and cook for a further 1 minute. Add other vegetables, with the exception of the beansprouts and cook for a further 30 seconds. Remove and refresh under cold running water and drain well.
4 Place a saucepan over a moderate heat and add a little oil.
5 Add onions and cook without colour until soft.
6 Mix in green Thai curry paste and cook for a further 1 minute.
7 Whisk in coconut cream, vegetable stock and coriander leaves.

8  Add soya sauce to taste.
9  Simmer over a low heat for approx. 5 minutes.
10 Add all vegetables and mix in thoroughly.
11 Cover with a tight fitting lid and cook for approx. 5 minutes, or until vegetables are heated through, stirring occasionally.
12 Mix cornflour with a little cold water. Add to the curried vegetables in small amounts mixing constantly until of a consistency that will coat the back of a spoon.
13 Mix in beansprouts.
14 Remove from heat. Season to taste and serve on a bed of steamed jasmine rice.

 **Notes**

Any other variety of vegetables, fresh or frozen, can be used for this dish provided the recommended weight remains the same.

**Green curry paste** is available from most suppliers and can also be substituted for red curry paste if a slightly different style of Thai curry is desired.

Additional herbs such as fresh coriander, lemon grass, purple basil and kaffir lime leaves can also be added during the cooking process to add extra flavour; this is optional and not essential to the recipe.

 **Health tip**    High in fibre.

# Ratatouille-style vegetable and mushroom casserole

This dish is suitable for a vegan diet if cheese is omitted.
Garnish: fresh sprigs of basil.

Ingredients

| | 25 | 50 | 100 |
|---|---|---|---|
| olive oil/vegetable oil | as required | | |
| **onions**, Spanish, large dice | 1 kg | 2 kg | 4 kg |
| **garlic**, cloves, peeled, finely chopped | 4 | 8 | 16 |
| **mushrooms**, button, washed, quartered | 1 kg | 2 kg | 4 kg |
| **basil**, leaves, fresh, finely chopped | 25 g | 50 g | 100 g |
| **marjoram**, dried | 25 g | 50 g | 100 g |
| **zucchini**, top, tail, 2 cm dice | 2 kg | 4 kg | 8 kg |
| **eggplants**, top, tail, 2 cm dice | 1 kg | 2 kg | 4 kg |
| **tomatoes**, cores removed, 2 cm dice | 1 kg | 2 kg | 4 kg |
| **tomatoes**, crushed, A10 tin | 1 | 2 | 4 |
| **bay-leaves**, dried | 2 | 4 | 8 |
| **sugar**, white | to taste | | |
| **salt and freshly milled black pepper** | to taste | | |
| **Cheddar cheese**, grated (optional) | 1 kg | 2 kg | 4 kg |
| **breadcrumbs** | 250 g | 500 g | 1 kg |
| **parsley**, finely chopped | 25 g | 50 g | 100 g |

continued

1 Pre-heat oven to moderate (150–180°C).
2 Heat a little oil in a pan over a moderate heat.
3 Add onions and garlic and cook without colour until onions are soft.
4 Mix in mushrooms, basil and marjoram. Cook for approx. 4 minutes.
5 Add zucchini, eggplant and diced tomato. Mix well.
6 Allow vegetables to sweat until softened, stirring occasionally.
7 Add crushed tomatoes and bay-leaves and mix well.
8 Place a tight fitting lid onto pan. Cook over a gentle heat for approx. 15–20 minutes or until vegetables are tender, stirring occasionally.
9 Add sugar, salt and freshly milled black pepper to taste to the mixture.
10 Remove from heat and place mixture into serving tray/s.
11 Combine cheese, breadcrumbs and parsley in a mixing bowl. Sprinkle evenly over vegetable mixture.
12 Place trays into oven and cook until cheese turns light golden brown.
13 Remove from oven and serve.

**♥ Health tip** Also suitable for low fat, cholesterol-lowering and diabetic diets. Reduce the fat content by using low fat cheese.

# Eggplant Parmigiana

Garnish: two whole chives.

Ingredients

| | 25 | 50 | 100 |
|---|---|---|---|
| Parmigiana sauce | see following recipe | | |
| flour, plain, lightly seasoned with paprika, salt and black pepper | as required | | |
| eggs | 10 | 20 | 40 |
| milk | 300 mL | 600 mL | 1.2 L |
| breadcrumbs | as required | | |
| eggplants, remove stalks, cut lengthways into 2 cm thick steaks | 25 | 50 | 100 |
| Cheddar cheese, grated | 1 kg | 2 kg | 4 kg |
| Parmesan cheese, grated | 50 g | 100 g | 200 g |
| parsley, finely chopped | 25 g | 50 g | 100 g |

Method

1 Pre-heat deep fryer to 165–170°C.
2 Prepare Parmigiana sauce.
3 Place flour into a bowl and the eggs, which have been beaten together with the milk, into a second bowl. Place the breadcrumbs into a third bowl.
4 Carefully dredge all eggplant steaks through flour, egg mixture and breadcrumbs. Gently shake off any excess breadcrumbs.
5 Place eggplant steaks gently into fat in small batches and cook to a light golden brown.

6 Remove eggplant from oil and drain any excess fat. Pre-heat oven to moderate (150–180°C).
7 Place eggplant steaks onto roasting tray/s and spoon over a little Parmigiana sauce. Top with a little Cheddar and Parmesan cheese.
8 Place trays into oven and cook until cheese has melted.
9 Remove from oven. Sprinkle each with a little parsley and serve one eggplant steak per portion.

## Parmigiana sauce

| Ingredients | | | 25 | 50 | 100 |
|---|---|---|---|---|---|
|  | olive oil/vegetable oil | | as required | | |
| | garlic, cloves, peeled, finely chopped | | 3 | 6 | 12 |
| | onions, finely sliced | | 500 g | 1 kg | 2 kg |
| | tomatoes, crushed, A10 tin | | 1 | 2 | 4 |
| | basil, fresh, finely chopped | | 40 g | 80 g | 160 g |
| | salt and freshly milled black pepper | | to taste | | |
| | vinegar, balsamic | | to taste | | |

Method
1 Heat a little oil in a saucepan over a moderate heat.
2 Add garlic and onions and cook without colour until onions are soft.
3 Add tomatoes and basil and mix well.
4 Simmer for approx. 30 minutes over a low heat or until sauce has thickened slightly. Season with salt, pepper and vinegar.
5 Remove from heat and use as required.

Health tip    Unsuitable for a low fat diet.

## Home-made Mexican chilli bean burgers

Garnish: refer to note.

| Ingredients | | | 25 | 50 | 100 |
|---|---|---|---|---|---|
|  | olive oil/vegetable oil | | as required | | |
| | garlic, cloves, peeled, finely chopped | | 4 | 8 | 16 |
| | onions, finely chopped | | 1.5 kg | 3 kg | 6 kg |
| | 3 bean mix, A10 tin, drained, finely chopped | | 2 | 4 | 8 |
| | potatoes, peeled, cooked | | 2 kg | 4 kg | 8 kg |
| | sweet chilli sauce | | to taste | | |
| | tomato sauce | | 150 mL | 300 mL | 600 mL |
| | eggs | | 8 | 16 | 32 |
| | salt and freshly milled black pepper | | to taste | | |
| | breadcrumbs | | as required | | |
| | burger buns | | 25 | 50 | 100 |

continued

1 Pre-heat oven to moderate (150–180°C).
2 Heat a little oil in a pan over a moderate heat. Add garlic and onions and cook without colour until onions are soft. Remove from heat.
3 In a large mixing bowl of a commercial mixer, place onion and garlic mix, bean mixture, cooked potatoes, sweet chilli sauce, tomato sauce, eggs and salt and pepper. Mix until beans are mashed and are thoroughly combined with other ingredients.
4 Gradually add breadcrumbs whilst mixing until a firm texture is achieved that can be moulded into patties.
5 Turn mixture out onto a lightly floured work bench and shape mixture into patties (approx. 200 g each, allowing one per portion).
6 Place patties onto tray/s one layer deep and place a piece of greaseproof paper between each layer and refrigerate until required.
7 Heat a sauté pan or grill plate lightly brushed with a little oil. Sear patties on each side until golden brown.
8 Place seared patties onto lightly greased roasting tray/s and place into oven. Cook for approx. 10–15 minutes or until heated through.
9 Serve one patty per portion on a toasted sesame seed bun.

 **Note** This is only a basic recipe and other ingredients such as: char-grilled pineapple rings, roasted red capsicum, guacamole, Swiss cheese, grilled tomato slices or a sautéed onion and mushroom compote can be used as a topping. The only limitation besides your budget is your imagination.

 **Health tip** An excellent meal for everyone, not only vegetarians. Very high in fibre.

# Vegetable moussaka

This dish is suitable for a vegan diet if cheese is omitted and white sauce is produced using margarine (with a vegetable oil base) and soya milk.
Garnish: freshly chopped parsley.

| Ingredients | | 25 | 50 | 100 |
|---|---|---|---|---|
| white sauce/béchamel (see following recipe) | | 4 L | 8 L | 16 L |
| vegetable mince (see note) | | 5 kg | 10 kg | 20 kg |
| olive oil/vegetable oil | | as required | | |
| garlic, cloves, peeled, finely chopped | | 4 | 8 | 16 |
| onions, finely sliced | | 500 g | 1 kg | 2 kg |
| tomato paste | | 300 g | 600 g | 1.2 kg |
| tomatoes, crushed, A10 tin | | 1/2 | 1 | 2 |
| stock, vegetable | | 1 L | 2 L | 4 L |
| salt and freshly milled black pepper | | to taste | | |
| eggplants, topped, tailed, thin slices | | 8 | 16 | 32 |
| Cheddar cheese, grated (optional) | | 1 kg | 2 kg | 4 kg |

**Method**

1 Pre-heat oven to moderate (150–180°C).
2 Heat a little oil in a saucepan over a moderate heat.
3 Add garlic and onions and cook without colour until soft.
4 Add vegetable mince and mix well with garlic and onion. Stirring occasionally, cook until hot.
5 Mix in tomato paste, tomatoes and stock. Bring sauce to a boil and then simmer gently. Reduce until it has thickened slightly.
6 Season to taste and remove from heat.
7 Place a layer of eggplant evenly into the bottom of serving tray/s. Lightly season and cover eggplant with a layer of vegetable mince.
8 Repeat process until 3.5 cm from the top of the tray.
9 Evenly cover with a layer of white sauce/béchamel.
10 Generously cover white sauce with grated Cheddar cheese and wipe edges of any spills.
11 Place tray/s into oven and cook for approx. 45 minutes to one hour or until moussaka is heated through, eggplant tender and the cheese golden brown.
12 Remove from oven, pre-portion and serve.

**Notes**

This famous dish comes from Greece and is also popular throughout the Near East. It is traditionally made with eggplant and minced lamb or beef but now has endless variations, such as this recipe.

To prepare vegetable mince, any variation of cooked vegetables can be used. They are prepared by finely chopping or blending in a food processor to a mince-like texture. Ideally vegetable mince should be made using equal quantities of four to six vegetables.

# White sauce (béchamel)

**Ingredients**

| | 25 | 50 | 100 |
|---|---|---|---|
| butter/polyunsaturated margarine | 300 g | 600 g | 1.2 kg |
| flour | 300 g | 600 g | 1.2 kg |
| milk/soya milk | 4 L | 8 L | 16 L |
| salt and white pepper | to taste | | |

**Method**

1 Melt the butter/margarine in a saucepan over a moderate heat.
2 Add the flour and mix well with butter using a wooden spoon.
3 Reduce heat. Cook for approx. 2–3 minutes without colouring.
4 Gently warm the milk/soya milk in a separate saucepan.
5 Slowly incorporate the milk/soya milk in small amounts, making sure each addition has mixed with the roux smoothly.
6 Reduce heat and cook out gently for approx. 10 minutes, stirring regularly.
7 Remove from heat, strain and use as required.

**Note**

When making a white sauce/béchamel it is always advisable when possible to use butter over margarine as it will give a slightly richer flavour. Nonetheless margarine will give a good finished result and is a non-animal-based product.

continued

To reduce fat content, use low fat milk and low fat cheese. This is then suitable for low fat, cholesterol-lowering and diabetic diets.

# Italian-style zucchini and Parmesan fritters with a fresh tomato and chilli salsa

Garnish: freshly chopped basil leaves.

**Ingredients**

| | 25 | 50 | 100 |
|---|---|---|---|
| **zucchini**, top and tail, finely grated | 6 kg | 12 kg | 24 kg |
| **Parmesan cheese**, finely grated | 150 g | 300 g | 600 g |
| **lemons**, zest | 2 | 4 | 8 |
| **eggs** | 12 | 24 | 48 |
| **salt and freshly milled black pepper** | to taste | | |
| **flour**, self-raising | as required | | |
| **olive oil/vegetable oil** | as required | | |
| **tomato and chilli salsa** | see following recipe | | |

**Method**

1 Place zucchini, Parmesan, lemon zest and eggs into a commercial mixing bowl. Mix well using a paddle attachment. Season to taste.
2 Gradually add flour until a firm but moist texture is achieved.
3 Heat a little oil in a large sauté pan or on a flat grill plate. Using a ladle place mixture onto sauté pan or grill plate: approx. 120 g per patty.
4 Gently fry until golden brown on both sides. Remove from heat. Repeat process until all mixture is used.
5 Serve, allowing two fritters per portion with fresh tomato and chilli salsa.

## Fresh tomato and chilli salsa

**Ingredients**

| | 25 | 50 | 100 |
|---|---|---|---|
| **tomatoes** | 13 | 25 | 50 |
| **chillies**, red, small | 4 | 8 | 6 |
| **onions**, Spanish, finely diced | 3 | 6 | 12 |
| **garlic**, cloves, peeled, finely diced | 2 | 4 | 8 |
| **olive oil** | 50 mL | 100 mL | 200 mL |
| **lemons/limes**, juice | 2 | 4 | 8 |
| **salt and freshly milled black pepper** | to taste | | |

1 Score bottoms of tomatoes and place into a pan of boiling water for approx. 20 seconds or until skin separates from tomatoes.
2 Refresh tomatoes under cold running water. Remove skin and drain.
3 Core and quarter tomatoes, removing seeds, and then finely dice the flesh.
4 Top and tail chillies, remove seeds and finely dice the flesh. Mix with tomatoes in a bowl.
5 Add Spanish onions and garlic to tomatoes. Combine.
6 Add olive oil, lemon/lime juice. Season to taste and gently combine.
7 Cover with cling wrap and refrigerate for at least 2–3 hours before serving.

 **Note**   **Salsa** is the Mexican word for sauce. It applies to cooked or uncooked mixtures classically made up of tomatoes, chillies and onions and can be used as an accompaniment to a wide variety of dishes.

# Stir-fried tofu with bok choy, button mushrooms and cashew nuts

This dish is suitable for a vegan diet.
Garnish: finely shredded red capsicum.

Ingredients

| | | 25 | 50 | 100 |
|---|---|---|---|---|
| tofu, 2 cm dice | | 4 kg | 8 kg | 16 kg |
| bok choy | | 3.5 kg | 7 kg | 14 kg |
| oil, sesame | | as required | | |
| ginger, peeled, minced | | 20 g | 40 g | 80 g |
| garlic, cloves, chopped | | 4 | 8 | 16 |
| onions, sliced | | 500 g | 1 kg | 2 kg |
| mushrooms, button, quartered | | 1 kg | 2 kg | 4 kg |
| cashews | | 500 g | 1 kg | 2 kg |
| honey | | 100 mL | 200 mL | 400 mL |
| oyster sauce | | 100 mL | 200 mL | 400 mL |
| soya sauce | | 50 ml | 100 mL | 200 mL |
| cornflour | | 75 g | 150 g | 300 g |
| salt and freshly milled black pepper | | to taste | | |
| beansprouts | | 500 g | 1 kg | 2 kg |

Method

1 Remove bottom 1 cm from whole bok choys and discard outer leaves. Separate all remaining leaves, tearing in half any that are very large, and blanch in a pan of boiling water for at least 10 seconds. Remove and refresh under cold running water and drain completely.
2 Heat a grill plate or brat pan until it is very hot. Add a liberal amount of sesame oil, then add ginger, garlic and onions and stir-fry until onions are softened.

continued

3 Add tofu, bok choy and mushrooms and stir-fry until all ingredients are heated through.

4 Add cashews, honey, oyster sauce and soya sauce and combine all ingredients.

5 Mix cornflour with a little cold water. Add to the stir-fried vegetables in small amounts, mixing constantly until all excess liquid thickens.

6 Season to taste. Add beansprouts and remove from heat.

7 Serve on a bed of steamed jasmine rice.

**Notes**

**Soya sauce** is an essential ingredient in Asian cuisine. It is produced by fermenting boiled soya beans and roasted wheat or barley.

**Bok choy** is a vegetable widely used in Asia that has become very popular in modern Australian cuisine. It has a crunchy stalk and dark green leaves: ideal raw, in salads, cooked as vegetables or as part of a stir-fry.

 **Health tip**
- A high protein meal for vegetarians.
- Also suitable for cholesterol-lowering diets.
- Tofu is a good source of antioxidants, which can help prevent cancer and heart disease.

# Puréed pumpkin and leek risotto

This dish is suitable for a vegan diet.
Garnish: finely diced tomato concassé mixed with freshly chopped parsley.

**Ingredients**

| | 25 | 50 | 100 |
|---|---|---|---|
| **olive oil/vegetable oil** | as required | | |
| **garlic**, cloves, finely chopped | 4 | 6 | 8 |
| **onions**, Spanish, finely chopped | 1 kg | 2 kg | 4 kg |
| **leeks**, trimmed, washed, finely sliced | 2 kg | 4 kg | 8 kg |
| **rice**, Arborio/long grain | 1.5 kg | 3 kg | 6 kg |
| **stock**, vegetable/water, warmed | 4 L | 8 L | 16 L |
| **pumpkin**, peeled, 2 cm dice | 2 kg | 4 kg | 8 kg |
| **parsley**, fresh, finely chopped | 50 g | 100 g | 200 g |
| **salt and freshly milled black pepper** | to taste | | |

**Method**

1 Heat a little oil in a saucepan over a moderate heat. Add garlic and Spanish onion and cook until onion is soft.

2 Add leeks and cook for a further 2–4 minutes.

3 Reduce heat and add rice. Stir continually, ensuring all rice is completely coated with oil; a little more oil can be added if necessary.

4 Slowly add warmed stock/water until all has been incorporated, stirring continuously.

5 Cook slowly, stirring regularly, until all stock has been absorbed and the rice is tender. Ensure the rice does not stick and burn to the bottom of the pan.

6 Whilst rice is cooking, steam diced pumpkin, then purée. Keep hot until required.
7 When rice is cooked and all liquid has been absorbed, mix in pumpkin and parsley thoroughly. Allow to re-heat.
8 Remove from heat. Season to taste and serve.

 **Note** Risotto is a classic Italian dish, usually made with Arborio rice. It is cooked slowly to allow the rice to absorb the many flavours and ingredients that can be used. Arborio rice, with its white core, stays firm while the rest of the grain leaks starch into the liquid, producing a velvety sauce. However, long grained rice can be substituted.

 **Health tip** Also suitable for low fat diets.

# Char-grilled marinated vegetable kebabs

This dish is suitable for a vegan diet.
Garnish: a sprig of continental parsley.

**Ingredients**

| | 25 | 50 | 100 |
|---|---|---|---|
| onions, Spanish, 3.5 cm dice | 1.5 kg | 3 kg | 6 kg |
| capsicums, red and green, 3.5 cm squares | 1 kg | 2 kg | 4 kg |
| mushrooms, button, halved | 1 kg | 2 kg | 4 kg |
| zucchini, 3.5 cm dice | 1 kg | 2 kg | 4 kg |
| tomatoes, 3.5 cm dice | 1 kg | 2 kg | 4 kg |
| olive oil/vegetable oil | as required | | |
| salt and freshly milled black pepper | to taste | | |
| **MARINADE:** | | | |
| olive oil | 200 mL | 400 mL | 800 mL |
| lemons, juice and zest | 3 | 6 | 12 |
| parsley, continental, leaves, finely chopped | 20 g | 40 g | 80 g |
| wine, white | 200 mL | 400 mL | 800 mL |

**Method**

1 Heat deep fryer oil to 170°C.
2 Place onions into fryer baskets and cook in the hot oil for 10 seconds agitating basket constantly. Remove from oil and drain thoroughly. Repeat process with capsicums and mushrooms and allow to cool.
3 Place alternately a piece of onion, capsicum, mushroom, zucchini and tomato onto pre-soaked bamboo skewers. Repeat process until skewers are full, pushing ingredients firmly together: two skewers per person, approx. 100 g each skewer.
4 Put all kebabs into lightly oiled roasting tray/s and place to one side.
5 Combine all marinade ingredients in a bowl.
6 Liberally brush each kebab on all sides with marinade; pour remaining marinade over kebabs.

continued

7 Cover trays with plastic wrap and refrigerate for 4–6 hours, turning kebabs every two hours.

8 Heat a sauté pan or grill plate and brush with a little oil. Pre-heat oven to moderate (150–180°C).

9 Place kebabs into sauté pan or onto grill plate and cook to a light brown on all sides.

10 Return kebabs to roasting tray/s and brush lightly with any remaining marinade. Season to taste and place tray/s into a pre-heated moderate oven for approx. 5–10 minutes or until vegetables are heated through. Serve.

**Note** Soak bamboo skewers in water before use for approx. 30 minutes to stop the skewers burning during cooking.

# Mexican-style vegetarian tacos

Garnish: sliced jalepeño peppers.

| Ingredients | | 25 | 50 | 100 |
|---|---|---|---|---|
| butter/margarine | | 100 g | 200 g | 400 g |
| onions, peeled, finely chopped | | 1 kg | 2 kg | 4 kg |
| garlic, cloves, peeled, finely chopped | | 4 | 8 | 16 |
| chillies, red, seeded, finely chopped | | 3 | 6 | 12 |
| flour, plain | | 100 g | 200 g | 400 g |
| tomatoes, crushed, A10 tin | | 1 | 2 | 4 |
| 3 bean mix, A10 tin, drained, roughly chopped | | 1 | 2 | 4 |
| salt and freshly milled black pepper | to taste | | | |
| taco shells | | 50 | 100 | 200 |
| guacamole (see following recipe) | | 1.5 kg | 3 kg | 6 kg |
| sour cream | | 1 kg | 2 kg | 4 kg |
| Cheddar cheese, grated | | 1 kg | 2 kg | 4 kg |

**Method**

1 Pre-heat oven to moderate (150–180°C).

2 Melt the butter/margarine in a saucepan over a moderate heat.

3 Add onions, garlic and chillies and cook until onions are soft.

4 Add flour gradually and mix well until all is incorporated and allow to cook for a further minute.

5 Add crushed tomatoes and bring to the boil. Reduce to a gentle simmer and cook for approx. 10 minutes stirring occasionally.

6 Add beans, mixing thoroughly. Remove pan from heat and season to taste.

7 Place mixture into serving trays and then into a bain-marie.

8 Warm taco shells through in a moderate oven and place next to bain-marie.

9 Serve taco shells half filled with bean mixture topped with a little guacamole, sour cream and grated Cheddar cheese, allowing two per portion.

# Guacamole

Ingredients

| | 25 | 50 | 100 |
|---|---|---|---|
| avocadoes, ripe, peeled, seeded | 1.25 kg | 2.5 kg | 5 kg |
| sour cream | 250 g | 500 g | 1 kg |
| lemon juice | 50 mL | 100 mL | 200 mL |
| tabasco sauce (optional) | to taste | | |
| salt and freshly milled black pepper | to taste | | |

Method
Combine all ingredients and blend until smooth. Season to taste and serve.

**Guacamole** is a classic Mexican accompaniment that can be served with a variety of dishes. Ideally it is made as close to service time as possible to avoid discoloration.

**Tabasco sauce** is made from the tabasco pepper. This very hot red pepper has its origins in the Mexican state of Tabasco. The peppers are fermented for approx. three years before being processed with vinegar and salt to produce the famous sauce, which has numerous uses.

♥ Health tip
Unsuitable for low fat diets. A high fibre dish.

# Red capsicum stuffed with yellow split pea dhal

This dish is suitable for a vegan diet.
Garnish: a sprig of fresh coriander.

Ingredients

| | 25 | 50 | 100 |
|---|---|---|---|
| split peas, yellow | 3.75 kg | 7.5 kg | 15 kg |
| stock, vegetable or water | enough to cover lentils by 4 cm | | |
| capsicums, red | 13 | 25 | 50 |
| olive oil/vegetable oil | as required | | |
| onions, peeled, finely chopped | 1 kg | 2 kg | 4 kg |
| garlic cloves, peeled, finely chopped | 3 | 6 | 12 |
| chilli powder | 30 g | 60 g | 120 g |
| turmeric | 20 g | 40 g | 80 g |
| salt and freshly milled black pepper | to taste | | |

Method
1 Place split peas into a bowl and cover with stock/water. Stand for 30 minutes. Pre-heat oven to moderate (150–180°C).
2 Cut capsicums in half lengthways, cutting through and retaining stalk and removing seeds.
3 Place a little oil in a saucepan over a moderate heat. Cook onions and garlic without colour until onions are tender.

continued

4 Add chilli powder, turmeric, peas and stock to onion mixture and mix well.

5 Bring to a gentle simmer and cook for approx. one hour, stirring regularly, or until peas have softened and broken down and a thickened sauce is achieved.

6 Remove from heat and cool slightly. Place a generous amount of mixture into each half capsicum.

7 Place filled capsicum halves onto baking/serving tray/s and put into oven for approx. 10–15 minutes or until heated through and capsicum is softened.

8 Remove from oven. Serve 1 capsicum half per portion.

 **Health tip**    High in fibre. Also suitable for low fat diets.

# Frittata with Provençale flavours

**G**arnish: layered slices of lemon and orange that have been lightly coated with chopped parsley.

**Ingredients**

| | 25 | 50 | 100 |
|---|---|---|---|
| olive oil/vegetable oil | as required | | |
| onions, Spanish, peeled, finely chopped | 500 g | 1 kg | 2 kg |
| garlic, cloves, peeled, finely chopped | 3 | 6 | 12 |
| capsicums, red and green, seeded, finely chopped | 750 g | 1.5 kg | 3 kg |
| tomatoes, blanched, seeded, rough dice | 750 g | 1.5 kg | 3 kg |
| eggs | 75 | 150 | 300 |
| milk | 500 mL | 1 L | 2 L |
| cream, single | 100 mL | 200 mL | 400 mL |
| Parmesan cheese, grated | 300 g | 600 g | 1.2 kg |
| parsley, finely chopped | 25 g | 50 g | 100 g |
| basil, roughly chopped | 25 g | 50 g | 100 g |
| salt and freshly milled black pepper | to taste | | |
| Cheddar cheese, grated | 500 g | 1 kg | 2 kg |
| mozzarella cheese, grated | 600 g | 1.2 kg | 2.4 kg |
| Parmesan cheese, grated | 100 g | 200 g | 400 g |

**Method**

1 Pre-heat oven to moderate (150–180°C).

2 Place a little oil in a pan over a moderate heat. Add onions and garlic and cook without colour until onions are tender.

3 Add capsicum and cook for a further 2–3 minutes or until capsicum is soft.

4 Remove from the heat and mix in tomatoes. Cool the mixture.

5 In a mixing bowl combine eggs, milk, cream and half the Parmesan cheese, half the parsley and basil and whisk. Season to taste.

6 Lightly grease a deep sided serving tray/s capable of holding egg mixture.

7 Place egg mixture into serving tray/s to half the depth of the tray/s. Add vegetable mixture evenly over egg mixture.

8 Place mixture into oven and cook until mixture is just set.

9 Top with remaining cheeses, parsley and basil.

10 Return to oven for a further 2–3 minutes until cheese has melted.

11 Remove from oven and leave to stand for approx. 2 minutes. Portion and serve immediately.

 **Notes**

**Parmesan cheese** is made from skimmed or partially skimmed cows' milk. Its complex flavour and granular texture are the results of the long ageing process, which can be between 2 and 4 years. The name comes from Parma in Italy where this cheese was originally made. It is now made in quite a few countries; the Italian variety is still thought to be the best.

Frittata is equally appetising served cold with a salad.

 **Health tip**    Unsuitable for low fat diets.

# Leek, tomato, potato and butternut pumpkin layered bake

This dish is suitable for a vegan diet if cheese is omitted and white sauce is produced using margarine and soya milk. Garnish: finely diced red capsicum.

Ingredients

| | 25 | 50 | 100 |
|---|---|---|---|
| white sauce (see following recipe) | 6 L | 12 L | 24 L |
| pumpkins, butternut, peeled, small dice | 2 kg | 4 kg | 8 kg |
| olive oil/vegetable oil | as required | | |
| garlic cloves, peeled, finely chopped | 4 | 8 | 16 |
| leeks, trimmed, washed, finely sliced | 2 kg | 4 kg | 8 kg |
| onions, finely sliced | 1.5 kg | 3 kg | 6 kg |
| butter/polyunsaturated margarine, melted | as required | | |
| potatoes, peeled, finely sliced | 3 kg | 6 kg | 12 kg |
| tomatoes, finely sliced | 2 kg | 4 kg | 8 kg |
| salt and freshly milled black pepper | to taste | | |
| Cheddar cheese, grated (optional) | 1 kg | 2 kg | 4 kg |

Method

1 Pre-heat oven to moderate (150–180°C).

2 Steam pumpkin until firm but tender. Refresh under cold running water and drain.

3 Heat a little oil in a saucepan over a moderate heat.

continued

4 Add garlic, leeks and onions and cook without colour until onions are soft. Remove from heat and cool.

5 Brush serving tray/s with a little melted butter or margarine. Place a thin layer of potatoes followed by a thin layer of the onion and leek mixture and then a thin layer of tomatoes followed by an even sprinkling of pumpkin and lightly season.

6 Cover the diced pumpkin with a thin layer of white sauce and then repeat step 5 until layers are 2 cm from the top of serving tray/s.

7 Cover vegetables with remaining white sauce and grated Cheddar cheese and wipe edges of any spills.

8 Place tray/s into oven and cook for approx. 45 minutes to one hour or until the bake is heated through, the potatoes tender and the cheese turned a light golden brown.

9 Remove from oven, pre-portion and serve.

♥ **Health tip**  A colourful dish. Also suitable for general eating. To reduce fat content, use low fat milk and low fat cheese.

# White sauce (béchamel)

**Ingredients**

| | 25 | 50 | 100 |
|---|---|---|---|
| butter/polyunsaturated margarine | 450 g | 900 g | 1.8 kg |
| flour, plain | 450 g | 900 g | 1.8 kg |
| milk/soya milk | 6 L | 12 L | 24 L |
| salt and white pepper | to taste | | |

**Method**

1 Melt the butter/margarine in a saucepan over a moderate heat.

2 Add the flour and mix well with butter using a wooden spoon.

3 Reduce heat and cook gently for approx. 2–3 minutes without colouring.

4 Gently warm the milk/soya milk in a separate saucepan.

5 Slowly incorporate the milk/soya milk in small amounts, making sure each addition has mixed with the roux smoothly.

6 Reduce heat and cook out gently for approx. 10 minutes stirring regularly.

7 Remove from heat, strain and use as required.

**Note**  When making a white sauce/béchamel it is always advisable when possible to use butter over margarine as it gives a slightly richer flavour. Nonetheless margarine will give a good result and is a non-animal-based product.

# Spinach, roasted red capsicum and feta cheese flan

Garnish: finely sliced chives.

| Ingredients | | 25 | 50 | 100 |
|---|---|---|---|---|
| butter, melted | | as required | | |
| pastry, filo | | as required | | |
| eggs | | 30 | 60 | 120 |
| milk | | 3 L | 6 L | 12 L |
| sour cream | | 500 g | 1 kg | 2 kg |
| salt and freshly milled black pepper | | to taste | | |
| spinach, stalks removed, leaves blanched, refreshed, drained, finely shredded, squeezed of any moisture | | 4 kg | 8 kg | 16 kg |
| capsicums, red, roasted, finely shredded (see note) | | 500 g | 1 kg | 2 kg |
| parsley, chopped | | 20 g | 40 g | 80 g |
| feta cheese, mild, crumbled | | 1 kg | 2 kg | 4 kg |

Method

1 Pre-heat oven to low-moderate (135–150°C).
2 Lightly brush serving tray/s with melted butter. Line the bottom and sides with sheets of filo pastry making sure each piece overlaps by at least 3 cm.
3 Lightly brush the top of the filo pastry with melted butter. Repeat process until filo pastry is four layers thick.
4 Whisk eggs, milk and sour cream together in a mixing bowl. Season to taste.
5 In another mixing bowl thoroughly combine spinach, capsicum, parsley and the crumbled feta cheese. Evenly distribute this mixture in the bottom of the serving tray/s.
6 Pour egg mixture into trays keeping mixture approx. 2 cm from the rim of the tray.
7 Carefully place tray/s into an oven and cook gently until egg is firm to the touch.
8 Remove from oven and allow to cool for approx. 2–3 minutes.
9 Pre-portion and serve.

Note

Roast capsicum by removing stalk and seeds, quartering and roughly chopping. Place capsicum into a deep sided roasting tray tossed with a little olive oil and place into a pre-heated moderate oven (150–180°C) and roast, turning regularly, for approx. 30–45 minutes or until the flesh is soft, and the skin is easily removed.

Health tip

To reduce fat content:
• use evaporated milk instead of sour cream
• use low fat milk.

# Chunky chat potato, cauliflower and chick pea curry

This dish is suitable for a vegan diet if margarine is used in place of butter.
Garnish: crispy pappadams and warm naan bread.

**Ingredients**

| | 25 | 50 | 100 |
|---|---|---|---|
| chick peas, soaked overnight and cooked till tender | 1.5 kg | 3 kg | 6 kg |
| potatoes, chat, quartered, cooked | 2 kg | 4 kg | 8 kg |
| cauliflower, small florets, blanched, refreshed and drained | 2 kg | 4 kg | 8 kg |
| butter/polyunsaturated margarine | 150 g | 300 g | 600 g |
| onions, peeled, finely sliced | 500 g | 1 kg | 2 kg |
| garlic, cloves, finely chopped | 4 | 8 | 16 |
| tomato paste | 100 g | 200 g | 400 g |
| curry powder, mild, approx. | 75 g | 150 g | 300 g |
| turmeric | 25 g | 50 g | 100 g |
| sugar, white | 50 g | 100 g | 200 g |
| flour, plain | 150 g | 300 g | 600 g |
| stock, vegetable, warm | 2.5 L | 5 L | 10 L |
| coconut cream | 250 mL | 500 mL | 1 L |
| salt and freshly milled black pepper | to taste | | |

**Method**

1 Cook chick peas in plenty of boiling water until tender. Refresh and drain. Prepare potatoes and cauliflower.
2 Melt butter/margarine in a saucepan over a moderate heat. Gently fry onions and garlic until onions are soft.
3 Mix in tomato paste, curry powder, turmeric and sugar.
4 Add flour and mix well.
5 Mix in small amounts of warmed stock until all is incorporated.
6 Simmer gently until it begins to thicken.
7 Once the sauce has reached the correct consistency, add coconut cream and season to taste.
8 Add cooked chick peas, potatoes and cauliflower; carefully incorporate into sauce.
9 When vegetables are heated through, serve on a bed of steamed rice.

**Notes**

Another ideal accompaniment to this dish is a small serving of dhal. See page 197.

**Curry powder** is widely used in Indian cookery and can vary in flavour and strength depending on the region where it is produced. Curry powder is made from a ground blend of approx. eighteen herbs, seeds and spices, predominantly: cardamom, chillies, cinnamon, cloves, coriander, cumin, fennel seeds, saffron, tamarind, turmeric and garlic.

 **Health tip**  A great source of protein. Also high in fibre.

# Thai-style potato and vegetable cutlets

**G**arnish: sprigs of fresh coriander and a little sweet chilli sauce.

**Ingredients**

| | 25 | 50 | 100 |
|---|---|---|---|
| lime leaves | 6 | 12 | 24 |
| potatoes, cooked until very soft | 2.5 kg | 5 kg | 10 kg |
| vegetable mince (see note) | 3 kg | 6 kg | 12 kg |
| eggs | 4 | 8 | 16 |
| coriander, sprigs, finely chopped | 50 g | 100 g | 200 g |
| spring onions, finely sliced | 500 g | 1 kg | 2 kg |
| beans, green, finely sliced | 500 g | 1 kg | 2 kg |
| garlic, cloves, peeled, finely chopped | 3 | 6 | 12 |
| ginger, peeled, finely grated | 30 g | 60 g | 120 g |
| chillies, red/green, seeded, finely chopped | 3 | 6 | 12 |
| breadcrumbs | as required | | |
| salt and freshly milled black pepper | to taste | | |
| eggs | 10 | 20 | 40 |
| milk | 300 mL | 600 mL | 1.2 L |
| breadcrumbs | as required | | |

**Method**

1 Place lime leaves into a small bowl and cover with boiling water. Stand for 2–3 minutes, remove from water and finely chop.

2 Using a paddle attachment in a commercial mixer combine lime leaves, potatoes, vegetable mince, eggs, coriander, spring onions, green beans, garlic, ginger and chillies. Mix well.

3 Season to taste. If required, adjust consistency with the addition of small amounts of breadcrumbs.

4 Place flour into a bowl and the eggs that have been beaten together with the milk in a second bowl. Place the breadcrumbs into a third bowl.

5 Mould mixture into large cutlets, approx. 250 g per cutlet.

6 Carefully dredge potato cutlets through flour, egg mixture and breadcrumbs, making sure potato cutlets are evenly coated at each stage. Gently shake off any excess breadcrumbs.

7 Carefully layer potato cutlets one layer deep between sheets of greaseproof paper and refrigerate for approx. 1–2 hours, allowing cutlets to firm.

8 Pre-heat deep fat fryer to 165–170°C. Place potato cutlets into fat in small batches and cook to a light golden brown.

9 Remove from oil and drain any excess fat.

10 Serve one cutlet per portion with a little sweet chilli sauce.

**Notes**

If lime leaves are unavailable substitute the zest and juice of lemons or limes. Ground roasted peanuts can also be added if desired.

To prepare vegetable mince, any variation of cooked vegetables can be used. They are prepared by finely chopping or blending in a food processor to a mince-like texture. Ideally vegetable mince should be made using an equal quantity of four to six vegetables.

**Health tip** Unsuitable for low fat diets.

# SALADS AND DRESSINGS

## Salads

continued

# Dressings

 **Health tip**  Salad dressings can be provided
separately for someone on a low
fat diet.

# SALADS

All salad recipes give a recommended dressing. These may be changed using the dressings section at the end of this chapter (pages 213–16). Any choice of dressing can be used. It should be remembered that dressings are to bind and enhance the flavour of a salad, not to overpower or drown it. All salad recipes will yield approx. 25 x 150 g portions. Ratios given are suggestions only.

## Mixed green salad

This salad, as indicated, requires the use of green salad vegetables. Any lettuce or combination of green lettuce, roughly torn, may be used with cucumber, onion, zucchini, green capsicum, spring onions and finely diced or sliced as well as roughly chopped fresh herbs. It is best served with a classic vinaigrette (page 213).

Ratio = 3 kg lettuce : 750 g vegetables.

## Italian beans with fresh basil and balsamic and lime vinaigrette

Top and tail beans and plunge into a pot of salted boiling water. Cook until beans are tender but firm; refresh and drain. Roughly chop a little basil and place ingredients into a bowl. Add small amounts of balsamic and lime vinaigrette (page 214) and mix together, making sure beans are lightly coated. Serve seasoned with freshly milled black pepper.

Quantity = 3.75 kg green beans.

 **Health tip**    A healthy addition to any meal. High in vitamins and fibre and low in fat.

## Sliced Roma tomato, Spanish onion and fresh basil salad with a dressing of extra virgin olive oil

Slice tomatoes approx. 5 mm thick. Place one layer of tomatoes into the bottom of a salad bowl. Sprinkle tomatoes with a little salt, freshly milled black pepper and a little finely minced Spanish onion. Finely chop basil and sprinkle over tomatoes. Drizzle olive oil and a small amount of balsamic vinegar over tomatoes. Repeat process until salad bowl is three-quarters full. Cover and refrigerate for approx. one hour before serving.

Ratio = 3.5 kg tomatoes : 250 g Spanish onions.

 **Health tip**    Extra virgin olive oil has a delicious strong flavour, so you do not need a large amount of it. Olive oil is recommended as the oil of first choice for good health.

# German potato, crispy bacon and spring onion salad bound in mayonnaise and sour cream

Cook chat potatoes until firm but tender. Refresh and allow to drain. Depending on size, cut into halves or quarters. Top and tail spring onions, wash and finely slice. In a bowl place potatoes, crisply cooked diced bacon and spring onions. Add enough mayonnaise and sour cream to lightly bind ingredients and mix well. Season to taste with salt and freshly milled black pepper. Mix through chopped parsley and serve.

Ratio = 3.5 kg potatoes : 150 g spring onions : 300 g bacon.
Equal quantities of sour cream and mayonnaise (page 214).

**Health tip**  Not desirable for low fat diets. To reduce fat: remove fat from bacon; use light sour cream; use dressing sparingly.

# Tomato, roasted green capsicum and feta cheese salad

Roast capsicum by removing stalk and seeds, quartering and roughly chopping. Place capsicum into a deep sided roasting tray tossed with a little olive oil and place into a pre-heated moderate (150–180°C) oven. Roast, turning regularly, for approx. 30–45 minutes or until the flesh is soft. Remove from oven and allow to cool. Cut tomatoes and feta cheese into 2 cm dice and place into a bowl. Add roughly chopped capsicum, then chopped parsley and vinaigrette (page 213). Mix well. Serve.

Ratio = 2.75 kg tomatoes : 500 g feta cheese : 1.5 kg uncooked green capsicum.

**Health tip**  Capsicum and tomatoes are both high in Vitamin C.
To reduce fat content of the dish, use less cheese.

# Broccoli, smoked ham and red pepper salad

Cut broccoli into small florets and plunge into salted boiling water for approx. 30 seconds until *al dente*. Refresh and drain. Cut capsicum and ham into strips approx. 3 mm x 10 cm. Place all ingredients into a bowl and lightly bind ingredients with a little English mustard vinaigrette (page 214). Serve.

Ratio = 3.2 kg broccoli florets : 300 g capsicum : 250 g smoked ham.

**Health tip**  Broccoli is a rich source of antioxidants. Antioxidants can help prevent cancer and heart disease. This is an excellent dish to encourage people to eat more healthy food.

## Niçoise salad

Top and tail French beans and cut into 3 cm pieces. Blanch, refresh and drain. Cook chat potatoes until tender, refresh and drain. Cut into quarters. Place beans and potatoes into a bowl and add tomatoes that have been cut into 2 cm dice. Add black olives that have been stoned and roughly chopped. Add a sprinkling of capers and a few finely chopped anchovy fillets. Season to taste with a little salt and freshly milled black pepper. Add sufficient herbed mayonnaise (page 215) to bind all ingredients lightly and serve.

Ratio = 1.2 kg potatoes : 1.2 kg tomatoes : 1.2 kg beans : 200 g olives.

**Health tip**    A nutritious and delicious salad. To reduce the fat content, use only a small amount of mayonnaise, or mix mayonnaise with some plain yoghurt. Alternatively, use low fat mayonnaise.

## Apple, celery, cashew nut and fresh coriander salad

Trim, wash and cut celery into 2 cm dice. Core and cut red apples into 2 cm dice. Finely chop a little coriander. Place all ingredients into a bowl and add cashew nuts and lightly bind with mayonnaise (page 214). Serve.

Ratio = 1.6 kg celery : 1.6 kg red apples : 550 g cashew nuts.

**Health tip**    A colourful way to enjoy this nutritious salad. The nuts make this salad particularly suitable for vegetarians. Use a low fat mayonnaise to reduce the fat content if desired.

# DRESSINGS

**A**ll dressing recipes will yield approx. 1 L.

**Health tip**    Olive oil is recommended as the oil of first choice for your health. Use dressings lightly on salads. Do not 'drown' the salad in dressing as it will spoil the salad.

## Classic vinaigrette

**Ingredients**

| | |
|---|---|
| olive oil | 800 mL |
| mustard, French | 40 g |
| vinegar | 200 mL |
| salt and freshly milled black pepper | to taste |

**Method**    Combine all ingredients, mixing well and serve.

## Herbed vinaigrette

**Ingredients**

| | |
|---|---|
| olive oil | 800 mL |
| mustard, French | 40 g |
| vinegar | 100 mL |

continued

| lemons, juice | 100 mL |
|---|---|
| chives, finely sliced | 10 g |
| parsley, finely chopped | 10 g |
| basil, finely chopped | 10 g |
| salt and freshly milled black pepper | to taste |

**Method**  Combine all ingredients, mixing well and serve.

# English mustard vinaigrette

**Ingredients**

| olive oil | 800 mL |
|---|---|
| mustard, English | 40 g |
| vinegar | 200 mL |
| sugar, castor | 100 g |
| salt and freshly milled black pepper | to taste |

**Method**  Combine all ingredients, mixing well and serve.

# Balsamic and lime vinaigrette

**Ingredients**

| olive oil | 800 mL |
|---|---|
| mustard, English | 40 g |
| balsamic vinegar | 50 mL |
| white vinegar | 50 mL |
| limes, juice | 100 mL |
| sugar, castor | 50 g |
| salt and freshly milled black pepper | to taste |

**Method**  Combine all ingredients, mixing well and serve.

# Mayonnaise

**Ingredients**

| egg, yolks | 8 |
|---|---|
| mustard, English | 25 g |
| vinegar | 50 mL |
| salt and freshly milled black pepper | to taste |
| olive oil, room temperature | 1 L |
| lemons, juice | to taste |

**Method**
1 Place egg yolks, mustard, vinegar, salt and pepper into a bowl. Whisk well.
2 Slowly add oil, whisking continuously until all oil has been incorporated.
3 Correct seasoning and use as required.

**Note**  If mixture curdles, add one egg yolk and a dash of vinegar to a clean mixing bowl and lightly whisk. Slowly add curdled mixture whisking continuously.

❤ **Health tip**   This mayonnaise contains a large percentage of monounsaturated fats, which is desirable for good health. For low fat diets, care needs to be taken to only have a small amount of mayonnaise.

# Fresh herb mayonnaise

Ingredients

| | |
|---|---|
| **egg**, yolks | 8 |
| **mustard**, English | 25 g |
| **vinegar** | 50 mL |
| **chives**, finely sliced | 10 g |
| **parsley**, finely chopped | 10 g |
| **basil**, finely chopped | 10 g |
| **salt and freshly milled black pepper** | to taste |
| **olive oil**, room temperature | 1 L |

Method

1 Place egg yolks, mustard, vinegar, herbs, salt and pepper into a bowl and whisk well.
2 Slowly add oil, whisking continuously until all oil has been incorporated.
3 Correct seasoning and use as required.

**Note**   If mixture curdles, place one egg yolk and a dash of vinegar in a clean mixing bowl and lightly whisk. Slowly add curdled mixture whisking continuously.

❤ **Health tip**   This mayonnaise contains a large percentage of monounsaturated fats, which is desirable for good health. For low fat diets, care needs to be taken to only have a small amount of mayonnaise.

# Roasted garlic mayonnaise

Ingredients

| | |
|---|---|
| **egg**, yolks | 8 |
| **mustard**, English | 25 g |
| **vinegar** | 50 mL |
| **garlic**, roasted | purée of 1 bulb (see note below) |
| **salt and freshly milled black pepper** | to taste |
| **olive oil**, room temperature | 1 L |

Method

1 Place egg yolks, mustard, vinegar, roasted garlic purée, salt and pepper into a bowl and whisk well.
2 Slowly add oil, whisking continuously until all oil has been incorporated.
3 Correct seasoning and use as required.

**Note**   If mixture curdles, place one egg yolk and a dash of vinegar in a clean mixing bowl and lightly whisk. Slowly add curdled mixture.

continued

**Note** To roast garlic, take whole bulbs and lightly prick cloves. Place onto a roasting tray and put into a pre-heated moderate oven (150–180°C) for approx. 20–30 minutes or until garlic cloves are soft to the touch. Remove from oven and cool completely. To extract roasted garlic purée, trim the base of the bulb and squeeze out the purée. The reason garlic is sometimes roasted is that it gives a milder, richer flavour.

**Health tip** This mayonnaise contains a large percentage of monounsaturated fats, which is desirable for good health. For low fat diets, care needs to be taken to only have a small amount of mayonnaise.

# POTATO DISHES

❤ **Health tip**   Recipes containing butter, cream or sour cream are unsuitable for a low fat diet. To reduce fat, use light sour cream or light cream.

# Mashed potatoes blended with sour cream

Ingredients

| | 25 | 50 | 100 |
|---|---|---|---|
| **potatoes**, peeled, rough dice | 5.75 kg | 11.5 kg | 23 kg |
| **butter**, room temperature | 200 g | 400 g | 800 g |
| **sour cream** | 400 g | 800 g | 1.6 kg |
| **salt and freshly milled black pepper** | to taste | | |

Method
1 Place potatoes into a saucepan and just cover with water.
2 Simmer until tender on a moderate heat. Drain water from potatoes and place into the bowl of a commercial mixer.
3 Using a paddle attachment, mash potatoes with butter and sour cream until smooth, thick and free of any lumps.
4 Season to taste and serve.

❤ Health tip To make suitable for inclusion in cholesterol-lowering, low fat, diabetic and weight-reduction diets, use canola margarine or polyunsaturated margarine instead of butter. Use skim evaporated milk instead of sour cream or use light sour cream.

# Baked cheese and mushroom potatoes with fresh herbs

Ingredients

| | 25 | 50 | 100 |
|---|---|---|---|
| **potatoes**, peeled, rough dice | 5.75 kg | 11.5 kg | 23 kg |
| **mushrooms**, button, finely sliced | 300 g | 600 g | 1.2 kg |
| **butter**, room temperature | 200 g | 400 g | 800 g |
| **sour cream** | 400 g | 800 g | 1.6 kg |
| **parsley**, fresh, finely chopped | 15 g | 30 g | 60 g |
| **basil**, fresh, finely chopped | 10 g | 20 g | 40 g |
| **chives**, fresh, finely sliced | 10 g | 20 g | 40 g |
| **salt and freshly milled black pepper** | to taste | | |
| **cheese**, Cheddar, grated | 300 g | 600 g | 1.2 kg |

Method
1 Pre-heat oven to moderate (150–180°C).
2 Place potatoes into a saucepan and just cover with water.
3 Simmer on a moderate heat until tender. Drain water from potatoes and place into the bowl of a commercial mixer.
4 In a sauté pan over a moderate heat, melt a little butter and gently sauté mushrooms until soft. Remove from heat.
5 Using a paddle attachment, mash potatoes, mushrooms, butter, sour cream and herbs until smooth, thick and free of any lumps. Season to taste.
6 Place potato mixture into serving trays and evenly top with cheese.
7 Place trays into oven and cook until cheese has melted and turned light golden brown. Remove from oven and serve.

# Mashed sweet potatoes with butter and cream

**Ingredients**

| | 25 | 50 | 100 |
|---|---|---|---|
| **potatoes**, sweet, peeled, rough dice | 3 kg | 6 kg | 12 kg |
| **potatoes**, peeled, rough dice | 3 kg | 6 kg | 12 kg |
| **butter**, room temperature | 200 g | 400 g | 800 g |
| **cream**, single | 200 mL | 400 mL | 800 mL |
| **salt and freshly milled black pepper** | to taste | | |

**Method**

1 Place sweet potatoes into a saucepan and just cover with water. Place over a moderate heat and simmer until tender.
2 Place regular potatoes into saucepan and just cover with water. Place over a moderate heat and simmer until tender.
3 Carefully drain water from potatoes and place into the bowl of a commercial mixer.
4 Using a paddle attachment, mash potatoes with butter and cream until smooth, thick and free of any lumps.
5 Season to taste and serve.

# Mashed potatoes with caramelised onions, black olives and sun-dried tomatoes

**Ingredients**

| | 25 | 50 | 100 |
|---|---|---|---|
| **potatoes**, peeled, rough dice | 5.75 kg | 11.5 kg | 23 kg |
| **onions**, white, finely chopped | 250 g | 500 g | 1 kg |
| **butter**, room temperature | 200 g | 400 g | 800 g |
| **sour cream** | 400 g | 800 g | 1.6 kg |
| **olives**, black, stoned, roughly chopped | 100 g | 200 g | 400 g |
| **sun-dried tomatoes**, finely shredded | 100 g | 200 g | 400 g |
| **salt and freshly milled black pepper** | to taste | | |

continued

**Method**

1 Place potatoes into a saucepan and just cover with water.
2 Place over a moderate heat and simmer until tender. Drain water from potatoes and place in the bowl of a commercial mixer.
3 In a sauté pan over a moderate heat, melt a little olive oil and gently sauté onions until lightly browned. Remove from heat.
4 Using a paddle attachment, mash potatoes with onions, butter, sour cream, olives and sun-dried tomatoes until smooth, thick, and free of any lumps.
5 Season to taste and serve.

**Health tip**

To make suitable for weight reduction, diabetic and cholesterol-lowering diets:
• use margarine instead of butter
• use skim evaporated milk instead of sour cream or light sour cream.

# Mashed potatoes flavoured with parsnip and pumpkin

**Ingredients**

| | 25 | 50 | 100 |
|---|---|---|---|
| potatoes, peeled, rough dice | 3 kg | 6 kg | 12 kg |
| parsnips, peeled, rough diced | 1 kg | 2 kg | 4 kg |
| pumpkin, peeled, seeded, rough diced | 1 kg | 2 kg | 4 kg |
| butter, room temperature | 200 g | 400 g | 800 g |
| sour cream | 400 g | 800 g | 1.6 kg |
| parsley, fresh, finely chopped | 15 g | 30 g | 60 g |
| salt and freshly milled black pepper | to taste | | |

**Method**

1 Place potatoes, pumpkin and parsnip into three separate saucepans, and just cover with water. Place onto a moderate heat and cook until vegetables are tender.
2 Carefully drain water from potatoes, parsnips and pumpkin and place into the bowl of a commercial mixer.
3 Using a paddle attachment, mash potatoes, parsnips and pumpkin with butter, sour cream and parsley until smooth, thick and free of any lumps.
4 Season to taste and serve.

**Health tip**

To make suitable for weight reduction, diabetic and cholesterol-lowering diets:
• use margarine instead of butter
• use skim evaporated milk instead of sour cream or light sour cream.

# Pontiac potatoes braised with beef stock, Spanish onions and garlic

**Ingredients**

| | 25 | 50 | 100 |
|---|---|---|---|
| **potatoes**, pontiac, peeled, sliced | 5.75 kg | 11.5 kg | 23 kg |
| **stock**, beef | 1.5 L | 3 L | 6 L |
| **onions**, Spanish, finely sliced | 500 g | 1 kg | 2 kg |
| **garlic**, cloves, peeled, finely chopped | 4 | 8 | 16 |
| **salt and freshly milled black pepper** | to taste | | |

**Method**

1 Layer potatoes, onions and garlic in suitably sized serving trays, seasoning each potato layer lightly, until all are used.
2 Carefully pour stock over potatoes and seal trays with aluminium foil. Place into a pre-heated moderate oven (150–180°C) and cook for approx. 1–1$^1$/$_2$ hours or until potatoes are tender.
3 Remove from oven and serve.

 **Health tip**  Suitable for low fat, diabetic, weight-reduction and cholesterol-lowering diets.

# Potatoes cooked with chicken stock, mushrooms and bacon

**Ingredients**

| | 25 | 50 | 100 |
|---|---|---|---|
| **potatoes**, peeled, sliced | 5.75 kg | 11.5 kg | 23 kg |
| **stock**, chicken | 1.5 L | 3 L | 6 L |
| **onions**, white, finely sliced | 500 g | 1 kg | 2 kg |
| **mushrooms**, button, finely sliced | 250 g | 500 g | 1 kg |
| **bacon**, fat removed, finely diced | 250 g | 500 g | 1 kg |
| **salt and freshly milled black pepper** | to taste | | |

**Method**

1 Pre-heat oven to moderate (150–180°C).
2 Layer potatoes, onions, mushrooms and bacon in baking tray/s seasoning each potato layer lightly.
3 Carefully pour stock over potatoes and seal trays with aluminium foil. Place into oven and cook for approx. 1–1$^1$/$_2$ hours or until potatoes are tender.
4 Remove from oven and serve.

**Health tip**  Suitable for low fat, diabetic, weight-reduction and cholesterol-lowering diets.

# Creamy chive potatoes

Ingredients

| | 25 | 50 | 100 |
|---|---|---|---|
| potatoes, peeled, sliced | 5.75 kg | 11.5 kg | 23 kg |
| onions, white, finely sliced | 200 g | 400 g | 800g |
| chives, finely sliced | 50 g | 100 g | 200 g |
| cream, single | 1 L | 2 L | 4 L |
| milk | 500 mL | 1 L | 2 L |
| salt and freshly milled black pepper | to taste | | |

Method

1 Pre-heat oven to moderate (150–180°C).
2 Layer potatoes, onions and chives in serving tray/s, seasoning each potato layer lightly.
3 Carefully pour cream and milk, which have been combined in a mixing bowl, over potatoes and seal trays with aluminium foil. Place into oven and cook for approx. 1–1¹/₂ hours or until potatoes are tender.
4 Remove from oven and serve.

♥ Health tip   To reduce fat content, use low fat milk. Use evaporated milk instead of cream.

# Classic fondant potatoes

Ingredients

| | 25 | 50 | 100 |
|---|---|---|---|
| potatoes, peeled, cut into uniform size | 5 kg | 10 kg | 20 kg |
| stock, chicken | 1 L | 2 L | 4 L |
| butter, melted | 150 g | 300 g | 600 g |

Method

1 Pre-heat oven to moderate (150–180°C).
2 Place potatoes one layer deep into a deep sided roasting tray/s. Pour over stock so the potatoes are half submerged.
3 Brush tops of potatoes with melted butter and place tray/s into oven. Cook until potatoes are tender and golden brown.
4 Remove from oven and serve.

♥ Health tip   To increase fibre content of the dish, leave the skin on the potatoes.

# Roasted Italian-style potatoes

Ingredients

| | 25 | 50 | 100 |
|---|---|---|---|
| potatoes, peeled, cut into 2 cm dice | 5 kg | 10 kg | 20 kg |
| garlic, cloves, peeled, finely minced | 6 | 12 | 24 |
| basil, dried | 10 g | 20 g | 40 g |
| oregano, dried | 10 g | 20 g | 40 g |
| rosemary, dried, finely chopped | 10 g | 20 g | 40 g |
| olive oil | 100 mL | 200 mL | 400 mL |
| salt and freshly milled black pepper | to taste | | |

**Method**
1 Pre-heat oven to moderate (150–180°C).
2 Place all ingredients into roasting tray/s and mix well. Season to taste.
3 Place tray/s into oven and cook until potatoes are tender and golden brown, gently turning potatoes every 15 minutes.
4 Remove from oven and serve.

❤ **Health tip**   Suitable for diabetic and cholesterol-lowering diets.

# Roasted potatoes with Spanish onion and paprika

**Ingredients**

| | 25 | 50 | 100 |
|---|---|---|---|
| **potatoes**, peeled, cut into 2 cm dice | 5 kg | 10 kg | 20 kg |
| **onions**, Spanish, minced | 250 g | 500 g | 1 kg |
| **garlic**, cloves, peeled, finely minced | 6 | 12 | 24 |
| **paprika** | 25 g | 50 g | 100 g |
| **olive oil** | 100 mL | 200 mL | 400 mL |
| **salt and freshly milled black pepper** | to taste | | |

**Method**
1 Pre-heat oven to moderate (150–180°C).
2 Place all ingredients into roasting tray/s and mix well. Season to taste.
3 Place tray/s into oven and cook until potatoes are tender and golden brown, gently turning potatoes every 15 minutes.
4 Remove from oven and serve.

❤ **Health tip**   Suitable for diabetic and cholesterol-lowering diets.

# Mexican potato wedges

**Ingredients**

| | 25 | 50 | 100 |
|---|---|---|---|
| **potatoes**, cut into required size wedges | 5 kg | 10 kg | 20 kg |
| **chilli**, powder | 25 g | 50 g | 100 g |
| **olive oil** | 100 mL | 200 mL | 400 mL |
| **salt and freshly milled black pepper** | to taste | | |

**Method**
1 Pre-heat oven to moderate (150–180°C).
2 Place all ingredients into roasting tray/s and mix well. Season to taste.
3 Place tray/s into oven and cook until potatoes are tender and golden brown, gently turning potatoes every 15 minutes.
4 Remove from oven and serve.

❤ **Health tip**   Suitable for diabetic and cholesterol-lowering diets.
Leaving the skin on potatoes will keep the fibre content high.

# Baked potato cups stuffed with sour cream, spring onion and roasted red capsicum

| Ingredients  | | 25 | 50 | 100 |
|---|---|---|---|---|
| | **potatoes**, whole, medium sized, washed | 13 | 25 | 50 |
| | **sour cream** | 250 g | 500 g | 1 kg |
| | **spring onions**, trimmed, finely sliced | 200 g | 400 g | 800 g |
| | **red capsicums**, roasted, finely diced | 2 | 4 | 8 |
| | **parsley**, fresh, finely chopped | 15 g | 30 g | 60 g |
| | **salt and freshly milled black pepper** | to taste | | |
| | **cheese**, Cheddar, grated | 500 g | 1 kg | 2 kg |

**Method**

1 Pre-heat oven to moderate (150–180°C).
2 Place potatoes into roasting trays and place into oven for approx. 1–1$^1$/$_2$ hours or until potatoes are cooked through.
3 Remove from oven. Cool and halve lengthways.
4 Gently scoop out potato flesh taking care not to damage skin and place into a bowl.
5 Add sour cream, spring onions, capsicums and parsley to flesh and combine well. Season to taste.
6 Spoon flesh back into potato skin cups and top with a little grated cheese.
7 Place potato cups onto baking trays and return to oven for approx. 10–15 minutes or until heated through and the cheese has turned a light golden brown.
8 Remove from oven and serve. Allow one potato cup per portion.

**Note** Roast capsicum by removing stalk and seeds, quartering and roughly chopping. Place capsicum into a deep sided roasting tray tossed with a little olive oil and place into a pre-heated moderate oven (150–180°C) and roast, turning regularly, for approx. 30–45 minutes or until the flesh is soft, and the skin is easily removed.

♥ **Health tip** To increase fat content, use low fat milk. Use evaporated milk instead of cream.

# Roasted chat potatoes

| Ingredients  | | 25 | 50 | 100 |
|---|---|---|---|---|
| | **potatoes**, chat, washed | 5 kg | 10 kg | 20 kg |
| | **olive oil** | 100 ml | 200 ml | 400 ml |
| | **salt and freshly milled black pepper** | to taste | | |
| | **parsley**, continental, finely chopped | 25 g | 50 g | 100 g |

**Method**

1 Pre-heat oven to moderate(150–180°C).
2 Place potatoes into roasting tray/s and toss with olive oil. (Cut any large potatoes in half to ensure uniform cooking time.) Season to taste.

3 Place tray/s into oven and cook for approx. 45 minutes–1 hour or until cooked through.
4 Remove from oven and toss with chopped parsley and serve.

 **Health tip**  Suitable for diabetic and cholesterol-lowering diets.

# Deep fried potato skins

|  | 25 | 50 | 100 |
|---|---|---|---|
| **potato**, skins, thoroughly washed and patted dry | 5.5 kg | 11 kg | 22 kg |
| **salt and freshly milled black pepper** | to taste | | |

**Ingredients**

**Method**
1 Place dry potato skins into deep fryer oil heated to approx. 165–170°C. Cook for approx. 2–3 minutes or until cooked through and a light golden brown.
2 Remove from fryer, and drain thoroughly. Season to taste and serve.

**Note** This dish utilises potato peel, which is often discarded. Potatoes should be thoroughly washed and then, using a vegetable knife, peeled in long thick strips. If not frying immediately, place peel into a container and cover with cold water, to avoid blackness.

**Health tip**  Unsuitable for a low-fat diet.

# Crispy potato curls with sour cream and chives

|  | 25 | 50 | 100 |
|---|---|---|---|
| **potato**, skins, thoroughly washed and patted dry | 5.5 kg | 11 kg | 22 kg |
| **salt and freshly milled black pepper** | to taste | | |
| **sour cream** | 1 kg | 2 kg | 4 kg |
| **Cheddar cheese**, grated | 300 g | 600 g | 1.2 kg |
| **chives**, finely sliced | 20 g | 40 g | 80 g |

**Ingredients**

**Method**
1 Pre-heat oven to moderate (150–180°C).
2 Place dry potato skins into deep fryer oil heated to approx. 165–170°C. Cook for approx. 2–3 minutes or until cooked through and light golden brown.
3 Remove from fryer, and drain thoroughly. Season to taste.
4 Place potato skins into roasting/serving tray/s and spread sour cream evenly over potato skins. Evenly sprinkle Cheddar cheese over sour cream and then sprinkle with chives.

continued

5 Return trays to oven and cook for approx. 5 minutes or until cheese has melted and the potatoes are heated through.

6 Remove from oven and serve.

 **Note**

This dish utilises potato peel, which is often discarded. Potatoes should be thoroughly washed and then, using a vegetable knife, peeled in long thick strips. If not frying immediately, place peel into a container and cover with cold water to avoid blackness.

 **Health tip**

Unsuitable for people on a low fat, diabetic, weight reduction or cholesterol-lowering diet.

# Deep fried chat potatoes tossed in balsamic vinegar and sea salt

| Ingredients | | 25 | 50 | 100 |
|---|---|---|---|---|
| potatoes, chat, washed | | 5 kg | 10 kg | 20 kg |
| sea salt and freshly milled black pepper | | to taste | | |
| vinegar, balsamic | | 100 mL | 200 mL | 400 mL |
| parsley, fresh, finely chopped | | 20 g | 40 g | 80 g |

**Method**

1 Pre-heat deep fryer to 165–170°C.

2 Boil or steam potatoes until cooked and tender, refresh and drain well.

3 Cut any large potatoes in half.

4 Place dry potatoes into deep fryer oil. Cook for approx. 2–3 minutes or until cooked through and light golden brown.

5 Remove from fryer. Drain well.

6 Place potatoes in a large bowl and sprinkle evenly with balsamic vinegar. Season to taste and toss vigorously.

7 Sprinkle with chopped parsley and serve.

 **Health tip**

Unsuitable for a low fat diet.

# Lyonnaise-style spiced potatoes

| Ingredients | | 25 | 50 | 100 |
|---|---|---|---|---|
| onions, white, finely diced | | 500 g | 1 kg | 2 kg |
| garlic, cloves, peeled, finely chopped | | 4 | 8 | 16 |
| potatoes, peeled, washed, 1.5 cm dice | | 5 kg | 10 kg | 20 kg |
| paprika | | 15 g | 30 g | 60 g |
| parsley, fresh, finely chopped | | 15 g | 30 g | 60 g |
| salt and freshly milled black pepper | | to taste | | |
| vegetable oil | | as required | | |

| Method | 1 Pre-heat deep fryer to 165–170°C. |
|---|---|

**Method**

1 Pre-heat deep fryer to 165–170°C.
2 In a sauté pan heat a little oil over a moderate heat. Cook onions and garlic until onions are soft. Remove from heat.
3 Place potatoes into deep fryer oil and cook for approx. 4–5 minutes or until cooked through and light golden brown.
4 Remove from fryer. Drain thoroughly. Pre-heat oven to moderate (150–180°C).
5 Place potatoes into roasting or serving tray/s and mix through onion and garlic mixture, paprika and parsley. Season to taste.
6 Place trays into oven and cook for approx. 4–5 minutes or until the potatoes are heated through.
7 Remove from oven and serve.

 **Health tip**   Unsuitable for a low fat diet.

# Swiss-style rösti potatoes

**Ingredients**

| | 25 | 50 | 100 |
|---|---|---|---|
| **potatoes**, washed and peeled | 6 kg | 12 kg | 24 kg |
| **salt and freshly milled black pepper** | to taste | | |
| **butter**, melted | 250 g | 500 g | 1 kg |
| **olive oil/vegetable oil** | 250 mL | 500 mL | 1 L |

**Method**

1 Pre-heat oven to moderate (150–180°C).
2 Boil or steam potatoes until cooked and tender. Refresh under cold running water and drain well.
3 Grate potatoes into mixing bowl and season generously.
4 Combine melted butter and oil and add a little to an omelette pan/s over a moderate heat. Add potato evenly to a 3 cm depth and cook for approx. 1–2 minutes or until bottom is golden brown.
5 Place pan/s into oven and allow the mix to firm for approx. 10–15 minutes.
6 Remove from oven and turn potato rösti out onto a chopping board, keeping the bottom as the presentation side. Cool.
7 Half or quarter röstis depending on required portion size. Re-heat in a moderate oven (150–180°C) and serve.

 **Note**   To save time, it is a good idea if extra omelette pans are available to produce several röstis at a time.

 **Health tip**   Unsuitable for a low fat diet.

continued

## VEGETABLES

continued

# Eggplant

| | |
|---|---|
| Eggplant ratatouille | 240 |
| Eggplant roasted with garlic, continental parsley and olive oil | 241 |
| Char-grilled seasoned sliced eggplant with fresh oregano | 241 |

# Leeks

| | |
|---|---|
| Creamy leeks sautéed with garlic and bacon | 242 |
| Leeks braised in chicken stock and balsamic vinegar | 242 |
| Whole roasted leeks | 243 |

# Mushrooms

| | |
|---|---|
| Mushrooms sautéed with spring onions and fresh basil | 243 |
| Deep fried mushrooms | 244 |
| Mushrooms braised with Spanish onions, bacon/ham and garlic | 244 |

# Onions

| | |
|---|---|
| Deep fried tempura onion rings | 245 |
| Caramelised roasted onions | 245 |
| Onions roasted with beef stock | 246 |

# Parsnips

| | |
|---|---|
| Roasted parsnip chips | 246 |
| Parsnip mash | 247 |
| Crispy shaved parsnips | 247 |

# Polenta

| | |
|---|---|
| Fresh herb polenta | 248 |
| Golden polenta triangles | 248 |

# Pumpkin

| | |
|---|---|
| Warmed pumpkin mousse | 249 |
| Roasted pumpkin with nutmeg, honey and parsley | 250 |
| Puréed butternut pumpkin with fresh coriander and sour cream | 250 |

# Spinach

| | |
|---|---|
| Spinach with garden peas and cream | 251 |
| Spinach stir-fried with pine nuts and bacon | 251 |
| Creamed spinach | 252 |

# Sweet corn

| | |
|---|---|
| Corn cobs tossed with butter, fresh Parmesan and black pepper | 253 |
| Spicy corn stir-fried with Spanish onion and capsicum | 253 |
| Corn wheels with fresh herb butter | 254 |

# Zucchini

| | |
|---|---|
| Zucchini with red capsicum and fresh basil leaves | 254 |
| Zucchini braised in beef stock with fresh rosemary | 255 |
| Zucchini tossed in garlic and fresh herb butter | 255 |

# BEANS, GREEN

## Seasonal availability
All year; peak November–March.

## Suitable methods of cookery
Sauté, stir-fry, steaming and boiling.

## Preparation
Wash beans thoroughly under cold running water, top and tail and cut into required size.

 **Note** — These are a member of a very large family including: butter beans, flat beans, borlotti beans and broad beans, all of which reach their seasonal peaks at different times of the year.

 **Health tip** — An excellent sourve of fibre and of vitamins A and C.

# Green beans sautéed in butter with continental parsley and Spanish onions

**Ingredients**

|  | 25 | 50 | 100 |
|---|---|---|---|
| **beans**, green | 2 kg | 4 kg | 8 kg |
| **butter** | 200 g | 400 g | 800 g |
| **garlic**, cloves, minced | 2 | 4 | 8 |
| **onions**, Spanish, finely sliced | 300 g | 600 g | 1.2 kg |
| **parsley**, continental, finely chopped | 25 g | 50 g | 100 g |
| **salt and freshly milled black pepper** | to taste | | |

**Method**

1 Blanch and refresh green beans. Drain well.
2 Melt butter in a saucepan over a moderate heat. Add garlic and onions and cook until onions are soft.
3 Add beans and mix well. Cook for approx. 1 minute, turning constantly until beans are heated through.
4 Add parsley, season to taste and serve.

# Thai-style green beans

**Ingredients**

|  | 25 | 50 | 100 |
|---|---|---|---|
| **beans**, green | 2 kg | 4 kg | 8 kg |
| **sweet chilli sauce** | 200 mL | 400 mL | 800 mL |
| **coriander**, fresh, finely chopped | 20 g | 40 g | 80 g |

**Method**

1 Cook beans in lightly salted boiling water for approx. 2–3 minutes and drain well.
2 Immediately toss sweet chilli sauce and coriander through beans and serve.

# Green beans coated with toasted almonds, butter and cracked pepper

| Ingredients | | 25 | 50 | 100 |
|---|---|---|---|---|
| beans, green | | 2 kg | 4 kg | 8 kg |
| butter, melted and warm | | 200 g | 400 g | 800 g |
| almonds, slivered, toasted until | | | | |
|    lightly browned | | 150 g | 300 g | 600 g |
| cracked black pepper | | 10 g | 20 g | 40 g |

Method

1 Cook beans in lightly salted boiling water for approx. 2–3 minutes. Drain well.
2 Immediately toss butter, almonds and cracked pepper through beans and serve.

# BROCCOLI

### Seasonal availability
All year; peak June–November.

### Suitable methods of cookery
Sauté, stir-fry, boiling, steaming.

### Preparation
Trim leaves and base of broccoli stalks, cut into required size florets, wash well under cold running water and drain well.

 Broccoli is a member of the cabbage, cauliflower and brussels sprouts family. Its name is derived from the Italian word meaning 'cabbage sprout'.

 Health tip    A good source of vitamins A and C.

# Steamed broccoli with julienne of red and green capsicum

| Ingredients | | 25 | 50 | 100 |
|---|---|---|---|---|
| broccoli | | 2 kg | 4 kg | 8 kg |
| red capsicum, julienne | | 200 g | 400 g | 800 g |
| green capsicum, julienne | | 200 g | 400 g | 800 g |

Method

1 Steam or boil broccoli florets until tender but crisp and drain well.
2 Place into serving tray/s and sprinkle evenly with capsicum. Serve.

# Broccoli florets cooked in a crisp tempura batter

Ingredients

|  | 25 | 50 | 100 |
|---|---|---|---|
| cornflour | 1 kg | 2 kg | 4 kg |
| rice flour | 1 kg | 2 kg | 4 kg |
| vinegar, white | 20 mL | 40 mL | 80 mL |
| water, iced | as required | | |
| salt | to taste | | |
| broccoli, florets cut with long stalks | 2 kg | 4 kg | 8 kg |
| flour, plain | 1 kg | 2 kg | 4 kg |

Method
1 Pre-heat deep fryer to 160–170°C.
2 In a mixing bowl combine cornflour, rice flour and vinegar. Slowly incorporate iced water until a consistency is reached that will thickly coat the back of a spoon. Season to taste.
3 Ensuring broccoli florets are dry, lightly coat with plain flour and dip florets into batter mix making sure all the florets are coated with the batter. Drain any excess mixture and carefully place florets into hot oil.
4 Allow florets to cook until they float to the surface of the oil and are a light golden brown.
5 Carefully remove florets from oil and drain excess fat. Serve.

# Broccoli florets tossed in a garlic and fresh herb butter

Ingredients

|  | 25 | 50 | 100 |
|---|---|---|---|
| broccoli, florets, small | 2 kg | 4 kg | 8 kg |
| butter | 200 g | 400g | 800 g |
| garlic, cloves, finely chopped | 3 | 6 | 12 |
| parsley, fresh, finely chopped | 20 g | 40 g | 80 g |
| basil, fresh, finely chopped | 10 g | 20 g | 40 g |
| salt and freshly milled black pepper | to taste | | |

Method
1 Cook broccoli florets in lightly salted boiling water. When water returns to the boil remove florets and drain well (do not refresh).
2 Whilst florets are cooking melt butter in saucepan over a moderate heat. Add garlic and cook for approx. 1 minute.
3 Add broccoli and herbs and agitate until all the broccoli florets are coated. Season to taste and serve.

Health tip    Use margarine instead of butter for cholesterol-lowering diets.

# CABBAGE

## Seasonal availability
All year; peak September–January

## Suitable methods of cookery
Sauté, stir-fry, boiling, steaming, braising.

## Preparation
Remove outer leaves, quarter, remove stalk and cut into required size.

 **Note** The cabbage is related to the same family as brussels sprouts, broccoli, cauliflower and kale. There are many varieties of cabbage, including red, white, savoy and Chinese.

 **Health tip** A good source of vitamins A and C. A good source of fibre. Colourful presentation of vegetables will encourage people to eat them.

# Braised cabbage with sultanas, apple and cinnamon

**Ingredients**

|  | 25 | 50 | 100 |
|---|---|---|---|
| cabbage, red, finely shredded | 3.5 kg | 7 kg | 14 kg |
| sultanas | 200 g | 400 g | 800 g |
| apples, peeled, cored, small dice | 350 g | 700 g | 1.4 kg |
| cinnamon, powdered | 1 tsp | 2 tsp | 4 tsp |
| vinegar, white | 100 mL | 200 mL | 400 mL |
| sugar | 50 g | 100 g | 200 g |
| salt and freshly milled black pepper | to taste | | |

**Method**

1 Place cabbage, sultanas, apple, cinnamon, vinegar, sugar and a little water in a saucepan over a low heat and cover with a tight fitting lid. Braise slowly for approx. 30–45 minutes or until tender. Stir thoroughly every 10 minutes making sure cabbage does not catch at the bottom of the pan; if it does, add a small amount of extra water.

2 Season to taste and serve.

# Asian-style stir-fried cabbage

Ingredients

|  | 25 | 50 | 100 |
|---|---|---|---|
| oil, sesame | as required | | |
| onions, finely sliced | 200 g | 400 g | 800 g |
| celery, finely sliced at 45° | 150 g | 300 g | 600 g |
| capsicums, red and green, julienne | 150 g | 300 g | 600 g |
| cabbage, white, finely shredded | 2 kg | 4 kg | 8 kg |
| carrots, halved, finely sliced at 45°, refreshed and drained | 150 g | 300 g | 600 g |
| beansprouts | 100 g | 200 g | 400 g |
| oyster sauce | 150 mL | 300 mL | 600 mL |

Method

1 Put a little sesame oil in a saucepan over a high heat. Heat through and add onion, celery, capsicum, cabbage and carrots and stir-fry for approx. 3–4 minutes.
2 Add beansprouts and oyster sauce and mix well. Remove from heat and serve.

# White cabbage baked with chicken stock, white onion and bacon

Ingredients

|  | 25 | 50 | 100 |
|---|---|---|---|
| cabbage, white, medium dice | 3.5 kg | 7 kg | 14 kg |
| stock, chicken | 500 mL | 1 L | 2 L |
| onions, white, finely diced | 250 g | 500 g | 1 kg |
| bacon, rind removed, medium dice | 250 g | 500 g | 1 kg |
| salt and freshly milled black pepper | to taste | | |

Method

1 Pre-heat oven to moderate (150–180°C).
2 Layer cabbage, chicken stock, onion and bacon in a roasting tray and cover tightly with aluminium foil. Place into oven and cook for approx. 30–45 minutes or until cabbage is tender.
3 Remove from oven, season to taste and serve.

# CARROTS

**Seasonal availability**
All year; peak April–August.

**Suitable methods of cookery**
Stir-fry, boiling, steaming, braising.

**Preparation**
Peel, top and tail and wash thoroughly under cold running water,
cut into required size.

**Note**   Carrot is the edible root of a plant belonging to the parsley family.

 **Health tip**   A good source of vitamin A.
To reduce the fat content, use light cream instead of regular cream and use
low fat milk.

## Mashed carrots with caraway seeds and butter

| Ingredients |  | | 25 | 50 | 100 |
|---|---|---|---|---|---|
| | | **carrots**, sliced | 3 kg | 6 kg | 12 kg |
| | | **caraway seeds**, dry roasted | 10 g | 20 g | 40 g |
| | | **butter**, room temperature | 200 g | 400 g | 800 g |
| | | **cream**, single | 50 mL | 100 mL | 200 mL |
| | | **salt and freshly milled black pepper** | to taste | | |

**Method**
1 Steam or boil sliced carrots until soft. Drain well.
2 Place carrots, caraway seeds, butter, cream and seasoning into a
  commercial mixing bowl. Mix until smooth.
3 Check seasoning and place mix into baking/serving tray/s and serve.

## Carrots braised with cream and lemon pepper

| Ingredients |  | | 25 | 50 | 100 |
|---|---|---|---|---|---|
| | | **carrots**, sliced lengthways | 3 kg | 6 kg | 12 kg |
| | | **onions**, white, finely sliced | 200 g | 400 g | 800 g |
| | | **parsley**, finely chopped | 15 g | 30 g | 60 g |
| | | **cream**, single | 1 L | 2 L | 4 L |
| | | **milk** | 500 mL | 1 L | 2 L |
| | | **lemon pepper seasoning** | to taste | | |

**Method**
1 Pre-heat oven to moderate (150–180°C).
2 Layer carrots, onions and parsley in baking tray/s, seasoning each carrot layer lightly.
3 Carefully pour cream and milk, which has been combined in a mixing bowl, over carrots. Seal trays with aluminium foil and place in oven. Cook for approx. 1–1$^1$/$_2$ hours or until carrots are tender.
4 Remove from oven, season and serve.

# Carrots glazed with fresh orange juice, honey and sesame seeds

**Ingredients**

|  | 25 | 50 | 100 |
|---|---|---|---|
| **carrots**, sliced | 3 kg | 6 kg | 12 kg |
| **oranges**, juice and zest | 1 | 2 | 4 |
| **honey** | 100 mL | 200 mL | 400 mL |
| **sesame seeds** | 50 g | 100 g | 200 g |
| **salt and freshly milled black pepper** | to taste | | |

**Method**
1 Steam or boil sliced carrots until tender; drain well.
2 Immediately toss drained carrots with all other ingredients together in a mixing bowl, season to taste and serve.

# CAULIFLOWER

## Seasonal availability
All year; peak June–September.

## Suitable methods of cookery
Stir-fry, boiling, steaming

## Preparation
Trim leaves and base of cauliflower stalks, cut into required size florets, wash well under cold running water and drain well.

 Cauliflower is a member of the cabbage, broccoli, brussels sprouts and kale family.

 **Health tip** A good source of vitamin C and iron.
A good source of fibre. Colourful presentation of vegetables will encourage people to eat them.

# Crispy fried cauliflower florets

**Ingredients**

| | | 25 | 50 | 100 |
|---|---|---|---|---|
| cauliflower, small florets | | 3 kg | 6 kg | 12 kg |
| flour, plain | | as required | | |
| salt and freshly milled black pepper | | to taste | | |

**Method**

1 Pre-heat deep fryer to 160–170°C.
2 Blanch, refresh and drain cauliflower florets.
3 Lightly coat dry florets with seasoned flour making sure all the florets are well coated. Place florets into hot oil.
4 Allow florets to cook until they float to the surface of the oil and are golden brown.
5 Remove florets from oil and drain excess fat. Serve.

# Cauliflower florets with fresh herbs and garlic

**Ingredients**

| | 25 | 50 | 100 |
|---|---|---|---|
| cauliflower, florets | 3 kg | 6 kg | 12 kg |
| butter | 250 g | 500 g | 1 kg |
| garlic, cloves, finely chopped | 3 | 6 | 12 |
| basil, fresh, finely chopped | 10 g | 20 g | 40 g |
| parsley, fresh, finely chopped | 10 g | 20 g | 40 g |

**Method**

1 Blanch and refresh cauliflower florets.
2 Melt butter in a saucepan over a moderate heat. Add garlic and herbs.
3 Add cauliflower florets and mix thoroughly until heated through. Serve.

# Cauliflower baked with a bacon and chive sauce

**Ingredients**

| | 25 | 50 | 100 |
|---|---|---|---|
| cauliflower, florets | 3 kg | 6 kg | 12 kg |
| butter | 150 g | 300 g | 600 g |
| flour, plain | 150 g | 300 g | 600 g |
| milk, warm | 2 L | 4 L | 8 L |
| bacon, rind removed, finely chopped | 200 g | 400 g | 800 g |
| chives, finely sliced | 20 g | 40 g | 80 g |
| salt and freshly milled black pepper | to taste | | |
| cheese, Cheddar, grated | 300 g | 600 g | 1.2 kg |

1 Pre-heat oven to moderate (150–180°C).
2 Blanch, refresh and drain cauliflower florets.
3 Melt butter in a saucepan over a moderate heat and add bacon. Gently cook out for approx. 2 minutes.
4 Add flour and incorporate thoroughly. Cook out gently for 2 minutes.
5 Gradually add warm milk until all milk is incorporated.
6 Add chives and season to taste. Cook gently for a further 2–3 minutes.
7 Place cauliflower florets evenly into serving tray/s and cover evenly with sauce. Sprinkle evenly with cheese.
8 Place tray/s into oven and cook until heated through and the cheese turns light golden brown. Serve.

# COUSCOUS

## Seasonal availability
n/a

## Suitable methods of cookery
Boiling, steaming

## Preparation
n/a

**Note**  Although not a vegetable, couscous has become popular as a vegetable or potato alternative. Couscous is made from wheat; the semolina grains are moistened and coated with flour, steamed and then dried. It is a popular dish in North African countries such as Tunisia, Algeria and Egypt and is the national dish of Morocco.

**Health tip**  A good source of iron, thiamin, protein and niacin.

**Ingredients**

|  | 25 | 50 | 100 |
|---|---|---|---|
| couscous | 2 kg | 4 kg | 8 kg |
| water, boiling | 8 L | 16 L | 32 L |
| butter | 400 g | 800 g | 1.6 kg |
| parsley, fresh, finely chopped | 15 g | 30 g | 60 g |
| salt and freshly milled black pepper | to taste | | |

**Method**

1 Place couscous into a saucepan and pour over boiling water.
2 Mix thoroughly with a wooden spoon and allow to stand for 5 minutes.
3 Add butter and cook over a very low heat stirring continually for 4–6 minutes.
4 Remove from heat. Add parsley, season to taste and mix well. Serve.

# EGGPLANT

### Seasonal availability
All year; peak November–March.

### Suitable methods of cookery
Stir-fry, roasting/baking, char-grill, braising

### Preparation
Remove stalk and wash well under cold running water, drain and cut into required size pieces.

**Note** This vegetable is thought to have originated in India. It is a member of the potato and tomato family. Many different varieties can be found throughout the world such as Japanese, Italian and Thai. Eggplant is actually a fruit (a berry).

**Health tip** A good source of vitamin C, potassium and iron.

# Eggplant ratatouille

| Ingredients | | 25 | 50 | 100 |
|---|---|---|---|---|
| **oil**, olive | | a small amount for frying | | |
| **onions**, Spanish, large dice | | 1 kg | 2 kg | 4 kg |
| **garlic**, cloves, peeled, finely chopped | | 4 | 8 | 16 |
| **basil leaves**, fresh, finely chopped | | 1/2 bunch | 1 bunch | 2 bunches |
| **marjoram**, dried | | 1 | 2 | 4 heaped tablespoons |
| **bay-leaves**, dried | | 2 | 4 | 8 |
| **eggplant**, top and tail, cut into 2 cm dice | | 2 kg | 4 kg | 8 kg |
| **zucchini**, top and tail, cut into 2 cm dice | | 1 kg | 2 kg | 4 kg |
| **tomatoes**, remove core, cut into 2 cm dice | | 1 kg | 2 kg | 4 kg |
| **tomatoes**, crushed, A10 tin | | 1 | 2 | 4 |
| **sugar**, castor | | to taste | | |
| **salt and freshly milled black pepper** | | to taste | | |

**Method**
1 Heat oil in a saucepan over a moderate heat.
2 Add onions and garlic and cook without colour until onions are soft.
3 Add basil, marjoram and bay-leaves.
4 Add eggplant, zucchini and tomatoes and mix well.
5 Allow vegetables to sweat until softened, stirring occasionally.
6 Add crushed tomatoes and mix well.
7 Place a tight fitting lid onto pan and cook over a gentle heat for approx. 20–30 minutes stirring occasionally.
8 Add sugar, salt and pepper to taste. Serve.

# Eggplant roasted with garlic, continental parsley and olive oil

| Ingredients | | 25 | 50 | 100 |
|---|---|---|---|---|
| **eggplant**, small dice | | 3 kg | 6 kg | 12 kg |
| **garlic**, cloves, finely chopped | | 3 | 6 | 12 |
| **parsley**, continental, finely chopped | | 20 g | 40 g | 80 g |
| **olive oil** | | 50 mL | 100 mL | 200 mL |
| **salt and freshly milled black pepper** | | to taste | | |

**Method**

1 Pre-heat oven to moderate (150–180°C).
2 Mix all ingredients together in a mixing bowl. Season to taste.
3 Place eggplant mixture onto roasting tray/s and place into oven. Cook for approx. 15–20 minutes or until eggplant is cooked through and lightly browned.
4 Remove from oven and serve.


# Char-grilled seasoned sliced eggplant with fresh oregano

| Ingredients | | 25 | 50 | 100 |
|---|---|---|---|---|
| **olive oil/vegetable oil** | | as required | | |
| **eggplant**, sliced lengthways 1 cm thick | | 3 kg | 6 kg | 12 kg |
| **salt and freshly milled black pepper** | | to taste | | |
| **oregano**, fresh, finely chopped | | 20 g | 40 g | 80 g |

**Method**

1 Pre-heat char-grill.
2 Lightly brush sliced eggplant with a little oil and season.
3 Place onto a char-grill/flat grill plate and cook for approx. 1 minute on either side.
4 Remove from grill. Lay neatly into serving trays and sprinkle with oregano, re-heat if necessary and serve.

# LEEKS

**Seasonal availability**
All year; peak October–May.

**Suitable methods of cookery**
Sauté, stir-fry, roasting/baking, braising.

**Preparation**
Trim ends and remove outer layer, cut in half lengthways and wash well under cold running water, drain and cut into required size pieces.

**Note**

The leek is thought to have come from the Mediterranean area where wild leeks still grow. The leek was introduced to the rest of Europe with the Roman conquests. The Welsh have worn the leek on their helmets during battle to distinguish themselves from the enemy and it has since become their national emblem. A member of the garlic and onion family.

**Health tip**

A good source of vitamin C, iron and fibre.

## Creamy leeks sautéed with garlic and bacon

| Ingredients | | 25 | 50 | 100 |
|---|---|---|---|---|
| butter | | 100 g | 200 g | 400 g |
| garlic, cloves, finely chopped | | 3 | 6 | 12 |
| bacon, rind removed, finely diced | | 150 g | 300 g | 600 g |
| leeks, finely sliced | | 3 kg | 6 kg | 12 kg |
| cream, single | | 300 mL | 600 mL | 1.2 L |
| salt and freshly milled black pepper | | to taste | | |

**Method**

1. Melt butter in a saucepan over a moderate heat and add garlic and bacon. Cook gently for approx. 2–3 minutes.
2. Add leeks and sauté for 2–4 minutes and then cover with a tight fitting lid. Cook, stirring regularly, for a further 3–4 minutes or until leeks are tender.
3. Add cream, mix well and cook for a further 1–2 minutes.
4. Season to taste. Remove from heat and serve.

## Leeks braised in chicken stock and balsamic vinegar

| Ingredients | | 25 | 50 | 100 |
|---|---|---|---|---|
| leeks, 3 cm pieces | | 3 kg | 6 kg | 12 kg |
| stock, chicken | | 500 mL | 1 L | 2 L |
| vinegar, balsamic | | to taste | | |

| Method | |
|---|---|
| | 1 Pre-heat oven to moderate (150–180°C). |
| | 2 Place leeks into baking or serving tray/s. |
| | 3 Mix chicken stock with balsamic vinegar to taste and pour over leeks. |
| | 4 Cover tray/s with aluminium foil and place into oven. Cook for approx. 1 hour or until leeks are tender. |
| | 5 Remove from oven and serve with a little of the remaining stock. |

# Whole roasted leeks

**Ingredients**

| | | 25 | 50 | 100 |
|---|---|---|---|---|
| leeks, whole, 10 cm long | | 25 | 50 | 100 |
| olive oil/vegetable oil | | as required | | |
| salt and freshly milled black pepper | | to taste | | |

**Method**

1 Pre-heat oven to moderate (150–180°C).
2 Brush roasting tray/s with a little olive oil and place leeks side by side one layer deep. Brush leeks with a little oil and season to taste.
3 Place into oven and cook for approx. 45 minutes–1 hour or until leeks are tender.
4 Remove tray/s from oven and serve.

# MUSHROOMS

## Seasonal availability
All year.

## Suitable methods of cookery
Sauté, stir-fry, char-grill, deep frying.

## Preparation
Wash well under cold running water, drain and cut into required size pieces.

 The mushroom was originally cultivated by the Greeks and Romans.
There are thousands of varieties of this fungus, many of which are poisonous.
Mushrooms come in varying shapes, sizes and colours.

 **Health tip**  The common cultivated variety are a good source of vitamin B.

# Mushrooms sautéed with spring onions and fresh basil

**Ingredients**

| | | 25 | 50 | 100 |
|---|---|---|---|---|
| butter | | 100 g | 200 g | 400 g |
| spring onions, cut at 45° | | 150 g | 300 g | 600 g |
| mushrooms, quartered | | 3 kg | 6 kg | 12 kg |
| basil leaves, fresh, cut into strips lengthways | | 10 g | 20 g | 40 g |
| salt and freshly milled black pepper | | to taste | | |

continued

**Method**

1 Melt butter in a saucepan over a moderate heat. Add spring onions and cook for approx. 1 minute.
2 Add mushrooms and basil and cook for approx. 5 minutes or until mushrooms are tender, stirring regularly.
3 Season to taste, remove from heat and serve.

# Deep fried mushrooms

| Ingredients | | 25 | 50 | 100 |
|---|---|---|---|---|
| flour, plain | | as required | | |
| salt and freshly milled black pepper | | to taste | | |
| eggs | | 10 | 20 | 40 |
| milk | | 300 mL | 600 mL | 1.2 L |
| breadcrumbs | | as required | | |
| mushrooms, whole, if large halve | | 3 kg | 6 kg | 12 kg |

**Method**

1 Pre-heat deep fryer to 160–170°C.
2 Place flour mixed with salt and pepper, eggs and milk which have been beaten together, and breadcrumbs into 3 separate mixing bowls.
3 Dredge mushrooms through flour and then the egg mixture followed by the breadcrumb mixture, shaking off any excess crumbs.
4 Place one layer of mushrooms into deep frying baskets and cook until golden brown. Drain well and serve.

♥ **Health tip**   Unsuitable for a low fat diet.

# Mushrooms braised with Spanish onions, bacon and garlic

| Ingredients | | 25 | 50 | 100 |
|---|---|---|---|---|
| mushrooms, quartered | | 3 kg | 6 kg | 12 kg |
| onions, Spanish, large dice | | 1 kg | 2 kg | 4 kg |
| bacon, rind removed, small dice | | 300 g | 600 g | 1.2 kg |
| garlic cloves, finely chopped | | 2 | 4 | 8 |
| stock, chicken | | 500 mL | 1 L | 2 L |

**Method**

1 Pre-heat oven to moderate (150–180°C).
2 Combine all ingredients in roasting tray/s and cover tightly with aluminium foil. Place into oven and cook for approx. 45 minutes–1 hour or until mushrooms are tender.
3 Remove from oven and serve with a little of the remaining stock.

# ONIONS

**Seasonal availability**
All year.

**Suitable methods of cookery**
Sauté, stir-fry, char-grill, deep frying, braising, roasting.

**Preparation**
Top and tail, remove outer skin and cut into required size.

 **Note**   Onions have been cultivated for thousands of years. They were a large part of the diet of the slaves who built the Pyramids in Egypt. A member of the lily family.

 **Health tip**   A good source of vitamin C.

# Deep fried tempura onion rings

| Ingredients | | | 25 | 50 | 100 |
| --- | --- | --- | --- | --- | --- |
| | | cornflour | 1 kg | 2 kg | 4 kg |
| | | rice flour | 1 kg | 2 kg | 4 kg |
| | | **vinegar**, white | 20 mL | 40 mL | 80 mL |
| | | **water**, iced | as required | | |
| | | salt | to taste | | |
| | | **onions**, cut into rings 1 cm thick | 3 kg | 6 kg | 12 kg |
| | | **flour**, plain | 1 kg | 2 kg | 4 kg |

**Method**
1. Pre-heat deep fryer to approx. 160–170°C.
2. Combine cornflour, rice flour and vinegar in a mixing bowl. Slowly incorporate iced water until a consistency is reached that will thickly coat the back of a spoon. Season to taste.
3. Ensuring onion rings are dry, lightly coat with flour and dip onion rings into batter mix. Make sure all the onion rings are coated well. Drain any excess mixture and carefully place into hot oil.
4. Cook onion rings until they float to the surface of the oil and are golden brown.
5. Carefully remove onion rings from oil and drain fat. Serve allowing 5–6 onion rings per portion.

 **Health tip**   Unsuitable for a low fat diet.

# Caramelised roasted onions

| Ingredients | | | 25 | 50 | 100 |
| --- | --- | --- | --- | --- | --- |
| |  | olive oil/vegetable oil | as required | | |
| | | **onions**, medium sized, quartered | 4 kg | 8 kg | 16 kg |
| | | **salt and freshly milled black pepper** | to taste | | |

continued

| | | Method | 1 Pre-heat oven to moderate (150–180°C). |

**Method**

1 Pre-heat oven to moderate (150–180°C).
2 Lightly grease roasting tray/s and place quartered onions one layer deep, cut side down.
3 Brush onions with a little oil, lightly season and place into oven. Cook for approx. 45 minutes–1 hour or until onions are cooked through and lightly browned.
4 Remove from oven and serve two quarters per portion.

# Onions roasted with beef stock

**Ingredients**

| | | 25 | 50 | 100 |
|---|---|---|---|---|
| onions, medium sized, quartered | | 4 kg | 8 kg | 16 kg |
| stock, beef | | 300 mL | 600 mL | 1.2 L |
| salt and freshly milled black pepper | to taste | | | |

**Method**

1 Pre-heat oven to moderate (150–180°C).
2 Place quartered onions one layer deep, cut side down onto roasting tray/s.
3 Pour over beef stock, lightly season and cover trays tightly with aluminium foil. Place into oven and cook for approx 45 minutes– 1 hour or until onions are cooked through and tender.
4 Remove from oven and serve two quarters per portion.

# PARSNIPS

**Seasonal availability**
All year; peak April–October.

**Suitable methods of cookery**
Boiling, steaming, deep frying, braising, roasting.

**Preparation**
Top and tail, peel, wash thoroughly under cold running water, drain and cut into required size.

 **Note**   Parsnips originated in Eastern Europe and have been cultivated for thousands of years essentially as a food for the poor. Parsnips were used in Tudor times in the making of bread; their popularity declined, however, with the introduction of the potato.

 **Health tip**   A good source of vitamin E.

# Roasted parsnip chips

**Ingredients**

| | | 25 | 50 | 100 |
|---|---|---|---|---|
| parsnips, cut into 2 cm x 8 cm chips | | 3 kg | 6 kg | 12 kg |
| olive oil/vegetable oil | | as required | | |
| salt and freshly milled black pepper | to taste | | | |

| Method | 1 Pre-heat oven to moderate (150–180°C). |
| --- | --- |
| | 2 Place parsnip chips onto lightly greased roasting tray/s and lightly season. |
| | 3 Add a little oil and mix well to ensure all chips are lightly coated with oil. |
| | 4 Place tray/s into oven and cook for approx. 45 minutes or until chips are tender and golden brown. |
| | 5 Remove from oven and serve. |

# Parsnip mash

Ingredients

| | 25 | 50 | 100 |
| --- | --- | --- | --- |
| **parsnips**, roughly chopped | 3 kg | 6 kg | 12 kg |
| **butter**, room temperature | 200 g | 400 g | 800 g |
| **cream**, single | 50 mL | 100 mL | 200 mL |
| **salt and freshly milled black pepper** | to taste | | |

Method

1 Steam or boil parsnips until soft. Drain well.
2 Place parsnips, butter, cream and seasoning into a commercial mixing bowl and mix until smooth.
3 Season and place mix into baking/serving tray/s and serve.

 Health tip    To reduce fat content, use evaporated milk instead of cream and use less butter.

# Crispy shaved parsnips

Ingredients

| | 25 | 50 | 100 |
| --- | --- | --- | --- |
| **parsnips**, finely sliced lengthways | 2.5 kg | 5 kg | 10 kg |
| **salt and freshly milled black pepper** | to taste | | |

Method

1 Pre-heat deep frying oil to 160–170°C. Place parsnips into hot fat in small batches and cook until the slices are crisp and a light golden brown.
2 Remove from oil and drain all excess oil. Season to taste and serve.

 Health tip    Unsuitable for low fat diets.

# POLENTA

**Seasonal availability**
n/a

**Suitable methods of cookery**
Sauté, boiling, steaming, deep frying, roasting.

**Preparation**
n/a

 Although not a vegetable, polenta has become popular as a vegetable or potato alternative. Polenta is a coarse yellow flour made from corn. It originated in northern Italy and was the main food ration of the Roman legionnaire. It has now been adopted by many other countries around the world.

 A good source of iron, thiamin, protein and niacin.

## Fresh herb polenta

| Ingredients | 25 | 50 | 100 |
|---|---|---|---|
| water/chicken stock | 2.3 L | 4.6 L | 9.2 L |
| chives, finely chopped | 10 g | 20 g | 40 g |
| basil, finely chopped | 10g | 20 g | 40 g |
| parsley, finely chopped | 10 g | 20 g | 40 g |
| polenta | 660 g | 1.3 kg | 2.6 kg |
| salt and freshly ground black pepper | to taste | | |

**Method**
1 Bring water to a simmer in a pan.
2 Add herbs and simmer for approx. 2 minutes, allowing herbs to infuse.
3 Add polenta and stir continuously until polenta absorbs all liquid and thickens. Stir for approx. 1 minute to cook out and remove from heat.
4 Season to taste and serve.

## Golden polenta triangles

| Ingredients | 25 | 50 | 100 |
|---|---|---|---|
| water/chicken stock | 2.3 L | 4.6 L | 9.2 L |
| polenta | 660 g | 1.3 kg | 2.6 kg |
| salt and freshly ground black pepper | to taste | | |
| olive oil/vegetable oil | as required | | |

**Method**
1 Bring water to a simmer in a pan.
2 Add polenta and stir continuously until polenta absorbs all liquid and thickens. Stir for approx. 1 minute to cook out and remove from heat. Season to taste.

3 Lightly grease baking trays and firmly press cooled polenta to a depth of $1^1/_2$ cm evenly into tray. Rest in a cool place for approx. 30–45 minutes.
4 Cut polenta into required size triangles.
5 Heat a little oil in a sauté pan over a moderate heat. Fry polenta triangles on each side until golden brown.
6 Remove triangles from pan. Drain any excess oil and serve.

# PUMPKIN

### Seasonal availability
All year; peak February–May.

### Suitable methods of cookery
Boiling, steaming, deep frying, roasting.

### Preparation
Quarter, remove seeds, cut into required size and remove skin.

 Pumpkin is a member of the gourd family which includes melons and squash. It originated in South America.

 Health tip    A good source of vitamins A and C.

# Warmed pumpkin mousse

Ingredients

| | 25 | 50 | 100 |
|---|---|---|---|
| pumpkin | 4 kg | 8 kg | 16 kg |
| butter | 100 g | 200 g | 400 g |
| eggs | 4 | 8 | 16 |
| salt and freshly milled black pepper | to taste | | |

Method
1 Pre-heat oven to moderate (150–180°C).
2 Steam or boil pumpkin until tender, drain and cool.
3 Place pumpkin, butter, eggs and a little seasoning into a commercial mixing bowl. Mix until smooth.
4 Place pumpkin evenly into lightly greased serving tray/s.
5 Place trays into oven and cook for approx. 20 minutes or until pumpkin is firm to the touch.
6 Remove from oven, pre-portion and serve.

# Roasted pumpkin with nutmeg, honey and parsley

| Ingredients | | 25 | 50 | 100 |
|---|---|---|---|---|
| olive oil/vegetable oil | | as required | | |
| pumpkin, skin on, 4 cm x 4 cm square | | 3 kg | 6 kg | 12 kg |
| nutmeg | | 10 g | 20 g | 40 g |
| honey | | 100 mL | 200 mL | 400 mL |
| parsley, fresh, finely chopped | | 10 g | 20 g | 40 g |

**Method**

1 Pre-heat oven to moderate (150–180°C).
2 Place pumpkin onto lightly greased roasting tray/s.
3 Add a little oil, nutmeg and honey and mix well. Arrange pumpkin pieces so that they are all skin side down.
4 Place tray/s into oven and cook for approx. 30–45 minutes or until pumpkin is tender.
5 Remove from oven, sprinkle with parsley and serve.


# Puréed butternut pumpkin with fresh coriander and sour cream

| Ingredients | | 25 | 50 | 100 |
|---|---|---|---|---|
| pumpkin, butternut | | 3 kg | 6 kg | 12 kg |
| coriander, fresh, finely chopped | | 10 g | 20 g | 40 g |
| butter, room temperature | | 200 g | 400 g | 800 g |
| sour cream | | 50 mL | 100 mL | 200 mL |
| salt and freshly milled black pepper | | to taste | | |

**Method**

1 Steam or boil pumpkin until tender. Drain well.
2 Place pumpkin, coriander, butter, sour cream and seasoning into a commercial mixing bowl. Mix until smooth.
3 Season and place mix into serving tray/s and serve.

 **Health tip**   To reduce fat content, use evaporated milk instead of cream and use less butter.

# SPINACH

### Seasonal availability
Peak March–November.

### Suitable methods of cookery
Sauté, stir-fry, boiling, steaming.

### Preparation
Discard any discoloured leaves, remove all stalks and wash leaves thoroughly under cold running water.

 Spinach originated in the Middle East and has been grown in Spain since the 8th century.

 **Health tip**  An excellent source of iron as well as vitamins A and C.

# Spinach with garden peas and cream

| Ingredients | | 25 | 50 | 100 |
|---|---|---|---|---|
| **spinach**, blanched, well drained | | 4 kg | 8 kg | 16 kg |
| **peas**, cooked | | 1 kg | 2 kg | 4 kg |
| **cream**, single | | 400 mL | 800 mL | 1.6 L |
| **salt and freshly milled black pepper** | to taste | | | |

**Method**

1 Squeeze all excess water from spinach and cut into thin strips. Place into a pan with peas, cream and seasoning.
2 Place pan over a moderate heat and warm through whilst mixing thoroughly.
3 Remove from heat and serve.

**Health tip**  To reduce fat content, use less cream.

# Spinach stir-fried with pine nuts and bacon

| Ingredients | | 25 | 50 | 100 |
|---|---|---|---|---|
| **butter** | | 100 g | 200 g | 400 g |
| **bacon**, rind removed, small dice | | 250 g | 500 g | 1 kg |
| **spinach**, finely shredded | | 5 kg | 10 kg | 20 kg |
| **pine nuts**, toasted to a light golden brown | | 250 g | 500 g | 1 kg |
| **salt and freshly milled black pepper** | to taste | | | |

continued

| Method | |
|---|---|
| | 1 Melt butter in a saucepan over a moderate heat. Add bacon and cook for 1 minute. |
| | 2 Add spinach and cook for a further 3–4 minutes stirring continuously. Add pine nuts and season to taste. |
| | 3 Remove from the heat and serve. |

# Creamed spinach

| Ingredients | | 25 | 50 | 100 |
|---|---|---|---|---|
| | spinach | 5 kg | 10 kg | 20 kg |
| | cream, single | 100 mL | 200 mL | 400 mL |
| | salt and freshly milled black pepper | to taste | | |

**Method**

1 Pre-heat oven to moderate (150–180°C).
2 Blanch, refresh and drain spinach. Squeeze out excess water from spinach leaves.
3 Place spinach into a food processor and blend with cream and seasoning until smooth.
4 Place spinach into serving tray/s, cover with aluminium foil and place into oven. Cook for a further 20–30 minutes or until heated through.
5 Remove from oven and serve.

# SWEET CORN

## Seasonal availability
All year; peak September–March.

## Suitable methods of cookery
Sauté, stir-fry, boiling, steaming, char-grill.

## Preparation
Remove outer leaves and husk, trim and wash well under cold running water and drain.

 Sweet corn originated in South America and has been cultivated there for thousands of years by Peruvian Indians. Sweet corn was introduced to the rest of the world by colonists and traders to the region.

 **Health tip** A good source of vitamin C and fibre.

# Corn cobs tossed with butter, fresh Parmesan and black pepper

| Ingredients | | | 25 | 50 | 100 |
|---|---|---|---|---|---|
|  | **corn**, cobs | | 17 | 34 | 68 |
| | **butter**, melted | | 200 g | 400 g | 800 g |
| | **Parmesan**, fresh, finely grated | | 100 g | 200 g | 400 g |
| | **freshly milled black pepper** | | to taste | | |

**Method**

1 Cut corn cobs into three even sized pieces and cook in boiling water until tender.
2 Remove corn cobs from water and drain briefly.
3 In a mixing bowl, toss corn cobs with butter, Parmesan and pepper thoroughly.
4 Serve immediately.

**Health tip**    Use less butter to reduce fat content.


# Spicy corn stir-fried with Spanish onion and capsicum

| Ingredients | | 25 | 50 | 100 |
|---|---|---|---|---|
|  | **corn**, niblets | 2.5 kg | 5 kg | 10 kg |
| | **olive oil/vegetable oil** | as required | | |
| | **onions**, Spanish, finely chopped | 500 g | 1 kg | 2 kg |
| | **garlic**, cloves, finely chopped | 2 | 4 | 8 |
| | **chillies**, fresh, finely chopped | 1 | 2 | 4 |
| | **capsicums**, red, cored, seeded, finely chopped | 1/2 | 1 | 2 |
| | **capsicums**, green, cored, seeded, finely chopped | 1/2 | 1 | 2 |
| | **parsley**, fresh, finely chopped | 20 g | 40 g | 80 g |

**Method**

1 Blanch, refresh and drain corn niblets.
2 Heat a little oil in a saucepan or on a flat grill plate. Add onions, garlic, chillies and capsicum and cook until onions are tender.
3 Add sweet corn and stir-fry for approx. 4–5 minutes or until sweet corn is heated through. Add parsley and mix well.
4 Remove from heat and serve.

# Corn wheels with fresh herb butter

| Ingredients | | 25 | 50 | 100 |
|---|---|---|---|---|
| corn cobs, cut widthways at 2 cm intervals | | 13 | 25 | 50 |
| butter, melted | | 500 g | 1 kg | 2 kg |
| parsley, fresh, finely chopped | | 10 g | 20 g | 40 g |
| basil, finely chopped | | 10 g | 20 g | 40 g |
| chives, finely sliced | | 10 g | 20 g | 40 g |
| salt and freshly milled black pepper | to taste | | | |

**Method**

1 Cook corn wheels in boiling water until tender.
2 Remove corn wheels from water and drain briefly.
3 In a mixing bowl, toss with the butter, parsley, basil and chives. Season to taste and serve.

**Health tip**   Use less butter to reduce fat content.

# ZUCCHINI

## Seasonal availability
All year; peak November–January.

## Suitable methods of cookery
Sauté, stir-fry, boiling, steaming, char-grill.

## Preparation
Top and tail and wash thoroughly under cold running water, drain and cut into required size.

**Note**   Zucchini originated in Italy; its name translates as 'sweetness'. Columbus is believed to have taken the seeds to North America.

**Health tip**   A good source of vitamin C.

# Zucchini with red capsicum and fresh basil leaves

| Ingredients | | 25 | 50 | 100 |
|---|---|---|---|---|
| olive oil/vegetable oil | | as required | | |
| garlic, cloves, finely chopped | | 3 | 6 | 12 |
| zucchini, cut into batons | | 2.5 kg | 5 kg | 10 kg |
| capsicums, red, cored, seeded, fine julienne | | 500 g | 1 kg | 2 kg |
| basil, leaves, shredded | | 10 g | 20 g | 40 g |
| salt and freshly milled black pepper | to taste | | | |

**Method**

1 Put a little oil in a saucepan or on a flat grill plate over a moderate heat. Add garlic and cook for 1 minute.
2 Add zucchini and capsicum and cook for approx. 4–5 minutes or until zucchini is tender.
3 Add basil and season to taste. Remove from heat and serve.

# Zucchini braised in beef stock with fresh rosemary

**Ingredients**

| | 25 | 50 | 100 |
|---|---|---|---|
| **zucchini**, medium sized, halved lengthways | 13 | 25 | 50 |
| **stock**, beef | 250 mL | 500 mL | 1 L |
| **rosemary**, fresh, leaves, roughly chopped | 15 g | 30 g | 60 g |

**Method**

1 Pre-heat oven to moderate (150–180°C).
2 Place zucchini halves one layer deep, cut side down into roasting tray/s.
3 Pour over beef stock and rosemary. Cover trays tightly with aluminium foil. Place tray/s into oven and cook for approx. 30 minutes or until zucchini is cooked through and tender.
4 Remove from oven and serve one half per portion.

# Zucchini tossed in garlic and fresh herb butter

**Ingredients**

| | 25 | 50 | 100 |
|---|---|---|---|
| **olive oil/vegetable oil** | as required | | |
| **garlic**, cloves, finely chopped | 3 | 6 | 12 |
| **zucchini**, $1/2$ cm rings | 3 kg | 6 kg | 12 kg |
| **butter** | 200 g | 400 g | 800 g |
| **parsley**, fresh, finely chopped | 10 g | 20 g | 40 g |
| **basil**, fresh, finely chopped | 10 g | 20 g | 40 g |
| **salt and freshly milled black pepper** | to taste | | |

**Method**

1 Place a little oil in a saucepan or on a flat grill plate over a moderate heat. Add garlic and cook for one minute.
2 Add zucchini and cook for approx. 4–5 minutes or until tender, mixing continuously.
3 Add all other ingredients and mix well. Season to taste. Remove from heat and serve.

 **Health tip**    To reduce fat content, use less butter.

# CAKES AND SLICES

## Cakes

## Biscuits

## Slices

## Muffins

# CAKES

## Pear and fresh ginger butter tea cake

|  | | 25 | 50 | 100 |
|---|---|---|---|---|
| **butter**, room temperature | | 740 g | 1.480 kg | 2.960 kg |
| **sugar**, castor | | 560 g | 1.120 g | 2.240 g |
| **eggs** | | 12 | 24 | 48 |
| **flour**, self-raising | | 480 g | 960 g | 1.920 kg |
| **flour**, plain | | 270 g | 540 g | 1.080 kg |
| **ginger**, fresh, minced | | 2 tbsp | 4 tbsp | 8 tbsp |
| **milk** | | 375 mL | 750 mL | 1.5 L |
| **pears**, peeled and cored, cut into 8 even-sized pieces lengthways | | 2 | 4 | 8 |

**Ingredients**

**Method**

1 Pre-heat oven to moderate (150–180°C).
2 Cream butter and sugar in a mixing bowl.
3 Fold in eggs one at a time until all are incorporated and gently mix in minced ginger.
4 Fold in sieved flours and slowly incorporate milk until mixed well.
5 Grease required amount of round cake tins, lining the base with lightly oiled greaseproof paper. Half fill with mixture.
6 Taking eight pieces of pear per tin, place evenly and neatly around the top of the cake mixture rounded side up.
7 Place cake tins into oven and cook for approx. 50 minutes or until cooked through.
8 Remove from oven. Cool for approx. 15 minutes before turning out onto cooling racks.
9 Dust cake prior to serving with a little sieved icing sugar and powdered ginger.

 **Note**

Pears should be prepared as close to the required time as possible as they discolour quickly. Tinned pears can be substituted if fresh ones are unavailable.

 **Health tip**

To increase fibre content, use wholemeal flour.
To reduce fat content, use skim milk instead of full cream milk.

## Iced almond summer cake

|  | | 25 | 50 | 100 |
|---|---|---|---|---|
| **butter**, room temperature | | 500 g | 1 kg | 2 kg |
| **sugar**, castor | | 720 g | 1.440 kg | 2.880 kg |
| **almond essence** | | 1/2 tsp | 1 tsp | 2 tsp |
| **eggs** | | 8 | 16 | 32 |
| **flour**, self-raising | | 720 g | 1.440 kg | 2.880 kg |
| **milk** | | 500 mL | 1 L | 2 L |
| **almonds**, slivered | | 125 g | 250 g | 500 g |

**Ingredients**

### ALMOND BUTTER ICING:

| | | | |
|---|---|---|---|
| **sugar**, icing | 400g | 800 g | 1.6 kg |
| **butter**, melted | 60 g | 120 g | 240 g |
| **almond essence** | to taste | | |

**Method**

1 Pre-heat oven to moderate (150–180°C).
2 Cream butter, sugar and almond essence in a mixing bowl.
3 Fold in eggs one at a time until all are incorporated.
4 Fold in sieved flour and add milk. Gently combine, then fold in almonds.
5 Grease required amount of round cake tins, lining the base with lightly oiled greaseproof paper; half fill with mixture.
6 Place cake tins into oven and cook for approx. 50 minutes or until cooked through.
7 Remove from oven. Cool for approx. 15 minutes before turning out onto cooling racks.
8 When cooled, lightly ice cake with almond butter icing.
9 When icing has set, serve.

**Almond Icing**

1 Combine icing sugar and butter in a mixing bowl and mix well.
2 Gradually add almond essence to taste.

**Health tip**

To increase fibre content, use wholemeal flour.
To reduce fat content, use skim milk instead of full cream milk.

# Fresh lemon and lime syrup cake

**Ingredients**

| | 25 | 50 | 100 |
|---|---|---|---|
| **butter**, room temperature | 500 g | 1 kg | 2 kg |
| **sugar**, castor | 720 g | 1.440 kg | 2.880 kg |
| **eggs** | 8 | 16 | 32 |
| **flour**, self-raising | 720 g | 1.440 kg | 2.880 kg |
| **milk** | 500 mL | 1 L | 2 L |
| **lemons**, zest, reserve juice for syrup | 2 | 4 | 8 |
| **limes**, zest, reserve juice for syrup | 2 | 4 | 8 |

### LEMON AND LIME SYRUP:

| | | | |
|---|---|---|---|
| **lemon**, juice | 125 mL | 250 mL | 500 mL |
| **lime**, juice | 125 mL | 250 mL | 500 mL |
| **water** | 125 mL | 250 mL | 500 mL |
| **sugar**, castor | 240 g | 480 g | 960 g |

continued

| | | | |

**Method**

1 Pre-heat oven to moderate (150–180°C).
2 Cream butter, sugar, lemon and lime zest in a mixing bowl.
3 Fold in egg yolks one at a time until all are incorporated.
4 Fold in sieved flour and slowly incorporate milk until thoroughly combined.
5 In a separate mixing bowl, whisk egg whites until soft peaks form. Fold through the cake mixture.
6 Grease required amount of round cake tins, lining the base with lightly oiled greaseproof paper; half fill with mixture.
7 Place cake tins into oven and cook for approx. 50 minutes or until cooked through.
8 Remove from oven. Cool for approx. 15 minutes before turning out onto cooling racks.
9 Whilst cakes are still warm, pour a little of the syrup over the top of each cake and allow to soak through. Cool and serve.

**Lemon and Lime Syrup**

1 Combine all syrup ingredients in a saucepan and place over a moderate heat.
2 Gently simmer for approx. 5 minutes and remove from heat. Cool.

 **Health tip**

To increase fibre content, use wholemeal flour.
To reduce fat content, use skim milk instead of full cream milk.

# Orange and poppy seed cake

**Ingredients**

| | 25 | 50 | 100 |
|---|---|---|---|
| **butter**, room temperature | 500 g | 1 kg | 2 kg |
| **sugar**, castor | 720 g | 1.440 kg | 2.880 kg |
| **oranges**, zest, reserve juice for syrup | 5 | 10 | 20 |
| **eggs**, yolks and whites separated | 8 | 16 | 32 |
| **poppy seeds** | 250 g | 500 g | 1 kg |
| **flour**, self-raising | 720 g | 1.440 kg | 2.880 kg |
| **milk** | 500 mL | 1 L | 2 L |
| **ORANGE SYRUP:** | | | |
| water | 250 mL | 500 mL | 1 L |
| orange juice | 125 mL | 250 mL | 500 mL |
| sugar | 240 g | 480 g | 960 g |

**Method**

1 Pre-heat oven to moderate (150–180°C).
2 Cream butter, sugar and orange zest in a mixing bowl.
3 Fold in eggs yolks one at a time until all are incorporated. Mix in poppy seeds.
4 Fold in sieved flour and slowly incorporate milk until thoroughly combined.

5 In a separate mixing bowl whisk egg whites until soft peaks form. Fold through the cake mixture.
6 Grease required amount of round cake tins, lining the base with lightly oiled greaseproof paper; half fill with mixture.
7 Place cake tins into oven and cook for approx. 50 minutes or until cooked through.
8 Remove from oven. Cool for approx. 15 minutes before turning out onto cooling racks.
9 While cakes are still warm, pour a little of the syrup over the top of each cake. Allow to soak through. Cool and serve.

**Orange Syrup**
1 Combine all syrup ingredients in a saucepan and place over a moderate heat.
2 Gently simmer for approx. 5 minutes and remove from heat. Cool.

**♥ Health tip**
To increase fibre content, use wholemeal flour.
To reduce fat content, use skim milk instead of full cream milk.

# Home-made walnut and carrot cake

**Ingredients**

| | 25 | 50 | 100 |
|---|---|---|---|
| **butter**, room temperature | 500 g | 1 kg | 2 kg |
| **sugar**, castor | 960 g | 1.920 kg | 3.840 kg |
| **eggs** | 12 | 24 | 48 |
| **flour**, self-raising | 240 g | 480 g | 960 g |
| **flour**, plain | 240 g | 480 g | 960 g |
| **carrots**, peeled, grated | 450 g | 900 g | 1.8 kg |
| **walnuts**, roughly chopped | 480 g | 960 g | 1.920 kg |

**Method**
1 Pre-heat oven to moderate (150–180°C).
2 Cream butter and sugar in a mixing bowl.
3 Fold in eggs one at a time until all are incorporated.
4 Fold in sieved flours, grated carrot and walnuts.
5 Grease required amount of round cake tins, lining the base with lightly oiled greaseproof paper; half fill with mixture.
6 Place cake tins into oven and cook for approx. 50 minutes or until cooked through.
7 Remove from oven. Cool for approx. 15 minutes before turning out onto cooling racks. Serve.

This cake can be iced if desired.

**♥ Health tip**
Use wholemeal flour to increase fibre content.

# Traditional English scones

**Yields:** 1 scone/person

|  |  | 25 | 50 | 100 |
|---|---|---|---|---|
| **flour**, self-raising | | 960 g | 1.920 kg | 3.840 kg |
| **sugar**, castor | | 120 g | 240 g | 480 g |
| **butter**, room temperature, small dice | | 120 g | 240 g | 480 g |
| **milk**, warm | | 500 mL | 750 mL | 1 L |
| **water**, warm | | 250 mL | 500 mL | 1 L |
| **milk** | | as required to brush scones | | |

*Ingredients* appears to the left of the ingredient list.

**Method**

1 Pre-heat oven to moderate (150–180°C).
2 Combine sieved flour and sugar in a mixing bowl.
3 Add butter and gently rub into flour until a sandy texture is achieved.
4 Gradually add milk and water, mixing thoroughly until a moist dough is achieved.
5 Turn dough out onto a lightly floured surface and gently form into a ball.
6 Roll out dough to approx. 2 cm with a lightly floured rolling pin.
7 Cut out required amount of scones using a 5 cm pastry cutter and place onto lightly floured and warmed baking trays approx. 3 mm apart.
8 Brush the top of each scone with a little of the milk. Place trays into oven for approx. 20–25 minutes or until golden brown.
9 Remove from oven. Cool slightly on baking trays before placing onto cooling racks.
10 Serve halved, topped with strawberry jam and whipped cream.

**Note** A little mixed spice can be added for variety if scones are made frequently.

**Health tip** Scones are suitable for low fat diets. Serve with low fat margarine and jam, not cream. Use wholemeal flour to increase the fibre.

# BISCUITS

# Home-made macadamia chocolate chip cookies

**Yields:** 2 cookies/person

|  |  | 25 | 50 | 100 |
|---|---|---|---|---|
| **butter**, room temperature | | 425 g | 850 g | 1.7 kg |
| **sugar**, castor | | 570 g | 140 g | 280 g |
| **bicarbonate of soda** | | 3¹/₂ tsp | 7 tsp | 14 tsp |
| **eggs** | | 2 | 4 | 8 |

*Ingredients* appears to the left of the ingredient list.

| | 2 tsp | 4 tsp | 8 tsp |
|---|---|---|---|
| **vanilla essence** | 2 tsp | 4 tsp | 8 tsp |
| **flour**, plain | 245 g | 490 g | 980 g |
| **oats**, rolled | 350 g | 700 g | 1.4 kg |
| **macadamia nuts**, roughly chopped | 350 g | 700 g | 1.4 kg |
| **chocolate**, dark, roughly chopped | 350 g | 700 g | 1.4 kg |

**Method**

1 Pre-heat oven to moderate (150–180°C).
2 Cream butter, sugar and vanilla essence until light and fluffy.
3 Beat in bicarbonate of soda and eggs one at a time until well combined.
4 In a separate bowl, combine sifted flour and oats and add this to the macadamia nuts and chocolate.
5 Add to the creamed butter and sugar and mix well.
6 Grease required amount of baking trays.
7 Taking a heaped teaspoon of mixture at a time, roll into balls and place onto baking trays pressing down lightly. Allow room for spreading on baking trays.
8 Bake in the oven for 10–15 minutes or until light golden brown.
9 Remove from oven. Cool on baking trays for 5 minutes and then transfer to cooling racks until required. Serve.

 **Health tip**     Unsuitable for low fat diets.

 # Almond shortbread biscuits

**Y**ields: 2 biscuits/person

**Ingredients**

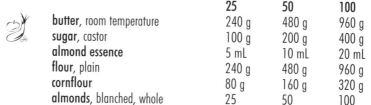

| | 25 | 50 | 100 |
|---|---|---|---|
| **butter**, room temperature | 240 g | 480 g | 960 g |
| **sugar**, castor | 100 g | 200 g | 400 g |
| **almond essence** | 5 mL | 10 mL | 20 mL |
| **flour**, plain | 240 g | 480 g | 960 g |
| **cornflour** | 80 g | 160 g | 320 g |
| **almonds**, blanched, whole | 25 | 50 | 100 |

**Method**

1 Pre-heat oven to moderate (150–180°C).
2 Cream butter, sugar and almond essence until light and fluffy.
3 Sift flours into creamed butter mixture and mix well.
4 Grease required amount of baking trays.
5 Taking a heaped teaspoon of mixture at a time, roll into balls and place onto baking trays pressing down lightly. Top each biscuit with a blanched almond. Allow room for spreading on baking trays.
6 Bake in the oven for 10–15 minutes or until a light golden brown.
7 Remove from oven. Cool on baking trays for 5 minutes and then transfer to cooling racks until required. Serve.

**Health tip**     Not recommended for low fat diets.

# Fig and macadamia cookies

Yields: 2 cookies / person

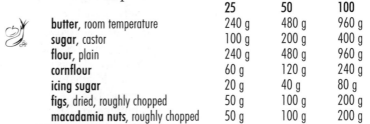

| Ingredients | | | 25 | 50 | 100 |
|---|---|---|---|---|---|
| | | butter, room temperature | 240 g | 480 g | 960 g |
| | | sugar, castor | 100 g | 200 g | 400 g |
| | | flour, plain | 240 g | 480 g | 960 g |
| | | cornflour | 60 g | 120 g | 240 g |
| | | icing sugar | 20 g | 40 g | 80 g |
| | | figs, dried, roughly chopped | 50 g | 100 g | 200 g |
| | | macadamia nuts, roughly chopped | 50 g | 100 g | 200 g |

**Method**

1 Pre-heat oven to moderate (150–180°C).
2 Cream butter and sugar until light and fluffy.
3 Sift flours and icing sugar into mixture, then add figs and macadamia nuts. Mix well.
4 Grease required amount of baking trays.
5 Taking a heaped teaspoon of mixture at a time, roll into balls and place onto baking trays pressing down lightly. Allow room for spreading on baking trays.
6 Bake in the oven for 10–15 minutes or until a light golden brown.
7 Remove from oven. Cool on baking trays for 5 minutes and then transfer to cooling racks until required. Serve.

 **Health tip** The figs and nuts make these biscuits high in fibre.

# Anzac biscuits

Yields 2 biscuits / person

| Ingredients | | | 25 | 50 | 100 |
|---|---|---|---|---|---|
| | | oats, rolled | 160 g | 320 g | 640 g |
| | | flour, plain | 250 g | 500 g | 1 kg |
| | | sugar, castor | 440 g | 880 g | 1.75 kg |
| | | coconut, desiccated | 180 g | 360 g | 720 g |
| | | butter | 250 g | 500 g | 1 kg |
| | | golden syrup | 120 mL | 240 mL | 480 mL |
| | | bicarbonate of soda | 5 g | 10 g | 20 g |
| | | water, boiling | 40 mL | 80 mL | 160 mL |

**Method**

1 Pre-heat oven to moderate (150–180°C).
2 Combine oats, sifted flour, sugar and coconut in a large mixing bowl.
3 Place butter and golden syrup into a saucepan and stir over a low heat until butter has melted. Remove from heat.
4 Add combined bicarbonate of soda and water to the butter mixture and combine.
5 Add butter mixture to the dry ingredients and mix well.
6 Grease required amount of baking trays.

7 Taking a heaped teaspoon of mixture at a time, roll into balls and place onto baking trays pressing down lightly. Allow room for spreading on baking trays.
8 Bake in the oven for 8–10 minutes or until a light golden brown.
9 Remove from oven. Cool and harden on baking trays for 5 minutes and then transfer to cooling racks until required. Serve.

 **Health tip**  Not recommended for low fat diets.
These biscuits are quite high in fibre.

# Orange poppy seed biscuits

Yields: 2 biscuits/person

Ingredients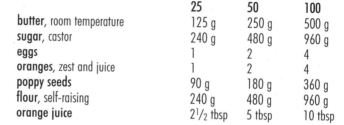

| | 25 | 50 | 100 |
|---|---|---|---|
| **butter**, room temperature | 125 g | 250 g | 500 g |
| **sugar**, castor | 240 g | 480 g | 960 g |
| **eggs** | 1 | 2 | 4 |
| **oranges**, zest and juice | 1 | 2 | 4 |
| **poppy seeds** | 90 g | 180 g | 360 g |
| **flour**, self-raising | 240 g | 480 g | 960 g |
| **orange juice** | 2$^{1}/_{2}$ tbsp | 5 tbsp | 10 tbsp |

Method
1 Pre-heat oven to moderate (150–180°C).
2 Cream butter and sugar in a bowl.
3 Add egg/s and mix well.
4 Add orange zest to butter mixture and mix well.
5 Add poppy seeds and sifted flour to butter mixture.
6 Add orange juice and mix well.
7 Grease required amount of baking trays.
8 Taking a heaped teaspoon of mixture at a time, roll into balls and place onto baking trays pressing down lightly. Allow room for spreading on baking trays.
9 Bake in the oven for 10–15 minutes or until a light golden brown.
10 Remove from oven. Cool on baking trays for 5 minutes and then transfer to cooling racks until required. Serve.

# Almond biscotti

Ingredients

| | 25 | 50 | 100 |
|---|---|---|---|
| **flour**, plain | 360 g | 720 g | 1.440 kg |
| **sugar**, castor | 360 g | 720 g | 1.440 kg |
| **bicarbonate of soda** | $^{1}/_{4}$ tsp | $^{1}/_{2}$ tsp | 1 tsp |
| **almonds**, blanched | 175 g | 350 g | 700 g |
| **eggs** | 3 | 6 | 12 |

 **Note**  This recipe **should not** be made using a blender or mixer but should be made by hand.

continued

1 Pre-heat oven to moderate (150–180°C).
2 Mix all dry ingredients together in a mixing bowl.
3 In a separate bowl lightly whisk eggs.
4 Slowly add whisked eggs to a well made in the centre of the dry ingredients. Mix gently.
5 Lightly knead mixture on a lightly floured surface for approx. 5 minutes.
6 Mould dough into cylindrical shapes approx. 8 cm in diameter and place onto lightly greased baking tray/s and gently press down on dough so it forms an oval shape.
7 Place tray/s into oven for approx. 35–40 minutes.
8 Remove tray/s from oven and cool for 5 minutes. Turn oven to low (130–150°C).
9 Slice cooked biscotti dough into thin oval slices, preferably with an electric knife.
10 Lay the slices carefully onto the baking trays and return to a *low* oven for a further 10–12 minutes or until light golden brown.
11 Remove from oven, cool and allow to crisp before removing from baking trays. Serve.

 Notes

This is a classic Italian twice baked crisp biscuit that is traditionally made with almonds or hazelnuts. Biscotti is ideally served with coffee, liqueurs or desserts such as crème brûlée or sweetened marscapone cheese.

Biscotti can be made in advance if stored in an airtight container.

 Health tip

These are very low in fat and therefore are suitable for low fat diets.

# SLICES

# White chocolate and blueberry cream cheese slice

Yields: 1 slice/person

| Ingredients | | | 25 | 50 | 100 |
|---|---|---|---|---|---|
|  | biscuits, sweet | | 500 g | 1 kg | 2 kg |
| | coconut, desiccated | | 45 g | 90g | 180 g |
| | butter, melted | | 500 g | 1 kg | 2 kg |
| | cream cheese | | 500 g | 1 kg | 2 kg |
| | milk, condensed | | 400 g | 800 g | 1.6 kg |
| | vanilla essence | | 2 mL | 4 mL | 8 mL |
| | chocolate, white, finely chopped | | 100 g | 200 g | 400 g |
| | blueberries, tinned, drained | | 250 g | 500 g | 1 kg |
| | gelatine, powdered | | 2 tbsp | 4 tbsp | 8 tbsp |
| | water, boiling | | 125 mL | 250 mL | 500 mL |

**Method**

1 Blend the biscuits and coconut until they resemble fine breadcrumbs.
2 Add half the melted butter and mix well.
3 Spread mixture out evenly over the base of lamington trays approx. 1 cm deep and refrigerate until set.
4 Blend cream cheese until smooth. Add to vanilla essence, condensed milk and the other half of the melted butter. Stir until combined.
5 Add white chocolate and mix well.
6 In a separate mixing bowl, dissolve the gelatine in the boiling water.
7 Add this to the cream cheese mixture and mix well. Gently fold in blueberries.
8 Place cream cheese mixture over biscuit base and spread out evenly.
9 Put back into refrigerator until fully set.
10 Remove from refrigerator, pre-portion and serve.

 **Health tip**    Unsuitable for low fat diets.

# Chocolate, walnut and pecan nut fudge brownies

Yields: 1 slice / person

**Ingredients**

| | 25 | 50 | 100 |
|---|---|---|---|
| butter | 250 g | 500 g | 1 kg |
| chocolate, dark, roughly chopped | 400 g | 800 g | 1.6 kg |
| sugar, castor | 480 g | 960 g | 1.920 kg |
| vanilla essence | 3 tsp | 6 tsp | 12 tsp |
| eggs | 4 | 8 | 16 |
| flour, plain | 240 g | 480 g | 960 g |
| walnuts, roughly chopped | 80 g | 160 g | 320 g |
| pecan nuts, roughly chopped | 80 g | 160 g | 320 g |
| **CHOCOLATE FUDGE TOPPING:** | | | |
| chocolate, dark, roughly chopped | 300 g | 600 g | 1.2 kg |
| golden syrup | 60 mL | 120 mL | 240 mL |

**Method**

1 Pre-heat oven to moderate (150–180°C).
2 Melt butter and chocolate in a saucepan over a low heat. Remove from heat.
3 Stir in sugar and add vanilla essence. Mix well.
4 Beat the eggs in a mixing bowl and add these to the chocolate mixture, mixing well.
5 Add the sifted flour, walnuts and pecan nuts to the chocolate mixture and mix well.

continued

6  Grease required amount of lamington trays and evenly distribute brownie mix.
7  Place trays into oven and cook for approx. 20–25 minutes or until cooked through.
8  Remove from oven. Cool for approx. 30 minutes then turn out onto a cooling rack.
9  Spread chocolate fudge topping with a spatula evenly over brownies. Refrigerate until topping has set.
10  Pre-portion, dust with icing sugar and serve.

**Chocolate Fudge Topping**

1  Melt chocolate in a double saucepan over boiling water.
2  Stir in golden syrup until combined and mixture thickens.
3  Use as required.

**Note**

For variation to this recipe substitute dark for white chocolate.

 **Health tip**

Unsuitable for low fat diets.

# Banana, walnut and mixed spice slice with lemon cream cheese icing

Yields: 1 slice / person

| Ingredients | | 25 | 50 | 100 |
|---|---|---|---|---|
| butter, room temperature | | 180 g | 360 g | 720 g |
| golden syrup | | 4 tbsp | 8 tbsp | 16 tbsp |
| sugar, castor | | 160 g | 320 g | 640 g |
| sugar, brown | | 90 g | 180 g | 360 g |
| eggs | | 2 | 4 | 8 |
| bananas, mashed | | 225 g | 450 g | 900 g |
| flour, self-raising | | 360 g | 720 g | 1.440 kg |
| bicarbonate of soda | | 1 tsp | 2 tsp | 4 tsp |
| ginger, powdered | | 1 tsp | 2 tsp | 4 tsp |
| cinnamon, powdered | | 2 tsp | 4 tsp | 8 tsp |
| walnuts, roughly chopped | | 120 g | 240 g | 480 g |
| milk | | 3 tbsp | 6 tbsp | 12 tbsp |
| **ICING:** | | | | |
| butter, room temperature | | 125 g | 250 g | 500 g |
| lemon, juice | | 60 mL | 120 mL | 240 mL |
| cream cheese | | 400 g | 800 g | 1.6 kg |
| sugar, icing | | 500 g | 1 kg | 2 kg |

| Method | |
|---|---|
| | 1 Pre-heat oven to moderate (150–180°C). |
| | 2 Cream butter, golden syrup and sugars together in a mixing bowl. |
| | 3 Add eggs one at a time until all are incorporated and then add mashed banana. |
| | 4 Sieve flour, bicarbonate of soda, ginger and cinnamon. Add to butter mixture with walnuts and combine. |
| | 5 Add milk and mix gently for approx. 5 minutes until creamy and smooth. |
| | 6 Grease required amount of lamington trays and evenly distribute cake mix. |
| | 7 Place trays into oven and cook for approx. 20–25 minutes or until cooked through. |
| | 8 Remove from oven. Cool completely and evenly ice with lemon cream cheese icing. Place into refrigerator until icing has set. |
| | 9 Pre-portion and serve. |

**Lemon Cream Cheese Icing**

1 Combine all ingredients and mix thoroughly until smooth.
2 Use immediately.

# MUFFINS

## Mixed berry muffins

Yields: 1 muffin / person

**Ingredients**

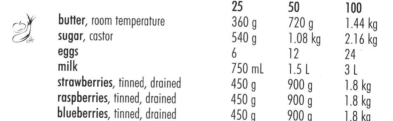

| | 25 | 50 | 100 |
|---|---|---|---|
| **butter**, room temperature | 360 g | 720 g | 1.44 kg |
| **sugar**, castor | 540 g | 1.08 kg | 2.16 kg |
| **eggs** | 6 | 12 | 24 |
| **milk** | 750 mL | 1.5 L | 3 L |
| **strawberries**, tinned, drained | 450 g | 900 g | 1.8 kg |
| **raspberries**, tinned, drained | 450 g | 900 g | 1.8 kg |
| **blueberries**, tinned, drained | 450 g | 900 g | 1.8 kg |
| **flour**, self-raising | 900 g | 1.8 kg | 3.6 kg |

**Method**

1 Pre-heat oven to moderate (150–180°C).
2 Cream butter and sugar in a mixing bowl.
3 Fold in eggs one at a time until all are incorporated.
4 Gradually add milk.
5 Carefully fold through drained berries.
6 Fold in sieved flour.
7 Grease required amount of muffin trays and half fill with mixture.
8 Place trays into oven and cook for 20–25 minutes or until cooked through.
9 Remove from oven. Cool for approx. 5 minutes before turning out onto cooling racks. Serve.

continued
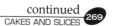

**Note** Other berries can be substituted such as blackberries or mulberries.

**❤ Health tip** These are not low fat muffins.
You can reduce the fat content by using low fat milk.
You can increase the fibre by using wholemeal flour.

# Banana and chocolate chip muffins

Yields: 1 muffin / person

Ingredients

| | 25 | 50 | 100 |
|---|---|---|---|
| **butter**, room temperature | 360 g | 720 g | 1.440 kg |
| **sugar**, castor | 320 g | 640 g | 1.280 kg |
| **eggs** | 3 | 6 | 12 |
| **bananas**, mashed | 750 g | 1.5 kg | 3 kg |
| **chocolate**, dark, roughly chopped | 300 g | 600 g | 1.2 kg |
| **flour**, self-raising | 660 g | 1.320 kg | 2.640 kg |
| **bicarbonate of soda** | ³/₄ tbsp | 1¹/₂ tbsp | 3 tbsp |

Method
1 Pre-heat oven to moderate (150–180°C).
2 Cream butter and sugar in a mixing bowl.
3 Fold in eggs one at a time until all are incorporated.
4 Carefully fold through mashed banana and chocolate chips.
5 Fold in sieved flour and bicarbonate of soda.
6 Grease required amount of muffin trays and half fill with mixture.
7 Place trays into oven and cook for 20–25 minutes or until cooked through.
8 Remove from oven. Cool for approx. 5 minutes before turning out onto cooling racks. Serve.

**❤ Health tip** Not recommended for a low fat diet.

# Apricot and pecan nut muffins

Yields: 1 muffin / person

Ingredients

| | 25 | 50 | 100 |
|---|---|---|---|
| **butter**, room temperature | 360 g | 720 g | 1.440 kg |
| **sugar**, castor | 400 g | 800 g | 1.6 kg |
| **eggs** | 6 | 12 | 24 |
| **milk** | 750 mL | 1.5 L | 3 L |
| **apricots**, dried, roughly chopped | 600 g | 1.2 kg | 2.4 kg |
| **pecan nuts**, roughly chopped | 170 g | 340 g | 680 g |
| **flour**, self-raising | 540 g | 1.080 kg | 2.160 kg |

**Method**

1 Pre-heat oven to moderate (150–180°C).
2 Cream butter and sugar in a mixing bowl.
3 Fold in eggs one at a time until all are incorporated.
4 Gradually add milk.
5 Gently mix in apricots and pecan nuts.
6 Fold in sieved flour.
7 Grease required amount of muffin trays and half fill with mixture.
8 Place trays into oven and cook for 20–25 minutes or until cooked through.
9 Remove from oven. Cool for approx. 5 minutes before turning out onto cooling racks. Serve.

♥ **Health tip**

These can be made more suitable for cholesterol-lowering diets by using margarine instead of butter.
Use low fat milk and wholemeal flour.

# Hot desserts

# Cold desserts

# HOT DESSERTS

## Apple and blueberry crumble with a brown sugar topping served with home-made vanilla custard

**G**arnish: a generous dusting of icing sugar.

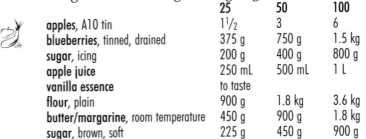

| Ingredients | | 25 | 50 | 100 |
|---|---|---|---|---|
| apples, A10 tin | | 1½ | 3 | 6 |
| blueberries, tinned, drained | | 375 g | 750 g | 1.5 kg |
| sugar, icing | | 200 g | 400 g | 800 g |
| apple juice | | 250 mL | 500 mL | 1 L |
| vanilla essence | | to taste | | |
| flour, plain | | 900 g | 1.8 kg | 3.6 kg |
| butter/margarine, room temperature | | 450 g | 900 g | 1.8 kg |
| sugar, brown, soft | | 225 g | 450 g | 900 g |

**Method**

1 Pre-heat oven to moderate (150–180°C).
2 Combine apples, blueberries, icing sugar, apple juice and vanilla essence in a commercial mixer.
3 Evenly distribute apple mixture into baking/serving trays.
4 Combine sieved flour and butter/margarine in a commercial mixer and gently mix until sandy texture is achieved. Add brown sugar and combine.
5 Evenly distribute flour mixture over apple mixture.
6 Place trays into oven and bake for approx. 20 minutes or until crumble has lightly browned. Serve.

## Home-made vanilla custard

| Ingredients | | 25 | 50 | 100 |
|---|---|---|---|---|
| milk | | 1.5 L | 3 L | 6 L |
| sugar, castor | | 250 g | 500 g | 1 kg |
| vanilla essence | | to taste | | |
| egg yolks | | 12 | 24 | 48 |

**Method**

1 Bring milk to the boil and cool slightly.
2 Mix together sugar, vanilla essence and egg yolks in a mixing bowl.
3 Pour hot milk onto egg mixture whisking quickly.
4 Return to a clean saucepan and place on a low heat. Cook gently until sauce thickens, stirring continuously, making sure the sauce does not boil.
5 Remove from heat, keep warm and use as required.

# Whole honey baked apples filled with dried fruits served with honey cream

Garnish: honey cream.

Ingredients

| | 25 | 50 | 100 |
|---|---|---|---|
| mixed dried fruit, finely chopped, any combination can be used | 2 kg | 4 kg | 8 kg |
| honey | 100 mL | 200 mL | 400 mL |
| sugar, brown, soft | 500 g | 1 kg | 2 kg |
| apples, cored | 25 | 50 | 100 |

Method
1 Pre-heat oven to moderate (150–180°C).
2 Combine dried fruits and honey with 200 g of brown sugar in a mixing bowl.
3 Lightly grease baking/serving tray/s.
4 Place a little of the dried fruit mixture into the centre of each apple, making sure it is compact.
5 Place apples into baking/serving tray/s one layer deep.
6 Place a small mound of the remaining brown sugar on top of each apple.
7 Place tray/s into oven and bake for approx. 25–35 minutes until apples are tender. Baste apples at regular intervals with any juices that collect in the tray/s.
8 Remove from oven and serve one per portion.

 There are a wide selection of dried fruits available today such as apples, apricots, dates, peaches, bananas, mangoes etc.

# Honey cream

Ingredients

| | 25 | 50 | 100 |
|---|---|---|---|
| cream, single | 1.25 L | 2.5 L | 5 L |
| vanilla essence | to taste | | |
| honey | 150 mL | 300 mL | 600 mL |

Method
1 Place cream and vanilla essence into a commercial mixing bowl and whisk until thickened.
2 Gently fold honey through thickened cream.
3 Refrigerate until required.

# Baked fresh orange and Grand Marnier sponge puddings served with a warm butterscotch sauce

Garnish: warm butterscotch and whipped cream.

| Ingredients | | 25 | 50 | 100 |
|---|---|---|---|---|
| flour, self-raising | | 600 g | 1.2 kg | 2.4 kg |
| baking powder | | 5 g | 10 g | 20 g |
| butter, room temperature | | 600 g | 1.2 kg | 2.4 kg |
| sugar, castor | | 500 g | 1 kg | 2 kg |
| vanilla essence | | to taste | | |
| oranges, zest and juice | | 2 | 4 | 8 |
| eggs | | 8 | 16 | 32 |
| Grand Marnier/orange essence (or to taste) | | 40 mL | 80 mL | 160 mL |

Method

1 Pre-heat oven to moderate (150–180°C).
2 Sift flour and baking powder and set aside.
3 Dice butter and cream with sugar and vanilla essence.
4 Zest all oranges and extract juice.
5 Add zest and juice and whilst beating add eggs one at a time until all is incorporated.
6 Add the Grand Marnier/orange essence to taste. Add the sieved flour and baking powder and mix well.
7 Grease required amount of dariole moulds or baking trays and fill three quarters full.
8 Place into oven for approx. 20–40 minutes depending on the quantity of sponge being cooked.
9 To test if sponge is cooked, pierce with a skewer to see if any sponge mix sticks to the skewer. If it does, further cooking is required.
10 When cooked, turn out of the individual moulds or pre-portion in baking trays.
11 Serve with warm butterscotch sauce and whipped cream.

## Butterscotch sauce

| Ingredients | | 25 | 50 | 100 |
|---|---|---|---|---|
| butter | | 750 g | 1.5 kg | 3 kg |
| golden syrup | | 500 mL | 1 L | 2 L |

Method

1 Place butter into a saucepan over a low heat and allow to melt.
2 Add golden syrup and increase heat to moderate and mix well using a wooden spoon.
3 When sauce begins to thicken, after approx. 1–2 minutes, remove from heat and serve.

# Pineapple and cherry upside-down cake served with a fresh banana custard .

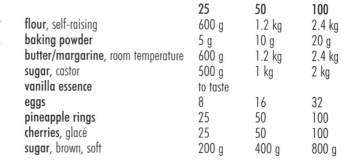

Garnish: fresh banana custard.

**Ingredients**

| | 25 | 50 | 100 |
|---|---|---|---|
| flour, self-raising | 600 g | 1.2 kg | 2.4 kg |
| baking powder | 5 g | 10 g | 20 g |
| butter/margarine, room temperature | 600 g | 1.2 kg | 2.4 kg |
| sugar, castor | 500 g | 1 kg | 2 kg |
| vanilla essence | to taste | | |
| eggs | 8 | 16 | 32 |
| pineapple rings | 25 | 50 | 100 |
| cherries, glacé | 25 | 50 | 100 |
| sugar, brown, soft | 200 g | 400 g | 800 g |

**Method**

1 Pre-heat oven to moderate (150–180°C).
2 Sift flour and baking powder and set aside.
3 Dice butter/margarine and cream with sugar and vanilla essence.
4 Add eggs one at a time and beat until mixed well.
5 Add the sieved flour and mix well.
6 Grease required amount of baking/serving trays.
7 Sprinkle baking/serving tray/s liberally with brown sugar.
8 Place a layer of pineapples one layer deep into trays, pushing them together to touch.
9 Place a cherry in the centre of each pineapple ring.
10 Carefully and evenly pour sponge mixture into trays.
11 Place trays into oven for approx. 20–40 minutes depending on the quantity of sponge being cooked.
12 To test if sponge is cooked, pierce with a skewer to see if any sponge mix sticks to the skewer. If it does, further cooking is required.
13 When cooked, turn out of the baking trays so that the bottom is served face upwards.
14 Serve with warmed banana custard.

## Home-made fresh banana custard

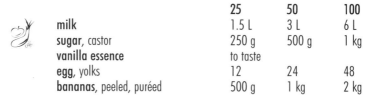

**Ingredients**

| | 25 | 50 | 100 |
|---|---|---|---|
| milk | 1.5 L | 3 L | 6 L |
| sugar, castor | 250 g | 500 g | 1 kg |
| vanilla essence | to taste | | |
| egg, yolks | 12 | 24 | 48 |
| bananas, peeled, puréed | 500 g | 1 kg | 2 kg |

**Method**

1 Bring milk to the boil and cool slightly.
2 Mix together sugar, vanilla essence and egg yolks in a mixing bowl.
3 Pour hot milk onto egg mixture, whisking vigorously.

continued

4 Return to a clean saucepan and place on a low heat. Cook gently until sauce thickens, stirring continuously, making sure the sauce does not boil.
5 Stir in puréed banana and heat through.
6 Remove from heat, keep warm and use as required.

# Baked peach and poppy seed pie topped with puff pastry served with chantilly cream

Garnish: a fine dusting of icing sugar.

**Ingredients**

| | 25 | 50 | 100 |
|---|---|---|---|
| peaches, A10 tin, drained | 1½ | 3 | 6 |
| poppy seeds | 100 g | 200 g | 400 g |
| sugar, icing | 100 g | 200 g | 400 g |
| pastry, puff | as required | | |
| eggs | 2 | 4 | 8 |

**Method**

1 Pre-heat oven to moderate (150–180°C).
2 Roughly chop peaches and combine with poppy seeds and sugar.
3 Place peach mixture into serving/baking trays and top with puff pastry rolled out to a thickness of approx. 3 mm. Crimp edges and trim excess pastry.
4 Brush pastry lightly with beaten egg.
5 Place pies into oven and bake for approx. 20–30 minutes or until pastry turns golden brown.
6 Pre-portion, dust with a little icing sugar and serve with a good quality ice-cream or chantilly cream.

## Chantilly cream

**Ingredients**

| | 25 | 50 | 100 |
|---|---|---|---|
| cream, single | 1.25 L | 2.5 L | 5 L |
| vanilla essence | to taste | | |
| sugar, castor | to taste | | |

**Method**

1 Place all ingredients into a commercial mixing bowl and whisk until thickened, forming soft peaks.
2 Refrigerate until required.

# Warm individual poached pear tarts with vanilla ice-cream

Garnish: vanilla ice-cream.

Ingredients

| | 25 | 50 | 100 |
|---|---|---|---|
| pears, whole, peeled, halved, then cored, stalk on | 13 | 25 | 50 |
| orange juice | 1.5 L | 3 L | 6 L |
| wine, white | 500 mL | 1 L | 2 L |
| cinnamon | 1 tsp | 2 tsp | 4 tsp |
| sugar, castor | 200 g | 400 g | 800 g |
| turmeric | 20 g | 40 g | 80 g |
| pastry, puff | as required | | |
| eggs, beaten | 3 | 6 | 12 |
| apricot jam | 150 g | 300 g | 600 g |
| water, boiling | as required | | |
| vanilla ice-cream | as required | | |

Method

1 Pre-heat oven to moderate (150–180°C).
2 In a mixing bowl combine orange juice, wine, cinnamon, sugar and turmeric, whisking thoroughly.
3 Place pears one layer deep into baking trays and pour over liquid until pears are three-quarters covered. Cover with aluminium foil.
4 Place pears into oven and bake until pears are cooked through and tender.
5 Remove pears from stock and place to one side to cool.
6 Cut puff pastry into 25, 50 or 100 as required, 14 cm x 9 cm rectangles.
7 Lightly brush pastry with beaten egg and place half a pear onto centre of each piece of pastry.
8 Place pastry and pears onto lightly greased baking tray/s and return to oven for approx. 15 minutes or until puff pastry is cooked.
9 Remove from oven, mix jam with a little boiling water and liberally brush pears with mixture.
10 Return trays to oven for approx. 1–2 minutes. Remove from oven.
11 Serve warm, allowing one half pear per portion with a scoop of vanilla ice-cream.

# COLD DESSERTS

## Fresh lemon tart

Garnish: a light dusting of icing sugar and a little honey cream.

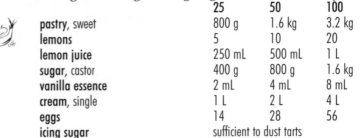

| Ingredients | | 25 | 50 | 100 |
|---|---|---|---|---|
| pastry, sweet | | 800 g | 1.6 kg | 3.2 kg |
| lemons | | 5 | 10 | 20 |
| lemon juice | | 250 mL | 500 mL | 1 L |
| sugar, castor | | 400 g | 800 g | 1.6 kg |
| vanilla essence | | 2 mL | 4 mL | 8 mL |
| cream, single | | 1 L | 2 L | 4 L |
| eggs | | 14 | 28 | 56 |
| icing sugar | | sufficient to dust tarts | | |

**Note**
This recipe has been written using 28 cm diameter 3 cm deep round baking trays with removable bases. Each flan yields 13–14 small slices.

**Method**
1. Pre-heat oven to moderate (150–180°C).
2. Grease lightly the required amount of baking trays.
3. Divide sweet pastry between the number of baking trays. Roll out pastry on a floured surface to a depth of 2.5 mm approx., sufficient to fill and overlap the baking trays.
4. Place greased baking trays onto flat baking trays and fold pastry into the tray making sure it is fitted snugly into the corners. Allow for a 1 cm overlap/overhang and trim away any extra pastry.
5. Line flans with greaseproof paper and cover paper with uncooked rice to support base and sides of tart.
6. Place into oven and bake for 10 minutes. Remove from oven and remove the greaseproof paper and rice. Return to the oven for a further 10–15 minutes until pastry is golden brown, then remove from oven. Turn oven to low (130–150°C).
7. Zest all lemons and extract juice. Add this to the extra lemon juice, sugar, vanilla essence, cream and eggs.
8. Mix this thoroughly and pour into the tart cases, return to a low oven and bake for approx. $1^1/_2$ hours or until just set.
9. Remove tarts from oven. Cool.
10. Carefully portion tarts and serve dusted with a little icing sugar and honey cream, or fresh fruit.

## Honey cream

| Ingredients | | 25 | 50 | 100 |
|---|---|---|---|---|
| cream, single | | 1.25 L | 2.5 L | 5 L |
| vanilla essence | | to taste | | |
| honey | | 150 mL | 300 mL | 600 mL |

| Method | 1 Place cream and vanilla essence into a commercial mixing bowl and whisk until thickened. |
|---|---|

Method

1 Place cream and vanilla essence into a commercial mixing bowl and whisk until thickened.
2 Gently fold honey through thickened cream.
3 Refrigerate until required.

# Strawberries Romanoff

Garnish: a rosette of whipped cream and a half-fanned strawberry.

| Ingredients | | 25 | 50 | 100 |
|---|---|---|---|---|
| strawberries, fresh, stalks removed, quartered | | 1 kg | 2 kg | 4 kg |
| cassis | | to taste | | |
| cream, single | | 1.25 L | 2.5 L | 5 L |
| sugar, castor | | 200 g | 400 g | 800 g |
| vanilla essence | | to taste | | |

Method

1 Divide strawberries in half, purée one half with cassis and finely chop the second half.
2 In a commercial mixer whip cream, sugar and vanilla essence until stiff.
3 Gently fold the prepared strawberries into the whipped cream.
4 Using a wide nozzle on a piping bag, neatly pipe mixture into individual serving dishes/glasses.
5 Refrigerate for at least one hour before service.
6 Serve garnished, allowing one per portion.

# Chocolate fudge profiteroles
# served on a warm white chocolate sauce

Garnish: a sprig of fresh mint.

| Ingredients | | 25 | 50 | 100 |
|---|---|---|---|---|
| water | | 1 L | 2 L | 4 L |
| butter | | 300 g | 600 g | 1.2 kg |
| flour, plain | | 450 g | 900 g | 1.8 kg |
| eggs | | 8–10 | 16–20 | 32–40 |
| cream, lightly whipped, with a little castor sugar and vanilla essence | | 1.5 L | 3 L | 6 L |
| chocolate, milk, roughly chopped | | 500 g | 1 kg | 2 kg |
| golden syrup | | 200 mL | 400 mL | 800 mL |

Method

1 Pre-heat oven to moderate (150–180°C).
2 Place water and butter into a saucepan and bring to a rolling boil.

3 Reduce to a low heat and stir in sieved flour with wooden spoon until a thick paste is formed.
4 Remove from heat and cool for 5–10 minutes.
5 Stir in eggs one at a time with a wooden spoon until a dropping consistency is achieved.
6 Grease required amount of baking trays. Place choux pastry into a piping bag fitted with a medium sized plain nozzle.
7 Pipe out small swirls of choux pastry allowing four profiteroles per portion.
8 Place trays into oven and bake until golden and dried: approx. 30–40 minutes.
9 Remove from oven and place profiteroles onto cooling racks. Cool.
10 Make a small incision into the bottom of each profiterole and fill with whipped cream.
11 Melt chocolate in a double saucepan, add golden syrup and mix well. Remove from heat.
12 Dip the top of each profiterole into sauce and cover generously. Return to cooling racks to allow sauce to set.
13 Serve four profiteroles per portion shaped into a pyramid on a small amount of warm white chocolate sauce.

## White chocolate sauce

| Ingredients | | | 25 | 50 | 100 |
|---|---|---|---|---|---|
| |  | chocolate, white, roughly chopped | 1 kg | 2 kg | 4 kg |
| | | cream, single approx. | 150 mL | 300 mL | 600 mL |

Method
1 Melt chocolate in a double saucepan over boiling water.
2 Add small amount of cream and mix well until it is smooth and coats the back of a spoon.

## Crème caramel

Garnish: a swirl of fresh cream with a sprig of fresh mint.

| Ingredients | | | 25 | 50 | 100 |
|---|---|---|---|---|---|
| |  | CARAMEL SAUCE: | | | |
| | | sugar, castor | 500 g | 1 kg | 2 kg |
| | | water | 625 mL | 1.25 L | 2.5 L |
| | | EGG CUSTARD: | | | |
| | | milk | 2.5 L | 5 L | 10 L |
| | | sugar, castor | 250 g | 500 g | 1 kg |
| | | eggs | 20 | 40 | 80 |
| | | vanilla essence | to taste | | |

<table>
<tr><td>Method</td><td>

1 Pre-heat oven to moderate (150–180°C).
2 Place sugar and water for caramel sauce into a saucepan and simmer until the mixture becomes light golden brown. Do not stir or shake the sauce while it is cooking.
3 Pour a little of the caramel sauce into the bottom of the required dariole moulds.
4 Bring the milk to a simmer.
5 Thoroughly whisk the eggs, sugar and vanilla essence together in a mixing bowl.
6 Add the milk to the egg mixture, whisking continuously.
7 Quarter fill a roasting tray with boiling water.
8 Fill each mould with the custard mixture. Place into water in tray.
9 Place roasting trays into oven and cook for approx. 30 minutes or until egg mixture is set.
10 Remove from oven and cool. Refrigerate until completely cooled.
11 Gently turn out and serve, allowing one per portion.

</td></tr>
</table>

# Vanilla bean bavarois served on a fresh raspberry coulis

Garnish: a sprig of fresh mint.

Ingredients

| | 25 | 50 | 100 |
|---|---|---|---|
| milk | 1.5 L | 3 L | 6 L |
| vanilla, pod, split | 1 | 2 | 4 |
| egg yolks | 10 | 20 | 40 |
| sugar, castor | 350 g | 700 g | 1.4 kg |
| gelatine, powdered | 50 g | 100 g | 200 g |
| water, boiling | 100 mL | 200 mL | 400 mL |
| cream, single, lightly whipped | 250 mL | 500 mL | 1 L |

Method

1 Place milk and contents of the split vanilla pod into a saucepan and heat until almost boiling.
2 Place egg yolks into a mixing bowl with sugar and whisk well.
3 Pour milk onto eggs, whisking continuously.
4 Place egg and milk mixture back into the saucepan and return to a low heat. Cook until mixture coats the back of a spoon.
5 Place boiling water into a small bowl to dissolve gelatine. Add this to the milk mixture and whisk in. Remove from heat and cool.
6 Place mixture into a freezer and cool, stirring regularly.
7 When mixture is almost set, gently fold in whipped cream and place into dariole moulds. Refrigerate until set.
8 Turn bavarois out of moulds. Serve on a bed of raspberry coulis, allowing one per portion.

continued

# Raspberry coulis

| Ingredients | | | 25 | 50 | 100 |
|---|---|---|---|---|---|
| |  | **raspberries**, frozen or fresh | 1.25 kg | 2.5 kg | 5 kg |
| | | **sugar**, icing | 125 g | 250 g | 500 g |

**Method**

1 Place all ingredients into a food processor and blend until smooth.
2 Refrigerate and use as required.

# Crème brûlée served with almond biscotti

| Ingredients | | | 25 | 50 | 100 |
|---|---|---|---|---|---|
| |  | **cream**, single | 3.75 L | 7.5 L | 15 L |
| | | **vanilla**, pod, split | 1 | 2 | 4 |
| | | **egg**, yolks | 25 | 50 | 100 |
| | | **sugar**, castor | 500 g | 1 kg | 2 kg |
| | | **TOFFEE SUGAR:** | | | |
| | | **sugar**, castor | 400 g | 800 g | 1.6 kg |

**Method**

1 Pre-heat oven to low (130–150°C).
2 Place cream and contents of the split vanilla pod into a saucepan. Heat until almost boiling. Remove from heat and cool for 5 minutes.
3 Place egg yolks into a mixing bowl with sugar and whisk well together.
4 Pour cream onto eggs, whisking continuously.
5 Pour mixture into ramekins allowing approx. 150 mL per portion.
6 Quarter fill a roasting tray with boiling water.
7 Place the filled ramekins into the water in the roasting tray.
8 Place roasting trays into oven and cook for approx. 1–1$^1$/$_2$ hours or just until egg mixture is set.
9 Remove from oven and cool. Refrigerate until completely cooled.
10 Place ramekins onto baking trays and evenly dust with sugar. Place under a very hot salamander until the sugar caramelises and turns light golden brown. Remove immediately.
11 Serve in the ramekins, allowing one per portion with almond biscotti (see following recipe).

# Almond biscotti

Ingredients

| | 25 | 50 | 100 |
|---|---|---|---|
| flour, plain | 360 g | 720 g | 1.440 kg |
| sugar, castor | 360 g | 720 g | 1.440 kg |
| bicarbonate of soda | 1/4 tsp | 1/2 tsp | 1 tsp |
| almonds, blanched | 175 g | 350 g | 700 g |
| eggs | 3 | 6 | 12 |

 **Note**

This recipe **should not** be made using a blender or mixer; it should be made by hand.

Method

1 Pre-heat oven to moderate (150–180°C).
2 Mix all dry ingredients together in a mixing bowl.
3 Lightly whisk eggs in a separate bowl.
4 Gradually pour whisked eggs into a well made in the centre of the dry ingredients and mix in until fully incorporated.
5 Lightly knead mixture on a lightly floured surface for approx. 5 minutes.
6 Mould dough into cylindrical shapes approx. 8 cm in diameter. Place onto lightly greased baking tray/s and gently press down on dough so it forms an oval shape.
7 Place tray/s into oven for approx 35–40 minutes.
8 Remove trays from oven. Cool for 5 minutes. Turn oven to low (130–150°C).
9 Slice cooked biscotti dough into thin oval slices, preferably with an electric knife.
10 Lay the slices carefully onto the baking trays and return to a *low* oven for a further 10–12 minutes or until light golden brown.
11 Remove from oven. Cool and allow to become crisp before removing from baking trays. Serve.

**Notes**

This is a classic Italian twice baked crisp biscuit that is traditionally made with almonds or hazelnuts. Biscotti are ideally served with coffee, liqueurs or desserts such as crème brûlée or sweetened marscapone cheese.

Biscotti can be made in advance if stored in an airtight container.

# DIETARY CONSIDERATIONS

# SPECIALISED DIETARY REQUIREMENTS

In some situations you may need to consider certain dietary requirements. These may be determined by lifestyles, medical conditions or religious convictions as shown in the following list.

**Lifestyle dietary requirements:**
- Semi-vegetarian
- Vegetarian
- Vegan

**Medical dietary requirements:**
- Diabetic
- Cholesterol-lowering and low cholesterol
- Weight reduction
- High fibre
- Low salt/sodium
- High energy
- Low potassium
- Low protein
- Low preservatives/colourings
- High iron
- Foods to avoid if suffering from gastric reflux or ulcers
- Foods to avoid for diverticulitis

**Religious dietary requirements:**
- Christian
- Kosher
- Islam
- Hindu
- Buddhist

When catering for large numbers of people on a regular basis, sooner or later the situation will arise where the caterer will be faced with a customer who has a specialised dietary requirement, be it lifestyle, medical or religious. This specialised dietary need must be approached professionally. This chapter gives a basic overall view of what we believe to be the main specialised dietary requirements. Its aim is to give readers a brief understanding of what may be required and expected of them as professional caterers.

## Lifestyle dietary requirements

### Vegetarianism
Many people — by choice, religious requirements or circumstance — are vegetarian in one form or another. The price of meat, a dislike of meat, philosophical objections to the killing of animals or famine, all may contribute to a person or persons becoming vegetarian, semi-vegetarian or vegan. The main danger when converting from a diet which consists of meat to a diet comprising mainly vegetables is that people may suffer protein deficiency. Vegetarians should aim for at least 60% pulses/beans to 30% grains and make up the remaining 10% with vegetables to have a balanced diet.

**Semi-vegetarian**

This is someone who will usually not eat any red meats including pork, which is a white meat, but may choose to eat chicken, seafood and dairy products.

**Vegetarian**

A strict vegetarian will not purchase or consume any meats, including chicken and seafood, but some individuals will eat certain dairy products; these are known as *ovo-lacto* vegetarians. Recipes suitable for vegetarians will be found in the vegetarian chapter. Vegetarians, like everyone else, need to have a nutritionally balanced diet and this must be provided for, taking into consideration all of the essential food groups.

**Vegan**

A vegan is a person who through personal choice believes the use of any animal products to be wrong. Usually a vegan will refuse to buy any item that utilises any animal products. This can be very perplexing, especially to a chef unfamiliar with this type of dietary requirement. Unlike a vegetarian, who may eat dairy products, a vegan will not, through choice or very occasionally medical restrictions, eat any animal based products. This includes the obvious, such as meats and seafoods, and also dairy products such as butter, milk, cream, eggs and yoghurt.

When catering for large numbers of people the need will eventually arise to cater for a vegan, especially with the current increase in this type of dietary preference. With a little careful pre-planning, when asked to produce a meal for a vegan a chef need not be unduly concerned. There are a few basic points that need to be adhered to, and like others with specialised dietary requirements, the needs of vegans must be respected. Listed below are five points that must be considered when catering for a vegan:

- No animal product must be used in the preparation and cooking of the planned dish.
- Pre-planning is essential. You must ensure your stores include the necessary ingredients to cater for a vegan.
- Any convenience foods planned for use should have their ingredients list closely scrutinised for any animal products.
- Vegans, like everyone else, need to have a nutritionally balanced diet and this must be provided for, taking into consideration all of the essential food groups.
- There should be variety in the chef's repertoire of dishes suitable for a vegan, especially when catering for this dietary requirement on a long-term basis.

Given below are the main vegan alternatives to commonly used food products:

| | |
|---|---|
| Animal fat based cooking media | vegetable oils, such as olive, grape seed and sesame |
| Butter | vegetable oil based margarines |
| Milk | soya milk, coconut milk/cream |
| Meat, fish and seafood | tofu, nuts, lentils and pulses, soya and vegetables |
| Breads and pastries | those utilising vegetable fats only |

# Medical dietary requirements

## Diabetic diet

**Main diet changes:**

- Diet needs to be very low in **sugar**. Avoid using all types of sweeteners like sugar, honey etc. in recipes. Artificial sweeteners may be used as a substitute e.g. Equal, Splenda. Ideally

the client would be served fruit (canned in natural juice or fresh, e.g. fresh fruit salad) instead of regular sweet desserts.
- Diet needs to be low in **fat**. This is for two reasons:
  - Most people with diabetes need to lose weight.
  - People with diabetes are more likely to get heart disease.

  Therefore avoid giving them fried foods, fatty meats, including processed meats like salami, creamy sauces, sour cream, coconut milk etc. Ideally meals are grilled, steamed, stir-fried in very little oil, or prepared by some other low fat cooking method.

  Diabetics should be offered reduced-fat dairy products i.e. milks, yoghurts, cheeses.

  Fats used should be polyunsaturated or monounsaturated.
- The client needs to be provided with some **carbohydrate**-containing food at each meal. This means they should be offered bread, rice, pasta, potato, legumes or cereals: e.g. rolled oats, Weet-Bix or fruit. The client should have approximately three serves of these carbohydrate foods per meal. Usually the client will know how much he or she is supposed to be eating of these foods.
- People with diabetes should be offered **vegetables** or salad with their lunch and evening meal. Ideally salads are provided without dressing.
- **Drinks:** Provide water. Maybe also offer artificially sweetened cordials or soft drink. Fruit juices need to be 100% juice. The person with diabetes should not be drinking more than 1–2 glasses of juice a day.
- **Snacks:** Unless the client is on insulin injections for their diabetes, they do *not* need snacks between meals. If they do want something, offer the following plain biscuits or fruit:
  - one piece of fresh fruit
  - 3 Sao, 3 Shredded Wheatmeal, 2 Ryvita, 2 Milk Arrowroot or Milk Coffee biscuits, 6 Salada.
- **Meal times:** people who are on medication for their diabetes need meals at regular times.
- **Hypoglycaemia:** This can be a dangerous situation in which the blood sugar level falls too low. If untreated, the person can go into a coma. Keep some soft drink which contains sugar, e.g. regular lemonade, to be used if the need arises.

## Cholesterol-lowering or low cholesterol diet

Most people with a high cholesterol level also need to lose weight. Therefore they should have a diet low in fat to lose the weight and low in saturated fats to help bring down the cholesterol.

**Main diet changes:**
- **Fats:** the type of fat used in cooking and offered for bread etc. should be monounsaturated or polyunsaturated. Monounsaturated oils include olive and canola oil.

  Avoid using saturated fats, i.e. butter, cream, coconut cream, sour cream, dripping, ghee, regular cheese. Remove all visible fat from meat and poultry. Avoid fatty meats such as processed meats, frankfurts, meat pies, sausages and fried fish.
- **Cooking methods** need to be low in fat as well. Grilling, steaming or stir-frying in very little oil are preferable to frying or covering in fatty sauces.
- **Sauces** need to be low in saturated fat. On salads, use 'no oil' dressings. On meats, use tomato-based sauces.
- **Quantity:** amounts of meat and chicken offered should be quite small. Fish should be offered three times a week.

- **Cereals:** rice, potato, pasta, legumes and bread are all suitable foods, and at least one or two of these should be offered with each meal.
- **Fruits and vegetables** should be offered generously with each meal.
- **Dairy** products need to be low in fat, i.e. milk, yoghurt, cheese.
- **Sweets/desserts:** fruit is ideal. Low fat recipes are usually suitable. Otherwise, modify an old recipe to use monounsaturated fats and low fat dairy products.

Dishes made with eggs, kidney, liver, brains or prawns should be offered infrequently, if ever.

Only serve meat, chicken or pork once a day.

## Weight reduction diet

**Main diet changes need to include low fat foods, and a reduced quantity of foods overall.**

- **Meats:** fish etc. need to be as lean as possible, and cooked in a low fat manner. Cut off all visible fat before cooking, remove skin from chicken. Grill, steam, stir-fry in minimal oil, or use low fat recipes. Avoid deep frying, or using creamy, cheesy sauces. All types of fat are equally fattening; therefore use as little as possible of all of them. Avoid serving fatty meats such as sausages, frankfurts, salami, meat pies etc. Serve only moderate to small quantities of meats or chicken.
- **Vegetables** should be offered in generous quantities, raw or cooked. Do not serve potato chips. Do not offer sour cream for potatoes. Serve salads without dressing. Offer 'no oil' dressings. Avocado is very fattening — avoid including this.
- **Fruits:** all are suitable and should ideally be served with each meal. Raw, cooked, or dried fruits are all suitable.
- **Dairy products:** offer low fat varieties of milk, cheese and yoghurt.
- **Breads, cereals, legumes, potatoes, rice and pasta** should all be presented in a low fat manner. Quantities of these offered can be quite generous, depending on the client's level of physical activity.
- **Drinks** should be water, tea, coffee, or artificially sweetened cordials and soft drinks.
- **Snacks:** fruit is the best choice. Ideally the client does not need snacks. Otherwise, offer low fat cracker-type biscuits. Avoid regular cakes, biscuits and desserts.

## High fibre diet

- **Cereals:** use wholemeal cereals as much as possible.

  Breakfast cereal — All-Bran, any cereal with 'bran' or 'fibre' in it, e.g. Weet-Bix Hi Bran, Bran Flakes, Fibreplus, rolled oats and muesli are high fibre.

  Flour — substitute wholemeal flour in all recipes, including cakes, biscuits, muffins, gravy. Use brown rice and wholemeal breads.

  Avoid white bread, highly processed cereals like Rice Bubbles, Corn Flakes and white flour products.
- **Legumes:** these are the highest fibre foods of all. Offer baked beans for any meal. Put other beans in recipes; e.g. kidney beans, chick peas, black-eyed beans, lentils or 4 bean mix can be mixed into salads or added to casseroles and soups.
- **Fruit:** very high fibre. Ideally offer fruit with every meal and perhaps also for snacks between meals. Dried fruit, including prunes, is high in fibre. Canned fruit has less fibre than fresh fruit. Ideally at least three pieces of fruit should be eaten a day. Berry fruits are high in fibre.
- **Vegetables:** all vegetables have fibre and should be offered in generous quantities. Ideally good serves of vegetables, twice a day.

- **Meats:** poultry etc. have no fibre. Perhaps only offer moderate amounts.
- **Cheese and dairy products** contain no fibre. Cheese can cause constipation; limit this.
- **Drinks:** juice has no fibre. Encourage sufficient water (ideally 2–3 litres a day) to ensure bowel will work properly.

## Low salt/low sodium diet

**Main diet changes:**
- Avoid using salt in cooking.
- Remove salt shaker from the serving table.
- Avoid serving high sodium foods.
- **High sodium foods:** processed meats like salami, devon, ham, bacon, sausages, smoked, salted or pickled foods; tinned vegetable juices; canned soups, stock cubes, stock powders e.g. chicken 'booster', packet sauces; cheese; canned baked beans, canned spaghetti, tuna, salmon in 'brine'; most breads; foods cooked with salt, such as rice, rolled oats etc.; cakes and biscuits cooked with salt as an ingredient. Baking powder and bicarbonate of soda contain a lot of sodium. MSG contains a lot of sodium. Commercial snack foods such as corn chips, crisps etc. contain a lot of sodium

  High sodium breakfast cereals — All-Bran, Corn Flakes, Rice Bubbles, Special K, Nutri-Grain.
- **Low sodium foods:** fresh or frozen fruits and vegetables; milk, yoghurt; eggs (cooked without salt); chicken, meat, fish; pasta, rice, oats cooked without salt, low sodium breads. Try using herbs and spices for added flavour in cooking.

  Low sodium breakfast cereals — Mini-Wheats, rolled oats, Lite Bix, puffed wheat, Sustain, Uncle Tobys Natural Muesli.

## High energy diet

Useful for all sportspeople and people whose daily job requires a lot of physical effort. Also a very healthy diet for all people.

A high energy diet needs to be a high carbohydrate diet; i.e. the greatest percentage of kilojoules in the diet need to come from carbohydrate. This means that only a small percentage of kilojoules should come from fats and fatty foods; i.e. it really needs to be a low fat diet as well.

Every meal and every snack needs to contain a large amount of carbohydrate and not too much fat.

**High carbohydrate low fat foods:**
- breakfast cereals (except toasted muesli)
- boiled rice, pasta with a low fat sauce, boiled or dry-baked potatoes, baked beans, all legumes
- bread, including Lebanese bread, pita bread, English muffins, crumpets, raisin bread
- cracker-type biscuits e.g. Ryvita, rice cakes
- biscuits, cakes, muffins, desserts, especially if made from a low fat recipe
- fruit, including fresh, canned and dried
- jam, honey, sugar, boiled lollies, jubes
- soft drink, cordial, fruit juice
- low fat milk, low fat yoghurt, including fruit flavoured ones.

**High fat foods which are unsuitable:**
- meat pies, hamburgers etc.
- fried potato chips, potatoes baked in fat, potatoes served with sour cream or butter
- pasta with cream and/or cheese sauces
- fried rice, fried noodles
- croissants
- chocolate
- most desserts, cakes, pastries
- cheese, regular milk and yoghurt, dairy desserts.

 Meat, poultry and fish do not contain carbohydrate. Therefore they will not provide extra energy; they should be served in moderate quantities, not high quantities.

## Low potassium diet

Potassium is found in most foods. Certain foods should be avoided with a low potassium diet.

**Foods to avoid:**
- all dried fruit
- more than one glass of fruit juice a day
- avocado, custard apple, coconut, rhubarb
- artichokes, bamboo shoots, leeks, mushrooms, silverbeet, spinach, tomato juice, tomato paste, tomato purée, vegetable juice, vegetable purée
- soups, gravy
- chutney, pickles, meat paste, fish paste
- potato crisps, corn chips etc.
- chocolate, carob, cocoa, Milo etc.

All wholemeal and wholegrain cereals have more potassium than the white refined products. Therefore it is best to avoid the following foods:
- wholemeal and multigrain breads
- fruit bread, fruit loaf
- bran cereals like All-Bran, Bran Flakes, cereals with dried fruits
- brown rice, wholemeal pasta and spaghetti.

**You can reduce the potassium in vegetables by following these instructions:**
- Peel vegetables and cut into small pieces.
- Soak the vegetables in a large volume of water for at least 1–2 hours.
- Discard the soaking water, then boil in a large volume of fresh water.
- Do not steam or microwave vegetables.
- Only roast or fry vegetables that have been cooked by the above method first.
- Do not serve vegetable soup.

All fruits contain potassium. The lowest potassium fruit is canned/stewed fruit which has been drained of its juice. If serving banana, only serve half a banana at one time.

## Low protein diet

The person on a strict low protein diet will probably know what he or she should be eating. The level of protein allowed would vary between clients, depending on their condition.

**As a guide:**
- no more than 60–90 grams (cooked weight) of meat, chicken, fish per day
- no more than 150–200 mL milk a day or 100–120 grams yoghurt or 30–45 grams cheese.

Bread, cereals, rice, pasta, potatoes and legumes all contain protein. On a strict low protein diet the protein content of these must also be taken into account.

Foods which are free of protein, which can be eaten relatively freely include: fruit, green and yellow vegetables, fruit drinks, cordial, soft drink, jam, honey, glucose lollies, butter, cream.

## Low preservatives, low colourings diet
By looking at the numbers on the backs of the packets of food you will be able to check which foods are not suitable. The following is a list of the numbers for foods which would be best avoided by someone who is trying to avoid preservatives and colourings.

**Colourings which are likely to cause a problem:**
102, 107, 110, 112–129, 133, 142, 151, 155, 160b.

No other colourings would be likely to cause any problems.

**Preservatives which are likely to cause a problem:**
200–203 (sorbates)
210–213 (benzoates)
220–224 (sulphites)
249–252 (nitrites, nitrates)
280–283 (propionates)
310–312, 320,321 (anti-oxidants)
620–623 (glutamates).

**Main things which you will need to watch:**
- Most breads have preservatives. Choose a bread without preservatives.
- Many processed meats and fish products contain preservatives. Best to serve fresh meats and fish.
- Processed cheeses often contain preservatives. Serve block cheese.
- Many bought biscuits and cakes contain colouring. Best to make your own.
- Most soft drinks, cordials and fruit juices contain preservatives. Buy juice with 'no preservatives' on the label.
- Most dried vegetables, e.g. dried potatoes, dried peas, contain preservatives. Serve fresh or frozen.
- Stock cubes, soup bases and packet sauces usually contain MSG and are therefore best avoided.

## Foods high in iron:
The best sources of iron (haem iron) are red meat (beef and lamb), oysters, mussels, liver and kidney. Sardines, salmon, fish and eggs are also good sources.

Iron from vegetables and cereals (non-haem iron) is only well absorbed if eaten at the same time as some food rich in vitamin C.

**Vegetables and cereals high in iron:**
- iron-fortified breakfast cereals, including Nutri-Grain, Special K and Sportsplus (Uncle Tobys)
- dried apricots and prunes
- broccoli, peas, spinach and silverbeet
- wholemeal breads and cereals; these have more iron than highly refined white breads and cereals.

# Foods to avoid if suffering from gastric reflux or ulcer:

- citrus juice, including orange, lemon and grapefruit
- tomato, any style, including tomato juice and tomato purée, in salad
- coffee
- caffeine-containing foods, including Coke and Pepsi
- chocolate
- alcohol, all varieties
- peppermint, including peppermint lollies and peppermint tea
- chilli, spices and spicy foods, e.g. Thai foods
- all fatty foods, including fried foods. Basically, follow the guidelines for a low fat diet.

Also, it may be necessary to avoid:
- celery, cucumber, onions, radishes, tomatoes and capsicums
- raw pineapple, oranges, apples, dried fruit and nuts.

# Foods to avoid with diverticulitis:

- peanuts and all other nuts
- coconut
- seeds, including poppy seeds
- sunflower seeds
- sesame seeds
- seeds in cucumber
- seeds in tomatoes
- seeds in passionfruit
- seeds in berries, including strawberries
- popcorn
- multigrain and wholegrain bread.

**Other guidelines for diverticulitis:**

Increase fibre in the diet (but avoid the above listed foods).
- Eat more high fibre breakfast cereals.
- Eat legumes regularly, e.g. baked beans.
- Eat wholemeal bread, not white.
- Eat more fruit and vegetables.
- Eat more dried fruit.
- Drink plenty of water.

# Religious dietary requirements
## Christian

This religion consists almost entirely of the Roman Catholic, Protestant and Eastern Orthodox Churches. Most of the nine hundred million followers are Roman Catholic. Most Protestant denominations have little or no dietary restrictions, with the exception of a number of sects that choose to avoid alcohol and tobacco and also choose vegetarian-type diets. The Eastern Orthodox Church observes total abstinence from animal products during the forty days of Lent and only fish is permitted during Annunciation Day and Palm Sunday. Easter is usually celebrated with lamb and Friday is the traditional day when fish is served.

## Kosher

Kosher cookery requires a complete separation of dairy and meat products, which encompasses the cooking areas and utensils. Strict guidelines extend to all food products, which must be rigorously investigated to obtain kosher approval. Certain animal parts and species are non-kosher, namely pork, any seafood without scales, shellfish and any portion of an animal from the twelfth rib down. Meat is killed and prepared in a specialised manner by kosher butchers to remove all blood and veins. All kosher catering outlets must have a representative from the Kashrut authority who constantly supervises the preparation and cooking of all food to authenticate its kosher standing. There are many festivals and religious days in the Jewish calender on which special food standards and regulations must be observed.

## Islamic

Founded by the prophet Muhammad, Islam has more than five hundred million followers throughout the world. In the second chapter of the Koran God reveals to Muhammad strict dietary laws. All alcohol is forbidden, as is pork, and all other meats must be ritually slaughtered. One of the main Muslim religious observations is the annual fast during the lunar month of Ramadan, when followers of this religion are forbidden to eat or drink between dawn and dusk.

## Hindu

Hinduism is the name given to the beliefs of most people living in India. Hindus believe no person should bulk his or her own flesh by eating that of other beings. Less orthodox Hindus eat meat with the exception of beef (they will use milk and its by-products, however); but other meats such as chicken and pork are used sparingly. Hindus will not eat fertilised eggs because they contain a live embryo. This religion's diet is strongly against any violence to other creatures.

## Buddhist

Buddhists believe strongly in love and compassion, so the slaughter of any living creature is considered a vice. They are usually vegetarian.

# HEALTHY DIET

by Sue Ross
Nutritionist/Dietician, BSc. (Hons), Grad.Dip.Nutr.Diet., MDAA.APD

Sue Ross is a practising dietician in Sydney and has experience in some of Sydney's major public and private hospitals. She is a consultant dietician in Sydney at Nutrition Decisions. Sue's wide range of experience includes talking to individuals about their own dietary and eating habits as well as teaching and designing courses for TAFE and working with the food industry.

## Introduction

While we eat food daily, there are a variety of factors that influence which foods we actually choose to eat in a day. As we move towards the year 2000 and beyond, more and more people are eating away from the home. We are therefore increasingly reliant on the foods which are prepared by people other than ourselves.

Our health is dependent on a healthy diet. The incidence of coronary heart disease, high blood pressure, diabetes, overweight and obesity and some cancers could be reduced if people ate healthier foods. In view of the fact that many people die each year of these nutrition-related diseases, I feel it is the responsibility of those providing food for other people to consider the health aspects of a menu.

More people are actually looking for the healthy alternative on a menu these days. Whatever group of people you are providing for, whatever age, sex or level of physical activity, they will almost all benefit from the healthier foods. By providing some foods which are in line with the Dietary Guidelines for Australians, you will be satisfying an increasing number of people in more ways than one.

The enjoyment of eating cannot be forgotten.

## Aspects of diet and health

The **Dietary Guidelines for Australians** have been designed to provide the general population with advice about healthy food choices. Healthy food choices will help to ensure that people's diets contribute to a healthy lifestyle, and are consistent with minimising the risk of developing diet-related diseases.

The Guidelines are published by the National Health and Medical Research Council. They were most recently updated in 1992. They are based upon current scientific knowledge about the relationships between diet and disease. The advice is targeted at healthy Australian adults.

The Guidelines are arranged in order of priority.

## Dietary Guidelines for Australians:

1  Enjoy a wide variety of nutritious foods.
2  Eat plenty of breads and cereals (preferably wholegrain), vegetables (including legumes) and fruits.
3  Eat a diet low in fat and, in particular, low in saturated fat.
4  Maintain a healthy body weight by balancing physical activity and food intake.
5  If you drink alcohol, limit your intake.
6  Eat only a moderate amount of sugars and foods containing added sugars.
7  Choose low salt foods and use salt sparingly.
8  Encourage and support breast feeding.

Of these, Guidelines 1, 2, 3, 6 and 7 are of direct concern to those in the food catering business.

## Guidelines on specific nutrients

1 Eat foods containing calcium. This is particularly important for girls and women.
2 Eat foods containing iron. This applies particularly to girls, women, vegetarians and athletes.

## How do the Dietary Guidelines for Australians relate to chefs?

Australians are eating an increasing number of meals away from home. We can no longer hope that the healthy foods eaten at home may counter-balance the foods eaten away from home. I believe the people who are providing meals to Australians have a responsibility to offer healthy meals as an alternative to more traditional foods which perhaps were not in keeping with the Dietary Guidelines for Australians.

70% of Australian men and 50% of Australian women eat too much sodium; i.e. they eat more than the **recommended daily intake**. As well as reducing or eliminating salt in cooking, you could offer less of the processed meats, as these are currently a major source of sodium in the diet. Also, buy reduced salt products where possible.

**Calcium** — Eat foods containing calcium. This is particularly important for women and girls.

Offer calcium-rich foods with each meal, including milk to drink, yoghurt and Cheddar-type cheese. Soya drinks need to be ones with added calcium. Salmon, sardines and oysters are good sources of calcium as well.

**Iron** — Eat foods containing iron. This applies particularly to girls, women, vegetarians and athletes.

- Liver, kidney, oysters and mussels are a good source of iron.
- Red meat, such as beef, has three times as much iron as chicken.
- Fish and eggs are also good sources of iron.
- Certain breakfast cereals are fortified with iron, and they should be offered every day, especially to all vegetarians.
- Fruit juice containing vitamin C will help the body to absorb iron, so should be offered at the same meal.

Your customers are relying on you to provide them with healthy foods. It is extremely important that the nutritional quality of the meals is considered when planning menus.

Many people will *want* to choose a healthy meal, as they are trying to look after their own health as much as possible. Obesity, diabetes, coronary heart disease, high blood pressure, cancer, diverticular disease, gall bladder disease and others are all influenced by a person's diet. Some people try to follow a healthy diet to prevent these diseases. Others will be advised by their doctor or dietitian to modify their diet as an important part of managing these diseases if they already exist.

## How can you modify your menus to take account of the Dietary Guidelines for Australians?

### Guideline 1: Enjoy a wide variety of nutritious foods.

- Provide a variety of foods over the week or fortnight. The more variety, the more likely your customers will get the nutrients they need to stay healthy.
- Offer a variety of vegetables and a variety of fruit.

### Guideline 2: Eat plenty of breads and cereals (preferably wholegrain), vegetables (including legumes) and fruits.

- Breads come in all shapes and sizes these days, and in a variety of types as well, from wholegrain, wholemeal, pumpernickel and rye breads, to French, Italian and Lebanese. Offer rolls, slices, different shaped loaves etc. Bread is not 'fattening'. (It was once thought to be so, and many people still think they should not eat much bread.) Australians should be encouraged to eat bread with every meal.
- Vegetables and fruits are full of vitamins and minerals.
- Vegetables should be offered in generous proportions, not just as decoration on the side of the plate.
- Fruits should be offered with every meal.
- Legumes are high in fibre and complex carbohydrates. Baked beans are one way of eating legumes.

**Guideline 3: Eat a diet low in fat and, in particular, low in saturated fat.**
- Most Australians eat far too much fat. The less fat you use in cooking, the healthier the meal will be for your clients.
- Saturated fats include butter, cream, sour cream, animal fats including the fat on meat, skin on chicken, dripping, lard, ghee, suet, fat in cheese and milk, coconut cream, palm oil, hydrogenated cooking fats, chocolate.
- You should try to offer low fat dairy products as an alternative to the full cream ones.
- You could also offer low fat or reduced fat sauces and spreads.
- You would ideally remove fat from meats and skin from chicken and offer these in preference to processed meats.
- The fats which are healthiest for cooking are the monounsaturated ones, including olive oil, canola oil, peanut oil and macadamia oil.
- You need to be careful of the amount of oils and fats used in dressings, sauces etc. as well.

**Guideline 6: Eat only a moderate amount of sugars and foods containing added sugar.**
- Sugar is not nearly as much of a health hazard as it was once thought to be.
- Certainly the amount and type of fat you eat is far more important than the sugars, as noted in the fact that fat is third on the list whereas sugars are only sixth.
- One of the biggest sources of sugars is soft drinks and fruit juices. Always offer water with meals.

**Guideline 7: Choose low salt foods and use salt sparingly.**

## General guidelines for reducing the fat content of recipes:
- For meat dishes — grill, bake, poach, roast or boil, rather than deep fry.
- Place roasts on a rack, so fat can drip away.
- Remove visible fat from meat. Remove skin from chicken.
- Use non-stick pans, and then only a smear of oil if necessary.
- Remove fat from cooked casseroles, soups, stocks etc. by placing in the refrigerator overnight, and scraping the hard fat off the top.

## Substitutions in recipes to make them lower in fat:
- Use light milk or skim milk instead of regular full cream milk.
- Use evaporated skim milk instead of cream.
- Low fat yoghurt is often a good substitute for sour cream.
- Reduce the amount of cheese which is called for in the recipe, and/or use low fat cheese.
- Reduce the amount of oil used to fry/sauté onions etc.

## Menu guidelines

In view of the fact that so many Australian are eating too much fat in their diets, and so many Australians are suffering health disorders as a result of this, it would seem appropriate to include some low fat foods in a menu. Perhaps you could offer one low fat dish and one not-so-low fat dish, so customers then have the option.

## General guidelines for making the menu suitable for a cholesterol-lowering diet:

The same guidelines generally apply as those for a low fat diet, as most people with a cholesterol problem would also benefit from keeping their diet low in fat. In addition, the type of fat is relevant. Use monounsaturated or polyunsaturated fats instead of saturated fats.
- Monounsaturated fats — canola oil or margarine, olive oil or margarine.
- Polyunsaturated fats — generally most vegetable oils will be polyunsaturated. The word 'polyunsaturated' will usually appear on the container.

## General guidelines for reducing the salt content of recipes:
- Ideally you would not use any salt in cooking. These recipes generally call for you to use salt according to taste.
- Remember your taste buds have been used to a different level of salt in your diet from those of many of your customers. If your customers have been avoiding using salt in cooking at home, and then you use salt in preparing food for them, they will quite likely taste your food as 'too salty'.

 It is possible for clients to add salt to a dish, but impossible for them to take it away.

- Herbs and spices might be appropriate modifications to recipes, instead of salt.
- You could also buy any processed products which are labelled 'low salt' or 'no added salt'.

## Guidelines for making a recipe suitable for someone trying to lose weight:
- The guidelines for reducing weight are focused on reducing the fat content of the diet; therefore apply guidelines for reducing the fat in recipes.
- Remember there are plenty of people who are trying to lose weight, and generally they will appreciate a low fat option on the menu.
- The quantity of food these people eat should also be moderate, not large. If you are responsible for serving the food, you should be careful to see that the quantity of food on the plate is not too much. It is mainly the quantity of meat, chicken etc. which needs to be small. The vegetables need to be prepared in a low fat manner, then they can be served generously.

## General guidelines for making a recipe suitable for a diabetic diet:
- Most people on a diabetic diet also need a low fat diet; therefore, the low fat guidelines also apply.
- Artificial sweeteners can sometimes be substituted for sugar in recipes for muffins, cakes and biscuits. Making this substitution may affect the texture of the food, however. It is important to remember that biscuits, cakes etc. tend to be high in fat, so they may still be unsuitable for a diabetic diet, even after substituting an artificial sweetener for sugar.

## General guidelines for making a recipe high in fibre:

- Use wholemeal flour instead of white flour.
- Use brown, not white, rice.
- Add more vegetables than the recipe suggests.
- Leave the skin on vegetables and fruit.
- Serve wholemeal bread, not white bread.

# FOOD PRESENTATION

# GARNISHING AND PRESENTATION

Successful garnishing and food presentation needs an understanding of its purpose, which is simply to present a finished product to its fullest potential. When catering for large numbers of people, thoughtful and careful food presentation combined with appropriate garnishing plays a significant role in the success of a dish or meal and ultimately in the success of the catering operation. It is therefore very important that professional caterers strive to market their food to its maximum potential whether it be the everyday sandwich, a salad or a full meal.

Marketing in the catering operation could be, at its simplest, a sprig of a fresh herb or, at its most complex, the overall impact of the catering operation. When used effectively, garnishing not only enhances the appearance of food; it can also complement it by adding extra colour, flavour and texture.

**'We eat with our eyes first'**

If a dish, be it on a salad bar, a sandwich counter or a hot and cold counter, is attractively garnished it will generate customer interest.

Before garnishing, consider the suitability of the garnish you intend to use. Where possible, try to not only improve the appearance, but also the flavour, colour contrast and texture.

Be careful not to over-garnish, or to garnish repetitively. This will lessen the visual impact for the customer.

# GARNISHING FOOD EFFECTIVELY

Listed are some straightforward and cost-effective garnishes that will suit many different dishes:

- A dash of sour cream with paprika and finely sliced chives (soups, casseroles and Mexican-style dishes).
- Home-made Parmesan or garlic croûtons (soups or salads).
- Finely diced Spanish onions tossed with finely chopped parsley (soups, most meat and fish dishes and salads).
- Finely chopped fresh herbs (most savoury dishes: bear flavour in mind).
- A dash of natural yoghurt with some finely grated carrot (soups and some wet dishes).
- A sprinkle of finely diced capsicum lightly fried or roasted until soft (soups, most meat and fish dishes, salads and vegetable dishes).
- A sprinkle of finely sliced button mushrooms lightly fried until soft (soups, meat dishes, vegetable dishes).
- A dash of freshly made pesto ( soups, pasta, grilled chicken and vegetable dishes).
- Finely diced tomato mixed with finely chopped fresh basil (most savoury dishes, bearing flavour in mind).
- Finely cut long strips of spring onion or capsicum left to curl in iced water before use (most savoury dishes).

- Finely sliced capsicum that has been roasted until soft (most savoury dishes).
- Finely diced bacon cooked till crisp (soup, pasta, wet dishes and some vegetable dishes).
- Sprigs of fresh herbs such as rosemary, basil, dill and coriander (most savoury dishes).
- A fine sprinkle of cracked black pepper (most savoury dishes, bearing flavour in mind).
- Almonds sliced or slivered and roasted to a light golden brown (soups, salads, fish dishes and desserts).
- Black olives with stones removed, roughly chopped (soups, pastas, salads, meat dishes, vegetable dishes).
- Golden breadcrumbs tossed with finely chopped fresh herbs (soups, pasta, salads, fish and vegetable dishes).
- A mixture of finely diced roasted nuts such as walnuts, pine nuts, peanuts (soups, salads and desserts).
- Fresh breadcrumbs mixed with Parmesan cheese roasted to a light golden brown (soups, salads, pasta and vegetable dishes).
- A slice of freshly made herb butter (grills, pasta and fish dishes).
- Grated zest of orange mixed with poppy seeds (hot and cold desserts).
- Sesame seeds roasted a light golden brown (soups, salads, Asian fish and vegetable dishes).
- A light sprinkle of poppy seeds (soups, salads, and hot and cold desserts).
- A fanned strawberry (hot and cold desserts, cold platters and salads).
- Finely grated or shaved chocolate (cold desserts).
- Passionfruit pulp (cold and hot desserts).
- A light sprinkle of finely diced mango and strawberry when in season (cold desserts).
- A light dusting with icing sugar (hot and cold desserts).
- Finely diced angelica and glacé cherries mixed (hot and cold desserts).
- Desiccated coconut toasted golden brown (hot and cold desserts).

---

**Your only limitation to original and effective garnishing besides your budget is your imagination**

---

# BAINS-MARIE, COUNTERS AND SANDWICH BARS

Presentation of hot and cold bains-marie, counters and sandwich bars is equally important. As aforementioned, potential customers 'eat with their eyes first'. Hot and cold bains-marie, counters and sandwich counters are the point where your product is marketed and one area where innovation is always essential.

Points to bear in mind with hot and cold bains-marie, counters and sandwich bars:

- Cleanliness is of the utmost importance and bains-marie and counters must be cleaned regularly. This includes the removal of display items and regular cleaning of the tops of bains-marie, counters etc. as well as general cleaning of bains-marie.

- Special attention should be given to the glass windows; clean regularly, paying special attention to the smears and grease marks.
- Any spills on bains-marie and counters that occur should be wiped immediately with a clean cloth.
- Serving utensils should be changed regularly, as should the containers and the water they are stored in during service times.
- Serving staff must be aware of all portion sizes before service begins. They must also be aware of all prices of food sold at the operation. A current price list should be available at the till(s) as reference for staff and customers alike.
- Food should always look fresh and this can be achieved by cooking food in smaller batches, wiping and changing serving trays regularly, topping up regularly, stirring wet dishes and re-garnishing continually from the beginning of service through to its completion.
- All dishes should be presented to complement one another and garnished in some way (refer to the list on the previous page or individual recipes in recipe chapters for appropriate ideas). Look at the counter from the customers' side to get their perspective of the food (remember colour co-ordination).
- All staff should be dressed in the required uniform, which should be clean and ironed, have their hair tied back and wear gloves during service times.
- Try to raise all food where possible. Terracotta dishes, tiles, woks and cast iron sauté pans look great with hot food. China bowls for salads, wicker baskets and small wooden boxes for sandwiches, fruit and confectionery.
- Carving roast meats on the hot bain-marie individually for customers looks great. Ensure the chef is in a fully cleaned and ironed uniform and wearing a hat and gloves.
- Dress bains-marie with whole vegetables such as capsicums, Spanish onions, whole garlic bulbs, zucchini, eggplant, tomatoes. These survive under the heat and lights very well in comparison to pre-cut garnishes (the vegetables can be used the following day for soups and sauces etc.)
- The tops of bains-marie and also counter areas should be utilised with products for sale. Decorate with olive oil cans, bottles filled with herb vinegars and oils, and glass jars containing preserved fruits and vegetables such as lemons, capsicums and kumquats.
- Utilise whole pumpkins and strings of garlic bulbs and dried chillies and stuff empty hessian sacks.
- Varnished dried bread in hessian filled baskets also looks great with wheat sheaves. Hessian and calico can also be used to cover the tops of cold bains-marie. Fresh vegetables can also be used to fill gaps or spare space in cold counters. Displays on bains-marie and counters should be altered or changed regularly to avoid their looking tired and dusty.
- Market your food through regular special days, such as Chinese New Year, Bastille Day and St Valentine's Day. Incorporate 'specials' on your menu; experiment with innovative and contemporary dishes to be found in this book. Ensure menu boards are written up daily and as neatly as possible, advertising any specials of the day or upcoming special days. Distribute your weekly menus, typed, throughout the building. Advertise anything you feel will attract and improve your custom and sales figures! Keep people interested, both staff and customers.

# APPENDIXES

# APPENDIX 1
# HERBS, SPICES,
# NUTS AND SEEDS

## HERBS AND SPICES

| Herb/Spice | Origin | Uses |
|---|---|---|
| **Aamchur** | India | Finely ground unripened mango, used as a meat tenderiser in marinades, grilled meats and vegetable dishes, and in condiments. |
| | **Example:** | Samosas |
| **Ajwain** | India | Very powerful spice. Used in chutneys and curries. |
| | **Example:** | Pappadams |
| **Allspice** | South America | Pickling, white meat casseroles, flavouring for desserts. |
| | **Examples:** | Christmas pudding, pork and veal pâtés |
| **Angelica** | Russia/Iceland | Used in the production of desserts. The crystallised stems used as an ingredient or garnish. Jams and jellies. |
| | **Example:** | Vermouth |
| **Anise** | Middle East | Topping for crusty breads, also used in the making of sweets, drinks, marinades, cakes, fruit salads. |
| | **Example:** | Anise cookies |
| **Annatto** | South America | The peppery taste of annatto adds flavour to fish, vegetables, and most meats. Mexican cuisine. Adds a yellow colour to foods such as red Leicester cheese and butter. |
| | **Example:** | Chinese roast pork |
| **Basil** | India/Persia | Any dish with tomato or with an Italian influence; soups, salads, zucchini, spinach, quiches, flans, pizza and pasta. |
| | **Example:** | Pesto |
| **Bay** | Mediterranean | Bouquet garni, stocks, sauces, soups. Compatible with most wet dishes. |
| | **Example:** | Chicken casserole |
| **Bergamot** | North America | Used to flavour vegetarian dishes, meatloaf, pork and veal. It can also be used to flavour sweet dishes and fruit salads. It is the herb that gives Earl Grey tea its distinctive flavour. |
| | **Example:** | Mixed green leaf salad |
| **Caraway seeds** | America/Europe | Pungent aniseed taste used in breads and confectionery. |
| | **Example:** | Caraway cake/rye bread |
| **Cardamom** | India/Sri Lanka | Pungent, sweet, spicy flavour. Adds flavour to curries, cakes, coffees and Danish pastries. Can be used with vegetables and all meat dishes. |
| | **Example:** | Pumpkin pie/Indian and Middle Eastern desserts |
| **Chervil** | Eastern Europe | Ingredient for *fines herbes*. Used in soups and cheese dishes. Goes well with potatoes, salads, poultry and fish. |
| | **Example:** | Spinach soup |
| **Chilli/cayenne pepper** | South America | Mexican, Italian and Asian cuisines. |
| | **Example:** | Chilli con carne |

| | | |
|---|---|---|
| Chives | Mediterranean | Sauces, salads, soups and dips; a mild onion flavour. |
| | **Example:** | Potato and chive soup |
| Cinnamon | Sri Lanka | Chutneys, apple pies, apple sauce, pumpkin and zucchini. |
| | **Example:** | Cinnamon bread |
| Cloves | China | Adds flavour to hams and fruits, bread sauce, pork, chutney and marinades. |
| | **Example:** | Honey glazed ham |
| Coriander | Mediterranean/Asia | Asian dishes, predominantly Thai; meat, vegetables, satay and curried sauces. Very sweet. |
| | **Example:** | Beef satay |
| Cumin | Mediterranean | Pickles, chutneys and rice dishes. Curries and Mexican style foods. |
| | **Example:** | Korma curry |
| Curry powder | India | This is a mixture of many herbs and spices. Powders vary depending upon the regions where they where created. They are usually made up with peppercorns, cardamom, coriander, cumin, nutmeg, cayenne and cloves along with up to twenty more herbs and spices. |
| Dill | Mediterranean | Chutneys, pickles, and seafood. Garnish for salads and soups. |
| | **Example:** | Gravlax |
| Fennel | Europe/Asia | Salads and salad dressings, fish and vegetable dishes. |
| | **Example:** | Potato cakes |
| Fenugreek | Asia/Europe | Chutneys, curries and stews. Seasoning for green beans and cauliflower. |
| | **Example:** | Curried vegetables |
| Garlic | Egypt | Mediterranean cuisine, soups, sauces, marinades, etc.; very versatile. |
| | **Example:** | Aïoli |
| Ginger | Asia | Used in the production of curries. Used in cakes and most Asian dishes. Acts as a tenderiser when used with meats. |
| | **Example:** | Gingerbread |
| Horseradish | Europe | Very strong pungent root. Used in moderation can add flavour to roasts, sauces and dressings. |
| | **Example:** | Horseradish sauce |
| Lemon grass | Asia | Important ingredient in Thai cuisine. Usually used in conjunction with chilli, curries, fish and chicken dishes. |
| | **Example:** | Most Thai-style soups |
| Lime leaves | Asia | Usually purchased dried and then soaked in water. Lime leaves add a refreshing lemon/lime flavour to most wet dishes. Used widely in Asian cuisine; complements most fish and chicken dishes. |
| | **Example:** | Thai fish cakes |
| Liquorice | Middle/Far East | Used to flavour drinks, fruits and confectionery. |
| | **Example:** | Liquorice ice-cream |
| Marjoram | Mediterranean | Bouquet garni. Italian dishes in the absence of oregano. Used in stews; complements poultry, fish and salads. |
| | **Example:** | Neapolitan sauce |
| Masalas | India | Masalas are mixtures of different herbs used in Indian cookery. Different mixes are traditionally used for different dishes. The most popular masala mix is garam masala, which is used in curries. Garam masala is a curry mix with the omission of turmeric. |
| | **Example:** | Chicken vindaloo |
| Mint | Mediterranean | Now synonymous with most lamb dishes, jelly, sauces and stuffing. Used in drinks, sauces and chutneys. Garnish for desserts. |
| | **Example:** | Mint sauce |
| Mustard | Mediterranean | Adds bite to most sauces. Served as a condiment to roast beef, ham and most cold meats. |
| | **Example:** | Vinaigrettes |

| | | |
|---|---|---|
| **Nutmeg** | Sri Lanka | Used in sweet dishes, milk puddings. Seasoning for vegetables, especially pumpkin, sweet potato and spinach. |
| | Example: | Creamed rice pudding |
| **Oregano** | Mediterranean | Strong flavour. Used with bay and basil to flavour most Italian-style dishes; most tomato based dishes; sprinkled over salads and in herb breads. |
| | Example: | Lasagne al forno |
| **Paprika** | Eastern Europe | Excellent garnish with its deep red colour for any white sauce. Good colour when used with rice dishes. Classically associated with goulash. |
| | Example: | Hungarian goulash |
| **Parsley** | Mediterranean | An all-purpose herb. Can be used in any form with most dishes. Classic garnish to most foods, either in sprigs or chopped. Stems used for stock production. |
| | Example: | Parsley sauce |
| **Pepper** | India | An accepted condiment on every table. Many different varieties and stages of ripeness of pepper are available, the most common being white and black. |
| | Example: | Green peppercorn sauce |
| **Rosemary** | Europe/Turkey | Used in conjunction with lemon in lamb dishes. Stuffings and most wet dishes in moderation. |
| | Example: | Lamb casserole |
| **Saffron** | Asia/Mediterranean | Because of the high cost of saffron, it is usually substituted with turmeric or artificial colouring. Adds a yellow colour to rice when mixing with water before rice is added. Colouring for poultry; excellent for presentation and adds a distinctive flavour. |
| | Example: | Spanish paella |
| **Sage** | Mediterranean | Powerful herb used mainly with pork and poultry and in the production of stuffings. |
| | Example: | Sage and onion stuffing |
| **Tarragon** | Europe | Vinegars, salad dressings, creamed soups and most poultry dishes. |
| | Example: | Bearnaise sauce |
| **Thyme** | Mediterranean | Bouquet garni. Goes well with any savoury dish, soups, fish, chicken and stuffings. |
| | Example: | Creole chicken |
| **Turmeric** | India/Africa | Curries, pickles and chutneys and as an alternative to saffron. |
| | Example: | Potato and chick pea curry |
| **Vanilla** | Central America | Adds flavour to any milk based dessert, pudding or ice-cream. |
| | Example: | Vanilla ice-cream |

# NUTS AND SEEDS

**Almond**
A creamy coloured nut high in dietary fibre, vitamin E and certain minerals. Can be purchased whole, crushed, sliced, slivered, flaked, ground and nibbed. Buying almonds whole prolongs their shelf life and allows for maximum flavour when used. The high percentage of oil contained in almonds dictates their storage in a refrigerator to prevent the oil going rancid. Almonds need shelling and then blanching before eating to remove the skin surrounding the nut.

**Uses** biscuits and cakes, confectionery, pastries, casseroles, vegetarian dishes, pastas, fish and chicken.

**Brazil nut**
A long, three sided nut, cream in colour and covered with a brown skin and then a shell. These nuts are usually bought whole, with or without the

shell, and should be kept in the refrigerator because of their high oil content. Shelled Brazil nuts can be eaten straight away.

**Uses**    biscuits and cakes, especially fruit cakes, confectionery, vegetarian dishes, served shelled with fresh fruit platters and cheese.

**Bunya nut**    Native to Australia, this nut has a very low fat content compared to other nuts. It is becoming more popular in kitchens today. Bunya nuts should be bought whole with unsplit shells and stored open in the refrigerator. They can be eaten raw or roasted and then shelled.

**Uses**    biscuits, cakes, flans, stews and soups.

**Candle nut**    Native to Asia and South Pacific regions, this nut is an excellent energy source due to its very high fat content. Candle nuts can be roasted and eaten.

**Uses**    candle nuts are usually roasted and ground and used to flavour rice, vegetables, relishes and other condiments.

**Caraway seed**    Because caraway seeds are used in such small amounts they have no nutritional value, but they aid digestion and palatability of the foods in which they are used. If purchased in an airtight container and stored in a cool, dry place, away from direct sunlight, they will keep for well over nine months.

**Uses**    stewed fruits, cakes, stews, vegetables, salads and in the production of certain cheeses.

**Cashew nut**    Cashews are high in oil and widely available. They are a cream coloured crescent shaped seed between 1–2 cm long. Cashew nuts should always be purchased pre-shelled, in airtight bags as the shell contains skin irritants. Once the airtight bag has been broken the nuts should be placed in an airtight container in the refrigerator.

**Uses**    Asian dishes, especially stir-fries, chicken dishes, as a snack food, salads, stuffings and vegetarian dishes.

**Celery seed**    Because celery seeds are used in such small amounts they have no nutritional value. If purchased in an airtight container and stored in a cool, dry place, away from direct sunlight, they will keep for well over nine months.

**Uses**    as a flavouring for soups, casseroles, fish, vegetables and as a flavouring for tomato juice.

**Chestnut**    High in fibre and very low in oil compared with other nuts. Always buy chestnuts in the shells, which should be undamaged, and store in a cool place for approx. one week. Cook chestnuts by either boiling or roasting. To boil, place chestnuts into boiling water and cook for approx. 25 minutes, remove, cool and then remove shells. To roast, slit shells a little with a sharp knife and place into a hot oven and cook for approx. 10 minutes, cool and remove from shells.

**Uses**    stuffings, especially turkeys at Christmas, puddings, desserts, vegetables and vegetarian dishes.

**Coconut**    Can be purchased whole in the shell. If so, insert a strong thin object into the markings at one end of the coconut. Two holes are required. Drain the juice from the coconut; this can be drunk or used in the production of

| | Asian-style dishes. Break the shell into small pieces, scrape away the white flesh and discard the shell. The tough flesh can be eaten raw. Coconuts can be bought prepared in desiccated form or as coconut milk or cream.<br>**Uses**    all Asian-style dishes, cakes and biscuits, desserts. |
|---|---|
| **Dill seed** | Because dill seeds are used in such small amounts they have no nutritional value but aid digestion of the foods in which they are used. If purchased in an airtight container and stored in a cool, dry place away from direct sunlight, they will keep for well over nine months.<br>**Uses**    with breads, cabbage, brussels sprouts, potatoes, white meats and in salads. |
| **Fennel seed** | Fennel seeds provide a little iron; they give an aniseed flavour to foods where they are used. If purchased in an airtight container and stored in a cool, dry place away from direct sunlight, they will keep for well over nine months.<br>**Uses**    vegetables, curries, pork, fish, pasta, dips, rice, soups and salads. |
| **Hazelnut** | High in oil and a good source of Vitamin E, these small, light brown, round nuts have a long shelf life. When purchasing, select the largest nuts with undamaged shells. Hazelnuts should be stored in a refrigerator whether they have been shelled or not. Hazelnuts can be eaten raw, purchased in the shell, shelled, whole or chopped.<br>**Uses**    biscuits, cakes, desserts, ice cream, stuffings. |
| **Macadamia nut** | An excellent source of fibre, these creamy coloured nuts are native to Australia with a taste and texture of their own. The ripe nuts are treated to reduce the moisture content and thus to prolong their shelf life, approx. 12 months in their shell. Once opened the macadamias should be stored in a refrigerator. These nuts are usually purchased shelled and whole.<br>**Uses**    as a snack, in biscuits, cakes, desserts, rice dishes, confectionery, ice cream, pastas. |
| **Palm nut** | Used widely in Indonesian cuisine, this nut resembles a gelatinous, transparent sap and can be purchased from speciality shops tinned. Once opened they should be stored in a separate clean container in the refrigerator for up to 2–3 days.<br>**Uses**    soups and desserts. |
| **Peanut** | Probably the most popular of all the nuts available. Peanuts can be purchased whole in their shells but more commonly they are purchased shelled, either whole or chopped. Peanuts are a high source of protein. Peanuts should be stored, if purchased shelled, in an airtight container in a cool place. They may be frozen. Peanuts are usually roasted before eating.<br>**Uses**    snacks, desserts, biscuits, cakes, with chicken and meats, fish, confectionery etc. |
| **Pecan nut** | These nuts, which are low in fibre and high in energy, can be purchased whole either shelled or unshelled. Pecans are usually purchased shelled in airtight bags. Pecans should be stored in the refrigerator in airtight containers. |

**Uses**    whole in cakes and breads or chopped in biscuits and
confectionery, pecan pie.

**Pine nut**    Small, creamy coloured, oval shaped nut with a multitude of uses.
Pine nuts are a good source of phosphorus, thiamin, iron and protein.
These nuts are usually roasted or grilled before use as this improves the
flavour. Pine nuts are usually purchased shelled. Pine nuts should be
stored in an airtight container in the refrigerator.
**Uses**    lamb, poultry, pasta dishes, salads, stuffings, vegetables, biscuits
and cakes, pesto sauce.

**Pistachio nut**    Like most other nuts the pistachio is high in oil and a very good source of
iron. The nut is encased in a brittle shell which is easily opened.
Unopened shells should be purchased in good condition; shelled nuts
should be purchased in an airtight bag. Pistachios should be stored in
airtight glass jars in the refrigerator. The skins around the edible nuts can
be removed by blanching for 30 seconds.
**Uses**    desserts, cakes, pastries, as a snack, in pâtés and terrines,
ice cream.

**Poppy seed**    Native to Asia, poppy seeds are tiny, round and a bluish-black in colour.
Poppy seeds are used in such small amounts they have no nutritional
value. If purchased in an airtight container and stored in a cool, dry place
away from direct sunlight, they will keep for well over nine months.
**Uses**    cakes and biscuits, breads and as a garnish to savouries.

**Pumpkin seed**    These seeds are an excellent source of vitamin C, iron and zinc.
These small, flat, oval seeds are gaining popularity the world over as a
healthy snack food. They are usually purchased ready to use and should
be stored in an airtight glass jar in the refrigerator. If stored correctly
pumpkin seeds can have a storage life of approx. six months.
**Uses**    as a snack food, in salads, cakes, slices and biscuits, vegetarian
dishes, casseroles and soups.

**Sesame seed**    Tiny, flat, cream coloured seeds native to Indonesia. They have been
cultivated there for over 300 years. Store in an airtight container in a cool,
dry place away from direct sunlight, and they will keep for well over nine
months. When adding to salads and dishes that require no cooking they
should be lightly dry fried, toasted or roasted.
**Uses**    salads, savouries, cakes, casseroles, fish, cheeses, quiches, flans
and as a garnish.

**Sunflower seed**    A good source of vitamin C, iron and zinc. Sunflower seeds are
small, flat, oval shaped, beige coloured seeds. Usually purchased ready to
use, they should be stored in an airtight glass jar in the refrigerator.
If stored correctly sunflower seeds can have a storage life of approx.
six months. Care should be taken when purchasing sunflower seeds to
ensure that there is no insect infestation. Sunflower seeds can be eaten
raw or roasted.
**Uses**    with vegetarian dishes, pastas, soups, casseroles, salads, cakes,
biscuits, puddings or served as they are as a snack.

**Walnut**          Walnuts can be purchased in their shell or shelled in airtight bags or tins. In their shell they can be stored for up to six months in a cool place away from direct sunlight or in the refrigerator. Shelled nuts should be kept in an airtight container in the refrigerator. Walnuts can be eaten raw or toasted.

**Uses**   desserts, cakes and biscuits, salads, stuffings; ground walnuts can be added to pastries.

# APPENDIX 2
# BULK ORDERING CHARTS

Recommended uncooked portion sizes, bulk ordering quantities and nutritional information.

| Product | Prepared Uncooked Portion Size | Approximate % In Preparation Wastage (Where relev) | Bulk Portion Sizes Allowing for Wastage % | | | Energy Value per 100 g (Unless Stated) | | Main Nutrients Contained In |
|---|---|---|---|---|---|---|---|---|
| | | | 25 | 50 | 100 | Cal | kJ | |
| **Fruits** | | | | | | | | |
| Apple | 100 g | 10% | 2.75 | 5.5 | 11 | 49 | 207 | Carb, Fib |
| Apricot | 100 g | 5% | 2.7 | 5.25 | 10.5 | 37 | 156 | Carb, A, Fib |
| Avocado | 110 g | 30% | 3.6 | 7.2 | 14.3 | 209 | 879 | Fat, A, C, Iron, B1, Fib |
| Banana | 110 g | 30% | 3.6 | 7.2 | 14.3 | 91 | 384 | C, Fib, Carb |
| Blackberry | 90 g | 0% | 2.25 | 4.5 | 9 | 30 | 130 | C, E, Fib, Iron Carb, Cal |
| Blueberry | 90 g | 0% | 2.25 | 4.5 | 9 | 57 | 240 | Carb, Fib, Iron |
| Cherries | 70 g | 25% | 2.2 | 4.4 | 8.75 | 53 | 224 | Carb |
| Cranberries | 80 g | 0% | 2 | 4 | 8 | 15 | 63 | C, Fib |
| Currants | 90 g | 0% | 2.25 | 4.5 | 9 | 24 | 100 | Fib, Carb, Mag, Iron, Cal, C |
| Dates | 40 g | 20% | 102 | 2.4 | 4.8 | 261 | 1100 | Carb, Iron, Mag, Cal, Fib |
| Figs | 40 g | 0% | 1 | 2 | 4 | 40 | 169 | C, Carb, Fib |
| Gooseberries | 90 g | 0% | 2.25 | 4.5 | 9 | 38 | 160 | C, Fib, A |
| Grapes | 90 g | 0% | 2.25 | 4.5 | 9 | 61 | 256 | Carb, Fib, C |
| Grapefruit | 1/2 p/portion | 0% | 13 | 25 | 50 | 26 | 111 | Carb, C |
| Kiwifruit | 80 g | 15% | 2.3 | 4.6 | 9.2 | 49 | 204 | C, Carb, Fib |
| Kumquat | 90 g | 0% | 2.25 | 4.5 | 9 | 59 | 250 | C, Carb |
| Lemon | n/a | varies | | | | 23 | 95 | C, Fib, Cal |
| Lime | n/a | varies | | | | 21 | 89 | C, Fib, Carb |
| Loquat | 30 g | 0% | 0.75 | 1.5 | 3 | 26 | 108 | A, C |
| Lychee | 80 g | 50% | 3 | 6 | 12 | 68 | 286 | C, Carb |
| Mandarin | 1 p/portion | | x25 | x50 | x100 | 38 | 160 | C, Carb |
| Mango | 1/2 p/portion | | x13 | x25 | x50 | 56 | 236 | A, Carb, C |
| Melon | 110 g | 20% | 3.3 | 6.6 | 13.2 | 20 | 84 | C, Carb |
| Nectarine | 1 p/portion | varies | x25 | x50 | x100 | 37 | 156 | Carb, Fib |
| Orange | 1 p/portion | varies | x25 | x50 | x100 | 37 | 156 | Carb, C, Fib |
| Papaw | 90 g | 40% | 3.2 | 6.3 | 12.6 | 28 | 120 | A, C, Fib, Carb |
| Passionfruit | 1 p/portion | varies | x25 | x50 | x100 | 46 | 193 | Fib, Carb |
| Peach | 1 p/portion | varies | x25 | x50 | x100 | 31 | 132 | A, Carb |
| Pear | 1 p/portion | varies | x25 | x50 | x100 | 50 | 211 | Carb |
| Pineapple | 80 g | 35% | 2.7 | 5.4 | 10.8 | 38 | 158 | C, Carb |
| Plum | 90 g | 20% | 2.7 | 5.4 | 10.8 | 37 | 155 | Carb, E, Fib |
| Pomegranate | 1/2 p/portion | varies | x13 | x25 | x50 | 66 | 278 | |
| Raspberries | 80 g | 0% | 2 | 4 | 8 | 25 | 105 | C, Iron, Fib, Mag |
| Rhubarb | 100 g | 25% | 3.2 | 6.25 | 12.5 | 18 | 76 | C, Cal, Fib |
| Starfruit | 90 g | 10% | 2.5 | 5 | 10 | 35 | 150 | A, C, Pot, Iron |
| Strawberry | 90 g | 0% | 2.25 | 4.5 | 9 | 20 | 84 | C, Fib |
| **Dried fruits** | | | | | | | | |
| Apple | 30 g | 0% | 0.75 | 1.5 | 3 | 285 | 1200 | Fib, Iron, Carb |
| Apricot | 30 g | 0% | 0.75 | 1.5 | 3 | 195 | 819 | Carb, Iron, Fib, A, Cal, B2 |
| Date | 35 g | 0% | 0.875 | 1.75 | 3.5 | 269 | 1130 | Fib, Carb, Mag, Iron, Cal |
| Peach | 30 g | 0% | 0.75 | 1.5 | 3 | 214 | 900 | Carb, A, B2, Fib |
| Prune | 60 g | 0% | 1.5 | 3 | 6 | 83 | 349 | Carb, A, Fib, Iron, B2 |
| Raisins | 20 g | 0% | 0.5 | 1 | 2 | 290 | 1220 | Fib, Carb Iron, Cal, B1 |
| Sultanas | 20 g | 0% | 0.5 | 1 | 2 | 305 | 1280 | E, Fib, Carb, Cal, Iron, B1 |

**Note** Weights and wastage percentages are only an approximate guide.

| Product | Prepared Uncooked Portion Size | Approximate % In Preparation Wastage (Where relev) | Bulk Portion Sizes Allowing for Wastage % 25 | 50 | 100 | Energy Value per 100 g (Unless Stated) Cal | kJ | Main Nutrients Contained In |
|---|---|---|---|---|---|---|---|---|

# Fish

| Product | Prepared Uncooked Portion Size | Approx % Wastage | 25 | 50 | 100 | Cal | kJ | Main Nutrients |
|---|---|---|---|---|---|---|---|---|
| Barramundi | 200 g | 0% | 5 | 10 | 20 | 92 | 390 | Pro, Cal, Mag |
| Bream | 200 g | 0% | 5 | 10 | 20 | 125 | 521 | Pro, B2, Cal |
| Cod | 200 g | 0% | 5 | 10 | 20 | 85 | 356 | Pro |
| Eel | 200 g | 0% | 5 | 10 | 20 | 166 | 700 | Pro, A, Iron |
| Flathead | 200 g | 0% | 5 | 10 | 20 | 94 | 395 | Pro, Cal, B2 |
| Gemfish | 220 g | 0% | 5 | 10 | 20 | 192 | 806 | Pro, Mag, Sod |
| Garfish | 2–4 p/portion | 0% | x50–100 | x100–200 | x200–400 | 95 | 400 | Pro, So, Cal |
| Hussar | 200 g | 0% | 5 | 10 | 20 | 95 | 400 | Pro, Cal |
| Jewfish | 200 g | 0% | 5 | 10 | 20 | 86 | 360 | Pro, Cal |
| John Dory | 200 g | 0% | 5 | 10 | 20 | 90 | 380 | Pro, Cal |
| King Fish | 200 g | 0% | 5 | 10 | 20 | 93 | 390 | Pro |
| Leather Jacket | 200 g | 0% | 5 | 10 | 20 | 83 | 350 | Pro, Cal |
| Ling | 200 g | 0% | 5 | 10 | 20 | 71 | 300 | Pro, Cal, Mag |
| Mackerel | 200 g | 0% | 5 | 10 | 20 | 222 | 930 | Pro, A, Iron |
| Mullet | 200 g | 0% | 5 | 10 | 20 | 131 | 549 | Pro, Iron, Mag |
| Orange Roughy | 200 g | 0% | 5 | 10 | 20 | 126 | 530 | Pro, Cal |
| Parrot fish | 200 g | 0% | 5 | 10 | 20 | | | Pro, Cal |
| Perch | 200 g | 0% | 5 | 10 | 20 | 83 | 350 | Pro, Cal |
| Red fish | 200 g | 0% | 5 | 10 | 20 | 119 | 500 | Pro |
| Sardines | 4–6 p/portion | varies | x100–150 | x200–300 | x400–600 | 162 | 680 | Pro, Fat, Iron, Mag |
| Shark | 200 g | 0% | 5 | 10 | 20 | 107 | 450 | Pro, Iron |
| Salmon | 200 g | 0% | 5 | 10 | 20 | 180 | 756 | Pro |
| Snapper | 200 g | 0% | 5 | 10 | 20 | 90 | 380 | Pro, B2 |
| Tailor | 200 g | 0% | 5 | 10 | 20 | 119 | 500 | Pro |
| Trevally | 200 g | 0% | 5 | 10 | 20 | 107 | 450 | Pro, Cal |
| Trout | 1 p/portion | 0% | x25 | x50 | x100 | 135 | 567 | Pro |
| Trumpeter | 200 g | 0% | 5 | 10 | 20 | 95 | 400 | Pro, Cal |
| Tuna | 200 g | 0% | 5 | 10 | 20 | 98 | 410 | Pro |
| Whitebait | 150 g | 0% | 3.75 | 7.5 | 15 | 95 | 400 | Pro, Cal, Phos |
| Whiting | 200 g | 0% | 5 | 10 | 20 | 86 | 362 | Pro, B2, Mag |

# Seafood

| Product | Prepared Uncooked Portion Size | Approx % Wastage | 25 | 50 | 100 | Cal | kJ | Main Nutrients |
|---|---|---|---|---|---|---|---|---|
| Abalone | 120 g | 0% | 3 | 6 | 12 | 142 | 600 | Carb, Sod, Zinc, Pro, Mag |
| Calamari | 140 g | 10% | 3.9 | 7.7 | 15.4 | | | Pro |
| Crab | 120 g | 70% | 5.1 | 10.2 | 20.4 | 86 | 360 | Pro |
| Cuttlefish | 140 g | 15% | 4.1 | 8.1 | 16.1 | 86 | 360 | Pro, Iron |
| Lobster | 180 g | 60% | 7.2 | 14.4 | 28.8 | 86 | 360 | Pro |
| Balmain Bugs | 120 g | 60% | 4.8 | 9.6 | 19.2 | 110 | 462 | Pro |
| Mussels | 10 p/portion | in shell | x250 | x500 | x1000 | 90 | 378 | Pro, Iron, Zinc |
| Octopus | 140 g | 15% | 4.1 | 8.1 | 16.1 | 67 | 280 | Pro |
| Prawns | 140 g | 30% | 4.6 | 9.1 | 18.2 | 98 | 410 | Pro, Cal |
| Scampi | 140 | 60% | 5.6 | 11.2 | 22.4 | 111 | 470 | Pro, Cal, Mag |
| Scallops | 7 p/portion | in shell | x175 | x350 | x700 | 53 | 224 | Pro, Pot |
| Squid | 140 g | 15% | 4.1 | 8.1 | 16.1 | 76 | 320 | Pro |
| Oysters | 6–12 p/portion | in shell | x90–180 | x150–300 | x300–600 | 73 | 306 | Pro, Cal, Iron, Zinc, B3 |

**Note** Weights and wastage percentages are only an approximate guide.

# Tinned and preserved seafoods

| Product | Prepared Uncooked Portion Size | Approximate % In Preparation Wastage (Where relev) | 25 | 50 | 100 | Cal | kJ | Main Nutrients Contained In |
|---|---|---|---|---|---|---|---|---|
| Anchovies | 12 g | 0% | 180 g | 300 g | 600 g | 45 (25 g) | 190 (25 g) | Sod, Pro, B |
| Caviar | 12 g | 0% | 180 g | 300 g | 600 g | 23 (20 g) | 100 (20 g) | Sod |
| Crab | 150 g | 0% | 3.75 | 7.5 | 15 | 60 | 254 | Pro, Sod, Cal |
| Dried Fish | 150 g | 0% | 3.75 | 7.5 | 15 | 145 | 610 | Pro, Sod, Iron |
| Lumpfish Roe | 12 g | 0% | 180 g | 300 g | 600 g | 2.3 (20 g) | 100 (20 g) | Phos, Sod |
| Mussels | x10 | 0% | x250 | x500 | x1000 | 193 | 812 | Pro, Iron, Zinc |
| Pilchards | 4 p/portion | 0% | x100 | x200 | x400 | 126 | 530 | Pro, Sod, B2, Cal, Iron |
| Salmon | 120 g | 0% | 3 | 6 | 12 | 146 | 615 | Pro, Sod, B2, Cal |
| Sardines | 4 p/portion | 0% | x100 | x200 | x400 | 227 | 952 | Pro, Fat, B2, Pot, Iron |
| Prawns | 140 g | 0% | 3.5 | 7 | 14 | 119 | 500 | Pro, Sod, Iron, Zinc |
| Tuna | 150 g | 0% | 3.75 | 7.5 | 15 | 123 | 518 | Pro, B2 |
| Seaweed | varies | | | | | 321 | 1350 | Cal, Carb |

*Approx 24 mussels to a kilo

# Beef

| Product | Prepared Uncooked Portion Size | Approximate % In Preparation Wastage (Where relev) | kg 25 | kg 50 | kg 100 | Cal | kJ | Main Nutrients Contained In |
|---|---|---|---|---|---|---|---|---|
| Fillet/Tenderloin | 200 g | 5% | 5.25 | 10.5 | 21 | 124 | 521 | Pro, Fat, Iron, A, Zinc, Pot, B2 |
| Sirloin (boneless) Striploin | 200 g | 10% | 5.5 | 11 | 22 | 138 | 580 | Pro, Fat, Iron, A, B2, Zinc |
| Rump | 200 g | 10% | 5.5 | 11 | 22 | 118 | 494 | Pro, Fat, Iron, A, B2, Zinc |
| Loin (boneless) | 200 g | 10% | 5.5 | 11 | 22 | 240 | 1008 | Pro, Fat, Iron, B2, Zinc, A |
| Silverside | 200 g | 10% | 5.5 | 11 | 22 | 80 | 335 | Pro, Zinc, Iron, A, Sod, Pot, B2, Foc |
| Topside | 200 g | 10% | 5.5 | 11 | 22 | 115 | 484 | Pro, Fat, Iron, A, B2, Zinc |
| Round | 200 g | 10% | 5.5 | 11 | 22 | 118 | 494 | Pro, Iron, Zinc, A, B2 |
| Chuck | 200 g | 15% | 5.75 | 11.5 | 23 | 108 | 456 | Pro, Iron, Zinc, B2, A |
| Ribs | 200 g | 0% | 5 | 10 | 20 | 132 | 556 | Pro, Fat, Iron, A, B2, Zinc |
| Mince | 180 g | 0% | 4.5 | 9 | 18 | 176 | 738 | Pro, Fat, Iron, A, B2, Zinc |
| Shin | 250 g | 0% | 6.25 | 12.5 | 25 | 223 | 940 | Pro, Iron, Min, A, Zinc |
| Sweetbreads | 70 g | 0% | 1.8 | 3.6 | 7.2 | 194 | 814 | Fat, C, A, Pro |
| Oxtail | 250 g | 0% | 6.25 | 12.5 | 25 | 307 | 1290 | Pro, Fat, B2, Zinc, A |
| Kidney | 110 g | 5% | 2.9 | 5.8 | 11.6 | 88 | 369 | Pro, Iron, A, B2, B3, Zinc |
| Liver | 200 g | 0% | 5 | 10 | 20 | 168 | 704 | A, Folate, Pro, Iron, B2, B3, Zinc |
| Sausages | 200 g | 0% | 5 | 10 | 20 | 260 | 1090 | Pro, Fat, Iron, Zinc, A |
| Tripe | 200 g | 0% | 5 | 10 | 20 | 72 | 302 | Pro, A, Zinc |

Bones (for stock) 2 kg of beef bones will yield 4 L of stock = 60 servings of a beef stock based sauce.

# Veal

| Product | Prepared Uncooked Portion Size | Approximate % In Preparation Wastage (Where relev) | 25 | 50 | 100 | Cal | kJ | Main Nutrients Contained In |
|---|---|---|---|---|---|---|---|---|
| Fillet/Tenderloin | 200 g | 5% | 5.25 | 10.5 | 21 | 148 | 624 | Pro, Iron, B2, A, Zinc |
| Leg (boneless) | 200 g | 5% | 5.25 | 10.5 | 21 | 88 | 370 | Pro, Iron, Zinc, A, B2, Zinc |
| Loin/Striploin | 200 g | 5% | 5.25 | 10.5 | 21 | 105 | 440 | Pro, Iron, B2, A, Zinc |
| Forequarter | 200 g | 5% | 5.25 | 10.5 | 21 | 108 | 453 | Pro, Iron, B2, Zinc, A |
| Shoulder (boneless) | 200 g | 5% | 5.25 | 10.5 | 21 | 114 | 478 | Pro, Iron, B2, Zinc, A |
| Knuckle/Shin/ Shank | 250 g | 5% | 6.6 | 31.2 | 26.3 | 90 | 379 | Pro, Iron, B2, A, Zinc |
| Schnitzel | 120 g | 0% | 3 | 6 | 12 | 110 | 462 | Pro, Iron, B2, A, Zinc |
| Rack/Best End | 1–2 cutlets | 10% | 25 | 50 | 100 | 170 | 714 | Pro, Iron, B2, A, Zinc |
| Cutlets | 1–2(if small) | 10% | 25–50 | 50–100 | 100–200 | 170 | 714 | Pro, Iron, B2, A, Zinc |

Bones (for stock) 2 kg of veal bones will yield 4 L of stock = 60 servings of a veal stock based sauce.

**Note** Weights and wastage percentages are only an approximate guide.

| Product | Prepared Uncooked Portion Size | Approximate % In Preparation Wastage (Where relev) | Bulk Portion Sizes Allowing for Wastage % | | | Energy Value per 100 g (Unless Stated) | | Main Nutrients Contained In |
|---|---|---|---|---|---|---|---|---|
| | | | 25 | 50 | 100 | Cal | kJ | |

# Lamb

| Product | Prepared Uncooked Portion Size | Approximate % Wastage | 25 | 50 | 100 | Cal | kJ | Main Nutrients Contained In |
|---|---|---|---|---|---|---|---|---|
| Fillet/Tenderloin | 200 g | 5% | 5.25 | 10.5 | 21 | 220 | 924 | Pro, Iron, Pot, B2, Zinc |
| Leg (boneless) | 200 g | 10% | 5 | 10 | 20 | 112 | 469 | Pro, Fat, Iron, B2, Pot, Zinc |
| Chump | 200 g | 10% | 5.5 | 11 | 22 | 140 | 589 | Pro, B2, Iron, Zinc, Fat |
| Loin | 200 g | 5% | 5.25 | 10.5 | 21 | 126 | 529 | Pro, Iron, Fat, Zinc, Pot |
| Shoulder (boneless) | 200 g | 0% | 5 | 10 | 20 | 114 | 478 | Pro, Iron, Fat, B2, Pot, Zinc |
| Forequarter (boneless) | 200 g | 0% | 5 | 10 | 20 | 310 | 1302 | Pro, Iron, B2, Zinc, Pot |
| Shank | 300 g | 0% | 7.5 | 15 | 30 | 114 | 477 | Pro, Fat, Iron, Zinc, Pot, B2 |
| Ribs | 300 g | 0% | 7.5 | 15 | 30 | 261 | 1100 | Pro, Iron, Zinc, Pot |
| Liver | 200 g | 0% | 5 | 10 | 20 | 162 | 680 | A, Fat, Pot, B2, B3, Zinc, Iron, Pro |
| Kidneys | 110 g | 5% | 2.9 | 5.8 | 11.6 | 91 | 383 | Pro, Iron, Pot, B2, B3, Zinc |
| Sweetbreads | 70 g | 0% | 1.8 | 3.6 | 7.2 | 214 | 900 | Fat, Pot, Pro |
| Cutlets | 2–3 p/person | 10% | 50–75 | 100–150 | 200–300 | 142 | 598 | Pro, Fat, Iron, Pot, B2, Zinc |
| Rack | 1 p/person | 20% | 25 | 50 | 100 | 300 | 1260 | Pro, Fat, Iron, Pot, B2, Zinc |
| Chops | 2–3 p/person | 5% | 50–75 | 100-150 | 200-300 | 326 | 1370 | Pro, Fat, Iron, Pot, B2, Zinc |

Bones (for stock) 2 kg of lamb bones will yield 4 L of stock = 60 servings of lamb stock based sauce.

# Pork

| Product | Prepared Uncooked Portion Size | Approximate % Wastage | 25 | 50 | 100 | Cal | kJ | Main Nutrients Contained In |
|---|---|---|---|---|---|---|---|---|
| Fillet/Tenderloin | 200 g | 5% | 5.25 | 10.5 | 21 | 108 | 452 | Pro, Pot, Mag, B1, B2 |
| Leg (boned) | 200 g | 0% | 5 | 10 | 20 | 102 | 429 | Pro, B1, B2, Pot |
| Loin (boneless) | 200 g | 10% | 5.5 | 11 | 22 | 109 | 456 | Pro, Fat, B1, B2 |
| Rump | 200 g | 10% | 5.5 | 11 | 22 | 114 | 478 | Pro, Fat, Zinc, B1, B2 |
| Forequarter (boneless) | 200 g | 0% | 5 | 10 | 20 | 106 | 447 | Pro, Zinc, B1, B2, Pot |
| Shoulder (boneless) | 200 g | 0% | 5 | 10 | 20 | 240 | 1008 | Pro, Fat, Mag, B1, B2 |
| Rib | 300 g | 0% | 7.5 | 15 | 30 | 309 | 1300 | Pro, Fat, B1, B2 |
| Ham steak | 200 g | 0% | 5 | 10 | 20 | 124 | 520 | Pro, Fat, B1, B2, Pot |
| Back bacon | 120 g | 5% | 3.2 | 6.3 | 12.6 | 400 | 1680 | Pro, Fat, Sod, Zinc, B1, B2 |
| Streaky bacon | 120 g | 5% | 3.2 | 6.3 | 12.6 | 404 | 1700 | Pro, Pot, Fat, Sod, Zinc, B1, B2 |
| Sausages | 180 g | 0% | 4.5 | 9 | 18 | 257 | 1080 | Pro, Fat, B1, Zinc, Sod |
| Hock | 1 p/person | 0% | 25 | 50 | 100 | 200 | 840 | Pro, B1, Pot |
| Chops | 1–2 p/person | 5% | 25–50 | 50–100 | 100–200 | 109 | 456 | Pro, Fat, B1, B2, Pot |

Bones (for stock) 2 kg of pork bones will yield 4 L of stock = 60 servings of a pork stock based sauce.

# Poultry and game

| Product | Prepared Uncooked Portion Size | Approximate % Wastage | 25 | 50 | 100 | Cal | kJ | Main Nutrients Contained In |
|---|---|---|---|---|---|---|---|---|
| Chicken | 1X1.5 kg = 4 portions | varies | 7 | 13 | 25 | 230 | 966 | Pro |
| Chicken breast | 1 p/portion | 0% | 25 | 50 | 100 | 112 | 469 | Pro |
| Chicken Thigh | 1–2 p/portion | 0% | 25–50 | 50–100 | 100–200 | 127 | 532 | Pro |
| Chicken Drumstick | 2 p/portion | 0% | 50 | 100 | 200 | 127 | 532 | Pro |
| Chicken Wing Tip | 6–8 p/portion | 0% | 150–200 | 300–400 | 600–800 | 127 | 532 | Pro |

Chicken Bones (for stock) 2 kg of Chicken Bones will yield 4 L of stock = 60 servings of a chicken stock based sauce

| Product | Prepared Uncooked Portion Size | Approximate % Wastage | 25 | 50 | 100 | Cal | kJ | Main Nutrients Contained In |
|---|---|---|---|---|---|---|---|---|
| Turkey | 1X9–11 kg = 30-35 portions | varies | 1 | 2 | 4 | 170 | 714 | Pro, Fat |
| Duck | 1X1–1.5 kg = 2 portions | varies | 13 | 25 | 50 | | | Pro, Fat |
| Spatchcock | 1 p/person | varies | 25 | 50 | 100 | 230 | 966 | Pro |
| Quail | 1 p/person | varies | 25 | 50 | 100 | 230 | 966 | Pro |
| Eggs | 1–2 p/person | 0% | 25–50 | 50–100 | 100–200 | 141 | 594 | Pro, Fat, A, D |

**Note** When serving poultry free from skin and bone we recommend a minimum portion size of 140 g

| Product | Prepared Uncooked Portion Size | Approximate % In Preparation Wastage (Where relev) | Bulk Portion Sizes Allowing for Wastage % | | | Energy Value per 100 g (Unless Stated) | | Main Nutrients Contained In |
|---|---|---|---|---|---|---|---|---|
| | | | 25 | 50 | 100 | Cal | kJ | |
| Rabbit | 150 g | 40% | 5.25 | 10.5 | 21 | 178 | 750 | Pro, Fat, Mag |
| Hare | 150 g | 40% | 5.25 | 10.5 | 21 | 190 | 800 | Pro, Fat |
| Venison | 150 g | 40% | 5.25 | 10.5 | 21 | 197 | 830 | Pro, Fat, Iron, Mag |

## Cooked and Cured Meats

| Product | Prepared Uncooked Portion Size | Approximate % In Preparation Wastage | 25 | 50 | 100 | Cal | kJ | Main Nutrients Contained In |
|---|---|---|---|---|---|---|---|---|
| Black Pudding | 100 | 0% | 2.5 | 5 | 10 | 257 | 1080 | Fat, Iron, Pro, Mag, Zinc, Sod |
| Bloodwurst | 100 | 0% | 2.5 | 5 | 10 | 283 | 1190 | Fat, Carb, Iron, Zinc, Sod |
| Bologna | 90 | 0% | 2.25 | 4.5 | 9 | 302 | 1270 | Fat, Sod, Iron, Zinc |
| Bratwurst | 90 g | 0% | 2.25 | 4.5 | 9 | 357 | 1500 | Fat, Sod, Iron, Zinc |
| Brawn | 80 | 0% | 2 | 4 | 8 | 216 | 909 | Fat, Sod, Iron, Zinc |
| Cabanossi | 80 | 0% | 2 | 4 | 8 | 363 | 1523 | Fat, Zinc, Sod |
| Chicken Roll | 90 | 0% | 2.25 | 4.5 | 9 | 150 | 631 | Zinc, Sod |
| Clobassy | 90g | 0% | 2.25 | 4.5 | 9 | 332 | 1393 | Fat, Zinc, Sod |
| Corned Beef | 110 | 0% | 2.75 | 5.5 | 11 | 98 | 412 | Iron, Zinc, Sod |
| Devon | 90 | 0% | 2.25 | 4.5 | 9 | 233 | 979 | Fat, Sod |
| Frankfurt | 110 | 0% | 2.75 | 5.5 | 11 | 248 | 1040 | Fat, Sod, Zinc |
| Hot Dog | 150 | 0% | 3.75 | 7.5 | 15 | 238 | 1000 | Fat, Sod, Zinc |
| Garlic Sausage | 110 | 0% | 2.75 | 5.5 | 11 | 238 | 1000 | Fat, Zinc, Sod |
| Ham | 110 | 0% | 2.75 | 5.5 | 11 | 108 | 453 | Pro, Fat, Zinc, Sod |
| Kielbasa | 90 | 0% | 2.25 | 4.5 | 9 | 392 | 1650 | Fat, Zinc, Sod |
| Kolbasa | 90 | 0% | 2.25 | 4.5 | 9 | 380 | 1600 | Fat, Zinc, Sod |
| Kransky | 90 g | 0% | 2.25 | 4.5 | 9 | 380 | 1600 | Fat, Pro, Sod |
| Liverwurst | 80 | 0% | 2 | 4 | 8 | 339 | 1422 | Fat, Iron, Zinc, A, Sod |
| Mortadella | 90 | 0% | 2.25 | 4.5 | 9 | 322 | 1354 | Fat, Sod, Zinc |
| Pastrami | 80 | 0% | 2 | 4 | 8 | 642 | 2700 | Fat, Sod |
| Pate | 70 | 0% | 1.75 | 3.5 | 7 | 312 | 1312 | Fat, Sod, Iron, A, Zinc |
| Salami | 70 | 0% | 1.75 | 3.5 | 7 | 428 | 1798 | Fat, Zinc, Pro, Sod |
| Saveloy | 100 g | 0% | 2.5 | 5 | 10 | | | Fat, Sod, Zinc |
| Tongue | 90 | 0% | 2.25 | 4.5 | 9 | 252 | 1057 | Fat, Zinc, Sod |
| Meat Pie | | 0% | 25 | 50 | 100 | 225 | 947 | Fat, Sod, Cal |

## Vegetables

| Product | Prepared Uncooked Portion Size | Approximate % In Preparation Wastage | 50 g | 100 g | 200 g | Cal | kJ | Main Nutrients Contained In |
|---|---|---|---|---|---|---|---|---|
| Alfalfa | 2 g | 0% | 50 g | 100 g | 200 g | 3 (10 g) | 15 (10 g) | C, E |
| Asparagus | 60 g | 20% | 1.8 | 3.6 | 7.2 | 17 | 71 | C, E |
| Aubergine/ Eggplant | 80 g | 10% | 2.2 | 4.4 | 8.8 | 17 | 73 | |
| Bamboo Shoot | 40 g | 5% | 1.1 | 2.2 | 4.4 | 8 | 33 | Pot |
| Bean, Broad | 60 g | 5% | 1.6 | 3.2 | 6.3 | 41 | 173 | Carb, A, C, Fib, B |
| French | 60 g | 5% | 1.6 | 3.2 | 6.3 | 21 | 87 | A, C, Fib |
| green | 60 g | 5% | 1.6 | 3.2 | 6.3 | 21 | 87 | A, C, Fib |
| runner | 60 g | 5% | 1.6 | 3.2 | 6.3 | 45 | 189 | A, C, Fib |
| snake | 60 g | 5% | 1.6 | 3.2 | 6.3 | 23 | 95 | A, C, Pot, Fib |
| Beansprouts | 30 g | 0% | 0.75 | 1.5 | 3 | 20 | 84 | C, Pot, Cal |
| Beetroot | 35 g | 10% | 1 | 2 | 4 | 41 | 173 | Carb, C, Fib |
| Broccoli | 70 g | 20% | 2.1 | 4.2 | 8.4 | 24 | 101 | A, C, E, Fib, Cal, B2 |
| Brussels Sprouts | 70 g | 10% | 2 | 3.9 | 7.7 | 27 | 114 | A, C, Fib |
| Cabbage | 60 g | 5% | 1.6 | 3.2 | 6.3 | 17 | 72 | A, C, Cal, Fib |
| Capsicum | 50 g | 5% | 1.4 | 2.7 | 5.25 | 19 | 79 | C |
| Carrot | 60 g | 5% | 1.6 | 3.2 | 6.3 | 25 | 103 | A, C, Fib, Cal |
| Cauliflower | 70 g | 25% | 2.2 | 4.4 | 8.75 | 19 | 80 | C, Fib, B |
| Celery | 50 g | 10% | 1.4 | 2.75 | 5.5 | 12 | 51 | Cal, Fib |

Note — Weights and wastage percentages are only an approximate guide

| Product | Prepared Uncooked Portion Size | Approximate % In Preparation Wastage (Where relev) | Bulk Portion Sizes Allowing for Wastage % | | | Energy Value per 100 g (Unless Stated) | | Main Nutrients Contained In |
|---|---|---|---|---|---|---|---|---|
| | | | 25 | 50 | 100 | Cal | kJ | |
| Corn Cobs | 1 | 1 | x25 | x50 | x100 | 92 | 388 | B, C, Fib, Carb |
| Corn Niblets | 40 g | 0% | 1 | 2 | 4 | 92 | 388 | B, C, Fib, Carb |
| Cucumber | 30 g | varies | 0.8 | 1.6 | 3.2 | 9 | 39 | |
| Leeks | 60 g | 25% | 1.9 | 3.75 | 7.5 | 26 | 111 | C, Iron, Fib, Cal |
| Lettuce 1½ average sized iceberg lettuce will yield 25 portions | | | | | | 6 | 27 | A, C |
| Mushroom | 50 g | 0% | 1.25 | 2.5 | 5 | 23 | 98 | B, Fol, B2 |
| Onion | 40 g | 10% | 1.1 | 2.2 | 4.4 | 26 | 111 | C, Cal |
| Parsnip | 60 g | 10% | 1.7 | 3.3 | 6.6 | 50 | 208 | C, E |
| Peas | 50 g | 0% | 1.25 | 2.5 | 5 | 59 | 249 | C, Fib, B1 |
| Potato | 150 g | 5% | 4 | 7.9 | 15.8 | 68 | 286 | C, Pot, Carb, B, Fib |
| Pumpkin (skin on) | 70 g | 15% | 2.1 | 4.1 | 8.1 | 38 | 158 | A, Fib |
| Radish | 30 g | 10% | 0.9 | 1.7 | 3.3 | 13 | 53 | C |
| Shallot | 30 g | 5% | 0.8 | 1.6 | 3.2 | 21 | 90 | C, Fol |
| Snow Peas | 50 g | 5% | 1.4 | 2.7 | 5.25 | 32 | 136 | C, Fib |
| Spinach | 80 g | 50% | 3 | 6 | 9 | 15 | 63 | A, C, E, Iron, Fib, Cal, B2 |
| Squash | 60 g | 5% | 1.6 | 3.2 | 6.3 | 24 | 100 | C |
| Tomatoes | 50 g | 0% | 1.25 | 2.5 | 5 | 13 | 56 | A, C |
| Turnip | 60 g | 5% | 1.6 | 3.2 | 6.3 | 19 | 81 | C, Cal, Mag, Fib |
| Water Chestnut | 40 g | 0% | 1 | 2 | 4 | 171 | 720 | C, Pot, Iron |
| Watercress | 15 g | 5% | 0.400 | 0.8 | 1.6 | 19 | 80 | A, C, Pot |
| Yam | 70 g | 10% | 2 | 3.9 | 7.7 | 135 | 567 | C, Pot, Carb, Fib |
| Zucchini | 60 g | 10% | 1.5 | 3 | 6 | 14 | 59 | C |

Note  Weights and wastage percentages are only an approximate guide.

# APPENDIX 3
# SEASONAL AVAILABILITY

## IN SEASON FOR JANUARY

### VEGETABLES

| | | | | | | |
|---|---|---|---|---|---|---|
| Asparagus | - green | Cucumbers | - baby | Onions | - Shemeji | Sprouts | - alfalfa |
| | - baby | | - green | | - Shitaki | | - beansprouts |
| Beans | - butter | | - Lebanese | | - Swiss brown | | - mung beans |
| | - green | | - telegraph | | - baby | | - snow pea sprouts |
| | - broad | Eggplant | - baby, black | | - brown | Squash | - baby, green |
| Beetroot | - baby | | - large, black | | - shallots | | - baby, yellow |
| Bok choy | - baby | Kale | | | - Spanish | | - large, green |
| | - regular | Leeks | - baby | | - spring | | - large, yellow |
| Broccoli | - Chinese | | - regular | | - white | | - two tone |
| | - regular | Lettuce | - butter | Peas | - garden | Swedes | - baby |
| Cabbage | - green | | - chicory | | - snap | Tomatoes | - cherry |
| | - red | | - coral, green | | - snow | | - egg/Italian |
| | - Savoy | | - coral, red | Potatoes | - chats | | - salad |
| Capsicum | - banana, red/green | | - corn | | - desirée | | - pear |
| | - black | | - endive | | - pink-eyed | Turnips | - baby |
| | - green | | - endive, baby | | - pontiac | Zucchini | - green |
| | - Hungarian | | - garden | Pumpkins | - butternut | | - yellow |
| | - red | | - marsh | | - golden nuggets | Baby veg | - beans |
| | - yellow | | - mizuna | | - gramma black | | - beetroot |
| Carrots | - baby | | - mignonette | | - minikins | | - bok choy |
| | - Dutch | | - oak, green | | - Queensland blue | | - carrots |
| Cauliflower | - baby | | - oak, red | | - small green & yellow | | - cauliflower |
| | - regular | | - rocket | | | | - cherry tomatoes |
| | - romaine | | - watercress | Radishes | - red | | - squash yellow/green |
| Chillies | - red | Mushrooms | - button, cup | | - white | | - swede |
| | - green | | - enoki | Spinach | - English | | - turnips |
| Corn | - regular | | - flat, oyster | | - baby, English | | |
| | | | - pine | | - silverbeet | | |

### FRUIT

| | | | | | | | |
|---|---|---|---|---|---|---|---|
| Apples | - green | | - green | Exotic fruit | - corella pears | | - paradise pears |
| | - red democrats | Melons | - honeydew | | - dry muscatel | | - passionfruit, black and yellow |
| | - red delicious | | - rockmelon | | - figs | | - pepinos |
| Bananas | - sugar | | - watermelon | | - guavas | | - persimmons |
| Berries | - strawberries | Stone fruit | - apricots | | - jackfruit | | - rambutans |
| | - youngberries | | - cherry | | - lychees | | - starfruit |
| Coconuts | - regular | | - nectarines | | - mangoes | | |
| | - green | | - peaches | | - nashi pears | | |
| Grapes | - red | Oranges | - valencia | | - papayas | | |

### HERBS

| | | | |
|---|---|---|---|
| Basil, purple/green | Dill | Peppermint | Thyme |
| Bay-leaves | Marjoram | Sage | Thyme, lemon |
| Chervil | Mints—apple, eau de col, spear | Sage pineapple | |
| Chives | Oregano | Sorrel | |
| Coriander | Parsley, curly/continental | Tarragon | |

### FISH

| | | |
|---|---|---|
| Barramundi | Jewie | Silver Jew |
| Blue Moki | Mackereal | Tailor |
| Butterfish | Mulloway | Teraglin |
| Jewfish | Prawns | Trumpeter, Striped, Tasmanian |

# IN SEASON FOR FEBRUARY

## VEGETABLES

| | | | | | | | |
|---|---|---|---|---|---|---|---|
| Asparagus | - green | Cucumbers | - Lebanese | | - Shemeji | | - beansprouts |
| | - baby | | - telegraph | | - Shitaki | | - mung beans |
| Beans | - butter | Eggplant | - baby, black | | - Swiss brown | | - snow pea sprouts |
| | - green | | - large, black | Onions | - baby | Squash | - baby, green |
| | - flat Italian | Kale | - green | | - brown | | - baby, yellow |
| | - snake | | - purple | | - shallots | | - large, green |
| Bok choy | - baby | | - white | | - Spanish | | - large, yellow |
| | - regular | Lettuce | - butter | | - spring | Swedes | - baby |
| Broccoli | - Chinese | | - chicory | Potatoes | - chats, new | Tomatoes | - cherry |
| | - regular | | - coral, green | | - chats, pontiac | | - egg/Italian |
| Cabbage | - green | | - coral, red | | - desirée | | - salad |
| | - red | | - corn | | - kiffler | | - pear |
| | - Savoy | | - endive, baby | | - orange, sweet | Turnips | - baby |
| Capsicum | - banana, | | - garden | | - pink-eye | | - large |
| | red/green | | - marsh | | - pontiac | Zucchini | - green |
| | - black | | - mizuna | | - white sweet | | - yellow |
| | - green | | - mignonette | Pumpkins | - butternut | Baby veg | - beans |
| | - red | | - mustard | | - golden nuggets | | - beetroot |
| | - yellow | | - oak, green | | - gramma | | - bok choy |
| Carrots | - baby | | - oak, red | | - Japanese black | | - carrots |
| | - Dutch | | - rocket | | - minikins | | - cauliflower |
| Cauliflower | - regular | | - watercress | | - Queensland blue | | - cherry tomatoes |
| | - baby | Mushrooms | - button | Radish | - red | | - squash, |
| Chillies | - red | | - cup | | - white | | yellow/green |
| | - green | | - enoki | Spinach | - English | | - swede |
| Corn | - regular | | - flat | | - silverbeet | | - turnips |
| | - baby | | - oyster | Sprouts | - alfalfa | | |

## FRUIT

| | | | | | | | |
|---|---|---|---|---|---|---|---|
| Apples | - green | | - green | | - custard apples | | - papayas |
| | - red delicious | Melons | - honeydew | | - feijoas | | - passionfruit |
| Bananas | - extra large | | - mini watermelon | | - figs | | - rambutans |
| | - sugar | | - rockmelon | | - guavas | | - starfruit |
| Berries | - blueberries | | - watermelon | | - jackfruit | | - tamarillos |
| | - strawberries | | - yellow melon | | - kiwano | | - tamarillos, red |
| Grapefruit | - regular | Oranges | - navel | | - kumquats | | |
| | - pink | Exotic fruit | - cape gooseberry | | - mangoes | | |
| Grapes | - black/red | | - corella pears | | - nashi pears | | |

## HERBS

| | | | |
|---|---|---|---|
| Basil, purple/green | Dill | Peppermint | Thyme, lemon |
| Bay-leaves | Marjoram | Sage | |
| Chervil | Mint—apple, eau de col, spear | Sorrel | |
| Chives | Oregano | Tarragon | |
| Coriander | Parsley, curly/continental | Thyme | |

## FISH

| | | | |
|---|---|---|---|
| Albacore, Anchovies | Ling | Sardine | Trumpeter, Striped, Tasmanian |
| Blue Grenadier, Blue Moki | Mirror Dory | Sea Perch, Snapper | Tuna |
| Coral Trout | Parrot Fish | Sprats | Whitebait |
| Dhu-fish | Perch, Pilchard | Tailor | |
| Leopard trout | Red Fish, Ribbon Fish | Teraglin | |

# IN SEASON FOR MARCH

## VEGETABLES

| | | | | | | | |
|---|---|---|---|---|---|---|---|
| Asparagus | - green | | - baby | | - oyster | Spinach | - English |
| | - baby | Cucumbers | - Lebanese | | - pine | | - English baby |
| Beans | - butter | | - telegraph | | - Shemeji | | - silverbeet |
| | - borlotto | Eggplant | - baby, black | | - Shitaki | Sprouts | - alfalfa |
| | - green | | - large, black | | - Swiss brown | | - beansprouts |
| | - flat Italian | | - white | Onions | - baby | | - mung beans |
| | - snake | Kale | - green | | - brown | | - snow pea sprouts |
| Beetroot | - baby | Leeks | - baby | | - shallot | Squash | - baby, green |
| Bok Choy | - baby | | - regular | | - Spanish | | - baby, yellow |
| | - regular | Lettuce | - butter | | - spring | | - large, green |
| Broccoli | - Chinese | | - chicory | | - white | | - large, yellow |
| | - regular | | - coral, green | Peas | - garden | | - two tone |
| | - purple | | - coral, red | | - snap | Tomatoes | - cherry |
| Cabbage | - green | | - corn | | - snow | | - egg, Italian |
| | - red | | - cos | Potatoes | - chats | | - salad |
| | - Savoy | | - endive | | - desirée | | - pear |
| Capsicum | - banana, | | - endive, baby | | - orange sweet | Turnips | - baby |
| | red/green | | - garden | | - pink-eyed | Zucchini | - green |
| | - black | | - marsh | | - pontiac | | - yellow |
| | - green | | - mizuna | Pumpkins | - butternut | Baby veg | - beans |
| | - Hungarian | | - mignonette | | - golden nuggets | | - beetroot |
| | - red | | - oak, green | | - gramma nuggets | | - cherry tomatoes |
| | - yellow | | - oak, red | | - Japanese green | | - Dutch carrots |
| Carrots | - baby | | - rocket | | - minikins | | - squash, |
| | - Dutch | | - watercress | | - Queensland blue | | yellow/green |
| Cauliflower | - regular | Mushrooms | - button | | - small green & | | - swede |
| Chillies | - red | | - cup | | yellow | | - turnips |
| | - green | | - enoki | Radish | - red | | |
| Corn | - regular | | - flat | | - white | | |

## FRUIT

| | | | | | | | |
|---|---|---|---|---|---|---|---|
| Apples | - green | Coconuts | - regular | | - nectarines | | (blk & yel) |
| | - red croft/ | | - green | | - peaches | | - nashi pears |
| | democrats | Grapes | - red | | - plums | | - passionfruit |
| | - red delicious | | - green | Exotic fruit | - corella pears | | - papayas |
| Avocados | - shepherd | | - currant | | - figs | | - paradise pears |
| Bananas | - extra large | Melons | - honey dew | | - guavas | | - pepinos |
| | - sugar | | - rockmelon | | - jackfruit | | - persimmons |
| Berries | - blackberry | | - watermelon | | - kiwanos | | - rambutans |
| | - blueberry | | - yellow melon | | - lychees | | |
| | - raspberry | Oranges | - valencia | | - mangoes, Bowen | | |
| | - strawberry | Stone fruit | - apricots | | - passionfruit | | |

## HERBS

| | | | |
|---|---|---|---|
| Basil, purple/green | Coriander | Oregano | Sorrel |
| Bay-leaves | Dill | Parsley, curly/continental | Tarragon |
| Chervil | Marjoram | Peppermint | Thyme |
| Chives | Mint—apple, eau de col, spear | Sage | Thyme, lemon |

## FISH

| | | |
|---|---|---|
| Albacore | Dhu-fish | Pilchard |
| Bream, silver/back | Flathead | Sardine |
| Barramundi | Mullet | Tailor |
| Bluefish | Perch | Tuna |

# IN SEASON FOR APRIL

## VEGETABLES

| | | | | | | | |
|---|---|---|---|---|---|---|---|
| Asparagus | - green | Eggplant | - baby, black | | - brown | | - snow pea sprouts |
| Artichoke | - globe | | - large, black | | - shallot | Squash | - baby, green |
| Beans | - borlotto | Horseradish | - fresh | | - Spanish | | - baby, yellow |
| | - butter | Lettuce | - butter | | - spring | | - large, green |
| | - green | | - chicory | Peas | - garden | | - large, yellow |
| | - snake | | - coral, green | | - snap | Swedes | - baby |
| Beetroot | - baby/golden | | - coral red | | - snow | Tomatoes | - cherry |
| Broccoli | - Chinese | | - corn | Potatoes | - chats | | - egg/Italian |
| | - regular | | - endive | | - orange, sweet | | - pear |
| Cabbage | - Chinese | | - endive, baby | | - pontiac | | - salad |
| | - green | | - garden | Pumpkins | - butternut | Turnips | - baby |
| | - red | | - marsh | | - golden nuggets | | - large/medium |
| | - Savoy | | - mizuna | | - gramma | Zucchini | - green |
| Capsicum | - black | | - mignonette | | - Japanese green | | - yellow |
| | - green | | - oak, green | | - minikins | Baby veg | - beans |
| | - red | | - oak, red | | - Queensland blue | | - beetroot |
| | - yellow | | - rocket | | - small green & | | - cherry tomatoes |
| Carrots | - baby | | - watercress | | yellow | | - corn |
| | - Dutch | Mushrooms | - button | Radishes | - red | | - Dutch carrots |
| Chillies | - red | | - cup | | - white | | - golden beetroot |
| | - green | | - oyster | Spinach | - English | | - squash, |
| Corn | - regular | | - pine | | - silverbeet | | yellow/green |
| | - baby | | - Shitaki | Sprouts | - alfalfa | | - swede |
| Cucumbers | - Lebanese | | - Swiss brown | | - beansprouts | | - turnips |
| | - telegraph | Onions | - baby | | - mung beans | | |

## FRUIT

| | | | | | | | |
|---|---|---|---|---|---|---|---|
| Apples | - golden delicious | Coconuts | - regular | Stone fruit | - chestnuts | | - lychees |
| | - green | | - green | | - kumquats | | - mangoes |
| | - red | Grapes | - black/red | | - nectarines | | - nashi pears |
| | - red delicious | | - green | | - peaches | | - papayas |
| Bananas | - sugar | Melons | - honey dew | | - plums | | - persimmons |
| Berries | - blackberry | | - rockmelon | Exotic fruit | - corella pears | | - pomegranates |
| | - blueberry | | - watermelon | | - custard apples | | - rambutans |
| | - raspberry | | - yellow melon | | - figs | | - starfruit |
| | - strawberry | Oranges | - valencia | | - kiwano | | - tamarillos |

## HERBS

| | | | |
|---|---|---|---|
| Basil, purple/green | Coriander | Oregano | Sorrel |
| Bay-leaves | Dill | Parsley, continental | Tarragon |
| Chervil | Marjoram | Peppermint | Thyme |
| Chives | Mint—apple, eau de col, spear | Sage | Thyme, lemon |

## FISH

| | | | |
|---|---|---|---|
| Albacore | Dhu-fish | Mullet | Sardine |
| Bluefish | Flathead | Perch | Tailor |
| Bream, silver/back | Kingfish | Pilchard | Tuna |

# IN SEASON FOR MAY

## VEGETABLES

| | | | | | | | |
|---|---|---|---|---|---|---|---|
| Asparagus | - green | | - telegraph | Onions | - baby | Squash | - baby, green |
| Beans | - borlotti | Eggplant | - baby, black | | - brown | | - baby, yellow |
| | - butter | | - large, black | | - shallot | | - large, green |
| | - flat Italian | Lettuce | - butter | | - Spanish | | - large, yellow |
| | - green | | - chicory | | - spring | Swedes | - baby |
| | - snake | | - coral, green | Peas | - garden | Tomatoes | - cherry |
| Beetroot | - baby | | - coral, red | | - snap | | - egg/Italian |
| Broccoli | - Chinese | | - corn | | - snow | | - salad |
| | - regular | | - endive | Potatoes | - chats | | - pear |
| Cabbage | - green | | - endive, baby | | - desirée | Turnips | - baby |
| | - red | | - garden | | - orange, sweet | | - large/medium |
| | - Savoy | | - marsh | | - pink-eyed | Zucchini | - green |
| Capsicum | - banana chillies | | - mizuna | | - pontiac | | - yellow |
| | - black | | - mignonette | Pumpkins | - butternut | Baby veg | - beans |
| | - green | | - oak, green | | - golden nuggets | | - beetroot |
| | - red | | - rocket | | - gramma | | - cherry tomatoes |
| | - yellow | | - watercress | | - minikins | | - corn |
| Carrots | - baby | Mushrooms | - button | Radishes | - red | | - Dutch carrots |
| | - Dutch | | - cup | | - white | | - squash |
| Chillies | - red | | - flat | Spinach | - English | | yellow/green |
| | - green | | - oyster | | - silverbeet | | - swedes |
| Corn | - regular | | - pine | Sprouts | - alfalfa | | - turnips |
| | - baby | | - Shitaki | | - beansprouts | | |
| Cucumbers | - Lebanese | | - Swiss brown | | - mung beans | | |

## FRUIT

| | | | | | | | |
|---|---|---|---|---|---|---|---|
| Apples | - green | Grapes | - black/red | Exotic fruit | - custard apples | | - papayas |
| | - red | | - green | | - feijoas | | - pepinos |
| | - red delicious | Melons | - honey dew | | - figs | | - persimmons |
| Avocados | | | - rockmelon | | - guavas | | - pomegranates |
| Bananas | - extra large | | - watermelon | | - kiwano | | - rambutans |
| | - medium | | - yellow melon | | - kumquats | | - starfruit |
| Berries | - raspberry | Oranges | - valencia | | - mangoes | | - tamarillos |
| | - strawberry | | - navel | | - nashi pears | | |

## HERBS

| | | | |
|---|---|---|---|
| Basil, purple/green | Coriander | Oregano | Tarragon |
| Bay-leaves | Dill | Parsley, curly/continental | Thyme |
| Chervil | Marjoram | Sage | Thyme, lemon |
| Chives | Mint—pepper, spear | Sorrel | |

## FISH

| | | | |
|---|---|---|---|
| Albacore | Dhu-fish | Ling | Ribbon fish |
| Bluefish | Flathead | Mirror Dory, Mullet | Salmon, Sardine |
| Blue Grenadier | Gemfish/hake | Orange Roughy | Sea Perch |
| Bream | Kingfish | Parrot fish | Tailor |
| Coral Trout | Leopard cod | Perch, Pilchard | Tuna |

# IN SEASON FOR JUNE

## VEGETABLES

| | | | | | | | | |
|---|---|---|---|---|---|---|---|---|
| Artichokes | - globe | | - telegraph | | - Swiss brown | | | - mung beans |
| | - Jerusalem | Eggplant | - baby, black | Onions | - baby | | | - snow pea |
| Asparagus | - green | | - large, black | | - brown | Squash | | - baby, green |
| Beans | - borlotti | Kale | - coloured | | - shallot | | | - baby, yellow |
| | - butter | | - green | | - Spanish | | | - large, green |
| | - green | Lettuce | - butter | | - spring | | | - large, yellow |
| | - snake | | - chicory | Peas | - garden | Swedes | | - baby |
| Beetroot | - baby | | - coral, green | | - snap | Tomatoes | | - cherry |
| Broccoli | - Chinese | | - coral, red | | - snow | | | - egg/Italian |
| | - regular | | - corn | Potatoes | - chats | | | - salad |
| Cabbage | - green | | - endive | | - desirée | | | - pear |
| | - red | | - endive, baby | | - pink-eyed | Turnips | | - baby |
| | - Savoy | | - garden | | - pontiac | | | - large |
| Capsicum | - banana red | | - marsh | Pumpkins | - butternut | Zucchini | | - green |
| | - black | | - mignonette | | - golden nuggets | | | - yellow |
| | - green | | - mizuna | | - gourds | Baby veg | | - beans |
| | - red | | - oak, green | | - gramma | | | - beetroot |
| | - yellow | | - rocket | | - minikins | | | - cherry tomatoes |
| Carrots | - baby | | - watercress | | - Queensland blue | | | - Dutch carrot |
| | - Dutch | Mushrooms | - button | Radishes | - red | | | - squash, |
| Chillies | - red | | - flat | | - white | | | yellow/green |
| | - green | | - cup | Spinach | - English | | | - swedes |
| Corn | - regular | | - oyster | | - silverbeet | | | - turnips |
| | - baby | | - Shimeji | Sprouts | - alfalfa | | | |
| Cucumbers | - Lebanese | | - Shitaki | | - bean | | | |

## FRUIT

| | | | | | | | |
|---|---|---|---|---|---|---|---|
| Apples | - green | | - green | | - custard apples | | - papayas |
| | - red | Melons | - honey dew | | - feijoas | | - pepinos |
| | - red delicious | | - rockmelon | | - figs | | - persimmons |
| Avocados | | | - watermelon | | - guavas | | - pomegranates |
| Bananas | - small | | - yellow | | - kiwano | | - rambutans |
| Berries | - raspberry | Oranges | - navel | | - kumquats | | - star fruit |
| | - strawberry | | - valencia | | - mangoes | | - tamarillos |
| Grapes | - black/red | Exotic fruit | - corello pear | | - nashi pears | | |

## HERBS

| | | | |
|---|---|---|---|
| Basil, purple/green | Coriander | spear | Sorrel |
| Bay-leaves | Dill | Oregano | Tarragon, lime |
| Chervil | Marjoram | Parsley, curly/continental | Thyme |
| Chives | Mint—apple, eau de col, pepper, | Sage | Thyme, lemon |

## FISH

| | | | |
|---|---|---|---|
| Albacore | Leopard Cod | Perch | Sprats |
| Anchovies | Ling | Pilchard | Tuna |
| Blue Grenadier | Mirror Dory | Ribbon fish | Whitebait |
| Coral Trout | Mullet | Salmon, Sardine | |
| Dhu-Fish | Orange Roughy | Sardine | |
| Gem Fish/hake | Parrot fish | Sea Perch | |

# IN SEASON FOR JULY

## VEGETABLES

| | | | | | | | |
|---|---|---|---|---|---|---|---|
| Beans | - baby | Cucumber | - baby | Onions | - Shitaki | Squash | - mung beans |
| | - borlotti | | - Lebanese | | - Swiss brown | | - snow pea |
| | - broad | | - telegraph | | - baby | | - baby, green |
| | - butter | Eggplant | - baby, black | | - brown | | - baby, yellow |
| | - flat Italian | | - large, black | | - shallot | | - large, green |
| | - green | | - white | | - Spanish | | - large, yellow |
| | - snake | Kale | - coloured | | - spring | Swedes | - baby |
| Beetroot | - baby | | - green | Peas | - garden | Tomatoes | - cherry |
| Broccoli | - Chinese | Lettuce | - butter | | - snap | | - egg/Italian |
| | - regular | | - chicory | | - snow | | - salad |
| Bok choy | - regular | | - coral, red | Potatoes | - chats, new | | - pear |
| | - baby | | - corn | | - chats, pontiac | Turnips | - baby |
| Cabbage | - green | | - endive | | - desirée | | - large |
| | - red | | - endive, baby | | - pink-eyed | Yams | - orange, sweet |
| | - Savoy | | - garden | | - pontiac | | - potato |
| Capsicum | - banana red green | | - marsh | | - white sweet | Zucchini | - green |
| | - black | | - mignonette | Pumpkins | - butternut | | - yellow |
| | - green | | - mizuna | | - golden nuggets | Baby Veg | - beans |
| | - red | | - oak, green | | - gramma | | - beetroot |
| | - yellow | | - rocket | | - minikins | | - cherry tomatoes |
| Carrots | - baby | | - watercress | | - Queensland blue | | - Dutch carrot |
| | - Dutch | Mushrooms | - button | Radishes | - red | | - squash, |
| Cauliflower | - regular | | - cup | | - white | | yellow/green |
| | - baby | | - enoki | Spinach | - English | | - swedes |
| Chillies | - red | | - flat | | - silverbeet | | - turnips |
| | - green | | - oyster | Sprouts | - alfalfa | | |
| Corn | - regular | | - Shimeji | | - bean | | |

## FRUIT

| | | | | | | | |
|---|---|---|---|---|---|---|---|
| Apples | - green | Grapes | - black/red | | - custard apples | | - papayas |
| | - red delicious | | - green | | - feijoas | | - passionfruit |
| Avocados | - fuerte | Melons | - honey dew | | - figs | | - quince |
| Bananas | - medium | | - rockmelon | | - guavas | | - rambutans |
| | - small | | - watermelon | | - jack fruit | | - star fruit |
| Berries | - raspberry | | - mini watermelon | | - kiwano | | - tamarillos, red |
| | - strawberry | Oranges | - navel | | - kumquats | | - tamarillos, yellow |
| Grapefruit | - regular | Exotic fruit | - Cape gooseberry | | - mangoes | | |
| | - pink | | - corello pears | | - nashi pears | | |

## HERBS

| | | | |
|---|---|---|---|
| Basil, purple/green | Coriander | spear | Sorrel |
| Bay-leaves | Dill | Oregano | Tarragon, lime |
| Chervil | Marjoram | Parsley, curly/continental | Thyme |
| Chives | Mint—apple, eau de col, pepper, | Sage | Thyme, lemon |

## FISH

| | | | |
|---|---|---|---|
| Albacore | Gemfish/Hake | Parrot fish | Sardine |
| Anchovies | Leopard Cod | Perch | Sea Perch |
| Blue Grenadier | Ling | Pilchard | Sprats |
| Coral Trout | Mirror Dory | Ribbon fish | Tuna |
| Dhu-Fish | Orange Roughy | Salmon | |

# IN SEASON FOR AUGUST

## VEGETABLES

| | | | | | | | |
|---|---|---|---|---|---|---|---|
| Beans | - broad | | - telegraph | | - brown | | - snow pea |
| | - butter | Eggplant | - baby, black | | - shallot | Squash | - baby, green |
| | - flat Italian | | - large, black | | - Spanish | | - baby, yellow |
| | - green | Kale | - green | | - spring | | - large, green |
| Broccoli | - Chinese | | - purple | Peas | - garden | | - large, yellow |
| | - regular | | - white | | - snap | Swedes | - baby |
| Bok choy | - regular | Lettuce | - butter | | - snow | Tomatoes | - cherry |
| | - baby | | - chicory | Potatoes | - chats, new | | - egg/Italian |
| Cabbage | - green | | - coral, red | | - chats, pontiac | | - salad |
| | - red | | - corn | | - desirée | | - pear |
| | - Savoy | | - endive | | - pink-eyed | Turnips | - baby |
| Capsicum | - banana red/green | | - endive, baby | | - pontiac | | - large |
| | - black | | - garden | | - orange, sweet | Zucchini | - green |
| | - green | | - marsh | | - white, sweet | | - yellow |
| | - red | | - mignonette | Pumpkins | - butternut | Baby veg | - beans |
| | - yellow | | - mizuna | | - golden nuggets | | - beetroot |
| Carrots | - baby | | - mustard | | - gramma | | - bok choy |
| | - Dutch | | - oak, green | | - minikins | | - carrots |
| | - Dutch round | | - oak, red | | - Queensland blue | | - cherry tomatoes |
| Cauliflower | - regular | | - rocket | | - Japanese black | | - Dutch carrot |
| | - baby | | - watercress | Radishes | - red | | - squash, |
| Chillies | - red | Mushrooms | - button | | - white | | yellow/green |
| | - green | | - cup | Spinach | - English | | - swede |
| Corn | - regular | | - flat | | - silverbeet | | - turnips |
| | - baby | | - oyster | Sprouts | - alfalfa | | |
| Cucumbers | - green | | - Shitaki | | - bean | | |
| | - Lebanese | Onions | - baby | | - mung beans | | |

## FRUIT

| | | | | | | | |
|---|---|---|---|---|---|---|---|
| Apples | - green | Grapes | - black/red | | - corello pears | | - papayas |
| | - red delicious | | - green | | - custard apples | | - passionfruit |
| Avocados | | Melons | - honey dew | | - feijoas | | - rambutans |
| Bananas | - small | | - rockmelon | | - guavas | | - star fruit |
| Berries | - blueberry | | - watermelon | | - jack fruit | | - tamarillo |
| | - strawberry | | - mini watermelon | | - kumquats | | red/yellow |
| | - raspberry | | - yellow | | - Kiwano | | |
| Grapefruit | - regular | Oranges | - navel | | - mangoes | | |
| | - pink | Exotic fruit | - Cape gooseberry | | - nashi pears | | |

## HERBS

| | | | |
|---|---|---|---|
| Basil, purple/green | Coriander | spear | Sorrel |
| Bay-leaves | Dill | Oregano | Tarragon |
| Chervil | Marjoram | Parsley, curly/continental | Thyme |
| Chives | Mint—apple, eau de col, pepper, | Sage | Thyme, lemon |

## FISH

| | | | |
|---|---|---|---|
| Albacore, Anchovies | Leopard Cod, Ling | Redfish | Trumpeter |
| Blue Grenadier, Blue Moki | Mirror Dory | Ribbon Fish | Trumpeter, Striped, Tasmanian |
| Coral Trout | Orange Roughy | Salmon, Sardine | Tuna, Whitebait |
| Dhu-Fish | Parrot Fish | Sea Perch | |
| Gemfish/Hake | Perch, Pilchard | Snapper, sprats | |

# IN SEASON FOR SEPTEMBER

## VEGETABLES

| | | | | | | | |
|---|---|---|---|---|---|---|---|
| Artichokes | - globe | | - large, black | | - Shemeji | Spinach | - English |
| Beans | - baby | | - orange | | - Shitaki | | - silverbeet |
| | - broad | | - white | | - Swiss brown | Sprouts | - alfalfa |
| | - butter | Kale | - green | Onions | - baby | | - bean |
| | - flat regular | | - purple | | - brown | | - mung beans |
| | - green | | - white | | - shallot | | - snow pea |
| Broccoli | - Chinese | Leeks | - regular | | - Spanish | Squash | - baby, green |
| | - regular | | - baby | | - spring | | - large, green |
| Bok choy | - baby | Lettuce | - butter | Peas | - garden | | - baby, yellow |
| Cabbage | - green | | - chicory | | - snap | | - large, yellow |
| | - red | | - coral, red | | - snow | Tomatoes | - cherry |
| | - Savoy | | - corn | Potatoes | - chats, new | | - egg/Italian |
| Capsicum | - banana red/green | | - endive, baby | | - chats, pontiac | | - salad |
| | - black | | - garden | | - desirée | | - pear |
| | - green | | - marsh | | - kiffler | Turnips | - baby |
| | - red | | - mignonette | | - pink-eyed | | - large |
| | - yellow | | - mizuna | | - pontiac | Zucchini | - green |
| Carrots | - baby | | - mustard | | - orange, sweet | | - yellow |
| | - Dutch | | - oak, green | | - white, sweet | Baby veg | - beans |
| Cauliflower | - regular | | - oak, red | Pumpkins | - butternut | | - beetroot |
| | - baby | | - rocket | | - golden nuggets | | - bok choy |
| Chillies | - red | | - watercress | | - gramma | | - carrots |
| | - green | Mushrooms | - button | | - minikins | | - cauliflower |
| Corn | - regular | | - ceps | | - Queensland blue | | - cherry tomatoes |
| | - baby | | - cup | | - Japanese black | | - squash, |
| Cucumbers | - Lebanese | | - enoki | | - swan neck | | yellow/green |
| | - telegraph | | - flat | Radishes | - red | | - swedes |
| Eggplant | - baby, black | | - oyster | | - white | | - turnips |

## FRUIT

| | | | | | | | |
|---|---|---|---|---|---|---|---|
| Apples | - green | Melons | - honey dew | | - corello pear | | - pomelo |
| | - red delicious | | - rockmelon | | - feijoas | | - passionfruit |
| Avocados | | | - watermelon | | - guavas | | - rambutans |
| Bananas | - sugar | | - mini watermelon | | - jack fruit | | - rosellas |
| Berries | - blueberry | | - yellow | | - kumquoats | | - star apples |
| | - mulberry | Oranges | - navel | | - kiwano | | - star fruit |
| | - strawberry | Stone fruit | - peaches | | - mango | | - tamarillos, red |
| Grapefruit | - regular | Exotic fruit | - bananas, | | - nashi pears | | - tamarillos, yellow |
| | - pink | | passionfruit | | - oranges, blood | | - tangello |
| Grapes | - black/red | | - black sapote | | - papayas | | |
| | - white | | - Cape gooseberry | | - pepino | | |

## HERBS

| | | | |
|---|---|---|---|
| Basil, purple/green | Coriander | spear | Sorrel |
| Bay-leaves | Dill | Oregano | Tarragon |
| Chervil | Marjoram | Parsley, curly/continental | Thyme |
| Chives | Mint—apple, eau de col, pepper, | Sage | Thyme, lemon |

## FISH

| | | | |
|---|---|---|---|
| Anchovies | Redfish | Sprats | Trumpeter, Striped, Tasmanian |
| Blue Moki | Sardine | Teraglin | Whitebait |
| Pilchard | Snapper | Trumpeter | |

# IN SEASON FOR OCTOBER

## VEGETABLES

| | | | | | | | |
|---|---|---|---|---|---|---|---|
| Artichokes | - globe | Cucumbers | - Lebanese | | - oyster | | - white |
| | - Jerusalem | | - telegraph | | - Shemeji | Spinach | - English |
| Asparagus | - green | Eggplant | - baby, black | | - Shitaki | | - English, baby |
| Beans | - broad | | - large, black | | - Swiss brown | | - silverbeet |
| | - butter | | - orange | Onions | - baby | | - silverbeet, baby |
| | - flat regular | Kale | - green | | - brown | Sprouts | - alfalfa |
| | - green | Leeks | - baby | | - shallot | | - bean |
| | - snake | | - regular | | - Spanish | Squash | - baby, green |
| Beetroot | | Lettuce | - butter | | - spring | | - baby, yellow |
| Broccoli | - Chinese | | - chicory | | - white | | - large, yellow |
| | - regular | | - coral, green | Peas | - garden | Tomatoes | - cherry |
| Bok choy | - baby | | - coral, red | | - snap | | - egg/Italian |
| Cabbage | - green | | - corn | | - snow | | - salad |
| | - red | | - cos | Potatoes | - chats, new | | - pear |
| | - Savoy | | - endive, baby | | - chats, pontiac | Turnips | - baby |
| Capsicum | - banana red/green | | - garden | | - desirée | | - large |
| | - black | | - marsh | | - kiffler | Zucchini | - green |
| | - green | | - mizuna | | - pink-eyed | | - yellow |
| | - red | | - mizuna baby | | - pontiac | Baby veg | - beans |
| | - yellow | | - mignonette | Pumpkins | - butternut | | - beetroot |
| Carrots | - baby | | - oak, green | | - golden nugget | | - cherry tomatoes |
| | - Dutch | | - oak, red | | - gourd | | - Dutch carrot |
| Cauliflower | - regular | | - rocket | | - gramma | | - squash, |
| | - baby | | - watercress | | - minikins | | yellow/green |
| Chillies | - red | Mushrooms | - button | | - Queensland blue | | - swede |
| | - green | | - cup | | - Japanese black | | - turnips |
| Corn | - regular | | - enoki | | - Swan neck | | |
| | - baby | | - flat | Radishes | - red | | |

## FRUIT

| | | | | | | | |
|---|---|---|---|---|---|---|---|
| Apples | - green | Grapes | - red | | - corello pear | | - peaches |
| | - red delicious | Melons | - crown prince | | - custard apples | | - pepino |
| Avocados | | | - honey dew | | - guavas | | - passionfruit |
| Bananas | - medium | | - rockmelon | | - jaboticabas | | - rambutans |
| | - sugar | | - watermelon | | - jack fruit | | - star apples |
| Coconut | - green | | - yellow | | - kiwano | | - star fruit |
| | - regular | Oranges | - navel | | - kumquats | | - tamarillos, |
| Berries | - blueberry | Stone fruit | - mangoes | | - mango | | red/yellow |
| | - Cape gooseberry | | - nectarines | | - nashi pears | | |
| | - mulberry | | - peaches | | - oranges, blood | | |
| | - strawberry | Exotic fruit | - Cape gooseberry | | - papayas | | |

## HERBS

| | | | |
|---|---|---|---|
| Basil, purple/green | Coriander | spear | Sorrel |
| Bay-leaves | Dill | Oregano | Tarragon |
| Chervil | Marjoram | Parsley, curly/continental | Thyme |
| Chives | Mint—apple, eau de col, pepper, | Sage | Thyme, lemon |

## FISH

| | | | |
|---|---|---|---|
| Anchovies | Jewie | Silver Jew | Trumpeter, Striped, Tasmanian |
| Barramundi | Mulloway | Snapper | Whitebait |
| Blue Moki | Pilchard | Sprats | |
| Butterfish | Redfish | Teraglin | |
| Jew Fish | Sardine | Trumpeter | |

# IN SEASON FOR NOVEMBER

## VEGETABLES

| | | | | | | | |
|---|---|---|---|---|---|---|---|
| Artichokes | - globe | Eggplant | - baby, black | Onions | - baby | Sprouts | - alfalfa |
| | - Jerusalem | | - large, black | | - brown | | - bean |
| Asparagus | - green | | - orange | | - shallot | | - snowpea cress |
| | - white | Kale | - green | | - Spanish | | yellow |
| | - baby | Leeks | - regular | | - spring | | - snowpea cress |
| Beans | - broad | | - baby | | - white | | green |
| | - butter | Lettuce | - butter | Peas | - garden | Squash | - baby, green |
| | - flat regular | | - chicory | | - snap | | - baby, yellow |
| | - green | | - coral, red | | - snow | | - large, yellow |
| | - snake | | - coral, green | Potatoes | - chats, new | Swedes | |
| Beetroot | | | - corn | | - chats, pontiac | Tomatoes | - cherry |
| Broccoli | - Chinese | | - cos | | - desirée | | - egg/Italian |
| | - regular | | - finesse | | - kiffler | | - salad |
| Bok choy | - baby | | - garden | | - new | | - pear |
| Cabbage | - green | | - marsh | | - old | Turnips | - baby |
| | - red | | - mignonette | | - pink-eyed | | - large |
| | - Savoy | | - mizuna | | - pontiac | Zucchini | - green |
| Capsicum | - banana red/green | | - mizuna, baby | Pumpkins | - butternut | | - yellow |
| | - black | | - oak, green | | - golden nugget | Baby veg | - beans |
| | - green | | - oak, red | | - gramma | | - beetroot |
| | - red | | - rocket | | - minikins | | - cherry tomatoes |
| | - yellow | | - watercress | | - Queensland blue | | - corn |
| Carrots | - baby | Mushrooms | - button | | - Japanese black | | - Dutch carrot |
| | - Dutch | | - cup | | - swan neck | | - squash, yellow & |
| Chillies | - red | | - enoki | Radishes | - red | | green |
| | - green | | - flat | | - white | | - swede |
| Corn | - regular | | - oyster | Spinach | - English | | - turnip |
| | - baby | | - Shemeji | | - English, baby | | |
| Cucumbers | - Lebanese | | - Shitaki | | - silverbeet | | |
| | - telegraph | | - Swiss brown | | - silverbeet, baby | | |

## FRUIT

| | | | | | | | |
|---|---|---|---|---|---|---|---|
| Apples | - green | | - youngberry | | - nectarines | | - mangoes |
| | - red delicious | Grapes | - red & green | Exotic Fruit | - banana | | Queensland |
| Avocado | | Melons | - honey dew | | passionfruit | | - nashi pears |
| Bananas | - sugar | | - rockmelon | | - Cape gooseberry | | - papayas |
| Coconut | - regular | | - watermelon | | - corello pears | | - pepinos |
| | - green | | - yellow | | - figs | | - rambutans |
| Berries | - blueberry | Oranges | - valencia | | - guavas | | - star apples |
| | - Cape gooseberry | Stone fruit | - cherry | | - jack fruit | | - star fruit |
| | - mulberry | | - peaches | | - kiwano | | - tamarillo |
| | - strawberry | | - mangoes | | - lychees | | red/yellow |

## HERBS

| | | | |
|---|---|---|---|
| Basil, purple/green | Coriander | spear | Sorrel |
| Bay-leaves | Dill | Oregano | Tarragon |
| Chervil | Marjoram | Parsley, curly/continental | Thyme |
| Chives | Mint—apple, eau de col, pepper, | Sage | Thyme, lemon |

## FISH

| | | | |
|---|---|---|---|
| Anchovies | Jewie | Redfish | Tailor |
| Barramundi | Mackereal | Sardine | Teraglin |
| Blue Moki | Mulloway | Silver Jew | Trumpeter |
| Butterfish | Pilchard | Snapper | Trumpeter, Striped, Tasmanian |
| Jew Fish | Prawns | Sprats | Whitebait |

# IN SEASON FOR DECEMBER

## VEGETABLES

| | | | | | | | |
|---|---|---|---|---|---|---|---|
| Artichokes | - globe | Cucumbers | - Lebanese | | - oyster | | - English, baby |
| Asparagus | - green | | - telegraph | | - Shemeji | | - silverbeet |
| | - white | Eggplant | - baby, black | | - Shitaki | Sprouts | - alfalfa |
| | - baby | | - large, black | | - Swiss brown | | - bean |
| Beans | - butter | Kale | - green | Onions | - baby | | - mung |
| | - green | Leeks | - regular | | - brown | | - snowpea |
| Broccoli | - Chinese | | - baby | | - shallot | Squash | - baby, green |
| | - regular | Lettuce | - butter | | - Spanish | | - large, green |
| Bok choy | - baby | | - chicory | | - spring | | - baby, yellow |
| | - regular | | - coral, red | | - white | | - large, yellow |
| Cabbage | - green | | - coral, green | Peas | - garden | Swedes | |
| | - red | | - corn | | - snap | Tomatoes | - cherry |
| | - Savoy | | - cos | | - snow | | - egg/Italian |
| Capsicum | - banana red/green | | - endive | Potatoes | - chats | | - salad |
| | - black | | - endive, baby | | - desirée | | - pear |
| | - green | | - garden | | - pink-eyed | Turnips | - baby |
| | - red | | - marsh | | - pontiac | | - large |
| | - yellow | | - mizuna | Pumpkins | - butternut | Zucchini | - green |
| | - Hungarian | | - mignonette | | - golden nugget | | - yellow |
| Carrots | - baby | | - oak, green | | - gramma | Baby veg | - beans |
| | - Dutch | | - oak, red | | - minikins | | - beetroot |
| Cauliflower | - regular | | - rocket | | - Queensland blue | | - cherry tomatoes |
| | - romaine | | - watercress | | - small green & | | - Dutch carrot |
| Chillies | - red | Mushrooms | - button | | yellow | | - squash, yellow & |
| | - green | | - cup | Radishes | - red | | green |
| Corn | - regular | | - enoki | | - white | | - swede |
| | - baby | | - flat | Spinach | - English | | - turnip |

## FRUIT

| | | | | | | | |
|---|---|---|---|---|---|---|---|
| Apples | - green | | - youngberry | | - peach | | - lychee |
| | - red delicious | Grapes | - red & green | | - plum | | - mangoes |
| | - red democrats | Melons | - honey dew | Exotic fruit | - banana | | - nashi pears |
| Bananas | - sugar | | - rockmelon | | passionfruit | | - passionfruit, black |
| Coconut | - regular | | - watermelon | | - corello pear | | & yellow |
| | - green | | - yellow | | - dry muscatel | | - papayas |
| Berries | - blueberry | Oranges | - valencia | | - figs | | - pepino |
| | - mulberry | Stone Fruit | - apricot | | - guava | | - persimmons |
| | - raspberry | | - cherry | | - jack fruit | | - rambutan |
| | - strawberry | | - nectarine | | - loquat | | - star fruit |

## HERBS

| | | | |
|---|---|---|---|
| Basil, purple/green | Coriander | spear | Sorrel |
| Bay-leaves | Dill | Oregano | Tarragon |
| Chervil | Marjoram | Parsley, curly/continental | Thyme |
| Chives | Mint—apple, eau de col, pepper, | Sage | Thyme, lemon |

## FISH

| | | | |
|---|---|---|---|
| Barramundi | Jewie | Silver Jew | Trumpeter, Striped, Tasmanian |
| Blue Moki | Mackereal | Tailor | |
| Butterfish | Mulloway | Teraglin | |
| Jew Fish | Prawns | Trumpeter | |

# APPENDIX 4
# CONVERSION CHARTS

Imperial measurements to rounded metric measurements

## LIQUIDS

| Fluid ounces (fl oz) | Millilitres (mL) | Fluid ounces (fl oz) | Millilitres (mL) | Fluid ounces (fl oz) | Millilitres (mL) | Pints (pt) | Litres (L) |
|---|---|---|---|---|---|---|---|
| $1/8$ | 3.5 | $4^1/_2$ | 128 | $12^1/_2$ | 355 | 2 (40 fl oz) | 1.0 |
| $1/4$ | 7.0 | 5 | 140 | 13 | 370 | 3 (60 fl oz) | 1.7 |
| $1/3$ | 9.5 | $5^1/_2$ | 155 | $13^1/_2$ | 384 | 4 (80 fl oz) | 2.3 |
| $3/8$ | 10.5 | 6 | 170 | 14 | 400 | 5 (100 fl oz) | 2.8 |
| $1/2$ | 14.0 | $6^1/_2$ | 185 | $14^1/_2$ | 410 | 6 (120 fl oz) | 3.4 |
| $5/8$ | 18.0 | 7 | 200 | 15 | 425 | 7 (140 fl oz) | 4.0 |
| $2/3$ | 19.0 | $7^1/_2$ | 215 | $15^1/_2$ | 440 | 8 (160 fl oz)(1 gal) | 4.5 |
| $3/4$ | 21.5 | 8 | 230 | 16 | 455 | **Gallons (gal)** | **Litres (L)** |
| $7/8$ | 25.0 | $8^1/_2$ | 242 | $16^1/_2$ | 470 | 1 | 4.5 |
| 1 | 30.0 | 9 | 255 | 17 | 485 | 2 | 9.0 |
| $1^1/_2$ | 42.5 | $9^1/_2$ | 270 | $17^1/_2$ | 500 | 3 | 13.5 |
| 2 | 55.0 | 10 | 285 | 18 | 510 | 4 | 18.0 |
| $2^1/_2$ | 71.0 | $10^1/_2$ | 300 | $18^1/_2$ | 525 | 5 | 22.75 |
| 3 | 85.0 | 11 | 310 | 19 | 540 | 6 | 27.0 |
| $3^1/_2$ | 100.0 | $11^1/_2$ | 325 | $19^1/_2$ | 555 | 7 | 32.0 |
| 4 | 115.0 | 12 | 340 | 20 (1 pint) | 570 | 8 | 36.5 |

## WEIGHTS

| Ounces (oz) | Grams (g) | Ounces (oz) | Grams (g) | Ounces (oz) | Grams (g) | Pounds (lb) | Kilograms (kg) |
|---|---|---|---|---|---|---|---|
| $1/8$ | 3.5 | 4 | 113 | $10^1/_2$ | 300 | 2 | 0.9 |
| $1/4$ | 7.0 | $4^1/_2$ | 128 | 11 | 310 | 3 | 1.3 |
| $3/8$ | 10.5 | 5 | 140 | $11^1/_2$ | 325 | 4 | 1.8 |
| $1/2$ | 14.0 | $5^1/_2$ | 155 | 12 | 340 | 5 | 2.2 |
| $5/8$ | 17.5 | 6 | 170 | $12^1/_2$ | 355 | 6 | 2.7 |
| $3/4$ | 21.0 | $6^1/_2$ | 185 | 13 | 370 | 7 | 3.1 |
| $7/8$ | 25.0 | 7 | 200 | $13^1/_2$ | 380 | 8 | 3.6 |
| 1 | 28.5 | $7^1/_2$ | 215 | 14 | 395 | 9 | 4.0 |
| $1^1/_2$ | 71.0 | 8 | 225 | $14^1/_2$ | 410 | 10 | 4.5 |
| 2 | 56.4 | $8^1/_2$ | 240 | 15 | 425 | 20 | 9.0 |
| $2^1/_2$ | 71.0 | 9 | 255 | $15^1/_2$ | 440 | 30 | 13.5 |
| 3 | 85.0 | $9^1/_2$ | 270 | 16 (1 pound) | 455 | 40 | 18.0 |
| $3^1/_2$ | 99.0 | 10 | 285 | | | 60 | 27.0 |

## LIQUID MEASUREMENTS

1/2 cup = 125 mL
1 cup = 250 mL
4 cups = 1 L

Imperial measurements to rounded metric measurements

# WEIGHTS AND MEASURES FOR SMALL QUANTITIES

| Commodity | Weight per 250 mL (8 oz) cup | Commodity | Weight per 250 mL (8 oz) cup |
|---|---|---|---|
| Baking powder | 185 g | Parmesan cheese (grated) | 115 g |
| Barbecue sauce | 265 g | Pepper (ground) | 115 g |
| Black beans | 105 g | Peppercorns (whole) | 175 g |
| Breadcrumbs | 70 g | Pine nuts | 140 g |
| Butter | 190 g | Polenta (uncooked) | 165 g |
| Cheddar cheese (grated) | 110 g | Poppy seeds | 150 g |
| Chicken stock powder | 180 g | Rice (uncooked) | 185 g |
| Corn-flour | 125 g | Salt | 240 g |
| Couscous (medium grain) | 160 g | Sesame seeds | 140 g |
| Flour | 120 g | Sour cream | 240 g |
| Garlic (crushed) | 235 g | Strawberry preserve | 310 g |
| Kidney beans (dried) | 175 g | Sugar (granulated) | 215 g |
| Herbs (dried) | 35 g | Sugar (raw) | 210 g |
| Mayonnaise | 280 g | Tomato paste | 255 g |
| Mint jelly | 310 g | Tomato sauce | 265 g |
| Mustard | 265 g | Walnuts | 85 g |
| Olives (natural) | 160 g | Yoghurt (natural) | 225 g |

| Commodity | Teaspoon | Tablespoon |
|---|---|---|
| Dried herbs | 2 g | 5 g |
| Cornflour | 3 g | 12 g |
| Oil | 3 g | 20 g |
| Salt | 3 g | 10 g |

# OVEN TEMPERATURES

| Description | Celsius | Fahrenheit |
|---|---|---|
| Very slow | 110–120 | 225–250 |
| Slow | 120–150 | 250–300 |
| Moderate | 150–175 | 300–350 |
| Hot | 175–230 | 350–450 |
| Very hot | 230–270 | 450–525 |

The temperatures given above are approximate only and may vary according to the oven used.

# APPENDIX 5
# GLOSSARY

(**F**) denotes French terminology

(**I**) denotes Italian terminology

## A

*à la* (**F**) 'in the style of', e.g. *à la français* means 'in the French style'

*à la broche* (**F**) cooked on a spit/skewer

*à la carte* (**F**) cooked to order and priced separately

*à la minute* (**F**) cooked to order

*al dente* (**I**) just cooked; literally, 'on the teeth'

*al forno* (**I**) baked

*al fresco* (**I**) out of doors

*abaisser* (**F**) to roll out pastry

**abalone** a mollusc of the gastropod group – one of two classifications of shellfish, the other being crustacean; *ormeau* (**F**)

*abats* (**F**) offal; heart, liver, kidney, sweetbreads etc.

*abats de volaille* (**F**) poultry offal

*abricot* (**F**) apricot

**acidify** to add lemon/lime juice or vinegar

**additives** flavourings, colours, stabilisers etc.; anything that changes the taste, texture or colour of a foodstuff

**agar-agar/agar** setting agent made from seaweed; used in Asia

*agneau* (**F**) lamb

*aile de poulet* (**F**) chicken wing

*aileron de poulet* (**F**) chicken winglet

*aïoli* (**F**) garlic flavoured mayonnaise; Provence, France

*airelles* (**F**) blueberries

*ajouter* (**F**) to add

**albumen** the white of an egg

*alla* (**I**) 'in the style of'

*allumettes* (**F**) 'matchsticks'; short rectangles of puff pastry with savoury fillings served as an *hors d'œuvre*

**almond** *amande* (**F**)

*aloyau de bœuf* (**F**) beef sirloin

*amande* (**F**) almond

**amino acids** material from which proteins are produced

**anchovy** *anchois* (**F**)

**angelica** a herb used for decorating desserts and flavouring liqueurs; *angélique* (**F**)

*anguille* (**F**) eel

*antipasto* (**I**) 'before the meal'; a selection of Italian-style *hors d'œuvres* consisting of pickled and marinated vegetables, fish, cheese and meats

*apéritif* (**F**) an alcholic drink taken before a meal to stimulate the appetite

*appareil* (**F**) a prepared mixture

**apple** *pomme* (**F**)

**apricot** *abricot* (**F**)

**Arborio rice** Italian rice used in risotto; its high starch content gives this dish its creamy flavour

*aromatiser* (**F**) to flavour

*arroser* (**F**) to baste

**arrowroot** powerful thickening agent that is tasteless and colourless when cooked; *marante* (**F**)

**artichoke, globe** *artichaut* (**F**)

**artichoke, Jerusalem** *topinambour* (**F**)

*arugula* (**I**) a peppery, green salad leaf; also known as **rocket**

**ascorbic acid** vitamin C

**asparagus** *asperge* (**F**)

**aspic** jelly used for larder work; begins in liquid form and solidifies when cold

*assaisonner* (**F**) to season

*assortiment* (**F**) an assortment of

*attendrir* (**F**) to tenderise

**avocado** *avocat* (**F**)

*avoine* (**F**) oats

*au beurre* (**F**) with butter

*au four* (**F**) oven-baked

***au jus* (F)** (meat) served in its own juice

***au lait* (F)** cooked in/with milk

***au naturel* (F)** served in its natural state

***au vin blanc* (F)** cooked with/containing white wine

***aubergine* (F)** eggplant

**B**

**baby chicken** *poussin, single* **(F)**

**bacon** *lard* **(F)**

**bacteria** microscopic organisms; some are harmful, others useful to the food industry such as in cheese production

**bagel** Jewish doughnut-shaped dense, chewy bread which is boiled before baking

***baguette* (F)** a long, crisp, cylindrical French loaf

***bain-marie* (F)** hot water storage container where cooked foods can be kept hot

**bake blind, to** to cook a pastry case before it is filled

**baked** *al forno* **(I)**

**baker** *boulanger* **(F)**

**baking powder** a combination of baking soda, an acid such as cream of tartar and a moisture absorber such as cornstarch; helps food to rise because carbon dioxide is created when it is mixed with water

**baking soda/bicarbonate of soda** acts as a rising agent for food such as batters. Baking soda was used to preserve the colour of vegetables that were boiled; research has shown that this destroys their vitamin C content

***ballottine* (F)** meat/fish that is boned, stuffed, rolled, tied and then braised or roasted

**balsamic vinegar** an Italian vinegar made from the white Trebbiano grape and aged for years in barrels of different woods

**banana** *banane* **(F)**

**bap** a soft white bread roll dusted with flour

***barder* (F)** to cover with strips of bacon

**barley** *orge* **(F)**

***barquettes* (F)** small boat-shaped pastry cases

**basmati rice** a long grained rice with a nutty flavour and distinctive aroma

***basse-côte de porc* (F)** pork spare ribs

**baste** to brush or spoon liquid of a meat while it is being cooked; ***arroser* (F)**

**bat out, to** to flatten raw meat with a meat tenderiser, e.g. schnitzel

**batter** a thick/thin semi-liquid that can be spooned or poured; usually made of flour, milk and eggs

***bavarois* (F)** a dessert; means 'Bavarian'

***bavette d'aloyau* (F)** beef, thick flank

**bean curd** tofu

**beat, to** to stir a liquid/semi-liquid very quickly

**beef** *bœuf* **(F)**

**beef, cuts of:**
    **boned out sirloin** *contrefilet* **(F)**
    **brisket** *poitrine* **(F)**
    **chuck ribs** *côtes du collier* **(F)**
    **fillet** *filet* **(F)**
    **fore ribs** *côtes* **(F)**
    **head of fillet** *chateaubriand* **(F)**
    **heart** *cœur* **(F)**
    **kidney** *rognon* **(F)**
    **liver** *foie* **(F)**
    **marrow** *moelle* **(F)**
    **middle fillet** *tournedos* **(F)**
    **rump** *culotte* **(F)**
    **shank** *jambe* **(F)**
    **shin** *jambe* **(F)**
    **silverside** *gîte à la noix* **(F)**
    **sirloin** *aloyau* **(F)**
    **sirloin steak** *entrecôte* **(F)**
    **thick flank** *tranche grasse* **(F)**
    **thin flank** *bavette d'aloyau* **(F)**
    **tongue** *langue* **(F)**
    **topside** *tranche tendre* **(F)**
    **tripe** *tripes* **(F)**
    **wing ribs** *côte* **(F)**

***beetroot* *betterave* (F)**

***beignets* (F)** savoury or sweet fritters

**best end, veal/lamb** *carré de veau / carré d'agneau* **(F)**

***betterave* (F)** beetroot

***beurrer* (F)** to spread with butter

***beurre* (F)** butter

***beurre fondu* (F)** melted butter

***beurre manié* (F)** method of thickening sauces using blended equal parts of butter and flour

***beurre noir* (F)** black butter

***beurre noisette* (F)** brown butter

**bind, to** to stir a thickening agent into hot liquid making a mixture hold together

**biscotti (I)**   small variously flavoured Italian biscuits served with coffee or desserts

**bisque (F)**   a thick, creamy soup of seafood, usually puréed

**bivalve**   a mollusc which has a soft flesh and two hinged shells

**black butter   beurre noir (F)**

**blackberry   mûre (F)**

**blackcurrant   cassis (F)**

**blanc (F)**   white, or:
- chicken breast
- cooking liquid of water, lemon juice and salt

**blancs d'oeufs (F)**   egg whites

**blanchaille (F)**   whitebait

**blanchir (F)**   to plunge into boiling water to:
- cook without colouring
- set and bring out the colour of certain vegetables
- help remove the skin of certain vegetables, e.g. tomatoes
- cook certain vegetables lightly to keep them crisp and firm

**blanquette (F)**   a white stew in which the sauce is made from the cooked meat liquid

**blend**   the complete incorporation of two or more ingredients mixed until smooth

**bleu (F)**   very underdone (meat/fish)

**blini**   a Russian yeast buckwheat pancake usually served with caviar and sour cream

**blonde (F)**   slightly coloured, e.g. blonde roux

**blueberries   airelles (F)**

**bocconcini (I)**   small non-matured mozzarella cheeses

**bœuf (F)**   beef

**boil, to   bouillir (F)**

**boiling fowl   poule au pot (F)**

**boiling water   eau bouillante (F)**

**bok choy**   a Chinese green-leafed vegetable

**bombe glacée (F)**   ice-cream shaped into large spheres

**bone out** .  to remove the bone from a joint of meat; usually the first stage of preparation; **désosser (F)**

**bordure (F)**   a ring of food, e.g. rice

**bortsch**   Russian beetroot soup garnished with sour cream

**bouchées (F)**   small pastry cases

**bouillabaisse (F)**   a thick seafood stew from Provence, France

**bouillir (F)**   to boil

**bouillon (F)**   unclarified stock; usually beef

**boulanger (F)**   baker

**bouquet garni (F)**   collation of parsley, thyme and bay-leaves tied to two small pieces of celery; used in stock production

**braise, to   braiser, cuire à l'étouffée (F)**

**braising**   a method of cookery in which food is first browned, covered and then cooked in liquid at a low temperature for a long time to break down tough connective tissues

**bran**   the outer layer of grains, e.g. wheat

**branche (F)**   whole, cooked leaves of spinach

**braiser (F)**   to braise

**brawn**   the gelatinised, pressed flesh of a pig's head

**bread   pain (F)**

**breadcrumbs   chapelure (F)**

**bream   brème (F)**

**breast, veal/lamb/pork   poitrine de veau/ poitrine d'agneau/poitrine de porc (F)**

**brème (F)**   bream

**bresaola (I)**   an aged, air-dried beef, thinly sliced; used for antipasto

**brider (F)**   to truss poultry

**brine**   a solution used for preserving certain foodstuffs; comprising water, saltpetre, salt and certain herbs and spices

**brioche (F)**   a very light French bread made with the addition of butter and eggs

**broccoli   brocoli (F)**

**brochette (F)**   a skewer

**brocoli (F)**   broccoli

**broth**   a soup that begins as the cooking liquid for vegetables or meats; **brodo (I)**

**brouillé (F)**   scrambled

**brown butter   beurre noisette (F)**

**brown, to   brunir (F)**

**brown sauce   espagnole (F)**

**brown stock   estouffade (F)**

**bruise**   to partially crush an ingredient, e.g. garlic clove to release flavour

**brûlé (F)**   burnt or browned under a grill, e.g. crème brûlée

**brun (F)**   brown

**brunoise (F)**   small dice

**bruschetta (I)**   bread roasted on open coals then rubbed with garlic

**Brussels sprouts**   *choux de Bruxelles* (F)

**buckwheat**   a flour obtained from a herb, not a cereal, but can be used as a cereal, e.g. blinis

**bulghur wheat**   kernels of wheat which are steamed, dried and then crushed; very common in the Middle East and used for tabbouleh

**buñuelo**   a Mexican pastry rolled very thin, deep fried and seasoned with sugar and cinnamon

**burrito**   tortilla; unleavened Mexican bread folded over a filling

**butter**   *beurre* (F)

**butter, melted**   *beurre fondu* (F)

**butter, with**   *au beurre* (F)

**butterfly cut**   to cut a piece of meat/seafood almost in half along the depth to almost double its size and halve the thickness

**C**

**cabanossi (I)**   type of Italian sausage

**cabbage**   *chou* (F)

**cabillaud (F)**   cod

**cacao**   the tree from which the seeds are cultivated to produce cocoa powder and chocolate

**cacciatore (I)**   'hunter's style'; Italian stew made with chicken, tomatoes, vegetables and wine

**Cajun**   a style of cookery synonymous with the French-Americans of Louisiana; different from the Creole style as it uses dark roux, plenty of spices and usually pork fat. Both styles utilise peppers and onions in their preparation

**calabrese (I)**   an Italian hot salami

**calamari**   squid

**calcium**   a mineral found in certain dairy products

**calorie**   a unit of measurement for energy or heat

**calzone (I)**   a closed, filled pizza that can be baked or deep fried

**canapé (F)**   ideally a small piece of bread topped with various items eaten with the fingers before the start of a meal with drinks; the bases can differ

**canard (F)**   duck

**caneton (F)**   duckling, male

**cannelloni (I)**   large pasta tubes that are cooked, filled and then baked with a sauce and cheese

**canola oil**   an oil extracted from the rape seed. Canola oil has the lowest saturated fat content and is also credited with containing more cholesterol-balancing monounsaturated fats than any other oil — with the exception of olive oil. Canola oil also contains Omega 3 fatty acids which are believed not only to reduce cholesterol but to enhance brain development

**caper**   *câpre* (F)

**capon**   *chapon* (F); a chicken less than one year old fed on a fattening diet

**caponata (I)**   Italian accompaniment made from onions, eggplant, tomatoes, olives, pine nuts, capers, anchovies, vinegar and olive oil

**cappelletti (I)**   stuffed squares of small pasta; similar to ravioli

**câpre (F)**   caper

**caramel**   the result of sugar which is cooked until it turns brown; caramel temperatures reach approximately 350°F

**caramelise, to**   to cook foods until their sugar content turns brown

**carbohydrate**   a nutrient which provides the body with energy

**carbonara (I)**   Italian dishes comprising eggs, cream, bacon and cheese; generally pasta

**carcass**   *carcasse* (F); carcass of chicken and other birds

**carotene**   found in certain fruits and vegetables; the liver converts carotene into vitamin C

**carotte (F)**   carrot

**carpaccio (I)**   an Italian appetiser consisting of thin slices of raw beef dressed with olive oil

**carpet bag steak**   a steak stuffed with oysters and then cooked. America claims this dish as theirs, although it is widely believed throughout the world to have originated in Australia

**carré d'agneau (F)**   best end of lamb

**carré de veau (F)**   best end of veal

**carte du jour (F)**   menu of the day

**casserole**   a moist method of cookery which uses a heat-resistant earthenware dish with a lid

**cassis (F)**   blackcurrant

**cauliflower**   *chou-fleur* (F)

**caviar**   roe/eggs of the sturgeon fish. Due to its cost, many other roes are available such as lumpfish caviar; *caviar* (F)

**celery**   *céleri* (F)

**Celsius** a scale for reading temperatures where 0°C represents freezing point and 100°C represents the boiling point of water; also called **Centigrade**

**cereal grain** any plant from the grass family that produces an edible seed such as barley, rice, millet, corn and oats

*cerise* **(F)** cherry

**chafing dish** a heated receptacle containing water, usually portable, where trays of food are placed to keep food warm on buffets and smörgåsbords

*champignon* **(F)** mushroom

**chapatti** an unleavened Indian bread which can be seasoned with herbs and spices and served hot

*chapelure* **(F)** breadcrumbs

*chapon* **(F)** capon

*chateaubriand* **(F)** head of a fillet of beef; grilled fillet served with béarnaise sauce

*chaud* **(F)** hot

**chaud-froid** a velouté thickened with aspic and coated to glaze on a prepared dish such as chicken

*chauffant* **(F)** boiling/simmering salted water to cook/re-heat or blanch foods

*chauffer* **(F)** to warm

**cheese** *fromage* **(F)**; *formaggio* **(I)**

**chef, assistant** *commis chef* **(F)**

*chef de cuisine* **(F)** head chef

**chef, second** *sous-chef* **(F)**

**cherry** *cerise* **(F)**

**chicken** *poulet* **(F)**

**chicken, cuts of:**
   breast *blanc* **(F)**
   carcass *carcasse* **(F)**
   drumstick *pilon* **(F)**
   thigh *gras de cuisse* **(F)**
   leg *cuisse* **(F)**
   offal *abats de volaille* **(F)**
   wing *aile* **(F)**
   winglet *aileron* **(F)**

**chicken, medium roasting** *poulet reine* **(F)**

**chicken, small roasting** *poulet de grain* **(F)**

*chiffonade* **(F)** something shredded; usually lettuce

*chinois* **(F)** a conical strainer

**chocolate** *chocolat* **(F)**

**chop, a** *côte* **(F)**

*chou* **(F)** cabbage

*choux de Bruxelles* **(F)** Brussels sprouts

*chou-fleur* **(F)** cauliflower

**choux pastry** a light pastry made from flour, butter, boiling water and eggs, used for profiteroles, éclairs etc; *pâte à choux* **(F)**

**chowder** a thick, hearty seafood soup; describes any soup containing large chunks of ingredients

**chutney** a thick accompaniment to curried dishes made from fruits, spices and sugar

**citric acid** a sharp tasting extract made from citrus fruits

*citron* **(F)** lemon

**citrus fruit** members of this family include: lemons, limes, grapefruits and oranges

*civet* **(F)** a brown game stew

**clarification/clarify** making clear/to make clear, e.g stock, butter

**clarified butter** butter that has been gently heated to evaporate all water and separate the milk solids that settle on the bottom. The top layer of clarified butter is skimmed off and used in cooking

**clostridium welchii** a harmful bacterium/pathogen

*clouté* **(F)** studded, e.g. an onion studded with cloves used in bread sauce

**club sandwich** a layered sandwich with layers of toasted bread, chicken, lettuce, bacon, tomato, etc.

**coagulation** the hardening of a protein; e.g. the reaction of the white of an egg when fried is irreversible

**coat, to** to cover with a sauce or liquid

**cochineal** a red food colouring derived from the Central American cochineal insect

**coconut cream** one part coconut liquid to four parts of coconut flesh; used in Asian cookery

**coconut milk** one part coconut liquid to one part coconut flesh; used in Asian cookery

*cocotte* **(F)** large earthenware stewpan

**cod** *cabillaud* **(F)**

*cœur d'agneau* **(F)** heart, lamb

*cœur de bœuf* **(F)** heart, beef

*colin* **(F)** hake

**collagen** protein found in the connective tissues and gristle of meat; yields gelatine and becomes tender during cooking

**combine** to mix two or more ingredients together to become one

*commis chef* (F)   assistant chef

*compote* (F)   stewed fruit

*concasser* (F)   roughly chopped vegetables, fruit or herbs

*concombre* (F)   cucumber

**condiment**   an accompaniment to a dish such as salt and pepper, sauces, chutneys, mustards, etc.

*confit* (F)   a method of preserving goose/duck by salting and then cooking slowly in their own fat

**confiture** (F)   fruit preserves

**conserves**   fruit mixtures that are cooked with sugar until thick

*consommé* (F)   a clear soup

*contre-filet de bœuf* (F)   a boned out sirloin of beef

**cook, to**   *cuire* (F)

**cooked**   *cuit* (F)

**cooked to order**   *à la minute* (F)

**cook out, to**   the process of cooking flour with fat, e.g. roux

*coquilles Saint-Jacques* (F)   scallops

*cordon* (F)   sauce placed onto a plate or dish in a fine line

**core**   the centre of fruit or vegetables which contains seeds or pips

**corn**   a widely used term for any cereal grains

**cornflour**   finely ground cornmeal used in baking; thickens wet dishes when mixed with a little water

*cornichons* (F)   small gherkins

**corn oil**   an oil that is excellent for deep frying due to its odourless, tasteless and low-smoke qualities; corn oil is high in polyunsaturates

**cornstarch**   see **cornflour**

**correct, to**   to adjust the seasoning, colouring or consistency of a dish near completion

*côte* (F)   a chop

*côte d'agneau* (F)   lamb chop

*côte de bœuf* (F)   beef, wing rib

*côte de porc* (F)   pork chop

*côte découverte* (F)   middle neck of lamb

*côtelette* (F)   a cutlet

*côtelette d'agneau* (F)   lamb cutlet

*côtelette de veau* (F)   veal cutlet

*côtes de bœuf* (F)   beef, fore ribs

*côtes du collier de bœuf* (F)   beef, chuck ribs

**cottonseed oil**   an oil obtained from the cotton plant and used in the production of margarines and other vegetables

*cou d'agneau* (F)   mid neck of lamb; scrag

*cou de veau* (F)   veal neck; scrag

*coulis* (F)   puréed fruit or vegetables of a similar consistency to a thin sauce

*coupe* (F)   a shallow glass dish in which fruits and ice-creams are served

*courgette* (F)   zucchini

*court-bouillon* (F)   cooking liquor used for fish

**couscous**   granular semolina; staple of North Africa

**cover, to**   *couvrir* (F)

**crab**   *crabe* (F)

**crackling**   the crispy skin on cooked pork

**cranberries**   *airelles coussinettes* (F)

**crayfish**   *écrevisse* (F)

**cream**   *crème* (F)

**cream of tartar**   an acetic stabiliser used with eggs and also added to baking powder to help produce the gases which cause cakes to rise

*crème* (F)   cream

*crème fouettée*   whipped cream

**Creole**   a style of cooking from the southern states of North America with Spanish influence utilising okra, peppers, rice and tomatoes

*crêpes* (F)   pancakes

*crespelles* (I)   filled, thin Italian pancakes

*cresson de fontaine* (F)   watercress

*crevette* (F)   prawn

**crimp**   to pinch the edges of pastry securing it to the dish it is cooked in

*croissant* (F)   a layered, flaky, rich butter and yeast roll which can be filled with savoury or sweet foods and served hot or cold

*croquettes* (F)   breadcrumbed foods which have been moulded into cylindrical shapes and deep fried

*croustade* (F)   an edible container made from bread or pastry which holds vegetable or meat stews

*croûtes* (F)   foods placed into either a puff pastry case or bread hollowed out and toasted

*croûtons* (F)   small squares of fried bread, usually served as a garnish with soup and salads, e.g. Caesar salad

**crudités (F)**   small vegetables served raw and eaten with the fingers

**crumb, to   paner (F)**

**crumble**   a dessert topped with rubbed flour, sugar and butter together forming a sandy texture, sprinkled over fruit and then baked

**crustacean**   one of the two classifications of shellfish such as prawns, lobster and Balmain bugs etc. The other classification is **mollusc**

**cucumber   concombre (F)**

**cuire (F)**   to cook

**cuisine (F)**   cooking in a certain style, e.g. Italian cuisine, Asian cuisine etc.

**cuisse (F)**   leg

**cuisse de poulet (F)**   chicken leg

**cuisseau/cuissot de veau (F)**   leg of veal

**cuissot de porc (F)**   leg of pork

**cuit (F)**   cooked

**culotte de bœuf (F)**   beef, rump

**curd**   the semi-solid portion of coagulated milk from which cheese is produced

**cure**   to preserve meats by smoking or pickling methods

**curry powder**   widely used in Indian cuisine; made from a blend of approximately eighteen herbs, seeds and spices, including: cinnamon, cloves, coriander, cumin, feenel seeds, saffron, tamarind and turmeric

**cutlet   côtelette (F)**

**D**

**damper**   traditional Australian outback bread made from flour, water and salt cooked in the hot ashes of a camp fire

**Danish pastry**   a sweetened multi-layered pastry, each layer brushed with butter to give a rich finish

**dariole mould**   small mould used for crème caramel

**darne (F)**   a slice of round fish containing the bone

**date   datte (F)**

**débarrasser (F)**   to clear away

**déglacer (F)**   to make a sauce by adding liquid to residue left over after cooking, e.g. roast

**dégraisser (F)**   to skim away fat, e.g. stock

**dehydrate**   to remove moisture from foods, increasing shelf life

**délice (F)**   a neatly folded fillet of fish

**demi-glace (F)**   equal quantities of espagnole/brown sauce and brown stock which have been reduced by half

**désosser (F)**   to bone out, e.g. poultry

**de-vein**   to remove the vein which runs along the back of prawns

**dhal**   a spiced Indian dish made of lentils, tomatoes and onions

**diced, small   brunoise (F)**

**dilute**   to weaken a liquid with the addition of water or to mix a powder with liquid, e.g. custard powder or cornflour; **diluér (F)**

**dinde (F)**   turkey

**dish of the day   plat du jour (F)**

**dissolve**   to incorporate a solid substance and a liquid so that none of the original dry ingredients are visible

**doily**   an attractive, intricately cut piece of paper for decorating plates, e.g. cakes

**doré (F)**   golden

**double baby chicken   poussin, double (F)**

**dough**   flour which is mixed with a liquid to create a pliable texture

**drain**   to allow liquid to escape from food, e.g. a collander or chinois

**dredge**   to pass food through flour or breadcrumbs until evenly coated

**dressing**   a mixture of oil and vinegar and various other ingredients used to enhance the flavour of salads

**dripping**   the fat which is left behind after a meat is cooked

**duck   canard (F)**

**duckling   caneton (F)**

**dumpling**   minced mixture of meat or vegetables with other ingredients, moulded into small balls and usually cooked in soup

**duxelles**   finely chopped mushrooms cooked in butter; used for garnishing fish and poultry

**E**

**earthenware**   heat resistant glazed clay dishes and bowls

**ébarber (F)**   to remove the beard from molluscs, e.g. mussels

**échalote (F)**   shallot

**écrevisse (F)**   crayfish

**écumer (F)** to skim

**eel** *anguille* **(F)**

**egg** *œuf* **(F)**

**egg noodles** noodles made from wheat flour and eggs and resembling spaghetti; used in Asian cuisine

**eggplant** *aubergine* **(F)**

**egg wash** beaten egg diluted with a little milk used for brushing pastry prior to cooking

**egg white** *blanc d'œufs* **(F)**

**émincer (F)** to slice meat into neat pieces

**entrecôte de bœuf (F)** sirloin steak; no bone

**entrée (F)** a small dish served before the main course (Australia). In other parts of the world, *entrée* refers to the main course

**entremettier (F)** vegetable chef

**épaule (F)** shoulder

**épaule d'agneau (F)** shoulder of lamb

**épaule de porc (F)** shoulder of pork

**épaule de veau (F)** shoulder of veal

**épinard (F)** spinach

**éplucher (F)** to remove the outer leaves or to peel

**escalope (F)** a thin slice of veal

**espagnole (F)** brown sauce

**estouffade (F)** brown stock

**étouffée (F)** to braise, stew or steam; to cook in its own juice

**étuvée** braised

**extracts** concentrated flavourings

**F**

**Fahrenheit** a scale for reading temperatures in which 32°F indicates freezing point and 212°F indicates the boiling point of water. Fahrenheit converted into Celsius/Centigrade: subtract 32 from the Fahrenheit reading, multiply by 5 and then divide by 9

**farce (F)** stuffing

**farcir (F)** to stuff

**farinaceous** pasta, cereal, beans and pulses; dishes containing flour

**farine (F)** flour

**feta** Greek cheese

**fig** *figue* **(F)**

**filet (F)** a slice of fish/beef free of bone

**filet d'agneau (F)** fillet of lamb

**filet mignon (F)** tender tail end of beef fillet

**filo pastry** very thin sheets of pastry; originally from Greece

**fish** *poisson* **(F)**

**fishmonger** *poissonnier* **(F)**

**flake, to** to lightly break fish into natural segments

**flamber (F)** to singe poultry removing small feathers

**flan** pastry case filled either with fruit or savoury filling

**flash point** the temperature oil must reach before it catches fire

**flavour, to** *aromatiser* **(F)**

**fleurons (F)** small crescent-shaped pieces of puff pastry which can be sweetened and served as a dessert accompaniment

**flour** *farine* **(F)**

**focaccia (I)** thick, flat Italian bread; can be drizzled with olive oil or seasoned with herbs, olives or vegetables prior to cooking

**foie (F)** liver

**foie d'agneau (F)** lamb's liver

**foie de bœuf (F)** beef liver

**foie de porc (F)** pork liver

**foie de veau (F)** veal liver

**fold** to lightly turn ingredients in a mixing bowl by gently folding one side over to the other until combined

**fondre (F)** to melt

**fondu (F)** melted

**formaggio (I)** cheese

**fouetter (F)** to whisk

**four (F)** oven

**frappé (F)** chilled iced drink at its slushy stage

**freeze, to** *glacer* **(F)**

**friandises (F)** dainty bite-sized cakes;
**petits fours (F)**

**fricassee** a white stew in which the meat is cooked in the sauce it is served with

**fried** *frit* **(F)**

**frire (F)** to fry

**frisé (F)** curled

**frit (F)** fried

**frittata (I)** similar to an omelette but without a pastry base. All ingredients are mixed with the egg mixture before cooking; usually served in the pan it is cooked in

**fritter**   a shallow deep fried cake of either chopped meat or vegetables which have been mixed with the batter mixture

**friture (F)**   a deep fat fryer

**fromage (F)**   cheese

**fructose**   the natural sweetener in fruits and honey

**fruit preserves   confiture (F)**

**fry, to   frire (F)**

**fumé (F)**   smoked

**fungo/funghi (I)**   mushroom/s

**G**

**galantine (F)**   boned and stuffed meat gently simmered then chilled, decorated and coated with aspic made from its own stock; slices served cold

**game   gibier (F)**

**garde-manger (F)**   larder chef

**garlic**   a member of the lily family related to leeks, chives and onions. The edible bulb grows underground and, stored properly in a cool, dark place, will keep up to eight weeks

**garnish**   to decorate a finished dish; **garnir (F)**

**gastronome (F)**   connoisseur of food; gourmet

**gastropod**   a form of mollusc, e.g. abalone, snail, whelk, etc.

**gâteau (F)**   a large cake

**gaufrette (F)**   fan-shaped wafer served with desserts

**gazpacho**   a chilled puréed vegetable soup from Spain

**gelatine**   a protein which is used to set foods; dissolved in hot water, gelatine forms into a jelly-like substance when cold

**gelato (I)**   ice-cream

**ghee**   clarified butter which is further cooked until it is brown in colour and has a nutty taste; ghee has a longer life and a higher smoke point than butter

**gherkins, small   cornichons (F)**

**gibier (F)**   game

**giblets**   liver and gizzards of a bird

**gigot d'agneau (F)**   leg of lamb

**ginger**   a spice found in tropical and sub-tropical regions; famous for its distinctive taste and aroma. Ginger is widely used in Asian cuisine and valued for its medicinal properties

**gîte a la noix de bœuf (F)**   silverside of beef

**glacé (F)**   frozen; can be referred to as ice-cream or flavoured ice, e.g. sorbet

**glacer (F)**   to freeze

**glaze, to**
- to brown a dish under a salamander
- to add a shine to desserts using preserves
- toss vegetables in honey giving a shiny finish

**gluten**   formed from protein when flour is mixed with water

**golden   doré (F)**

**goujon (F)**   a fillet of fish which has been cut into strips

**grapefruit   pamplemousse (F)**

**grapes   raisins (F)**

**gras de cuisse de poulet (F)**   chicken thigh

**grate, to**   to reduce a food to small strips by rubbing it against a surface of small serrated holes; **râper (F)**

**gratin (F)**   topped with a cheese/breadcrumb crust and lightly browned in an oven or under a salamander

**gravy**   a sauce made from the juices of cooked meat

**grill chef   grilladin (F)**

**grill, to   griller (F)**

**grilladin (F)**   grill chef

**griller (F)**   to grill

**grind**   to reduce food into small particles

**guacamole**   a Mexican dish of avocado puréed with lemon juice and chilli powder

**H**

**haché (F)**   minced or finely chopped

**hake   colin (F)**

**ham   jambon (F)**

**hareng (F)**   herring

**head chef   chef de cuisine (F)**

**heart   cœur (F)**

**herbs   herbes (F)**

**herring   hareng (F)**

**homard (F)**   lobster

**honey   miel (F)**

**hors d'œuvre (F)**   an appetiser

**hot   chaud (F)**

**hot water pastry**   the pastry used for making pork pies

**huile (F)**   oil

**huile d'olives (F)**   olive oil

**huîtres (F)**   oysters

**hummus**   a sauce from the Middle East made with chick-peas, lemon juice and garlic

## I

**ice-cream/flavoured ice   glacé (F); gelato (I)**

**infusion**   flavour which is extracted out of an ingredient into a liquid in which it rests, e.g. tea

## J

**jam**   a simmered mixture of fruits and sugar; **confiture (F)**

**jambe de bœuf (F)**   beef, shank or shin

**jambon (F)**   ham

**jardiniere (F)**   mixed vegetables cut into batons

**jarret de veau (F)**   veal knuckle/shin/shank

**jasmine rice**   a long grained rice grown in Asia with a distinctive fragrant aroma and flavour, also known as Thai rice

**jell, to**   to set a liquid

**John Dory   saint-pierre (F)**; fish

**jus-lié (F)**   thickened gravy

**julienne (F)**   fine strips of food

## K

**kebabs**   cubes of meat, seafood or vegetables placed onto a skewer and then cooked; **shaslik**

**kidney   rognon (F)**

**kneaded   manie (F)**

**kneading**   the technique used in bread making to stretch and expand the gluten content

**knuckle, veal   jarret de veau (F)**

**korma**   a spicy curry dish native to India and Pakistan; usually made with lamb or chicken with the addition of onions and various vegetables

**kosher**   describes food acceptable to Orthodox Jewish people, having strict guidelines at all production points

## L

**lactic acid**   found in dairy products and pickles; it is the result of certain bacteria combined with sugar in the milk by-product, lactose

**lactose**   the sugar found in milk and milk by-products

**lait (F)**   milk

**laitance (F)**   roe

**laitue (F)**   lettuce

**lamb   agneau (F)**

**lamb, cuts of**
   best end   **carré (F)**
   breast   **poitrine (F)**
   chop   **côte (F)**
   cutlet   **côtelette (F)**
   fillet   **filet (F)**
   heart   **cœur (F)**
   kidney   **rognon (F)**
   leg   **gigot (F)**
   liver   **foie (F)**
   loin   **carré (F)**
   mid neck   **côte découverte/cou (F)**
   saddle   **selle (F)**
   scrag   **cou (F)**
   shoulder   **épaule (F)**
   sweetbread   **ris (F)**
   tongue   **langue (F)**

**lamb stew   navarin (F)**

**langue (F)**   tongue

**langue d'agneau (F)**   lamb tongue

**langue de bœuf (F)**   beef tongue

**langoustine (F)**   scampi

**lard**   rendered port fat; **saindoux (F)**

**lard (F)**   bacon

**larder (F)**   to insert strips of bacon into a joint of meat

**larder chef   garde-manger (F)**

**lardons (F)**   batons of thick streaky bacon

**leek   poireau (F)**

**leg   cuisse (F)**

**leg, lamb   gigot d'agneau (F)**

**leg, pork   cuissot de porc (F)**

**leg, veal   cuisseau de veau (F)**

**légumes (F)**   vegetables; more specifically, vegetables which have a seed pod that splits in two when ripe

**lemon   citron (F)**

**lemon sole   limande (F)**

**lettuce   laitue (F)**

**levure (F)**   yeast

**liaison**   thickening or binding mixture, usually with an egg yolk *lier* (F)   to bind

*limande* (F)   lemon sole

liver   *foie* (F)

lobster   *homard* (F)

loin   *longe* (F)

*longe de porc* (F)   loin of pork

**M**

*macédoine* (F)   vegetables (or sometimes fruit) cut into approximately ½ cm dice sometimes used with fruit and vegetables

macerate   to marinate fruit; *macerer* (F)

maize   *maïs* (F); sweet corn

malic acid   a natural acid found in fruits

*manie* (F)   kneaded

*marante* (F)   arrowroot

*margarine* (F)   margarine

marinade   a liquid which imparts its flavour into food that is soaked in it; can also act as a tenderiser with meat

marinate   to soak food in a marinade

*mariné* (F)   pickled

*marinière* (F)   in the style of a sailor or mariner

marmalade   a preserve made from the rind of fruits

*marmite* (F)   stock pot

*marquer* (F)   to prepare for cooking

marrow   the soft brown centre of bones; *moelle* (F)

matzo   Jewish unleavened bread

meat   *viande* (F)

*médaillon*   a small round piece of meat

*mélanger* (F)   to mix

*melon* (F)   melon

melt, to   *fondre* (F)

melted   *fondu* (F)

menu   bill of fare

menu of the day   *carte du jour* (F)

meringue   egg whites beaten together with a little sugar until stiff and then slowly baked in a low oven

*merlan* (F)   whiting

miro-organisms   bacteria, yeasts and moulds

*miel* (F)   honey

*mignonette* (F)   coarsely ground pepper

*mijoter* (F)   to simmer

milk   *lait* (F)

milled pepper   pepper which is ground at the table onto a dish using a hand held pepper-mill

*mille-feuille* (F)   a dessert of puff pastry, fruits, cream and custard

minced   *haché* (F)

minnows   whitebait

*mirepoix* (F)   roughly cut vegetables, e.g. onions, carrots and celery used for braising

mirin   a Japanese rice wine

*mise en place* (F)   preparation of ingredients prior to cooking

mixed   *panaché* (F)

mix, to   *mélanger* (F)

*moelle de bœuf* (F)   beef marrow

moki   a variety of fish found in parts of the west Pacific

mollusc   one of the two classifications of shellfish, the other being **crustacean** – mollusc includes abalone, snails, mussels, clams, oysters etc.

monosodium glutamate (MSG)   flavour enhancer widely used in Asian cuisine

mortar and pestle   a vessel with a grinder for grinding ingredients

*moules* (F)   mussels

*mousse* (F)   froth; a hot or cold dish of a light consistency

*mousseline* (F)   a sauce which has had whipped egg white or cream added to it

*moutarde* (F)   mustard

MSG   see **monosodium glutamate**

*mûre* (F)   blackberry

mushroom/s   *champignon/s* (F); *fungo/ funghi* (I)

mussels   *moules* (F)

mustard   *moutarde* (F)

**N**

naan   flat Indian bread which is traditionally baked in a tandoor oven

nap   to lightly coat food with a sauce

*napper* (F)   to coat with a sauce

*navarin* (F)   lamb stew

*navet* (F)   turnip

niacin   part of the vitamin B group found in

foodstuffs such as liver, bacon and meat extracts

***noisette* (F)** a small, boneless round cut of lamb

***noix* (F)** nut

***noix de veau* (F)** veal, cushion

**nut *noix* (F)**

**nutrients** components of food; vitamins, carbohydrates, minerals etc.


## O

**oats *avoine* (F)**

***œuf* (F)** egg

**offal** head, heart, liver, kidney, sweetbreads etc; ***abats* (F)**

***oignon* (F)** onion

**oil *huile* (F)**

***olive* (F)** olive

**olive oil** the oil extracted from pressed olives. Olive oils are graded in accordance with the degree of acidity they contain, the best being extra virgin olive oil. Olive oil is extracted by the gentle pressing of olives between two boards. Olive oil is a monounsaturated oil which is cholesterol free; a very versatile oil used for cooking, marinades, dressings and most importantly *flavouring* food – ***huile d'olive* (F)**

**onion *oignon* (F)**

**onion, studded *clouté* (F)**

***orange* (F)** orange

***orge* (F)** barley

***ormeau* (F)** abalone

***osso buco* (I)** Italian dish made from veal knuckle cut through the bone simmered with tomato, vegetables, wine and lemon peel until the marrow and meat become tender

**oven *four* (F)**

**oven-baked *au four* (F)**

**oysters *huîtres* (F)**


## P

**paella** Spanish rice, chicken and seafood dish

***pain* (F)** bread

***pamplemousse* (F)** grapefruit

***panaché* (F)** mixed

***panais* (F)** parsnip

**pancakes *crêpes* (F)**

***pancetta* (I)** Italian cured pork

***paner* (F)** to pass through flour, beaten egg and breadcrumbs; to crumb

***panforte* (I)** a rich, dense Italian cake made with citrus peel, nuts and honey

***papillote* (F)** cooked in greaseproof paper

***pappadam*** an Indian wafer-thin crisp made from lentil flour

**paprika** a spice produced by grinding certain sweet red capsicum pods into powder; Hungarian paprika is considered the best and is used for the famous Hungarian goulash

***parer* (F)** to trim

***parfait* (F)** a chilled dessert of egg, cream and puréed fruits

**parsley** most popular fresh herb and an excellent source of vitamins A and C; ***persil* (F)**

**parsnip *panais* (F)**

**pass** to sieve or strain

***pasta* (I)** a generic term for noodles

**pastry** a mixture of flour, butter and water mixed to a pliable texture; used for topping wet dishes/pies and in the production of certain desserts, pies and slices

**pastry chef *pâtissier* (F)**

***pâté*** pie; smooth texture of coarsely-ground minced meats with herbs, chilled and sliced or spread onto biscuits/bread

***pâte à choux* (F)** choux pastry

***pâte feuilletée* (F)** puff pastry

**pathogen** harmful bacterium

***pâtissier* (F)** pastry chef

***paupiette* (F)** a fillet of fish or a finely sliced meat layered with stuffing and neatly rolled

***paysanne* (F)** to cut vegetables into rough shapes

**peach *pêche* (F)**

**pear *poire* (F)**

**peas *pois/petit pois* (F)**

***pêche* (F)** peach

**pectin** a natural substance in fruit which helps the setting of food, e.g. preserves

**peel, to *peler* (F)**

***peler* (F)** to peel

**pepper, coarsely ground *mignonette* (F)**

**peppercorn *poivre* (F)**

**peppercorn, types**
**black**   picked when the berry is unripened and dried; left either whole or ground
**green**   picked when the berry is soft and unripened; usually preserved whole
**white**   picked when the berry is ripened; skin removed, dried and usually ground

*pepperoni* **(I)**   Italian pork sausage

*persillé* **(F)**   parsley

*peser* **(F)**   to weigh

**pesto**   an uncooked sauce of basil, olive oil, garlic, pine nuts and Parmesan cheese

*petits fours* **(F)**   small, decorated cakes

*petits pois* **(F)**   peas

**phosphorus**   a mineral found in fish which helps the body to build bones and teeth

**pickled**   *mariné* **(F)**

**pickles**   foods preserved in vinegar and brine

*pieds de cochon* **(F)**   pig's trotters

**pilaff rice**   rice cooked in liquid on a stove and left to stand to complete cooking

*pilon de cuisse* **(F)**   drumstick; poultry

*piquant* **(F)**   sharply flavoured

*piqué* **(F)**   studded, e.g. cloves pushed into an onion or garlic cloves securely placed into small incisions on a joint of meat etc.

**pit, to**   to remove the seed or stone from fruit

**pitta bread**   a round of double-layered flat bread which can filled

*plat du jour* **(F)**   dish of the day

**poach**   *pocher* **(F)**

*poire* **(F)**   pear

*poireau* **(F)**   leek

*pois/petits pois* **(F)**   peas

*poisson* **(F)**   fish

*poissonnier* **(F)**   fishmonger

*poitrine* **(F)**   breast

*poitrine d'agneau* **(F)**   lamb breast

*poitrine de bœuf* **(F)**   beef brisket

*poitrine de porc* **(F)**   pork belly

*poitrine de veau* **(F)**   veal breast

*poivre* **(F)**   pepper

**polenta** **(I)**   a coarse granular flour made from corn or maize; a staple food in many ethnic cuisines

*pomme* **(F)**   apple

*pomme de terre* **(F)**   potato

**pork**   *porc* **(F)**

**pork, cuts of**
   **belly**   *poitrine* **(F)**
   **chop**   *côte* **(F)**
   **head**   *tête* **(F)**
   **kidney**   *rognon* **(F)**
   **leg**   *cuissot* **(F)**
   **liver**   *foie* **(F)**
   **loin**   *longe* **(F)**
   **shoulder**   *épaule* **(F)**
   **spare ribs**   *basse-côte/echine* **(F)**
   **trotters**   *pieds de cochon* **(F)**

*potage* **(F)**   a thickened puréed soup

**potato**   *pomme de terre* **(F)**

**pot roast**   meat slowly braised in a little liquid in a covered pot

*poularde* **(F)**   large roasting chicken; boiling chicken

*poule* **(F)**   boiling fowl

*poulet* **(F)**   chicken; hen

*poulet de grain* **(F)**   small roasting chicken

*poulet reine* **(F)**   medium-sized roasting chicken

**poultry**   *volaille* **(F)**

**poultry offal, giblets**   *abats de volaille* **(F)**

**pour, to**   *verser* **(F)**

*poussin, double* **(F)**   double baby chicken

*poussin, single* **(F)**   baby chicken

**praline**   nuts mixed with hot caramelised sugar and then cooled to form a brittle confectionery

**prawn**   *crevette* **(F)**

**preserve**   treat foods to extend their shelf life, e.g. by pickling, drying, freezing, canning etc.

**preserves**   jams

*prosciutto* **(I)**   Italian raw, cured ham

**protein**   nutrient needed to promote growth and repair in the body

**prove**   to allow yeast products to rise and expand

*provolone* **(I)**   an Italian pear-shaped cheese

**puff pastry**   multi-thin layers of dough and fat; when baked, moisture from the butter causes all the layers to rise from each other giving a high, light, buttery pastry; *pâte feuilletée* **(F)**

**pulses**   vegetables grown in a pod

**purée**   any food minced or blended to a smooth consistency

**Q**

*quasi de veau* **(F)**   veal, thick flank

*queue de bœuf* **(F)**   beef, tail

*quiche* **(F)**   savoury egg custard with a little bacon, leek and onion baked in a short pastry shell; anything else is a flan

**R**

**rack of lamb**   portion of the rib section

**radish**   *radis* **(F)**

*rafraîchir* **(F)**   to refresh

*raie* **(F)**   ray/skate

*raisins* **(F)**   grapes

*raper* **(F)**   to grate

*ratatouille* **(F)**   a Provençal dish of tomatoes, onions, capsicum, eggplant, zucchini and garlic

*ravioli* **(I)**   small squares of pasta filled with vegetables or meats and then boiled

**ray/skate**   *raie* **(F)**

*réchauffer* **(F)**   to re-heat food

**reduce**   to allow a liquid or sauce to simmer until evaporation of the liquid thickens it; *réduire* **(F)**

*réduire* **(F)**   to reduce

**refresh**   to stop the cooking process under cold running water; *refraîchir* **(F)**

*rémoulade* **(F)**   a mixture of mayonnaise, capers, gherkins, mustard, herbs and anchovies

**riboflavin**   vitamin B$_2$, found in yeast and liver

**rice**   *riz* **(F)**

*ris de veau* **(F)**/*ris d'agneau* **(F)**   sweetbreads, veal/lamb

*risotto* **(I)**   Italian Arborio rice (usually) which is coated in melted butter and then has small amounts of stock added; as soon as the stock is absorbed, more stock is added until the rice is cooked

*rissoler* **(F)**   to brown; usually in hot oil

*riz* **(F)**   rice

**roast, to**   *rôtir* **(F)**

**roast chef**   *rôtisseur* **(F)**

**rocket**   a peppery, green salad leaf also known as *arugula* **(I)**

**roe**   *laitance* **(F)**

*rognon* **(F)**   kidney

*rognons d'agneau* **(F)**   kidneys, lamb

*rognons de bœuf* **(F)**   kidneys, beef

*rognons de porc* **(F)**   kidneys, pork

*rognons de veau* **(F)**   kidneys, veal

**romano cheese**   pecorino cheese

**rosemary**   a member of the mint family with a highly aromatic flavour native to the Mediterranean; associated with lamb

**rösti**   Swiss-style, golden, crisp, grated potatoes

*rôtir* **(F)**   to roast

*rôtisseur* **(F)**   roast chef

*roulade* **(F)**   a thin slice of meat folded around a filling; also a dessert

*roux* **(F)**   a thickening agent usually made of equal quantities of fat and flour

*rutabaga* **(F)**   swede

**S**

*sabayon* **(F)**   egg yolks and marsala beaten and cooked until creamy

**saccharin**   a sugar subsititute

**saddle, lamb**   *selle d'agneau* **(F)**

**saffron**   yellow stigmas from a certain variety of crocus, which produce a yellow colouring

*saindoux* **(F)**   lard

*saint-pierre* **(F)**   John Dory

**salamander**   heating equipment which heats, cooks and glazes food from above

*saler* **(F)**   to add salt

**salmon**   *saumon* **(F)**

**salmonella**   a harmful bacterium/pathogen

**salt**   *sel* **(F)**

*saltimbocca* **(I)**   a slice of veal wrapped with prosciutto, cheese and sage

**sambal**   an accompaniment to Asian dishes made from chillies, lemon/lime juice and spices

*sardine* **(F)**   sardine; a soft boned salt water fish which is a member of the herring family

**sashimi**   Japanese-style finely sliced raw fish

**sauce chef**   *saucier* **(F)**

*saucier* **(F)**   sauce chef

*saumon* **(F)**   salmon

*sauté* **(F)**   to cook quickly in a little fat

**scallop**   *coquille Saint-Jacques* **(F)**

*scallopine* **(I)**   describes thinly sliced meat; usually veal

**scampi**   *langoustine* **(F)**

**score, to** to make small incisions in foods to help penetration of marinade flavours or to help hasten cooking in thick foods

**scrambled** *brouillé* **(F)**

**seal, to** to quickly cook/brown the outer portion of meat in a little fat to close all meat pores so the juices cannot excape during further cooking

**sear, to** to brown meats quickly in a little fat

**season, to** *assaisonner* **(F)**

**second chef** *sous chef* **(F)**

*sel* **(F)** salt

*selle d'agneau* **(F)** saddle of lamb

*selle de veau* **(F)** saddle of veal

*servir* **(F)** to serve

**set** to harden and hold colour

**shallot** *échalote* **(F)**

**sharply flavoured** *piquant* **(F)**

**shaslik** a kebab

**shoulder** *épaule* **(F)**

**shred** to cut foodstuffs into fine strips, e.g. lettuce, ham

**shrimp** a small prawn

**shuck** to remove the meat from a shell, e.g. to shuck an oyster

**sieve, to** *tamiser* **(F)**

**sift** to pass ingredients such as flour through a fine mesh

**simmer** to boil a liquid very gently; *mijoter* **(F)**

**singe** to remove any remaining small feathers from a plucked chicken; to brown/colour food

**skewer** *brochette* **(F)**

**skim, to** to remove any impurities which rise to the surface of a liquid; *écumer* **(F)**

**slice, a** *tranche* **(F)**

**smoked** *fumé* **(F)**

**smoke point** the temperature oil reaches before it smokes, signifying oil breakdown

**smörgåsbord** a buffet-style selection of hot and cold foods; originating from Sweden

**sodium** salt

*sole* **(F)** sole

*sorbet* **(F)** flavoured ice used to cleanse the palate before the next course; ideally after a fish course

*soufflé* **(F)** a hot or cold dish with a light consistency, sweet or savoury

*sous-chef* **(F)** second chef

*sous noix de veau* **(F)** veal, under cushion

**soya sauce** an essential ingredient in Asian cuisine; produced by fermenting boiled soya beans and roasted wheat

**spinach** *épinard* **(F)**

**squid** calamari

**staphylococcus** a harmful bacterium/pathogen

**starch** a carbohydrate found in flour, cereals and farinaceous dishes

**steel, a** a long, thin, hand held piece of rough metal used to sharpen knives

**stew, a** *ragout* **(F)**

**stewed fruit** *compote* **(F)**

**stir-fry** to cook foods quickly in a little oil; usually in a wok

**stock** the resultant liquid from liquid and foods simmered together

**stock pot** *marmite* **(F)**

**strain** to pass food through a strainer, chinois or fine mesh

**stuff, to** *farcir* **(F)**

**stuffing** *farce* **(F)**

*sucre* **(F)** sugar

*sucrer* **(F)** to sweeten

*suer* **(F)** to sweat vegetables

**sugar** *sucre* **(F)**

**sweat, to** to cook gently without colour

**swede** *rutabaga* **(F)**

**sweetbreads, veal/lamb** *ris de veau* **(F)**/*ris d'agneau* **(F)**

**sweet corn** *maïs* **(F)**

**sweeten, to** *sucrer* **(F)**

**T**

**Tabasco sauce** a very hot pepper sauce originally from the Mexican state of Tabasco. Tabasco peppers are fermented for approximately three years before being processed with vinegar and salt to produce this famous sauce

**tabbouleh** a dish originating in the Middle East comprising bulghur wheat, onions, tomatoes, mint, oil and lemon juice

*table d'hôte* **(F)** a meal at a fixed price

**tahini** ground sesame seeds

**tamiser (F)**   to sieve

**tapenade (F)**   a paste made from anchovies, capers, olives, olive oil and lemon

**tartaric acid**   the natural acid found in grapes

**tempura**   a light Japanese batter made with iced water and flour

**tenderise, to   attendrir (F)**

**terrine (F)**   a dish used for pâté production

**tête de porc (F)**   pig's head

**thiamine**   part of the vitamin B group ($B_1$) found in yeast and wholemeal products; helps the nervous system function properly

**timbale (F)**   puréed or minced vegetables/meat with added egg white, cream etc. cooked in a mould and set using aspic or gelatine

**tofu**   bean curd; made from curdled soya milk – very popular with Asian and vegetarian cuisine

**tomato   tomate (F)**

**tongue   langue (F)**

**topinambour (F)**   Jerusalem artichoke

**toss**   to coat food with a liquid, e.g. dressing on salad leaves, gently flipping the ingredients in a bowl

**tourner (F)**   to shape vegetables into barrel shapes, e.g. potatoes, carrots etc.

**tournedos de bœuf (F)**   beef, middle fillet

**tranche (F)**   a slice

**tranche grasse de bœuf (F)**   beef, thick flank

**tranche tendre de bœuf (F)**   beef, topside

**trim, to   parer (F)**

**tripe, beef   tripe de bœuf (F)**

**tronchon (F)**   a slice of flat fish on the bone

**trout**   generally a freshwater fish; a member of the salmon family; **truite (F)**

**truss**   to firmly secure a chicken with string

**turkey   dinde (F)**

**turmeric**   a spice which can be used as a yellow colouring in lieu of saffron; turmeric is also known as **haldi**

**turn, to**   to shape vegetables into barrel shapes, e.g. potatoes, carrots, etc.

**turnip   navet (F)**

**tongue   langue (F)**

**U**

**UHT**   ultra heat tested

**V**

**veal**   a young calf; **veau (F)**

**veal, cuts of**
  **best end   carré (F)**
  **breast   poitrine (F)**
  **cushion   noix (F)**
  **cutlet   côtelette (F)**
  **kidneys   rognons (F)**
  **knuckle/shin   jarret (F)**
  **leg   cuisseau/cuissot (F)**
  **liver   foie (F)**
  **loin   longe (F)**
  **neck end   cou/côte découverte (F)**
  **saddle   selle (F)**
  **scrag   cou (F)**
  **shoulder   épaule (F)**
  **sweetbreads   ris (F)**
  **thick flank   quasi (F)**
  **under cushion   sous noix (F)**

**veau (F)**   veal

**vegan**   person who does not eat any animal products or by-products

**vegetables   légumes (F)**
  **bulbs**   onions, shallots, leeks, garlic
  **flowers**   broccoli, cauliflower
  **fruits**   cucumber, tomato, avocado, eggplant
  **leaves**   lettuce, spinach, sprouts, cabbage
  **legumes**   beans, peas
  **roots**   carrots, swedes, turnips, radishes, parsnips, beetroot
  **stems**   asparagus, celery, chicory
  **tubers**   potatoes

**vegetable chef   entremettier (F)**

**vegetable oil**   any oil which is a derivative of a vegetable or seed

**vegetarian**   person who will not eat meat

**vegetarian, semi**   someone who won't eat red meat

**velouté (F)**   a basic sauce made with a white stock or a soup of creamy consistency

**verser (F)**   to pour

**viande (F)**   meat

**Vichyssoise (F)**   a chilled potato and leek soup

**vider (F)**   to clean out poultry; to empty

**vinaigre (F)**   vinegar

**vinaigrette (F)**   a basic salad dressing made from oil, vinegar and seasoning

**vinegar**   used over hundreds of years, vinegars are made by bacterial activity which converts fermented liquids such as beer, cider or wine into a weak solution of acetic acid. Many countries have developed their own varieties such as English malt and Italian balsamic vinegar; **vinaigre (F)**

**vitamins**   nutrients which help regulate bodily functions

**vol-au-vent (F)**   a puff pastry case

**volaille (F)**   poultry

## W

**warm, to   chauffer (F)**

**watercress   cresson de fontaine (F)**

**weigh, to   peser (F)**

**whey**   the liquid part of milk strained off during cheese-making

**whipped cream   crème fouettée (F)**

**whisk   fouetter (F)**

**whitebait   blanchaille (F)**; minnows

**whiting   merlan (F)**

**wok**   a round bottomed frying pan used in Asian cookery

**Worcestershire sauce**   orginally developed by the British in India, but first bottled in Worcester, England. Its main ingredients are soya sauce, tamarind, garlic, onions, molasses, anchovies, vinegar and limes

## Y

**yeast**   living single cell organism which converts food into alcohol and carbon dioxide; these gases allow bread and flour products to rise; **levure (F)**

**yoghurt**   produced by fermenting milk and allowing it to coagulate; thought to have been first made by nomadic Balkan tribes as a means of preserving milk

## Z

**zest**   the outer layer of fruit

**zucchini   courgette (F)**

# INDEX

*ht* = health tip; *n* = note